PART FIRST.

PROSE AND VERSE.

BY

THOMAS HOOD.

NEW EDITION, COMPLETE IN ONE VOLUME.

NEW YORK:
GEO. P. PUTNAM & CO., 10 PARK PLACE.
M.DCCC.LIII.

CONTENTS

OF

THE FIRST PART.

CONTENTS

OF

THE SECOND PART.

EDITOR'S PREFACE.

It is designed to embrace in the present collection of the writings of Thomas Hood, a miscellany which shall include his more serious and earnest writings—those which were written most directly from the heart, which reflect most faithfully his life and opinions, which may be emphatically called (as he himself gave name to a book which has contributed largely to these pages) Hood's Own, and not the bookseller's own, the magazine's own, or the newspaper's own. If a pension had been given to Hood earlier in his life, it would have probably added much to his fame. He would have had the opportunity of writing only when his better genius prompted him; he would not have been compelled for ever to glean a scanty crop from the surface; he might oftener with time and labor have penetrated to the ore beneath. He might have been less of a Punster, but he would have been more of a Wit. The Poet—the higher title—might have been better known than the prose writer.

With the exception of a few of his later poems—the Bridge of Sighs, the Song of a Shirt, and his earlier Eugene Aram—the writings of Hood which have been circulated in America have been his puns and jests, comic verses from his annuals, farcical letters of servants and others, after the manner of Winifred Jenkins—clever extravagances, seldom deficient in literary merit, but which oftener conceal the man from the reader than lead the latter to suspect the tender heart, the delicate fancy, hidden beneath.

There are whole volumes of Hood's writings which appear mere whimsicality and grotesqueness; there are pages which indicate the genius of the man, and will be worth more to posterity than the volumes. Frequently since his recent death Hood has been called *a great author*, a phrase used not inconsiderately or in vain. He will take his place among the English classics. How he was great is a question which will not be fully answered till his Life, his Correspondence, his Complete Writings—his Poetical works especially—have been given to the world. Many good men and great men among his friends will add their tribute of recollections; and the next generation will see the man, twin brother in heart and mind to Elia whom he loved. That this volume, undertaken in a spirit of reverence for the author, in admiration of his genius, with the desire that he should be wisely known, will be cordially received, cannot be doubted; but it is sent forth accompanied by a sigh of regret. The task of the editor and critic seems an impertinence, a piece of bitter hypocrisy, while the rights of the author (in his representatives) to the profits of his own labor are denied. Hood died poor, and his widow was anticipating the small pittance of her next quarter's government pension to pay the undertaker while the American public was laughing over his latest jest. No man with a soul capable of enjoying the honest, heartfelt appeals of this truly humorous writer can deny the injustice of a system by which Hood was deprived of the least participation in the profits of his own works in America. In the second part of this Miscellany will be found his own views of this matter, simply, manfully stated, as it is incumbent upon every man to assert, in whatever case may come under his experience or observation, the laws of Justice. Self-respect, self-interest no less than a sense of justice, require the recognition, on our statute book, of the rights of the foreign author. The present system has reached that point in the development of evil where a wrong being committed, every one suffers, no one is benefited. It is the nature of wrong to end in precisely this predicament. The foreign author confessedly is injured; the American author (where the system allows such a person to exist at all) is at a disadvantage at every turn; the bookselling interest is deprived of that security of property, based upon right, which is essential to give honor and dignity to trade; and the public are not the gainers. In what respect is the nation better or wiser for the floods of reprints of every kind and quality which have been poured over the land? In every respect the people are worse for this deluge—less beneficial, more destructive than the natural rain. In the physical world there are laws, which, if violated, would destroy the harvest. If it were all rain or all sunshine, the crops would cease. A similar law governs our intellectual and moral well-being. Property is a blessing, but it is only so when acquired righteously and honestly. Riches are valuable by the stamp which virtue and privation set upon them. The grand law of morality which protects the rights of the author, and distributes his works to the world in accordance with those rights, will be found to be the just measure by which his writings can be received with any advantage. A complicated system of checks and counter-checks—all of them necessary—depends upon the recognition of that primary right. The due responsibility of the author, the force of his character depend upon it. A just competition, the sacred right to be "free and equal" between the native and the foreign author, depend upon it. A proper Nationality in our case depends upon it. Follow out the system where you will, it will be found here as elsewhere, that only the just and right are profitable.

JULY 1, 1845.

PROSE AND VERSE.

PREFACE TO HOOD'S OWN.

BEING

AN INAUGURAL DISCOURSE ON A CERTAIN SYSTEM OF PRACTICAL PHILOSOPHY.

COURTEOUS READER!

Presuming that you have known something of the Comic Annual from its Child-Hood, when it was first put into half binding and began to run alone, I make bold to consider you as an old friend of the family, and shall accordingly treat you with all the freedom and confidence that pertain to such ripe connexions.

How many years is it, think you, "since we were first acquent?"

"By the deep *nine!*" sings out the old bald *Count Fathom* with the lead-line: no great lapse in the world's chronology, but a space of infinite importance in individual history. For instance, it has wrought a serious change on the body, if not on the mind, of your very humble servant;—it is not, however, to bespeak your sympathy, or to indulge in what Lord Byron calls "the gloomy vanity of drawing from self," that I allude to my personal experience. The Scot and lot character of the dispensation forbids me to think that the world in general can be particularly interested in the state of my Household Sufferage, or that the public ear will be as open to my Maladies as to my Melodies. The simple truth is, that, being a wiser but not sadder man, I propose to admit you to my Private View of a system of Practical Cheerful Philosophy, thanks to which, perchance, the cranium of your Humorist is still secure from such a lecture as was delivered over the skull of Poor Yorick.

In the absence of a certain thin "blue-and-yellow" visage, and attenuated figure,—whose effigies may one day be affixed to the present work,—you will not be prepared to learn that some of the merriest effusions in the forthcoming numbers have been the relaxations of a gentleman literally enjoying bad health —the carnival, so to speak, of a personified Jour Maigre. The very fingers so aristocratically slender, that now hold the pen, hint plainly of the "*ills* that *flesh* is heir to:"—my coats have become great coats, my pantaloons are turned into trowsers, and by a worse bargain than Peter Schlemihl's, I seem to have retained my shadow and sold my substance. In short, as happens to prematurely old port wine, I am of a bad color with very little body. But what then? That emaciated hand still lends a hand to embody in words and sketches the creations or recreations of a Merry Fancy: those gaunt sides yet shake heartily as ever at the Grotesques and Arabesques and droll Picturesques that my Good Genius (a Pantagruelian Familiar) charitably conjures up to divert me from more sombre realities. It was the whim of a late pleasant Comedian, to suppose a set of spiteful imps sitting up aloft, to aggravate all his petty mundane annoyances; whereas I prefer to believe in the ministry of kindlier Elves that "nod to me and do me courtesies." Instead of scaring away these motes in the sunbeam, I earnestly invoke them, and bid them welcome; for the tricksy spirits make friends with the animal spirits, and do not I, like a father romping with his own urchins,—do not I forget half my cares whilst partaking in their airy gambols? Such sports are as wholesome for the mind as the other frolics for the body. For on our own treatment of that excellent Friend or terrible Enemy the Imagination, it depends whether we are to be scared and haunted by a Scratching Fanny, or tended by an affectionate Invisible Girl—like an unknown Love, blessing us with "favors secret, sweet, and precious," and fondly stealing us from this worky-day world to a sunny sphere of her own.

This is a novel version, Reader, of "Paradise and the Peri," but it is as true as it is new. How else could I have converted a serious illness into a comic wellness—by what other agency could I have transported myself, as a Cockney would say, from *Dull*age to *Grin*nage? It was far from a practical joke to be laid up in ordinary in a foreign land, under the care of Physicians quite as much abroad as myself with the case; indeed the shades of the gloaming were stealing over my prospect; but I resolved that, like the sun, so long as my day lasted, I would look on the bright side of everything. The raven croaked, but I persuaded myself that it was the nightingale: there was the smell of the mould, but I remembered that it nourished the violets. However my body might cry craven, my mind luckily had no mind to give in. So, instead of mounting on the black long-tailed coach horse, she vaulted on her old Hobby that had capered in the Morris-Dance, and began to exhort from his back. To be sure, said she, matters look darkly enough; but the more need for the lights. Allons! Courage! Things may take a turn, as the pig said on the spit. Never throw down your cards, but play out the game. The more certain to lose, the wiser to get all the play you can for your money. Come—give us a song! chirp away like that best of cricket-players, the cricket himself. Be bowled out or caught out, but never throw down the bat. As to Health, it's the weather of the body—it hails, it rains, it blows, it snows, at present, but it may clear up by-and-by. You cannot eat, you say, and you must not drink; but laugh and make believe, like the Barber's wise brother at the Barmecide's feast. Then, as to thinness, not to flatter, you look like a lath that has had a split with the carpenter and a fall out with the plaster; but so much the better: remember how the smugglers trim the sails of the lugger to escape the notice of the cutter. Turn your edge to the old enemy, and mayhap he won't see you! Come—be alive! You have no more right to slight your life than to neglect your wife—they are the two better halves that make a man of you! Is not life your means of living? so stick to thy business and thy business will stick to thee. Of course, continued my mind, I am quite disinterested in this advice—for I am aware of my own immortality—but for that very reason, take care of the mortal body, poor body, and give it as long a day as you can!

Now, my mind seeming to treat the matter very pleasantly as well as profitably, I followed her counsel, and instead of calling out for relief according to the fable, I kept along on my journey, with my bundle of sticks,—*i. e.* my arms and legs. Between ourselves it would have been "extremely inconvenient," as I once heard the opium-eater declare, to pay the debt of nature at that particular juncture; nor do I quite know, to be candid, when it would altogether suit me to settle it, so, like other parties in narrow circumstances, I laughed, and gossipped, and played the agreeable with all my might, and as such pleasant behavior sometimes obtains a respite from a human creditor, who knows but that it may prove successful with the Universal Mortgagee? At all events, here I am, humming "Jack's Alive!" and my own dear skilful native physician gives me hopes of a longer lease than appeared from the foreign reading of the covenants. He declares indeed, that, anatomically, my heart is lower hung than usual—but what of that? *The more need to keep it up!* So huzza! my boys! Comus and Momus for ever! No Heraclitus! Nine times nine for Democritus! And here goes my last bottle of Elixir at the heads of the Blue Devils—be they Prussian blue or indigo, powder-blue or ultramarine!

Gentle reader, how do you like this Laughing Philosophy? The joyous cheers you have just heard, come from a crazy vessel that has clawed, by miracle, off a lee-shore, and I, the skipper, am sitting down to my grog, and re-counting to you the tale of the past danger, with the manœuvres that were used to escape the perilous Point. Or rather, consider me as the Director of a Life Assurance, pointing out to you a most beneficial policy, whereby you may eke out your natural term. And, firstly, take precious care of your precious health,—but how, as the housewives say, to make it keep? Why then, don't cure and smoke-dry it—or pickle it in everlasting acids—like the Germans. Don't bury it in a potato-pit, like the Irish. Don't preserve it in spirits, like the Barbadians. Don't salt it down, like the Newfoundlanders. Don't pack it in ice, like Captain Back. Don't parboil it in Hot Baths. Don't bottle it, like gooseberries. Don't pot it—and don't hang it. A rope is a bad Cordon Sanitaire. Above all, don't despond about it. Let not anxiety "have thee on the hyp." Consider your health as your best friend, and think as well of it, in spite of all its foibles, as you can. For instance, never dream, though you may have a "clever hack," of galloping consumption, or indulge in the Meltonian belief, that you are going the pace. Never fancy every time you cough, that you are going to coughypot. Hold up, as the shooter says, over the heaviest ground. Despondency in a nice case is the over-weight that may make you kick the beam and the bucket both at once. In short, as with other cases, never meet trouble half-way, but let him have the whole walk for his pains; though it should be a Scotch mile and a bittock. I have even known him to give up his visit in sight of the house. Besides, the best fence against care is a ha! ha!—wherefore take care to have one all round you wherever you can. Let your "lungs crow like Chanticleer," and as like a GAME cock as possible. It expands the chest, enlarges the heart, quickens the circulation, and "like a trumpet makes the spirits dance."

A fico then for the Chesterfieldian canon, that laughter is an ungenteel emotion. Smiles are tolerated by the very pinks of politeness; and a laugh is but the full-blown flower of which a smile is the bud. It is a sort of vocal music—a glee in which everybody can take a part:—and "he who hath not laughter in his soul, let no such man be trusted." Indeed, there are two classes of Querists particularly to be shunned; thus when you hear a Cui Bono? be sure to leave the room; but if it be Quid Rides? make a point to quit the house, and forget to take its number. None but your dull dogs would give tongue in such a style;—for, as Nimrod says in his "Hunt after Happiness," "A single *burst* with Mirth is worth a whole season of *full cries* with Melancholy."

Such, dear reader, is the cheerful Philosophy which I practise as well as preach. It teaches to "make a sunshine in a shady place," to render the mind independent of external foul weather, by compelling it, as old Absolute says, to get a sun and moon of its own. As the system has worked so well in my own case, it is a duty to recommend it to others: and like certain practitioners, who not only prescribe but dispense their own medicines, I have prepared a regular course of light reading, whereof I now present the first packet, in the humble hope that your dull hours may be amused, and your cares diverted, by the laughing lucubrations which have enlivened Hood's Own.

THE PUGSLEY PAPERS.

How the following correspondence came into my hands must remain a Waverley mystery. The Pugsley Papers were neither rescued from a garret, like Evelyn,—collected from cartridges like the Culloden,—nor saved, like the Garrick, from being shredded into a snow storm at a Winter Theatre. They were not snatched from a tailor's shears, like the original parchment of Magna Charta. They were neither the Legacy of a Dominie, nor the communications of My Landlord,—a consignment, like the Clinker Letters, from some Rev. Jonathan Dustwich,—nor the waifs and strays of a Twopenny Post Bag. They were not unrolled from ancient papyri. They were none of those that "line trunks, clothe spices," or paper the walls of old attics. They were neither given to me nor sold to me,—nor stolen,—nor borrowed and surreptitiously copied,—nor left in a hackney coach, like Sheridan's play,—nor misdelivered by a carrier pigeon,—nor dreamt of, like Coleridge's Kubla Khan,—nor turned up in the Tower, like Milton's Foundling MS.,—nor dug up,—nor trumped up, like eastern tales of Horam harum Horam the son of Asmar,—nor brought over by Rammohun Roy,—nor translated by Doctor Bowring from the Scandinavian, Batavian, Pomeranian, Spanish, or Danish, or Russian, or Prussian, or any other language dead or living. They were not picked from the Dead Letter Office, nor purloined from the British Museum. In short, I cannot, dare not, will not, hint even at the mode of their acquisition: the reader must be content to know, that, in point of authenticity, the Pugsley Papers are the extreme reverse of Lady L.'s celebrated Autographs, which were all written by the proprietor.

No. I.—*From Master* Richard Pugsley, *to Master* Robert Rogers, *at Number* 132, *Barbican.*

Dear Bob,

Huzza!—Here I am in Lincolnshire! It's good-bye to Wellingtons and Cossacks, Ladies' double channels, Gentlemen's stout calf, and ditto ditto. They've all been sold off under prime cost, and the old Shoe Mart is disposed of, goodwill and fixtures, for ever and ever. Father has been made a rich Squire of by will, and we've got a house and fields, and trees of our own. Such a garden, Bob!—It beats White Conduit.

Now, Bob, I'll tell you what I want. I want you to come down here for the holidays. Don't be afraid. Ask your Sister to ask your Mother to ask your Father to let you come. It's only ninety miles. If you're out of pocket money, you can walk, and beg a lift now and then, or swing by the dickeys. Put on cordroys, and don't care for cut behind. The two prentices, George and Will, are here to be made farmers of, and brother Nick is took home from school to help in agriculture. We like farming very much, it's capital fun. Us four have got a gun, and go out shooting: it's a famous good un, and sure to go off if you don't full cock it. Tiger is to be our shooting dog as soon as he has left off killing the sheep. He's a real savage, and worries cats beautiful. Before Father comes down, we mean to bait our bull with him.

There's plenty of New Rivers about, and we're going a fishing as soon as we have mended our top joint. We've killed one of our sheep on the sly to get gentles. We've a pony too, to ride upon when we can catch him, but he's loose in the paddock, and has neither mane nor tail to signify to lay hold of. Isn't it prime, Bob? You *must* come. If your Mother won't give your Father leave to allow you,—run away. Remember, you turn up Goswell Street to go to Lincolnshire, and ask for Middlefen Hall. There's a pond full of frogs, but we won't pelt them till you come, but let it be before Sunday, as there's our own orchard to rob, and the fruit's to be gathered on Monday.

If you like sucking raw eggs, we know where the hens lay,

and mother don't; and I'm bound there's lots of birds' nests. Do come, Bob, and I'll show you the wasps' nest, and everything that can make you comfortable. I dare say you could borrow your father's volunteer musket of him without his knowing of it; but be sure anyhow to bring the ramrod, as we have mislaid ours by firing it off. Don't forget some bird-lime, Bob—and some fish-hooks—and some different sorts of shot—and some gut and some gunpowder—and a gentle-box, and some flints,—some May flies,—and a powder horn,—and a landing net and a dog-whistle—and some porcupine quills, and a bullet mould—and a trolling-winch, and a shot-belt and a tin can. You pay for 'em, Bob, and I'll owe it you.

Your old friend and schoolfellow,
RICHARD PUGSLEY.

No. II.—*From the Same to the Same.*

DEAR BOB,

When you come, bring us a 'bacco-pipe to load the gun with. If you don't come, it can come by the wagon. Our Public House is three mile off, and when you've walked there it's out of everything. Yours, &c.,

RICH. PUGSLEY.

No. III.—*From Miss* ANASTASIA PUGSLEY, *to Miss* JEMIMA MOGGRIDGE, *at Gregory House Establishment for Young Ladies, Mile End.*

MY DEAR JEMIMA,

Deeply solicitous to gratify sensibility, by sympathizing with our fortuitous elevation, I seize the epistolary implements to inform you, that, by the testamentary disposition of a remote branch of consanguinity, our tutelary residence is removed from the metropolitan horizon to a pastoral district and its congenial pursuits. In futurity I shall be more pertinaciously superstitious in the astrological revelations of human destiny. You remember the mysterious gipsy at Hornsey Wood?—Well, the eventful fortune she obscurely intimated, though couched in vague terms, has come to pass in the minutest particulars; for I perceive perspicuously, that it predicted that papa should sell off his boot and shoe business at 133, Barbican, to Clack & Son, of 144, Hatton Garden, and that we should retire, in a station of affluence, to Middlefen Hall, in Lincolnshire, by bequest of our great-great maternal uncle, Pollexfen Goldsworthy Wrigglesworth, Esq., who deceased suddenly of apoplexy at Wisbeach Market, in the ninety-third year of his venerable and lamented age.

At the risk of tedium, I will attempt a cursory delineation of our rural paradise, altho' I feel it would be morally arduous, to give any idea of the romantic scenery of the Lincolnshire Fens. Conceive, as far as the visual organ expands, an immense sequestered level, abundantly irrigated with minute rivulets, and studded with tufted oaks, whilst more than a hundred wind-mills diversify the prospect and give a revolving animation to the scene. As for our own gardens and grounds they are a perfect Vauxhall—excepting of course the rotunda, the orchestra, the company, the variegated lamps, the fire-works, and those very lofty trees. But I trust my dear Jemima will supersede topography by ocular inspection; and in the interim I send for acceptance a graphical view of the locality, shaded in Indian ink, which will suffice to convey an idea of the terrestrial verdure and celestial azure we enjoy, in lieu of the sable exhalations and architectural nigritude of the metropolis.

You who know my pastoral aspirings, and have been the indulgent confidant of my votive tributes to the Muses, will conceive the refined nature of my enjoyment when I mention the intellectual repast of this morning. I never could enjoy Bloomfield in Barbican,—but to-day he read beautifully under our pear-tree. I look forward to the felicity of reading Thomson's Summer with you on the green seat, and if engagements at Christmas permit your participation in the bard, there is a bower of evergreens that will be delightful for the perusal of his Winter.

I enclose, by request, an epistolary effusion from sister Dorothy, which I know will provoke your risible powers, by the domesticity of its details. You know she was always in the homely characteristics a perfect Cinderella, though I doubt whether even supernatural agency could adapt her foot to a diminutive vitrified slipper, or her hand for a prince of regal primogeniture. But I am summoned to receive, with family members, the felicitations of Lincolnshire aristocracy; though whatever necessary distinctions may prospectively occur between respective grades in life, they will only superficially affect the sentiments of eternal friendship between my dear Jemima and her affectionate friend,

ANASTASIA PUGSLEY.

No. IV.—*From Miss* DOROTHY PUGSLEY *to the Same.*

MY DEAR MISS JEMIMA,

Providence having been pleased to remove my domestic duties from Barbican to Lincolnshire, I trust that I shall have strength of constitution to fulfil them as becomes my new allotted line of life. As we are not sent into this world to be idle, and Anastasia has declined housewifery, I have undertaken the Dairy, and the Brewery, and the Baking, and the Poultry, the Pigs and the Pastry,—and though I feel fatigued at first, use reconciles to labors and trials, more severe than I at present enjoy. Altho' things may not turn out to wish at present, yet all well-directed efforts are sure to meet reward in the end, and altho' I have chumped and churned two days running, and it's nothing yet but curds and whey, I should be wrong to despair of eating butter of my own making before I die. Considering the adulteration committed by every article in London, I was never happier in any prospect, than of drinking my own milk, fattening my own calves, and laying my own eggs. We cackle so much I am sure we new-lay somewhere, tho' I cannot find out our nests; and I am looking every day to have chickens, as one pepper-and-salt-colored hen has been sitting these two months. When a poor ignorant bird sets me such an example of patience, how can I repine at the hardest domestic drudgery! Mother and I have worked like horses to be sure, ever since we came to the estate; but if we die in it, we know it's for the good of the family, and to agreeably surprise my Father, who is still in town winding up his books. For my own part, if it was right to look at things so selfishly, I should say I never was so happy in my life; though I own I have cried more since coming here than I ever remember before. You will confess my crosses and losses have been unusual trials, when I tell you, out of all my makings, and bakings, and brewings, and preservings, there has been nothing either eatable or drinkable; and what is more painful to an affectionate mind,—have half poisoned the whole family with home-made ketchup of toadstools, by mistake for mushrooms. When I reflect that they are preserved, I ought not to grieve about my damsons and bullaces, done by Mrs. Maria Dover's receipt.

Among other things we came into a beautiful closet of old China, which, I am shocked to say, is all destroyed by my preserving. The bullaces and damsons fomented, and blew up a great jar with a violent shock that smashed all the tea and coffee cups, and left nothing but the handles hanging in rows on the tenter-hooks. But to a resigned spirit there's always some comfort in calamities, and if the preserves work and foment so, there's some hope that my beer will, as it has been a month next Monday in the mash tub. As for the loss of the elder wine, candor compels me to say it was my own fault for letting the poor blind little animals crawl into the copper; but experience dictates next year not to boil the berries and kittens at the same time.

I mean to attempt cream cheese as soon as we can get cream,—but as yet we can't drive the Cows home to be milked for the Bull—he has twice hunted Grace and me into fits, and kept my poor Mother a whole morning in the pigstye. As I know you like country delicacies, you will receive a pound of my fresh butter when it comes, and I mean to add a cheese as soon as I can get one to stick together. I shall send also some family pork for Governess, of our own killing, as we wring a pig's neck on Saturday. I did hope to give you the unexpected treat of a home-made loaf, but it was forgot in the oven from ten to six, and so too black to offer. However, I hope to surprise you with one by Monday's carrier. Anastasia bids me add she will send a nosegay for respected Mrs. Tombleson, if the plants don't die off before, which I am sorry to say is not improbable.

It's really shocking to see the failure of her cultivated taste, and one in particular, that must be owned a very pretty idea. When we came, there was a vast number of flower roots, but jumbled without any regular order, till Anastasia trowelled them all up, and set them in again, in the quadrille figures. It must have looked sweetly elegant, if it had agreed with them, but they have all dwindled and drooped like deep declines and consumptions. Her dahlias and tulips too have turned out nothing but onions and kidney potatoes, and her ten-week stocks have not come up in twenty. But as Shakspeare says, Adversity is a precious toad—that teaches us Patience is a jewel.

Considering the unsettled state of coming in, I must conclude, but could not resist giving your friendliness a short account of the happy change that has occurred, and our increase of comforts. I would write more, but I know you will excuse my listening to the calls of dumb animals. It's the time I always scald the little pigs' bread and milks, and put saucers of clean water for the ducks and geese. There are the fowls' beds to make with fresh straw, and a hundred similar things that country people are obliged to think of.

The children, I am happy to say, are all well, only baby is a little fractious, we think from Grace setting him down in the nettles, and he was short-coated last week. Grace is poorly with a cold, and Anastasia has got a sore throat, from sitting up fruitlessly in the orchard to hear the nightingale; perhaps there may not be any in the Fens. I seem to have a trifling ague and rheumatism myself, but it may be only a stiffness from so much churning, and the great family wash-up of everything we had directly we came down, for the sake of grass bleaching on the lawn. With these exceptions, we are all in perfect health and happiness, and unite in love, with

Dear Miss Jemima's affectionate friend,

DOROTHY PUGSLEY.

No. V.—*From* Mrs. Pugsley *to* Mrs. Mumford, *Bucklersbury.*

My dear Martha,

In my ultimatum I informed of old Wrigglesworth paying his natural debts, and of the whole Middlefen estate coming from Lincolnshire to Barbican. I charged Mr. P. to send bulletings into you with progressive reports, but between sisters, as I know you are very curious, I am going to make myself more particular. I take the opportunity of the family being all restive in bed, and the house all still, to give an account of our moving. The things all got here safe, with the exception of the Crockery and Glass, which came down with the dresser, about an hour after its arrival. Perhaps if we hadn't overloaded it with the whole of our breakables, it wouldn't have given way,—as it is, we have only one plate left, and that's chipt, and a mug without a spout to keep it in countenance. Our furniture, &c., came by the wagon, and I am sorry to say a poor family at the same time, and the little idle boys with their knives have carved and scarified my rosewood legs, and, what is worse, not of the same patterns: but as people say, two Lincolnshire removes are as bad as a fire of London.

The first thing I did on coming down, was to see to the sweeps going up,—but I wish I had been less precipitous, for the sooty wretches stole four good flitches of bacon, as was up the kitchen chimbly, quite unbeknown to me. We have filled up the vacancy with more, which smoke us dreadfully, but what is to be cured must be endured. My next thing was to have all holes and corners cleared out, and washed, and scrubbed, being left, like bachelor's places, in a sad state by old single W.; for a rich man, I never saw one that wanted so much cleaning out. There were heaps of dung about, as high as haystacks, and it cost me five shillings a load to have it all carted off the premises; besides heaps of good-for-nothing littering straw, that I gave to the boys for bonfires. We are not all to rights yet, but Rome wasn't built in St. Thomas's day.

It was providential I hampered myself with cold provisions, for except the bacon there were no eatables in the house. What old W. lived upon is a mystery, except salads, for we found a whole field of beet-root, which, all but a few plants for Dorothy to pickle, I had chucked away. As the ground was then clear for sowing up a crop, I directed George to plough it up, but he met with agricultural distress. He says as soon as he whipped his horses, the plough stuck its nose in the earth, and tumbled over head and heels. It seems very odd when ploughing is so easy to look at, but I trust he will do better in time. Experience makes a King Solomon of a Tom-noddy.

I expect we shall have bushels upon bushels of corn, tho' sadly pecked by the birds, as I have had all the scarecrows taken down for fear of the children dreaming of them for Bogies. For the same dear little sakes I have had the well filled up, and the nasty sharp iron spikes drawn out of all the rakes and harrows. Nobody shall say to my teeth, I am not a good Mother. With these precautions I trust the young ones' will enjoy the country when the gipsies have left, but till then, I confine them to round the house, as it's no use shutting the stable door after you've had a child stole.

We have a good many fine fields of hay, which I mean to have reaped directly, wet or shine; for delays are as dangerous as pickles in glazed pans. Perhaps St. Swithin's is in our favor, for if the stacks are put up dampish they won't catch fire so easily, if Swing should come into these parts. The poor boys have made themselves very industrious in shooting off the birds, and hunting away all the vermin, besides cutting down trees. As I knew it was profitable to fell timber, I directed them to begin with a very ugly straggling old hollow tree next the premises, but it fell the wrong way, and knocked down the cow-house. Luckily the poor animals were all in the clover-field at the time. George says it wouldn't have happened but for a violent sow, or rather sow-west,—and it's likely enough, but it's an ill wind that blows nothing to nobody.

Having writ last post to Mr. P., I have no occasion to make you a country commissioner. Anastasia, indeed, wants to have books about everything, but for my part and Dorothy's we don't put much faith in authorized receipts and directions, but trust more to nature and common sense. For instance, in fatting a goose, reason points to sage and onions,—why our own don't thrive on it, is very mysterious. We have a beautiful poultry yard, only infested with rats,—but I have made up a poison, that I know by the poor ducks, will kill them if they eat it.

I expected to send you a quantity of wall-fruit, for preserving, and am sorry you bought the brandy beforehand, as it has all vanished in one night by picking and stealing, notwithstanding I had ten dozen of bottles broke on purpose to stick a top of the wall. But I rather think they came over the pales, as George, who is very thoughtless, had driven in all the new tenter-hooks with the points downwards. Our apples and pears would have gone too, but luckily we heard a noise in the dark, and threw brickbats out of window, that alarmed the thieves by smashing the cowcumber frames. However, I mean on Monday to make sure of the orchard, by gathering the trees,—a pheasant in one's hand is worth two cock-sparrows in a bush. One comfort is, the house-dog is very vicious, and won't let any of us stir in or out after dark—indeed, nothing can be more furious, except the bull, and at me in particular. You would think he knew my inward thoughts, and that I intend to have him roasted whole when we give our grand house-warming regalia.

With these particulars, I remain, with love, my dear Dorcas, your affectionate sister,

BELINDA PUGSLEY.

P. S.—I have only one anxiety here, and that is, the likelihood of being taken violently ill, nine miles off from any physical powers, with nobody that can ride in the house, and nothing but an insurmountable hunting horse in the stable. I should like, therefore, to be well doctor-stuff'd from Apothecaries' Hall, by the wagon or any other vehicle. A stitch in the side taken in time saves nine spasms. Dorothy's tincture of the rhubarb stalks in the garden doesn't answer, and it's a pity now they were not saved for pies.

No. VI.—*From Mrs.* Pugsley *to Mrs.* Rogers.

Madam,

Although warmth has made a coolness, and our having words has caused a silence—yet as mere writing is not being on speaking terms, and disconsolate parents in the case; I waive venting of animosities till a more agreeable moment. Having perused the afflicted advertisement in the *Times*, with interesting description of person, and ineffectual dragging of New River,—beg leave to say that Master Robert is safe and well,—having arrived here on Saturday night last, with almost not a shoe to his foot, and no coat at all, as was supposed to be with the approbation of parents. It appears, that not supposing the distance between the families extended to him, he walked the whole way down on the footing of a friend, to visit my son Richard, but hearing the newspapers read, quitted suddenly, the same day with the gipsies, and we haven't an idea what is become of him. Trusting this statement will relieve of all anxiety, remain, Madam, your humble servant,

Belinda Pugsley.

No. VII.—*To Mr.* Silas Pugsley, *Parisian Depôt, Shoreditch.*

Dear Brother,

My favor of the present date is to advise of my safe arrival on Wednesday night, per opposition coach, after ninety miles of discomfort, absolutely unrivalled for cheapness, and a walk of five miles more, through lanes and roads, that for dirt and sludge may confidently defy competition, not to mention turnings and windings, too numerous to particularise, but morally impossible to pursue on undeviating principles. The night was of so dark a quality as forbade finding the gate, but for the house-dog flying upon me by mistake for the late respectable proprietor, and almost tearing my clothes off my back by his strenuous exertions to obtain the favor of my patronage.

Conscientiously averse to the fallacious statements, so much indulged in by various competitors, truth urges to acknowledge that on arrival, I did not find things on such a footing as to ensure universal satisfaction. Mrs. P., indeed, differs in her statement, but you know her success always surpassed the most sanguine expectations. Ever emulous to merit commendation by the strictest regard to principles of economy, I found her laid up with lumbago, through her studious efforts to please, and Doctor Clarke of Wisbeach in the house prescribing for it, but I am sorry to add—no abatement. Dorothy is also confined to her bed, by her unremitting assiduity and attention in the house-keeping line, and Anastasia the same, from listening for nightingales, on a fine July evening, but which is an article not always to be warranted to keep its virtue in any climate,—the other children, large and small sizes, ditto, ditto, with Grace too ill to serve in the nursery,—and the rest of the servants totally unable to execute such extensive demands. Such an unprecedented depreciation in health makes me doubt the quality of country air, so much recommended for family use, and whether constitutions have not more eligibility to offer that have been regularly town-made.

Our new residence is a large lonely Mansion, with no connexion with any other House, but standing in the heart of Lincolnshire fens, over which it looks through an advantageous opening: comprising a great variety of windmills, and drains, and willow-pollards, and an extensive assortment of similar articles, that are not much calculated to invite inspection. In warehouses for corn, &c., it probably presents unusual advantages to the occupier, but candor compels to state that agriculture in this part of Lincolnshire is very flat. To supply language on the most moderate terms, unexampled distress in Spitalfields is nothing to the distress in ours. The corn has been deluged with rain of remarkable durability, without being able to wash the smut out of its ears; and with regard to the expected great rise in hay, our stacks have been burnt down to the ground, instead of going to the consumer. If the hounds hadn't been out, we might have fetch'd the engines, but the hunter threw George on his head, and he only revived to be sensible that the entire stock had been disposed of at an immense sacrifice. The whole amount I fear will be out of book,—as the Norwich Union refuses to liquidate the hay, on the ground that the policy was voided by the impolicy of putting it up wet. In other articles I am sorry I must write no alteration. Our bull, after killing the house-dog, and tossing William, has gone wild and had the madness to run away from his livelihood, and, what is worse, all the cows after him—except those that had burst themselves in the clover field, and a small dividend, as I may say, of one in the pound. Another item, the pigs, to save bread and milk, have been turned into the woods for acorns, and is an article producing no returns—as not one has yet come back. Poultry ditto. Sedulously cultivating an enlarged connexion in the Turkey line, such the antipathy to gypsies, the whole breed, geese and ducks inclusive, removed themselves from the premises by night, directly a strolling camp came and set up in the neighborhood. To avoid prolixity, when I came to take stock, there was no stock to take—namely, no eggs, no butter, no cheese, no corn, no hay, no bread, no beer—no water even—nothing but the mere commodious premises, and fixtures, and good will—and candor compels to add, a very small quantity on hand of the last-named particular.

To add to stagnation, neither of my two sons in the business nor the two apprentices have been so diligently punctual in executing country orders with despatch and fidelity, as laudable ambition desires, but have gone about fishing and shooting—and William has suffered a loss of three fingers, by his unvarying system of high charges. He and Richard are likewise both threatened with prosecution for trespassing on the Hares in the adjoining landed interest, and Nick is obliged to decline any active share, by dislocating his shoulder in climbing a tall tree for a tom-tit. As for George, tho' for the first time beyond the circumscribed limits of town custom, he indulges vanity in such unqualified pretensions to superiority of knowledge in farming, on the strength of his grandfather having belonged to the agricultural line of trade, as renders a wholesale stock of patience barely adequate to meet its demands. Thus stimulated to injudicious performance he is as injurious to the best interests of the country, as blight and mildew, and smut and rot, and glanders, and pip, all combined in one texture. Between ourselves, the objects of unceasing endeavors, united with uncompromising integrity, have been assailed with so much deterioration, as makes me humbly desirous of abridging sufferings, by resuming business as a Shoe

Marter at the old established House. If Clack & Son, therefore, have not already taken possession and respectfully informed the vicinity, will thankfully pay reasonable compensation for loss of time and expense incurred by the bargain being off. In case parties agree, I beg you will authorize Mr. Robins to have the honor to dispose of the whole Lincolnshire concern, tho' the knocking down of Middlefen Hall will be a severe blow on Mrs. P. and Family. Deprecating the deceitful stimulus of advertising arts, interest commands to mention,—desirable freehold estate and eligible investment—and sole reason for disposal, the proprietor going to the continent. Example suggests likewise, a good country for hunting for fox-hounds—and a prospect too extensive to put in a newspaper. Circumstances being rendered awkward by the untoward event of the running away of the cattle, &c., it will be best to say—"The Stock to be taken as it stands;"—and an additional favor will be politely conferred, and the same thankfully acknowledged, if the auctioneer will be so kind as bring the next market town ten miles nearer, and carry the coach and the wagon once a day past the door. Earnestly requesting early attention to the above, and with sentiments of,

R. Pugsley, Sen.

P. S. Richard is just come to hand dripping and half dead out of the Nene, and the two apprentices all but drowned each other in saving him. Hence occurs to add, fishing opportunities among the desirable items.

THE DREAM OF EUGENE ARAM.*

'Twas in the prime of summer time,
An evening calm and cool,
When four-and-twenty happy boys
Came bounding out of school;
There were some that ran, and some that leapt,
Like troutlets in a pool.

Away they sped, with gamesome minds
And souls untouch'd by sin;
To a level mead they came, and there
They drave the wickets in:
Pleasantly shone the setting sun
Over the town of Lynn.

Like sportive deer they coursed about,
And shouted as they ran—
Turning to mirth all things of earth,
As only boyhood can:
But the usher sat remote from all,
A melancholy man!

* The late Admiral Burney went to school at an establishment where the unhappy Eugene Aram was usher, subsequent to his crime. The Admiral stated that Aram was generally liked by the boys; and that he used to discourse to them about *murder*, in somewhat of the spirit which is attributed to him in this poem.

His hat was off, his vest apart,
  To catch Heaven's blessed breeze ;
For a burning thought was on his brow,
  And his bosom ill at ease :
So he leaned his head on his hands, and read
  The book between his knees.

Leaf after leaf he turn'd it o'er,
  Nor ever glanced aside ;
For the peace of his soul he read that book,
  In the golden eventide :
Much study had made him very lean
  And pale and leaden-eyed.

At last he shut the ponderous tome;
  With a fast and fervid grasp—
He strained the dusky covers close,
  And fixed the brazen hasp ;
"O God! could I so close my mind,
  And clasp it with a clasp."

Then leaping on his feet upright,
  Some moody turns he took—
Now up the mead, then down the mead,
  And past a shady nook—
And, lo! he saw a little boy
  That pored upon a book.

"My gentle lad, what is 't you read—
  Romance, or fairy fable!
Or is it some historic page,
  Of kings and crowns unstable?"
The young boy gave an upward glance—
  "It is the Death of Abel."

The usher took six hasty strides,
  As smit with sudden pain—
Six hasty strides beyond the place,

Then slowly back again;
And down he sat beside the lad,
And talked with him of Cain.

And long since then, of bloody men,
Whose deeds tradition saves;
Of lonely folk, cut off unseen,
And hid in sudden graves;
Of horrid stabs in groves forlorn,
And murders done in caves!

And how the sprites of injured men
Shriek upward from the sod—
And how the ghostly hand will point
To show the burial clod;
And unknown facts of guilty acts
Are seen in dreams from God!

He told how murderers walked the earth
Beneath the curse of Cain—
With crimson clouds before their eyes,
And flames about their brain;
For blood had left upon their souls
Its everlasting stain!

"And well," quoth he, "I know, for truth,
Their pangs must be extreme—
Wo, wo, unutterable wo—
Who spill life's sacred stream!
For why? Methought, last night, I wrought
A murder in a dream!

"One that had never done me wrong—
A feeble man and old;
I led him to a lonely field,
The moon shone clear and cold;
Now here, said I, this man shall die,
And I will have his gold!

"Two sudden blows with a ragged stick,
And one with a heavy stone,
One horrid gash with a hasty knife—
And then the deed was done;
There was nothing lying at my feet,
But lifeless flesh and bone!

"Nothing but lifeless flesh and bone,
That could not do me ill;
And yet I feared him all the more,
For lying there so still;
There was a manhood in his look,
That murder could not kill!

"And lo! the universal air
Seemed lit with ghastly flame—
Ten thousand thousand dreadful eyes
Were looking down in blame;
I took the dead man by the hand,
And called upon his name!

"Oh God! it made me quake to see
Such sense within the slain!
But when I touched the lifeless clay,
The blood gushed out amain!
For every clot, a burning spot
Was scorching in my brain!

My head was like an ardent coal,
My heart was solid ice;
My wretched, wretched soul, I knew,
Was at the Devil's price;
A dozen times I groan'd; the dead
Had never groan'd but twice!

"And now from forth the frowning sky,
From the heaven's topmost height
I heard a voice—the awful voice

Of the blood-avenging sprite ;
'Thou guilty man! take up thy dead,
And hide it from my sight!'

"I took the dreary body up,
And cast it in a stream—
A sluggish water, black as ink,
The death was so extreme
(My gentle boy, remember this
Was nothing but a dream).

"Down went the corse with a hollow plunge
And vanish'd in a pool ;
Anon I cleaned my bloody hands,
And wash'd my forehead cool,
And sat among the urchins young
That evening in the school.

"Oh heaven! to think of their white souls,
And mine so black and grim!
I could not share in childish prayer,
Nor join in evening hymn ;
Like a devil of the pit I seem'd
'Mid holy cherubim.

"And peace went with them one and all,
And each calm pillow spread ;
But Guilt was my grim chamberlain
That lighted me to bed,
And drew my midnight curtains round,
With fingers bloody red!

"All night I lay in agony,
From weary chime to chime,
With one besetting horrid hint,
That racked me all the time,
A mighty yearning, like the first,
Fierce impulse unto crime!

One stern, tyrannic thought, that made
All other thoughts its slave;
Stronger and stronger every pulse
Did that temptation crave—
Still urging me to go and see
The dead man in his grave!

"Heavily I rose up—as soon
As light was in the sky—
And sought the black, accursed pool,
With a wild misgiving eye,
And I saw the dead in the river bed,
For the faithless stream was dry!

"Merrily rose the lark, and shook
The dew-drop from its wing;
But I never marked its morning flight,
I never heard it sing:
For I was stooping once again
Under the horrid thing.

"With breathless speed, like a soul in chase,
I took him up and ran—
There was no time to dig a grave
Before the day began!
In a lonesome wood with heaps of leaves,
I hid the murdered man!

"And all that day I read in school,
But my thought was otherwhere;
As soon as the mid-day task was done,
In secret I was there:
And a mighty wind had swept the leaves,
And still the corse was bare!

"Then down I cast me on my face,
And first began to weep,
For I knew my secret then was one

That Earth refused to keep;
Or land or sea, though he should be
Ten thousand fathoms deep!

'So wills the fierce avenging sprite
Till blood for blood atones!
Ay, though he 's buried in a cave,
And trodden down with stones,
And years have rotted off his flesh—
The world shall see his bones!

"Oh God, that horrid, horrid dream
Besets me now awake!
Again—again, with a dizzy brain,
The human life I take;
And my red right hand grows raging hot,
Like Cranmer's at the stake.

"And still no peace for the restless clay
Will wave or mould allow;
The horrid thing that pursues my soul—
It stands before me now!"
The fearful boy looked up and saw
Huge drops upon his brow!

That very night, while gentle sleep
The urchin's eyelids kissed,
Two stern-faced men set out from Lynn,
Through the cold and heavy mist;
And Eugene Aram walked between,
With gyves upon his wrist.

BLACK, WHITE, AND BROWN.

All at once Miss Morbid left off sugar.

She did not resign it as some persons lay down their carriage, the full-bodied family coach dwindling into a chariot, next into a fly, and then into a sedan-chair. She did not shade it off artistically, like certain household economists, from white to whitey brown, brown, dark-brown, and so on, to none at all. She left it off, as one might leave off walking on the top of a house, or on a slide, or on a plank with a further end to it, that is to say, slapdash, all at once, without a moment's warning. She gave it up, to speak appropriately, in the lump. She dropped it,—as Corporal Trim let fall his hat,—dab. It vanished, as the French say, *toot sweet.* From the 30th of November, 1830, not an ounce of sugar, to use Miss Morbid's own expression, ever "darkened her doors."

The truth was she had been present the day before at an Anti-Slavery Meeting; and had listened to a lecturing Abolitionist, who had drawn her sweet tooth, root and branch, out of her head. Thenceforth sugar, or as she called it "shugger," was no longer white, or brown, in her eyes, but red, blood-red—an abomination, to indulge in which would convert a professing Christian into a practical Cannibal. Accordingly, she made a vow, under the influence of moist eyes and refined feelings, that the sanguinary article should never more enter her lips or her house; and this pretty parody of the famous Berlin decree against our Colonial produce was rigidly enforced. However others might countenance the practice of the Slave Owners by consuming "shugger," she was resolved for her own part, that "no suffering sable son of Africa should ever rise up against her out of a cup of Tea!"

In the mean time, the cook and house-maid grumbled in concert at the prohibition: they naturally thought it very hard to be deprived of a luxury which they enjoyed at their own proper cost; and at last only consented to remain in the service, on condition that the privation should be handsomely considered in their wages. With a hope of being similarly remembered in her will, the poor relations of Miss Morbid continued to drink the "warm without," which she administered to them every Sunday, under the name of Tea: and Hogarth would have desired no better subject for a picture than was presented by their physiognomies. Some pursed up their lips, as if resolved that the nauseous beverage should never enter them; others compressed their mouths, as if to prevent it from rushing out again. One took it mincingly, in sips,—another gulped it down in desperation,—a third, in a fit of absence, continued to stir very superfluously with his spoon; and there was one shrewd old gentleman, who, by a little dexterous by-play, used to bestow the favor of his small souchong on a sick geranium. Now and then an astonished Stranger would retain a half cupful of the black dose in his mouth, and stare round at his fellow guests, as if tacitly putting to them the very question of Matthews's Yorkshireman, in the mail-coach—"Coompany!—oop or doon?"

The greatest sufferers, however, were Miss Morbid's two nephews, still in the morning of their youth, and boy-like, far more inclined to "sip the sweets" than to "hail the dawn." They had formerly looked on their Aunt's house as peculiarly a Dulce Domum. Prior to her sudden conversion, she had been famous for the manufacture of a sort of hard bake, commonly called Toffy or Taffy,—but now, alas! "Taffy was not at home," and there was nothing else to invite a call. Currant tart is tart indeed without sugar; and as for the green gooseberries, they always tasted, as the young gentlemen affirmed, "like a quart of berries sharpened to a pint." In short, it always required six pennyworth of lollipops and bulls'-eyes, a lick of honey, a dip of treacle, and a pick at a grocer's hogshead, to sweeten a visit at Aunt Morbid's.

To tell the truth, her own temper soured a little under the prohibition. She could not persuade the Sugar-eaters that they were Vampyres;—instead of practising, or even admiring her self-denial, they laughed at it; and one wicked wag even compared her, in allusion to her acerbity and her privation, to a crab, without *the nippers*. She persevered notwithstanding in her system; and to the constancy of a martyr added something of the wilfulness of a bigot:—indeed, it was hinted by patrons and patronesses of white charities, that European objects had not their *fair* share in her benevolence. She was pre-eminently the friend of the blacks. Howbeit, for all her sacrifices, not a lash was averted from their sable backs. She had raised discontent in the kitchen, she had disgusted her acquaintance, sickened her friends, and given her own dear little nephews the stomach-ache, without saving Quashy from one cut of the driver's whip, or diverting a single kick from the shins of Sambo. Her grocer complained loudly of being called a dealer in human gore, yet not one hogshead the less was imported from the Plantations. By an error common to all her class she mistook a negative for a positive principle; and persuaded herself that by *not* preserving damsons, she preserved the Niggers; that by *not* sweetening her own cup, she was dulcifying the lot of all her sable brethren in bondage. She persevered accordingly in setting her face against sugar instead of slavery; against the plant, instead of the planter; and had actually abstained for six months from the forbidden article, when a circumstance occurred that roused her sympathies into more active exertions. It pleased an American lady to import with her a black female servant, whom she rather abruptly dismissed, on her arrival in England. The case was considered by the Hampshire Telegraph of that day, as one of GREAT HARDSHIP; the paragraph went the round of the papers —and in due time attracted the notice of Miss Morbid. It was precisely addressed to her sensibilities, and there was a "Try Warren" tone about it, that proved irresistible. She read—and wrote,—and in the course of one little week, her domestic establishment was maliciously but truly described as consisting of "two white Slaves and a black Companion."

The adopted protégée was, in reality, a strapping clumsy Negress, as ugly as sin, and with no other merit than that of being of the same color as the crow. She was artful, sullen, gluttonous, and, above all, so intolerably indolent, that if she had been literally "carved in ebony," as old Fuller says, she could scarcely have been of less service to her protectress. Her notion of Free Labor seemed to translate it into laziness, and taking liberties; and, as she seriously added to the work of her fellow-servants, without at all contributing to their comfort, they soon looked upon her as a complete nuisance. The house-maid dubbed her "a Divil,"—the cook roundly compared her to "a mischivus beast, as runs out on a herd o' black cattle;"—and both concurred in the policy of laying all household sins upon the sooty shoulders—just as slatterns select a color that hides the dirt. It is certain that shortly after the instalment of the negress in the family, a moral disease broke out with considerable violence, and justly or not, the odium was attributed to the new comer. Its name was theft. First, there was a shilling short in some loose change—next, a missing half-crown from the mantel-piece—then there was a stir with a tea-spoon—anon, a piece of work about a thimble. Things went, nobody knew how —the "Divil" of course excepted. The Cook *could*, the House-maid *would*, and Diana *should*, and *ought* to take an oath, declaratory of innocence, before the mayor; but as Diana did not volunteer an affidavit, like the others, there was no doubt of her guilt, in the kitchen.

Miss Morbid, however, came to a very different conclusion. She thought that whites who could eat sugar, were capable of any atrocity, and had not forgotten the stand which had been made by the "pale faces," in favor of the obnoxious article. The cook especially incurred suspicion; for she had been notorious aforetime for a lavish hand in sweetening, and was accordingly quite equal to the double turpitude of stealing and bearing false witness. In fact, the mistress had arrived at the determination of giving both her white hussies their month's warning, when unexpectedly the thief was taken, as the lawyers say, "in the manner," and with the goods upon the person. In a word, the ungrateful black was detected in the very act of levying what might be called her "Black Mail."

The horror of Emilia, on discovering that the Moor had murdered her mistress, was scarcely greater than that of Miss Morbid! She hardly, she said, believed her own senses. You might have knocked her down with a feather! She did not know whether she stood on her head or her heels. She was rooted to the spot! and her hair, if it had been her own, would have stood upright upon her head! There was no doubt in the case. She saw the transfer of a portion of her own bank-stock, from her escritoire into the right-hand pocket of her protégée—she heard it chink as it dropped downwards,—she was petrified!—dumb-founded!—thunder-bolted!—"annilliated." She was as white as a sheet, but she felt as if all the blacks in the world had just blown in her face.

Her first impulse was to rush upon the robber, and insist on restitution—her second was to sit down and weep,—and her third was to talk. The opening, as usual, was a mere torrent of ejaculations intermixed with vituperation—but she gradually fell into a lecture with many heads. First, she described all she had done for the Blacks, and then, alas! all that the Blacks had done for her. Next she insisted on the enormity of the crime, and, anon, she enlarged on the nature of its punishment. It was here that she was most eloquent. She traced the course of human justice, from detection to conviction, and thence to execution, liberally throwing dissection into the bargain: and then descending with Dante into the unmentionable regions, she painted its terrors and tortures with all the circumstantial fidelity that certain very Old Masters have displayed on the same subject.

"And now, you black wretch," she concluded, having just given a finishing touch to a portrait of Satan himself; "and now, you black wretch, I insist on knowing what I was robbed for. Come, tell me what tempted you! I'm determined to hear it! I insist, I say, on knowing what was to be done with the wages of iniquity!"

She insisted, however, in vain. The black wretch had seriously inclined her ear to the whole lecture, grinning and blubbering by turns. The Judge with his black cap, the Counsel and their wigs, the twelve men in a box, and Jack Ketch himself—whom she associated with that pleasant West Indian personage, John Canoe—had amused, nay, tickled her fancy; the press-room, the irons, the rope, and the Ordinary, whom she mistook for an overseer, had raised her curiosity, and excited her fears; but the spiritualities, without any reference to Obeah, had simply mystified and disgusted her, and she was now in a fit of the sulks. Her mistress, however, persisted in her question; and not the less pertinaciously, perhaps, from expecting a new peg whereon to hang a fresh lecture. She was determined to learn the destination of the stolen money; and by dint of insisting, cajoling, and, above all, threatening—for instance, with the whole Posse Comitatus—she finally carried her point.

"Cuss him money! Here's a fuss!" exclaimed the culprit, quite worn out at last by the persecution. "Cuss him money! here's a fuss! What me 'teal him for? What me do wid him? What anybody 'teal him for? Why, for sure, *to buy sugar!*"

I REMEMBER, I REMEMBER.

I REMEMBER, I remember,
  The house where I was born,
The little window where the sun
  Came peeping in at morn:
He never came a wink too soon,
  Nor brought too long a day;
But now, I often wish the night
  Had borne my breath away.

I remember, I remember,
  The roses—red and white;
The violets and the lily-cups,
  Those flowers made of light!
The lilacs where the robin built,
  And where my brother set
The laburnum on his birth-day,—
  The tree is living yet!

I remember, I remember,
  Where I was used to swing;
And thought the air must rush as fresh
  To swallows on the wing:
My spirit flew in feathers then,
  That is so heavy now,
And summer pools could hardly cool
  The fever on my brow!

I remember, I remember,
  The fir trees dark and high;

I used to think their slender tops
  Were close against the sky:
It was a childish ignorance,
  But now 'tis little joy
To know I'm farther off from heaven
  Than when I was a boy.

THE PORTRAIT:

BEING AN APOLOGY FOR NOT MAKING AN ATTEMPT ON MY OWN LIFE

THE late inimitable Charles Mathews, in one of his amusing entertainments, used to tell a story of a certain innkeeper, who made it a rule of his house, to allow a candle to a guest, only on condition of his ordering a pint of wine. Whereupon the guest contends, on the reciprocity system, for a light for every half-bottle, and finally drinks himself into a general illumination.

Something of the above principle seems to have obtained in the case of a Portrait and a Memoir, which in literary practice have been usually dependent on each other—a likeness and a life,—a candle and a pint of wine. The mere act of sitting probably suggests the idea of hatching; at least an author has seldom nested in a painter's chair, without coming out afterwards with a brood of Reminiscences, and accordingly, no sooner was my effigy about to be presented to the Public, than I found myself called upon by my Publisher, with a finished proof of the engraving in one hand, and a request for an account of myself in the other. He evidently supposed, as a matter of course, that I had my auto-biography in the bottle, and that the time was come to un-cork and pour it out *with a Head.*

To be candid, no portrait, perhaps, ever stood more in need of such an accompaniment. The figure has certainly the look of one of those practical jokes whereof the original is oftener suspected than really culpable. It might pass for the sign of "The Grave Maurice." The author of Elia has declared that he once sat as substitute for a whole series of British Admirals,* and a physiognomist might reasonably suspect that

* He perhaps took the hint from Dibdin, who lays down the rule in his Sea Songs, that a Naval Hero ought to be a Lion in battle, but afterwards a Lamb.

in wantonness or weariness, instead of giving my head I had procured myself to be painted by proxy. For who, that calls himself stranger, could ever suppose that such a pale, pensive, peaking, sentimental, sonneteering countenance—with a wry mouth as if it always laughed on its wrong side—belonged bonâ fide to the Editor of the Comic—a Professor of the Pantagruelian Philosophy, hinted at in the preface of the present work? What unknown who reckons himself decidedly serious, would recognize the head and front of my "offending," in a visage not at all too hilarious for a frontispiece to the Evangelical Magazine! In point of fact the owner has been taken sundry times, ere now, for a Methodist Minister, and a pious turn has been attributed to his hair—lucus a non lucendo—from its having no turn in it at all.* In like manner my literary contemporaries who have cared to remark on my personals, have agreed in ascribing to me a melancholy bias; thus an authority in the New Monthly Magazine has described me as "a grave anti-pun-like-looking person," whilst another—in the Book of Gems—declares that "my countenance is more grave than merry," and insists, therefore, that I am of a pensive habit, and "have never laughed heartily in company or in rhyme." Against such an inference, however, I solemnly protest, and if it be the fault of my features, I do not mind telling my face to its face that it insinuates a false Hood, and grossly misrepresents a person notorious amongst friends for laughing at strange times and odd places, and in particular when he has the worst of the rubber. For it is no comfort for the loss of points, by his theory, to be upon thorns. And truly what can be more unphilosophical, than to sit ruefully as well as whistfully, with your face inconsistently playing at longs and your hand at shorts,—getting hypped as well as pipped,—"talking of Hoyle," as the city lady said, "but looking like winegar," and betraying as keen a sense of the profit and loss, as if the *pack* had turned you into a *pedlar*.

But I am digressing; and turning my back, as Lord Castlereagh would have said, on my face. The portrait, then, is genuine—"an ill-favored thing, Sir," as Touchstone says, "but

* On a march to Berlin, with the 19th Prussian Infantry, I could never succeed in passing myself off as anything but the Regimental Chaplain.

mine own." For its quarrel with the rules of Lavater there is precedent. I remember seeing on Sir Thomas Lawrence's easel, an unfinished head of Mr. Wilberforce, so very merry, so rosy, so good-fellowish, that nothing less than the Life and Correspondence recently published could have persuaded me that he was really a serious character. A memoir, therefore, would be the likeliest thing to convince the world that the physiognomy alluded to, is actually Hood's own:—indeed a few of the earlier chapters would suffice to clear up the mystery, by proving that my face is only answering in the affirmative, the friendly inquiry of the Poet of all circles—"Has sorrow thy young days shaded?"—and telling the honest truth of one of those rickety constitutions which, according to Hudibras, seem

"——— as if intended
For nothing else but to be mended."

To confess the truth, my vanity pricked up its ears a little at the proposition of my publisher. There is something vastly flattering in the idea of appropriating the half of a quarter of a century, mixing it up with your personal experience, and then serving it out as your own Life and Times. On casting a retrospective glance however across Memory's waste, it appeared so literally a waste, that vanity herself shrank from the enclosure act, as an unpromising speculation. Had I foreseen indeed, some five-and-thirty years ago, that such a demand would be made upon me, I might have laid myself out on purpose, as Dr. Watts recommends, so as "to give of every day some good account at last." I would have lived like a Frenchman, for effect, and made my life a long dress rehearsal of the future biography. I would have cultivated incidents "pour servir," laid traps for adventures, and illustrated my memory like Rogers's, by a brilliant series of Tableaux. The earlier of my Seven Stages should have been more Wonder Phenomenon Comet and Balloon-like, and have been timed to a more Quicksilver pace than they have travelled; in short, my Life, according to the tradesman's promise, should have been "fully equal to bespoke." But, alas! in the absence of such a Scottish second-sight, my whole course of existence up to the present moment would hardly furnish materials for one of those "bald biographies" that content the old gentlemanly pages of Sylvanus Urban. Lamb, on being applied to for a Memoir of himself, made answer that it would go into an epigram; and I really believe that I could compress my own into that baker's dozen of lines called a sonnet. Montgomery, indeed, has forestalled the greater part of it, in his striking poem on the "Common Lot," but in prose, nobody could ever make anything of it, except Mr. George Robins. The lives of literary men are proverbially barren of interest, and mine, instead of forming an exception to the general rule, would bear the application of the following words of Sir Walter Scott, much better than the career of their illustrious author. "There is no man known at all in literature, who may not have more to tell of his private life than I have. I have surmounted no difficulties either of birth or education, nor have I been favored by any particular advantages, and my life has been as void of incidents of importance as that of the weary knife-grinder—'Story! bless you, I have none to tell, sir.'"

Thus my birth was neither so humble that, like John Jones, I have been obliged amongst my lays to lay the cloth, and to court the cook and the muses at the same time; nor yet so lofty, that, with a certain lady of title, I could not write without letting myself down. Then, for education, though on the one hand I have not taken my degree, with Blucher; yet, on the other, I have not been rusticated, at the Open Air School, like the Poet of Helpstone. As for incidents of importance, I remember none, except being drawn for a soldier, which was a hoax, and having the opportunity of giving a casting vote on a great parochial question, only I didn't attend. I have never been even third in a duel, or crossed in love. The stream of time has flowed on with me very like that of the New River, which everybody knows has so little romance about it, that its Head has never troubled us with a Tale. My own story then, to possess any interest, must be a fib.

Truly given, with its egotism and its barrenness, it would look too like the chalked advertisements on a dead wall. Moreover, Pope has read a lesson to self-importance in the Memoirs of P. P., the parish Clerk, who was only notable after all amongst his neighbors as a swallower of loaches. Even in such practical whims and oddities I am deficient,—for instance, eschewing razors, or bolting clasp-knives, riding on painted ponies, sleeping for weeks, fasting for months, devouring raw tripe, and similar eccentricities, which have entitled sundry knaves, quacks, boobies, and brutes, to a brief biography in the Wonderful Magazine. And, in the absence of these distinctions, I am equally deficient in any spiritual pretensions. I have had none of those experiences which render the lives of saintlings, not yet in their teens, worth their own weight in paper and print, and consequently my personal history, as a Tract, would read as flat as the Pilgrim's Progress without the Giants, the Lions, and the grand single combat with the Devil.

To conclude, my life,—" upon my life,"—is not worth giving, or taking. The principal just suffices for me to live upon; and of course, would afford little interest to any one else. Besides, I have a bad memory; and a personal history would assuredly be but a middling one, of which I have forgotten the beginning and cannot foresee the end. I must, therefore, respectfully decline giving my life to the world—at least till I have done with it—but to soften the refusal, I am willing, instead of a written character of myself, to set down all that I can recall of other authors, and, accordingly, the next number will contain the first instalment of

MY LITERARY REMINISCENCES.

LITERARY REMINISCENCES.

"Commençons par le commencement."

The very earliest of one's literary recollections must be the acquisition of the alphabet; and in the knowledge of the first rudiments I was placed on a par with the Learned Pig, by two maiden ladies that were called Hogsflesh. The circumstance would be scarcely worth mentioning, but that being a day-boarder, and taking my dinner with the family, I became aware of a Baconian brother, who was never mentioned except by his Initial, and was probably the prototype of the sensitive "Mr. H.," in Lamb's unfortunate farce. The school in question was situated in Token-house Yard, a convenient distance for a native of the Poultry, or Birchin-lane, I forget which, and in truth am not particularly anxious to be more certainly acquainted with my parish. It was a metropolitan one, however, which is recorded without the slightest repugnance; firstly, for that, practically, I had no choice in the matter; and secondly, because, theoretically, I would as lief have been a native of London as of Stoke Pogis or Little Pedlington. If such local prejudices be of any worth, the balance ought to be in favor of the capital. The Dragon of Bow Church, or Gresham's Grasshopper, is as good a terrestrial sign to be born under as the dunghill cock on a village steeple. Next to being a citizen of the world, it must be the best thing to be born a citizen of the world's greatest city. To a lover of his kind, it should be a welcome dispensation that cast his nativity amidst the greatest congregation of the species; but a literary man should exult rather than otherwise that he first saw the light—or perhaps the fog—in the same metropolis as Milton, Gray, De Foe, Pope, Byron, Lamb, and other town-born authors, whose fame has nevertheless triumphed over the

Bills of Mortality. In such a goodly company I cheerfully take up my livery; and especially as Cockneyism, properly so called, appears to be confined to no particular locality or station in life. Sir Walter Scott has given a splendid instance of it in an Orcadian, who prayed to the Lord to bless his own tiny ait, "not forgetting the neighboring island of Great Britain;" and the most recent example of the style I have met with, was in the Memoirs of Sir William Knighton, being an account of sea perils and sufferings during a passage across the Irish Channel by "the First Gentleman in Europe."

Having alluded to my first steps on the ladder of learning, it may not be amiss in this place to correct an assertion of my biographer in the Book of Gems, who states, that my education was finished at a certain suburban academy. In this ignorant world, where we proverbially live and learn, we may indeed leave off school, but our education only terminates with life itself. But even in a more limited sense, instead of my education being finished, my own impression is, that it never so much as progressed towards so desirable a consummation at any such establishment, although much invaluable time was spent at some of those institutions where young gentlemen are literally boarded, lodged, and *done for*. My very first essay was at one of those places improperly called *semi*-naries, because they do not half teach anything; the principals being probably aware that the little boys are as often consigned to them to be "out of a mother's way," as for anything else. Accordingly, my memory presents but a very dim image of a pedagogical powdered head, amidst a more vivid group of females of a composite charter-part dry-nurse, part housemaid, and part governess,—with a matronly figure in the back-ground, very like Mrs. S., allegorically representing, as Milton says, "our universal mother." But there is no glimpse of Minerva. Of those pleasant associations with early school days, of which so much has been said and sung, there is little amongst my retrospections, excepting, perhaps, some sports which, like charity, might have been enjoyed at home, without the drawbacks of sundry strokes, neither apoplectic nor paralytic, periodical physic, and other unwelcome extras. I am not sure whether an invincible repugnance to early rising may not be attributable to our precocious wintry summonses, from a warm bed into a dim damp school-room, to play at filling our heads on an empty stomach; and perhaps I owe my decided sedentary habits to the disgust at our monotonous walks, or rather processions, or maybe to the sufferings of those longer excursions of big and little, where a pair of compasses had to pace as far and as fast as a pair of tongs. Nevertheless, I yet recall, with wonder, the occasional visits of grown-up ex-scholars to their old school, all in a flutter of gratitude and sensibility at recognizing the spot where they had been caned, and horsed, and flogged, and fagged, and brimstone-and-treacled, and black-dosed, and stick-jawed, and kibed, and fined,—where they had caught the measles and the mumps, and been overtasked, and undertaught—and then, by way of climax, sentimentally offering a presentation snuff-box to their revered preceptor, with an inscription, ten to one, in dog Latin on the lid!

For my own part, were I to revisit such a haunt of my youth, it would give me the greatest pleasure, out of mere regard to the rising generation, to find Prospect House turned into a Floor Cloth Manufactory, and the playground converted to a bleach-field. The tabatière is out of the question. In the way of learning, I carried off nothing in exchange for my knife and fork, and spoon, but a prize for Latin without knowing the Latin for prize, and a belief which I had afterwards to unbelieve again, that a block of marble could be cut in two with a razor.

To be classical, as Ducrow would say, the Athenians, the day before the Festival of Theseus, their Founder, gratefully sacrificed a ram, in memory of Corridas the schoolmaster, who had been his instructor; but in the present day, were such offerings in fashion, how frequently would the appropriate animal be a donkey, and especially too big a donkey to get over the Pons Asinorum!

From the preparatory school, I was transplanted in due time to what is called by courtesy, a finishing one, where I was immediately set to begin everything again at the beginning. As this was but a backward way of coming forward, there seemed little chance of my ever becoming what Mrs. Malaprop calls "a progeny of learning;" indeed my education was pursued very much after the plan laid down by that feminine authority. I had nothing to do with Hebrew, or Algebra, or Simony, or Fluxions, or Paradoxes, or such inflammatory branches; but I obtained a supercilious knowledge of accounts, with enough of geometry to make me acquainted with the contagious countries. Moreover, I became fluent enough in some unknown tongue to protect me from the French Mark; and I was sufficiently at home (during the vacations) in the quibbles of English grammar, to bore all my parents, relations, friends, and acquaintance, by a pedantical mending of their "cakeology." Such was the sum total of my acquirements; being, probably, quite as much as I should have learned at a Charity School, with the exception of the parochial accomplishment of hallooing and singing of anthems.

I have entered into these personal details, though pertaining rather to illiterate than to literary reminiscences, partly because he important subject of Education has become of prominent in terest, and partly to hint that a writer may often mean in earnest what he says in jest. One of my readers at least has given me credit for a serious purpose. A schoolmaster called, during the vacation, on the father of one of his pupils, and in answer to his announcement of the re-opening of his establishment, was informed that the young gentleman was not to return to the academy. The worthy parent declared that he had read the "Carnaby Correspondence," in the Comic Annual, and had made up his mind. "But, my dear Sir," expostulated the pedagogue, "you cannot be serious; why the Comic Annual is nothing but a book full of jokes!" "Yes, yes," returned the father, "but it has let me into a few of your tricks. I believe Mr. Hood. James is not coming again!"

And now, it may be reasonably asked, where I did learn anything if not at these establishments, which promise Universal Knowledge—extras included—and yet unaccountably produce so very few Admirable Crichtons?* It may plausibly be objected, that I did not duly avail myself of such overflowing

* In spite of hundreds of associates, it has never happened to me, amongst the very many distinguished names connected with science or literature, to recognize *one* as belonging to a school-fellow.

opportunities to dabble, dip, duck in, and drink deeply of, the Pierian spring, that I was an Idler, Lounger, Tatler, Rambler, Spectator, anything rather than a student. To which my reply must be, first, that the severest punishment ever inflicted on my shoulders was for a scholar-like offence, the being "fond of my book," only it happened to be Robinson Crusoe; and secondly, that I did go ahead at another guess sort of academy, a reference to which will be a little flattering to those Houses which claim Socrates, Aristotle, Alfred, and other *Learnedissimi Worthii*, as their Sponsors and Patron Saints. The school that really schooled me being comparatively of a very humble order—without sign—without prospectus—without ushers—without ample and commodious premises—in short, without pretension, and, consequently, almost without custom.

The autumn of the year 1811, along with a most portentous comet, "with fear of change perplexing monarchs," brought, alas! a melancholy revolution in my own position and prospects, by the untimely death of my father; and my elder brother shortly following him to the grave, my bereaved mother naturally drew the fragments of the family more closely around her, so that thenceforward her dearest care was to keep her "only son, myself, at home." She did not, however, neglect my future interest, or persuade herself by any maternal vanity that a boy of twelve years old could have precociously finished his education; and, accordingly, the next spring found me at what might have been literally called a High School, in reference to its distance from the ground.

In a house, formerly a suburban seat of the unfortunate Earl of Essex—over a grocer's shop—up two pair of stairs, there was a very select day-school, kept by a decayed Dominie, as he would have been called in his native land. In his better days, when my brother was his pupil, he had been master of one of those wholesale concerns in which so many ignorant men have made fortunes, by favor of high terms, low ushers, gullible parents, and victimized little boys. As our worthy Dominie, on the contrary, had failed to realize even a competence, it may be inferred logically, that he had done better by his pupils than by himself; and my own experience certainly went to prove that he attended to the interests of his scholars, however he might have neglected his own. Indeed, he less resembled, even in externals, the modern worldly trading Schoolmaster than the good, honest, earnest, olden Pedagogue—a pedant, perchance, but a learned one, with whom teaching was "a labor of love," who had a proper sense of the dignity and importance of his calling, and was content to find a main portion of his reward in the honorable proficiency of his disciples. Small as was our College, its Principal maintained his state, and walked gowned and covered. His cap was of faded velvet, of black, or blue, or purple, or sad green, or as it seemed, of all together, with a *nuance* of brown. His robe, of crimson damask, lined with the national tartan. A quaint, carved, high-backed, elbowed article, looking like an *émigré*, from a set that had been at home in an aristocratical drawing-room, under the *ancien régime*, was his Professional Chair, which, with his desk, was appropriately elevated on a dais, some inches above the common floor. From this moral and material eminence, he cast a vigilant yet kindly eye over some dozen of youngsters; for adversity, sharpened by habits of authority, had not soured him, or mingled a single tinge of bile with the peculiar red-streak complexion, so common to the healthier natives of the North. On one solitary occasion, within my memory, was he seriously, yet characteristically discomposed, and that was by his own daughter, whom he accused of "forgetting all regard for common decorum," because, forgetting that he was a Dominie as well as a Parent, she had heedlessly addressed him in public as "Father," instead of "Papa." The mere provoking contrariety of a dunce never stirred his spleen, but rather spurred his endeavor, in spite of the axiom, to make Nihil fit for anything. He loved teaching for teaching's sake; his kill-horse happened to be his hobby: and doubtless, if he had met with a penniless boy on the road to learning, he would have given him a lift, like the charitable Waggoner to Dick Whittington—for love. I recall, therefore, with pleasure, the cheerful alacrity with which I used to step up to recite my lesson, constantly forewarned—for every true schoolmaster has his stock joke—not to "stand in my own light." It was impossible not to take an interest in learning what he seemed so interested in teaching; and in a few months my education progressed infinitely farther than it had done in as many years under the listless superintendance of B. A., and LL. D. and Assistants. I picked up *some* Latin, was a tolerable English Grammarian, and so good a French scholar, that I earned a few guineas—my first literary fee—by revising a new edition of "Paul et Virginie" for the press. Moreover, as an accountant, I could work a *summum bonum*—i. e., a good sum.

In the meantime,—so generally unfortunate is the courtship of that bashful undertoned wooer, Modest Merit, to that loud, brazen masculine, worldly heiress, Success—the school did not prosper. The number of scholars diminished rather than increased. At least no new boys came—but one fine morning, about nine o'clock, a great "she gal," of fifteen or sixteen, but so remarkably well grown that she might have been "any of our mothers," made her unexpected appearance with bag and books. The sensation that she excited is not to be described! The apparition of a Governess, with a Proclamation of a Gynecocracy, could not have been more astounding! Of course SHE instantly formed a class; and had any form SHE might prefer to herself:—the most of us being just old enough to resent what was considered as an affront on the corduroy sex, and just young enough to be beneath any gallantry to the silken one. The truth was, sub rosâ, that there was a plan for translating us, and turning the unsuccessful Boys' School into a Ladies' Academy, to be conducted by the Dominie's eldest daughter—but it had been thought prudent to be well on with the new set before being off with the old. A brief period only had elapsed, when, lo! a leash of female school *Fellows*—three sisters, like the Degrees of Comparison personified, Big, Bigger, and Biggest—made their unwelcome appearance, and threatened to push us from our stools. They were greeted, accordingly, with all the annoyances that juvenile malice could suggest. It is amusing, yet humiliating, to remember the nuisances the sex endured at the hands of those who were thereafter to honor the shadow of its shoe-tie—to groan, moan, sigh, and sicken for its smiles,—to become poetical, prosaical, nonsensical, lack-a-daisical, and perhaps even melodramatical for its sake. Numberless were the desk-quakes, the ink-spouts, the book-bolts, the pea-showers, and other unregistered phenomena, which likened the studies of those four unlucky maidens to the "Pursuit of Knowledge under Difficulties,"—so that it glads me to reflect, that I was in a very small minority against the persecution; having already begun to read poetry, and even to write something which was egregiously mistaken for something of the same nature. The final result of the struggle in the academic nest—whether the hen-cuckoos succeeded in ousting the cock-sparrows, or vice versâ—is beyond my record; seeing that I was just then removed from the scene of contest, to be introduced into that Universal School, where, as in the preparatory one, we have very unequal shares in the flogging, the fagging, the task-work, and the pocket-money; but the same breaking up to expect, and the same eternity of happy holidays to hope for in the Grand Recess.

In brief, a friend of the family having taken a fancy to me, proposed to initiate me in those profitable mercantile mysteries which enabled Sir Thomas Gresham to gild his grasshopper; and like another Frank Osbaldestone, I found myself planted on a counting-house stool, which nevertheless served occasionally for a Pegasus, on three legs, every foot, of course, being a dactyl or a spondee. In commercial matters, the only lesson imprinted on my memory is the rule, that when a ship's crew from Archangel come to receive their L. S. D., you must lock up your P. Y. C.

MY APOLOGY.

GENTLE READERS,

For the present month, there must be what Dr. Johnson called a solution of continuity in my "Literary Reminiscences." Confined to my chamber by what ought to be termed *room*atism—then attacked by my old livery complaint—and finally, by a minor, but troublesome malady, the Present has too much prevailed over the Past, to let me indulge in any retrospective reviews. In such cases, on the stage, when a Performer is unable to support his character, a substitute is usually found to read the part; but unfortunately, in the present case there is no part written, and consequently it cannot be read. But apropos of theatricals—there is an anecdote in point.

In the Olympic days of the great Elliston, there was one evening a tremendous tumult at his Theatre, in consequence of the absence of a favorite performer. One man in the pit—a Butcher—was especially vociferous in his cry for "Carl! Carl! Carl!" Others called for the Manager, who duly made his appearance, and black as the weather looked, he was the very sort of pilot to weather the storm. With one of his princely bows he proceeded to address the House. "Ladies and Gentlemen—but by your leave I will address myself to a single individual. I will ask that gentleman (pointing to the vociferous Butcher) what right he has to demand the appearance of Mr. Carl?" "'Cos," said the Butcher, "'cos he's down in the Bill." Such an undeniable answer would have staggered any other Manager than Elliston, but he was not easily to be disconcerted. "Because he is down in the bill!" he echoed, in a tone of the loftiest indignation: "Ladies and Gentlemen, the Mr. Carl, so unseasonably, so vociferously, and so unfeelingly called for, is at this very moment laboring under severe illness—he is in bed. And let me ask, is a man, a fellow-creature, a human being, to be torn from his couch, from his home, on a cold night, from the affectionate attention of his wife and family, at the risk of his valuable life perhaps, to go through a fatiguing part because he happens to be DOWN IN THE BILL?" [Cries of "Shame! shame!" from all parts of the house.] "And yet, ladies and gentlemen, there stands a man—if I may call him so—a Butcher, that for his own selfish gratification—the amusement of a few short hours—would risk the very existence of a deserving member of society, a good husband, father, friend, and one of your favorite actors, and all, forsooth, because he is DOWN IN THE BILL!" [Universal hooting, with cries of "Turn him out."] "By all means," acquiesced the Manager, with one of his best bows—and the indignant pittites actually hooted and kicked their own champion out of the theatre, as something more than a Butcher, and less than a Christian.

Now I am myself, gentle readers, in the same predicament with Mr. Carl. Like him I am an invalid—and like him I am unfortunately down in the Bill. It would not become me to set forth my own domestic or social virtues, or to hint what sort of gap my loss would make in society—still less would it consist with modesty to compare myself with a favorite actor—but as a mere human being I throw myself on your mercy, and ask, in common charity, would you have had me leave my warm bed, to shiver in a printer's damp sheets, at the risk of my reputation perhaps, and for the mere amusement of some half hour, or more probably for no amusement at all—simply because I was "*down in the Bill?*"

But there is no such Butcher, or Butcheress, or little Butcherling, amongst you; and by your good leave and patience, the instalment of my Reminiscences that is over due, shall be paid with interest in the next number.

LITERARY REMINISCENCES.

No I.

TIME was, I sat upon a lofty stool,
At lofty desk, and with a clerkly pen
Began each morning, at the stroke of ten,
To write in Bell and Co.'s commercial school;
In Warnford Court, a shady nook and cool,
The favorite retreat of merchant men;
Yet would my quill turn vagrant even then,
And take stray dips in the Castalian pool.
Now double entry—now a flowery trope—
Mingling poetic honey with trade wax—
Blogg, Brothers—Milton—Grote and Prescott—Pope—
Bristles—and Hogg—Glyn Mills and Halifax—
Rogers—and Towgood—Hemp—the Bard of Hope—
Barilla—Byron—Tallow—Burns—and Flax!

MY commercial career was a brief one, and deserved only a sonnet in commemoration. The fault, however, lay not with the muses. To commit poetry indeed is a crime ranking next to forgery in the counting-house code; and an Ode or a song dated Copthall Court, would be as certainly noted and protested as a dishonored bill. I have even heard of an unfortunate clerk, who lost his situation through being tempted by the jingle to subscribe under an account current

"Excepted all errors
Made by John Ferrers,"

his employer emphatically declaring that Poetry and Logwood could never coexist in the same head. The principal of *our* firm on the contrary had a turn for the Belles Lettres, and would have winked with both eyes at verses which did not intrude into an invoice or confuse their figures with those of the Ledger. The true cause of my retirement from Commercial affairs was more prosaic. My constitution, though far from venerable, had begun to show symptoms of decay: my appetite failed, and its principal creditor, the stomach, received only an ounce in the pound. My spirits daily became a shade lower—my flesh was held less and less firmly—in short, in the language of the price current, it was expected that I must "submit to a decline." The Doctors who were called in, declared imperatively that a mercantile life would be the death of me—that by so much sitting, I was hatching a whole brood of complaints, and that no Physician would insure me as a merchantman from the Port of London to the next Spring. The Exchange, they said, was against me, and as the Exchange itself used to ring with "Life let us Cherish," there was no resisting the advice. I was ordered to abstain from Ashes, Bristles, and Petersburg yellow candle, and to indulge in a more generous diet—to take regular country exercise instead of the Russia Walk, and to go to bed early even on Foreign Post nights. Above all I was recommended change of air, and in particular the bracing breezes of the North. Accordingly I was soon shipped, as per advice, in a Scotch Smack, which "*smacked* through the breeze," as Dibdin sings, so merrily, that on the fourth morning we were in sight of the prominent old Steeple of "Bonny Dundee."

My Biographer, in the Book of Gems, alludes to this voyage, and infers from some verses—"Gadzooks! must one swear to the truth of a song?"—that it sickened me of the sea. Nothing can be more unfounded. The marine terrors and disagreeables enumerated in the poem, belong to a Miss Oliver, and not to me, who regard the ocean with a natural and national partiality. Constitutionally proof against that nausea which extorts so many wave-offerings from the afflicted, I am as constant as Captain Basil Hall himself, in my regard "for the element that never tires." Some washy fellows, it is true, *Fresh*-men from Cambridge and the like, affect to prefer river or even pond water for their aquatics—the tame ripple to the wild wave, the prose to "the poetry of motion." But give *me* "the mu' itudinous sea," resting or rampant, with all its variable moods and changeable coloring. Methought, when pining under the *maladie du pays*, on a hopeless, sick bed, inland, in Germany, it would have relieved those yearnings but to look across an element so instinct with English associations, that it would seem rather to unite me to than sever me from my native island. And, truly, when I did at last stand on the brink of the dark blue sea, my home-sick wishes seemed already half fulfilled, and it was not till many months afterwards that I actually crossed the Channel. But I am, besides, personally under deep obligations to the great deep. Twice, indeed, in a calm and in a storm, has my life been threatened with a salt-water catastrophe; but that quarrel has long been made up, and forgiven, in gratitude for the blessing and bracing influence of the breezes that smack of the ocean brine. Dislike the sea !—With what delight aforetime used I to swim in it, to dive in it, to sail on it! Ask honest Tom Woodgate, of Hastings, who made of me, for a landsman, a tolerable boatsman. Even now, when do I feel so easy in body, and so cheerful in spirit, as when walking hard by the surge, listening, as if expecting some whispering of friendly but distant voices, in its eternal murmuring. Sick of the sea! If ever I have a water-drinking fancy, it is a wish that the ocean brine had been sweet, or sour instead of salt, so as to be potable; for what can be more tempting *to the eye* as a draught, than the pure fluid, almost invisible with clearness, as it lies in some sandy scoop, or rocky hollow, a true "Diamond of the Desert," to say nothing of the same living liquid in its effervescing state, when it sparkles up, hissing and bubbling in the ship's wake—the very Champaigne of water! Above all, what intellectual solar and soothing syrup have I not derived from the mere contemplation of the boundless main,—the most effectual and innocent of mental sedatives, and often called in aid of that practical philosophy it has been my wont to recommend in the present work. For whenever, owing to physical depression, or a discordant state of the nerves, my personal vexations and cares, real or imaginary, become importunate in my thoughts, and acquire, by morbid exaggeration, an undue prominence and importance, what remedy then so infallible as to mount to my solitary seat in the look-out, and thence gaze awhile across the broad expanse, till in the presence of that vast horizon, my proper troubles shrink to their true proportions, and I look on the whole race of men, with their insignificant pursuits, as so many shrimpers! But this is a digression—we have made the harbor of Dundee, and it is time to step ashore in "stout and original Scotland," as it is called by Doctor Adolphus Wagner, in his German edition of Burns.*

Like other shipments, I had been regularly addressed to the care of a consignee;—but the latter, not anxious, probably, to take charge of a hobbledehoy, yet at the same time unwilling to incur the reproach of having a relative in the same town and not under the same roof, peremptorily declined the office. Nay, more, she pronounced against me a capital sentence, so far as returning to the place from whence I came, and even proceeded to bespeak my passage and reship my luggage. Judging from such vigorous measures the temper of my customer, instead of remonstrating, I affected resignation, and went with a grave face through the farce of a formal leave-taking; I even went on board, but it was in company with a stout fellow who relanded

* The Baron Dupotet de Sennevoy and Doctor Elliotson will doubtless be glad to be informed, that the inspired Scottish Poet was a believer in their magnetismal mysteries—at least in the article of reading a book behind the back. In a letter to Mr. Robert Ainslie, is the following passage in proof. "I have no doubt but scholarcraft may be caught, as a Scotchman catches the itch—by friction. How else can you account for it that born blockheads, by mere dint of *handling* books, grow so wise that even they themselves are equally convinced of, and surprised at their own parts? I once carried that philosophy to that degree, that in a knot of country folks, who had a library amongst them, and who, to the honor of their good sense, made me factotum in the business; one of our members, a little wiselook, squat, upright, jabbering body of a tailor, I advised him instead of turning over the leaves, *to bind the book on his back.* Johnnie took the hint, and as our meetings were every fourth Saturday, and Pricklouse having a good Scots mile to walk in coming, and of course another in returning, Bodkin was sure to lay his hand on some heavy quarto or ponderous folio; with and under which, wrapt up in his grey plaid, he grew wise as he grew weary all the way home. He carried this so far, that an old musty Hebrew Concordance, which we had in a present from a neighboring priest, *by mere dint of applying it as doctors do a blistering plaster, between his shoulders*, Stitch, in a dozen pilgrimages, acquired as much rational theology as the said priest had done by forty years' perusal of its pages."

my baggage; and thus, whilst my transporter imagined, good easy soul! that the rejected article was sailing round St. Abb's Head, or rolling off the Bass, he was actually safe and snug in Dundee, quietly laughing in his sleeve with the Law at his back. I have a confused recollection of meeting, some three or four days afterwards, a female cousin on her road to school, who at sight of me turned suddenly round, and galloped off towards home with the speed of a scared heifer.

My first concern was now to look out for some comfortable roof, under which "for a consideration" one would be treated as one of the family. I entered accordingly into a treaty with a respectable widower, who had no sons of his own, but in spite of the most undeniable references, and a general accordance as to terms, there occurred a mysterious hitch in the arrangement, arising from a whimsical prepossession which only came afterwards to my knowledge—namely, that an English laddie, instead of supping parritch, would inevitably require a rump-steak to his breakfast! My next essay was more successful; and ended in my being regularly installed in a boarding-house, kept by a Scotchwoman, who was not so sure of my being a beefeater. She was a sort of widow, with a seafaring husband "as good as dead," and in her appearance not unlike a personification of *rouge et noir*, with her red eyes, her red face, her yellow teeth, and her black velvet cap. The first day of my term happened to be also the first day of the new year, and on stepping from my bed-room, I encountered our Hostess—like a witch and her familiar spirit—with a huge bottle of whiskey in one hand, and a glass in the other. It was impossible to decline the dram she pressed upon me, and very good it proved, and undoubtedly strong, seeing that for some time I could only muse its praise in expressive silence, and indeed, I was only able to speak with "a *small still* voice" for several minutes afterwards. Such was my characteristic introduction to the Land of Cakes, where I was destined to spend the greater part of two years, under circumstances likely to materially influence the coloring and filling up of my future life.

To properly estimate the dangers of my position, imagine a boy of fifteen, at the Nore, as it were, of life, thus left dependent on his own pilotage for a safe voyage to the Isle of Man; or conceive a juvenile Telemachus, without a Mentor, brought suddenly into the perilous neighborhood of Calypso and her enchantments. It will hardly be expected, that from some half-dozen of young bachelors, there came forth any solemn voice didactically warning me in the strain of the sage Imlac to the Prince of Abyssinia. In fact, I recollect receiving but one solitary serious admonition, and that was from a she cousin of ten years old, that the Spectator I was reading on a Sunday morning, "was not the Bible." For there was still much of this pious rigor extant in Scotland, though a gentleman was no longer committed to Tolboothia Infelix, for an unseasonable promenade during church time. It was once, however, my fortune to witness a sample of the *ancien régime* at an evening party composed chiefly of young and rather fashionable persons, when lo! like an Anachronism confounding times past with times present, there came out of some corner an antique figure, with quaintly cut blue suit and three-cornered hat, not unlike a very old Greenwich Pensioner, who taking his stand in front of the circle, deliberately asked a blessing of formidable length on the thin bread and butter, the short cake, the marmalade, and the Pekoe tea. And here, *en passant*, it may be worth while to remark, for the benefit of our Agnews and Plumtres, as illustrating the intrinsic value of such sanctimonious pretension, that the elder Scotland, so renowned for armlong graces, and redundant preachments, and abundant psalm-singing, has yet bequeathed to posterity a singularly liberal collection of songs, the reverse of Divine and Moral, such as "can only be sung when the punch-bowl has done its work and the wild wit is set free." *

To return to my boarding-house, which, with all its chairs, had none appropriated to a Professor of Moral Philosophy. In the absence of such a monitor, nature, fortunately for myself, had gifted me with a taste for reading, which the languor of ill-health, inclining me to sedentary habits, helped materially to encourage. Whatever books, good, bad, or indifferent, happen

* A. Cunningham.

ed to come within my reach, were perused with the greatest avidity, and however indiscriminate the course, the balance of the impressions thence derived was decidedly in favor of the allegorical lady, so wisely preferred by Hercules when he had to make his election between Virtue and Vice. Of the material that ministered to this appetite, I shall always regret that I did not secure, as a literary curiosity—a collection of halfpenny Ballads, the property of a Grocer's apprentice, and which contained, amongst other matters, a new version of Chevy Chase, wherein the victory was transferred to the Scots. In the mean time, this bookishness acquired for me a sort of reputation for scholarship amongst my comrades, and in consequence my pen was sometimes called into requisition, in divers and sometimes delicate cases. Thus for one party, whom the Gods had not made poetical, I composed a love-letter in verse; for another, whose education had been neglected, I carried on a correspondence with reference to a tobacco manufactory in which he was a sleeping-partner; whilst, on a graver occasion, the hand now peacefully setting down these reminiscences, was employed in penning a most horrible peremptory invitation to pistols and twelve paces, till one was nicked. The facts were briefly these. A spicy-tempered captain of Artillery, in a dispute with a superior officer, had rashly cashiered himself by either throwing up or tearing up his commission. In this dilemma he arrived at Dundee, to assume a post in the Customs, which had been procured for him by the interest of his friends. To his infinite indignation, however, he found that instead of a lucrative surveyorship, he had been appointed a simple tide-waiter! and magnificent was the rage with which he tore, trampled, and danced on the little official paper book wherein he had been set to tick off, bale by bale, a cargo of "infernal hemp." Unluckily, on the very day of this revelation, a forgery was perpetrated on the local Bank, and those sapient Dogberries, the town officers, saw fit to take up our persecuted ex-captain, on the simple ground that he was the last stranger who had entered the town. Rendered almost frantic by this second insult, nothing would serve him in his paroxysm but calling somebody out, and he pitched at once on the cashier of the defrauded Bank. As the state of his nerves would not permit him to write, he entreated me earnestly to draw up a defiance, which I performed, at the expense of an agony of suppressed laughter, merely to imagine the effect of such a missive on the man of business—a respectable powdered, bald, pudgy, pacific little body, with no more idea of "going out" than a cow in a field of clover. I forget the precise result—but certainly there was no duel.

LITERARY REMINISCENCES.

No II.

To do justice to the climate of "stout and original Scotland," it promised to act kindly by the constitution committed to its care. The air evidently agreed with the natives; and auld Robin Grays and John Andersons were plenty as blackberries, and Auld Lang Syne himself seemed to walk bonneted amongst these patriarchal figures in the likeness of an old man covered with a mantle. The effect on myself was rather curious—for I seemed to have come amongst a generation that scarcely belonged to my era; mature spinsters, waning bachelors, very motherly matrons, and experienced fathers, that I should have set down as uncles and aunts, called themselves my cousins; reverend personages, apparently grandfathers and grandmothers, were simply great uncles and aunts: and finally I enjoyed an interview with a relative oftener heard of traditionally, than encountered in the body—a great-great-grandmother—still a tall woman and a tolerable pedestrian, going indeed down the hill, but with the wheel well locked. It was like coming amongst the Struldbrugs; and truly, for any knowledge to the contrary, many of these Old Mortalities are still living, enjoying their sneeshing, their toddy, their cracks, and particular reminiscences. The very phrase of being "Scotch'd, but not killed," seems to refer to this Caledonian tenacity of life, of which the well-known Walking Stewart was an example: he was an annuitant in the County-office, and as the actuaries would say, died very hard. It must be difficult for the teatotallers to reconcile this longevity with the imputed enormous consumption of ardent spirits beyond the Tweed. Scotia, according to the evidence of

Mr. Buckingham's committee, is an especially drouthie bodie, who drinks whiskey at christenings, and at buryings, and on all possible occasions besides. Her sons drink not by the hour or by the day, but by the week,—witness Souter Johnny :—

> "Tam lo'ed him like a vera brither,
> They had been fou for weeks thegither."

Swallowing no thin washy potation, but a strong overproof spirit, with a smack of smoke—and "where there is smoke there is fire," yet without flashing off, according to temperance theories, by spontaneous combustion. On the contrary, the canny northerns are noted for soundness of constitution and clearness of head, with such a strong principle of vitality as to justify the poetical prediction of C***, that the world's longest liver, or Last Man, will be a Scotchman.

All these favorable signs I duly noted; and prophetically refrained from delivering the letter of introduction to Doctor C——, which was to place me under his medical care. As the sick man said, when he went into the gin-shop instead of the hospital, "I trusted to natur." Whenever the weather permitted, therefore, which was generally when there were no new books to the fore, I haunted the banks and braes, or paid flying visits to the burns, with a rod intended to punish that rising generation amongst fishes called trout. But I whipped in vain. Trout there were in plenty, but like obstinate double teeth, with a bad operator, they would neither be pulled out nor come out of themselves. Still the sport, if so it might be called, had its own attractions, as, the catching excepted, the whole of the Waltonish enjoyments were at my command, the contemplative quiet, the sweet wholesome country air, and the picturesque scenery—not to forget the relishing the homely repast at the shealing or the mill; sometimes I went alone, but often we were a company, and then we had for our attendant a journeyman tobacco-spinner, an original, and literary withal, for he had a reel in his head, whence ever and anon he unwound a line of Allan Ramsay, or Beattie, or Burns. Methinks I still listen, trudging homeward in the gloaming, to the recitation of that appropriate stanza, beginning—

"At the close of the day when the hamlet was still,"

delivered with a gusto, perhaps only to be felt by a day-laboring mechanic, who had "nothing but his evenings to himself." Methinks I still sympathize with the zest with which he dwelt on the pastoral images and dreams so rarely realized, when a chance holiday gave him the fresh-breathing fragrance of the living flower in lieu of the stale odor of the Indian weed: and philosophically I can now understand why poetry, with its lofty aspirations and sublime feelings, seemed to sound so gratefully to the ear from the lips of a "squire of low degree." There is something painful and humiliating to humanity in the abjectness of mind, that too often accompanies the sordid condition of the working classes; whereas it is soothing and consolatory to find the mind of the poor man rising superior to his estate, and compensating by intellectual enjoyment for the physical pains and privation that belong to his humble lot. Whatever raises him above the level of the ox in the garner, or the horse in the mill, ought to be acceptable to the pride, if not to the charity, of the fellow creature that calls him brother; for instance music and dancing, but against which innocent unbendings some of our magistracy persist in setting their faces, as if resolved that a low neighborhood should enjoy no dance but St. Vitus's, and no fiddle but the Scotch.

To these open-air pursuits, sailing was afterwards added, bringing me acquainted with the boatmen and fishermen of The Craig, a hardy race, rough and ready-witted, from whom perchance was first derived my partiality for all marine bipeds and sea-craft, from Flag Admirals down to Jack Junk, the proud first-rate to the humble boatie that "wins the bairns' bread." The Tay at Dundee is a broad noble river, with a raging tide, which, when it differs with a contrary wind, will get up "*jars*" (Anglicé waves) quite equal to those of a family manufacture. It was at least a good preparatory school for learning the rudiments of boat craft; whereof I acquired enough to be able at need to take the helm without either going too near the wind or too distant from the port. Not without some boyish pride I occasionally found myself intrusted with the guidance of the Coach-Boat,—so called from its carrying the passengers by the Edinburgh Mail—particularly in a calm, when the utmost exertions of the crew, four old man-of-war's-men, were required at the oars. It not unfrequently happened, however, that "the laddie" was unceremoniously ousted by the unanimous vote, and sometimes by the united strength, of the ladies, who invariably pitched upon the oldest old gentleman in the vessel to

Steer her up and haud her gaun"

The consequence being the landing with all the baggage, some mile above or below the town—and a too late conviction, that the *Elder* Brethren of our Trinity House were not the best Pilots.

It was during one of these brief voyages, that I witnessed a serio-comic accident, at which the reader will smile or sigh according to his connexion with the Corporation of London. I forget on what unconscious pilgrimage it was bound, but amongst the other passengers one day, there was that stock-dove of a gourmand's affection, a fine lively turtle. Rich and rare as it was, it did not travel unprotected like Moore's heroine, but was under the care of a vigilant guardian, who seemed as jealous of the eyes that looked amorously at his charge, as if the latter had been a ward in Chancery. So far—namely, as far as the middle of the Tay—so good; when the spirit of mischief, or curiosity, or humanity, suggested the convenience of a sea-bath, and the refreshment the creature might derive from a taste of its native element. Accordingly, Testudo was lifted over the side, and indulged with a dip and a wallop in the wave, which actually revived it so powerfully, that from a playful flapping with its fore-fins it soon began to struggle most vigorously, like a giant refreshed with brine. In fact, it paddled with a power which, added to its weight, left no alternative to its guardian but to go with it, or without it. The event soon came off. The man tumbled backward into the boat, and the turtle plunged forward into the deep. There was a splash—a momentary glimpse of the broad back-shell—the waters closed, and all was over—or at least under! In vain one of the boatmen aimed a lunge with his boat-hook, at the fatal spot in particular—in vain another made a blow with his oar at the Tay in general—whilst a third, in his confusion, heaved a coil of rope, as he would, could, should, might, or ought to have done to a drowning Christian. The Amphibious was beyond their reach, and no doubt, making westward and homeward with all its might, with an instinctive feeling that

> "The world was all before it where to choose
> Its place of rest, and Providence its guide."

Never shall I forget, whilst capable of reminiscences, the face of that mourning mate thus suddenly bereaved of his turtle! The unfortunate shepherd, Ding-dong, in Rabelais, could hardly have looked more utterly and unutterably dozed, crazed, miz-mazed, and flabbergasted, when his whole flock and stock of golden-fleeced sheep suicidally sheepwashed themselves to death, by wilfully leaping overboard! He said little in words, but more eloquently clapped his hands to his waistcoat, as if the loss, as the nurses say, had literally "flown to his stomach." And truly, after promising it both callipash and callipee, with the delicious green fat to boot, what cold comfort could well be colder than the miserable chilling reflection that there was

> "Cauld kail in Aberdeen?"

LITERARY REMINISCENCES.

No. III.

My first acquaintance with the press—a memorable event in an author's experience—took place in Scotland. Amongst the temporary sojourners at our boarding-house, there came a legal antiquarian who had been sent for from Edinburgh, expressly to make some unprofitable researches amongst the mustiest of the civic records. It was my humor to think, that in Political as well as Domestic Economy, it must be better to sweep the Present than to dust the Past; and certain new brooms were recommended to the Town Council in a quizzing letter, which the then editor of the Dundee Advertiser or Chronicle thought fit to favor with a prominent place in his columns. "'Tis pleasant sure," sings Lord Byron, "to see one's self in print," and according to the popular notion I ought to have been quite up in my stirrups, if not standing on the saddle, at thus seeing myself, for the first strange time, set up in type. Memory recalls, however, but a very moderate share of exaltation, which was totally eclipsed, moreover, by the exuberant transports of an accessary before the fact, whom, methinks, I still see in my mind's eye, rushing out of the printing-office with the wet sheet steaming in his hand, and fluttering all along the High Street, to announce breathlessly that "we were in." But G. was an indifferent scholar, even in English, and therefore thought the more highly of this literary feat. It was this defective education, and the want of a proper vent for his abundant love of nonsense in prose or verse, that probably led to the wound he subsequently inflicted on his own throat, but which was luckily remedied by "a stitch in time." The failure of a tragedy is very apt to produce some thing like a comedy, and few afterpieces have amused me more than the behavior of this Amicus Redivivus, when, thus dramatising the saying of "cut and come again," he made what ought to have been a posthumous appearance amongst his friends. In fact, and he was ludicrously alive to it, he had placed himself for all his supplementary days in a false position. Like the old man in the fable, after formally calling upon Death to execute a general release, he had quietly resumed his fardel, which he bore about with exactly the uneasy ridiculous air of a would-be fine gentleman, who is sensitively conscious that he is carrying a bundle. For the sake of our native sentimentalists who profess dying for love, as well as the foreign romanticists who affect a love for dying, it may not be amiss to give a slight sketch of the bearing of a traveller who had gone through half the journey. I had been absent some months, and was consequently ignorant of the affair, when lo! on my return to the town, the very first person who accosted me in the market-place was our felo-de-se; and truly, no Bashful Man, "with all his blushing honors thick upon him," in the presence of a damp stranger, could have been more divertingly sheepish, and awkwardly backward in coming forward as to manner and address. Indeed, something of the embarrassment of a fresh introduction might naturally be felt by an individual, thus beginning again, as the lawyers say, *de novo*, and renewing ties he had virtually cast off. The guilty hand was as dubiously extended to me as if it had been a dyer's,—its fellow meanwhile performing sundry involuntary motions and manipulations about his cravat, as if nervously mistrusting the correctness of the ties or the stability of a buckle. As for his face, there was a foolish, deprecatory smile upon it that would have puzzled the pencil of Wilkie; and even Liston himself could scarcely have parodied the indescribable croak with which, conscious of an unlucky notoriety, he inquired "if I had heard"—here, a short husky cough—"of anything particular?"

"Not a word," was the answer.

"Then you don't know"—(more fidgetting about the neck, the smile rather sillier, the voice more guttural, and the cough worse than ever)—"then you don't know"—but, like Macbeth's amen, the confession literally stuck in the culprit's throat; and I was left to learn, an hour afterwards, and from another source, that "Jemmy G * * * had *fought a duel with himself*, and cut his own weazand, about a lady."

For my own part, with the above figure, and all its foolish features vividly imprinted on my memory, I do not think that I could ever seriously attempt "what Cato did, and Addison approved," in my own person. On the contrary, it seems to me that the English moralist gave but an Irish illustration of "a brave man struggling with the storms of fate," by representing him as wilfully scuttling his own hold, and going at once to the bottom. As for the Censor, he plainly laid himself open to censure, when he used a naked sword as a stomachic—a very sorry way, by the way, when weary of conjectures, of enjoying the benefit of the doubt, and for which, were I tasked to select an inscription for his cenotaph, it should be the exclamation of Thisby, in the Midsummer Night's Dream—

"This is old Ninny's tomb."

Mais revenons à nos moutons, as the wolf said to her cubs. The reception of my letter in the Dublin Newspaper encouraged me to forward a contribution to the Dundee Magazine, the Editor of which was kind enough, as Winifred Jenkins says, to "wrap my bit of nonsense under his Honor's Kiver," without charging anything for its insertion. Here was success sufficient to turn a young author at once into "a scribbling miller," and make him sell himself, body and soul, after the German fashion, to that minor Mephistophiles, the Printer's Devil! Nevertheless, it was not till years afterwards, and the lapse of term equal to an ordinary apprenticeship, that the Imp in question became really my Familiar. In the meantime, I continued to compose occasionally, and, like the literary performances of Mr. Weller Senior, my lucubrations were generally committed to paper, not in what is commonly called written hand, but an imitation of print. Such a course hints suspiciously of type and antetype, and a longing eye to the Row, whereas, it was adopted simply to make the reading more easy, and thus enable me the more readily to form a judgment of the effect of my little efforts. It is more difficult than may be supposed to decide on the value of a work in MS., and especially when the handwriting presents only a swell mob of bad characters, that must be severally examined and re-examined to arrive at the merits or demerits of the case. Print settles it, as Coleridge used to say: and to be candid, I have more than once reversed, or greatly modified a previous verdict, on seeing a rough proof from the press. But, as Editors too well know, it is next to impossible to retain the tune of a stanza, or the drift of an argument, whilst the mind has to scramble through a patch of scribble scrabble, as stiff as a gorse cover. The beauties of the piece will as naturally appear to disadvantage through such a medium, as the features of a pretty woman through a bad pane of glass; and without doubt, many a tolerable article has been consigned hand over head to the Balaam Box for want of a fair copy. Wherefore, O ye Poets and Prosers, who aspire to write in Miscellanies, and above all, O ye palpitating Untried, who meditate the offer of your maiden essays to established periodicals, take care, pray ye take care, to cultivate a good, plain, bold, round text. Set up Tomkins as well as Pope or Dryden for a model, and have an eye to your pothooks. Some persons hold that the best writers are those who write the best hands, and I have known the conductor of a magazine to be converted by a crabbed MS. to the same opinion. Of all things, therefore, be legible; and to that end, practise in penmanship. If you have never learned, take six lessons of Mr. Carstairs. Be sure to buy the best paper, the best ink, the best pens, and then sit down and do the best you can; as the schoolboys do—put out your tongue, and take pains. So shall ye haply escape the rash rejection of a jaded editor; so, having got in your hand, it is possible that your head may follow; and so, last not least, ye may fortunately avert those awful mistakes of the press which sometimes ruin a poet's sublimest effusion, by pantomimically transforming his roses into noses, his angels into angles, and all his happiness into pappiness.

LITERARY REMINISCENCES.

No. IV.

> "And are ye sure the news is true?
> And are ye sure he's well?"—Old Scotch Song.

The great Doctor Johnson—himself a sufferer—has pathetically described, in an essay on the miseries of an infirm constitution, the melancholy case of an Invalid, with a willing mind in a weak body. "The time of such a man," he says, "is spent in forming schemes which a change of wind prevents him from executing; his powers fume away in projects and in hope, and the day of action never arrives. He lies down delighted with the thoughts of to-morrow; but in the night the skies are overcast; the temper of the air is changed; he wakes in languor, impatience, and distraction; and has no longer any wish but for ease, nor any attention but for misery." In short the Rambler describes the whole race of Valetudinarians as a sort of great Bitumen Company, paving a certain nameless place, as some of the Asphalticals have paved Oxford Street, with not very durable good intentions. In a word, your Invalid promises like a Hogmy, and performs like a Pigmy.

To a hale hearty man, a perfect picture of health in an oaken frame, such abortions seem sufficiently unaccountable. A great hulking fellow, revelling, as De Quincey used emphatically to say, "in rude BOVINE health,"—a voracious human animal, camel-stomached and iron-built, who could all but devour and digest himself like a Kilkenny cat,—can neither sympathize with nor understand those frequent failures and down-breakings which happen to beings not so fortunately gifted with indelicate constitutions. Such a half-horse half-alligator monster cannot judge, like a *Puny* Judge, of a case of feebleness. The broad-chested cannot allow for the narrow-breasted; the robust for the no-bust. Nevertheless, even the stalwart may sometimes fall egregiously short of their own designs—as witness a case in point.

Amongst my fellow passengers, on a late sea voyage, there was one who attracted my especial attention. A glance at his face, another at his figure, a third at his costume, and a fourth at his paraphernalia, sufficed to detect his country: by his light hair, nubbly features, heavy frame, odd-colored dressing-gown, and the national meerschaum and gaudy tobacco-bag, he was undeniably a German. But, besides the everlasting pipe, he was provided with a sketching apparatus, an ample note-book, a gun, and a telescope; the whole being placed ready for immediate use. He had predetermined, no doubt, to record his German sentiments on first making acquaintance with the German Ocean; to sketch the picturesque craft he might encounter on its surface; to shoot his first sea-gull; and to catch a first glimpse of the shores of Albion, beyond the reach of the naked eye. But alas! all these intentions fell—if one may correctly say so with only sky and water—to the ground. He ate nothing—drank nothing—smoked nothing—drew nothing—wrote nothing—shot nothing—spied nothing—nay he merely stared, but replied nothing to my friendly inquiry (I am ill at the German tongue and its pronunciation), "Wie befinden *sea sick?*"

Now, my own case, gentle reader, has been precisely akin to that of our unfortunate Cousin German. Like him I have promised much, projected still more, and done little. Like him, too, I have been a sick man, though not at sea, but on shore—and in excuse of all that has been left undone, or delayed, with other Performers, when they do not perform, I must proffer the old theatrical plea of indisposition. As the Rambler describes, I have erected schemes which have been blown down by an *ill* wind; I have formed plans and been weather-beaten, like another Murphy, by a change in the weather. For instance, the Comic Annual for 1839 ought properly to have been published some forty days earlier; but was obliged, as it were, to perform quarantine, for want of a clean Bill of Health. Thus, too, the patron of the present Work, who has taken the trouble to peruse certain chapters under the title of Literary Reminiscences, will doubtless have compared the tone of them with an Apology in Number Six, wherein, declining any attempt at an Auto-biography, a promise was made of giving such anecdotes as a bad memory and a bad hearing might have retained of my literary friends and acquaintance. Hitherto, however, the fragments in question have only presented desultory glimpses of a goose-quill still in its green-gosling-hood, instead of any recollections of "celebrated pens." The truth is that my malady forced me to temporise:—wherefore the kind reader will be pleased to consider the aforesaid chapters but as so many "false starts," and that Memory has only now got away, to make play as well as she can.

Whilst I am thus closeted in the Confessional, it may be as well, as the Pelican said, to make a clean breast of it, and at once plead guilty to all those counts—and some, from long-standing, have become very Old Baily counts—that haunt my conscience. The most numerous of these crimes relate to letters that would not, could not, or at least did not answer. Others refer to the receipt of books, and, as an example of their heinousness, it misgives me that I was favored with a little volume by W. and M. Howitt, without ever telling them *how-it* pleased me. A few offences concern engagements which it was impossible to fulfil,' although doubly bound by principle and interest. Seriously I have perforce been guilty of many, many, and still many sins of omission; but Hope, reviving with my strength, promises, granting me life, to redeem all such pledges. In the meantime, in extenuation, I can only plead particularly that deprecation which is offered up, in behalf of all Christian defaulters every Sunday,—"We have left undone those things which we ought to have done,—*And there is no* HEALTH *in us.*"

It is pleasant after a match at Chess, particularly if we have won, to try back, and reconsider those important moves which have had a decisive influence on the result. It is still more interesting, in the game of Life, to recal the critical positions which have occurred during its progress, and review the false or judicious steps that have led to our subsequent good or ill fortune. There is, however, this difference, that chess is a matter of pure skill and calculation, whereas the chequered board of human life is subject to the caprice of Chance—the event being sometimes determined by combinations which never entered into the mind of the player.* To such an accident it is, perhaps, attributable, that the hand now tracing these reminiscences is holding a pen instead of an etching-point: jotting down these prose pleasures of memory, in lieu of furnishing articles "plated on steel," for the pictorial periodicals.

It will be remembered that my mental constitution, however weak my physical one, was proof against that type-us fever which parches most scribblers till they are set up, done up, and may be, cut up, in print and boards. Perhaps I had read, and trembled at the melancholy annals of those unfortunates, who, rashly undertaking to write for bread, had poisoned themselves, like Chatterton, for want of it, or choked themselves, like Otway, on obtaining it. Possibly, having learned to think humbly of myself—there is nothing like early sickness and sorrow for "taking the conceit" out of one—my vanity did not presume to think, with certain juvenile Tracticians, that I "had a call" to hold forth in print for the edification of mankind. Perchance, the very deep reverence my reading had led me to entertain for our Bards and Sages, deterred me from thrusting myself into the fellowship of Beings that seemed only a little lower than the angels. However, in spite of that very common excuse for publication, "the advice of a friend," who seriously recommended the submitting of my MSS. to a literary authority, with a view to his imprimatur, my slight acquaintance with the press was pushed no farther. On the contrary, I had selected a branch of the Fine Arts for my serious pursuit. Prudence, the daughter of Wisdom, whispering, perhaps, that the engraver, Pye, had a better chance of beef-steak inside, than Pye the Laureate; not that the verse-spinning was quite given up.

* To borrow an example from fiction, there is that slave of circumstances, Oliver Twist. There are few authors whom one would care to see running two heats with the same horse. It is intended, therefore, as a compliment, that I wish Boz would re-write the history in question from page 122, supposing his hero NOT to have met with the Artful Dodger on his road to seek his fortune.

Though working in *aqua fortis*, I still played with Castaly, now writing — all monkeys are imitators, and all young authors are monkeys — now writing a Bandit, to match the Corsair, and anon, hatching a Lalla Crow, by way of companion to Lalla Rookh. Moreover, about this time, I became a member of a private select Literary Society that "waited on Ladies and Gentlemen at their own houses." Our Minerva, allegorically speaking, was a motley personage, in blue stockings, a flounced gown, quaker cap and kerchief, French flowers, and a man's hat. She held a fan in one hand and a blowpipe in the other. Her votaries were of both sexes, old and young, married and single, assenters, dissenters, High Church, Low Church, No Church; Doctors in Physics, and Apothecaries in Metaphysics; dabblers in Logic, Chemistry, Casuistry, Sophistry, natural and unnatural History, Phrenology, Geology, Conchology, Demonology; in short, all kinds of Colledgy-Knowledgy-Ology, including "Cakeology," and tea and coffee. Like other Societies, we had our President—a sort of Speaker who never spoke; at least within my experience he never unbosomed himself of anything but a portentous shirt frill. According to the usual order of the entertainment, there was, first—Tea and Small Talk; secondly, an original essay, which should have been followed, thirdly, by a Discussion, or Great Talk; but nine times in ten, it chanced, or rather mumchanced, that, between those who did not know what to think, and others, who did not know how to deliver what they thought, there ensued a dead silence, so "very dead indeed," as Apollo Belvi says, that it seemed buried into the bargain. To make this awkward pause more awkward, some misgiving voice, between a whisper and a croak, would stammer out some allusion to a Quaker's Meeting, answered from right to left by a running titter, the speaker having innocently, or perhaps wilfully forgotten, that one or two friends in drab coats, and as many in slate-colored gowns, were sitting, thumb-twiddling, in the circle. Not that the Friends contented themselves with playing *dumby* at our discussions They often spoke, and very characteristically, to the matter in hand. For instance, their favorite doctrine of non-resistance was once pushed—if Quakers ever push—a little "beyond beyond." By way of clencher, one fair, meek, sleek Quakeress, in dove color, gravely told a melo-dramatic story of a conscientious Friend, who, rather than lift even his finger against a Foe, passively, yea, lamb-like, suffered himself to be butchered in bed by an assassin, and died consistently, as he thought, with Fox principles, very like a Goose. As regards my own share in the Essays and Arguments, it misgives me, that they no more satisfied our decidedly serious members, than they now propitiate Mr. Rae Wilson. At least, one Society night, in escorting a female Fellow towards her home, she suddenly stopped me, taking advantage, perhaps, of the awful locality, and its associations, just in front of our chief criminal prison, and looking earnestly in my face, by the light of a Newgate lamp, inquired somewhat abruptly, "Mr. Hood! are you not an Infidel?"*

In the meantime, whilst thus playing at Literature, an event was ripening which was to introduce me to Authorship in earnest, and make the Muse, with whom I had only flirted, my companion for life. It had often occurred to me, that a striking, romantical, necromantical, metaphysical, melo-dramatical, Germanish story, might be composed, the interest of which should turn on the mysterious influences of the fate of A over the destiny of B, the said parties having no more natural or apparent connection with each other than Tenterden Steeple and the Goodwin Sands. An instance of this occult contingency occurred in my own case; for I did not even know by sight the unfortunate gentleman on whose untimely exit depended my entrance on the literary stage. In the beginning of the year 1821, a memorable duel, originating in a pen-and-ink quarrel, took place at Chalk Farm, and terminated in the death of Mr. John Scott, the able Editor of the London Magazine. The melancholy result excited great interest, in which I fully participated, little dreaming that his catastrophe involved any consequences of importance to myself. But, on the loss of its conductor, the Periodical passed into other hands. The new Proprietors were my friends; they sent for me, and after some preliminaries,

* In justice to the Society, it ought to be recorded, that two of its members have since distinguished themselves in print: the authoress of "London in the Olden Time," and the author of a "History of Moral Science"

I was duly installed as a sort of sub-Editor of the London Magazine.

It would be affectation to say, that engraving was resigned with regret. There is always something mechanical about the art—moreover, it is as unwholesome as wearisome to sit copper-fastened to a board, with a cantle scooped out to accommodate your stomach, if you have one, painfully ruling, ruling, and still ruling lines straight or crooked, by the long hundred to the square inch, at the doubly-hazardous risk which Wordsworth so deprecates, of "growing double." So farewell Woollett! Strange! Bartolozzi! I have said, my vanity did not rashly plunge me into authorship; but no sooner was there a legitimate opening than I jumped at it, à la Grimaldi, head foremost, and was speedily behind the scenes.

To judge by my zeal and delight in my new pursuit, the bowl had at last found its natural bias.* Not content with taking articles, like candidates for holy orders—with rejecting articles like the Belgians—I dreamt articles, thought articles, wrote articles, which were all inserted by the editor, of course with the concurrence of his deputy. The more irksome parts of authorship, such as the correction of the press, were to me labors of love. I received a revise from Mr. Baldwin's Mr. Parker, as if it had been a proof of his regard; forgave him all his slips, and really thought that printers' devils were not so black as they are painted. But my top-gallant glory was in "our Contributors!" How I used to look forward to Elia! and backward for Hazlitt, and all round for Edward Herbert, and how I used to *look up* to Allan Cunningham! for at that time the London had a goodly list of writers—a rare company. It is now defunct, and perhaps no ex-periodical might so appropriately be apostrophized with the Irish funereal question—"Arrah,

* There was a dash of ink in my blood. My father wrote two novels, and my brother was decidedly of a literary turn, to the great disquietude for a time of an anxious parent. She suspected him, on the strength of several amatory poems of a very desponding cast, of being the victim of a hopeless attachment; so he was caught, closeted, and catechised, and after a deal of delicate and tender sounding, he confessed, not with the anticipated sighs and tears, but a very unexpected burst of laughter, that he had been guilty of translating some fragments of Petrarch.

honey, why did you die?" Had not you an editor, and elegant prose writers, and beautiful poets, and broths of boys for criticism and classics, and wits and humorists.—Elia, Cary, Procter, Cunningham, Bowring, Barton, Hazlitt, Elton, Hartley Coleridge, Talfourd, Soane, Horace Smith, Reynolds, Poole, Clare, and Thomas Benyon, with a power besides. Hadn't you Lions' Heads with Traditional Tales? Hadn't you an Opium Eater, and a Dwarf, and a Giant, and a Learned Lamb, and a Green Man? Had not you a regular Drama, and a Musical Report, and a Report of Agriculture, and an Obituary and a Price Current, and a current price, of only half-a-crown? Arrah, why did you die? Why, somehow the contributors fell away—the concern went into other hands—worst of all, a new editor tried to put the Belles Lettres in Utilitarian envelopes; whereupon, the circulation of the Miscellany, like that of poor Le Fevre, got slower, slower, slower,—and slower still—and then stopped for ever! It was a sorry scattering of those old Londoners! Some went out of the country: one (Clare) went into it. Lamb retreated to Colebrooke. Mr. Cary presented himself to the British Museum. Reynolds and Barry took to engrossing when they should pen a stanza, and Thomas Benyon gave up literature.

It is with mingled feelings of pride, pleasure, and pain, that I revert to those old times, when the writers I had long known and admired in spirit were present to me in the flesh—when I had the delight of listening to their wit and wisdom from their own lips, of gazing on their faces, and grasping their right hands. Familiar figures rise before me, familiar voices ring in my ears, and, alas! amongst them are shapes that I must never see, sounds that I can never hear, again. Before my departure from England, I was one of the few who saw the grave close over the remains of one whom to know as a friend was to love as a relation. Never did a better soul go to a better world! Never perhaps (giving the lie direct to the common imputation of envy, malice, and hatred, amongst the brotherhood), never did an author descend—to quote his favorite Sir T. Browne—into "the land of the mole and the pismire" so hung with golden opinions, and honored and regretted with such sincere eulogies and elegies, by his contemporaries. To HIM, the first of these, my reminiscences, is eminently due, for I lost in him not only a dear and kind friend, but an invaluable critic; one whom, were such literary adoptions in modern use, I might well name, as Cotton called Walton, my "father." To borrow the earnest language of old Jean Bertaut, as Englished by Mr. Cary—

"Thou, chiefly, noble spirit, for whose loss
Just grief and mourning all our hearts engross,
Who seeing me devoted to the Nine,
Did'st hope some fruitage from those buds of mine;
Thou did'st excite me after thee t'ascend
The Muses' sacred hill; nor only lend
Example, but inspirit me to reach
The far-off summit by thy friendly speech.
* * * * *
May gracious Heaven, O honor of our age!
Make the conclusion answer thy presage,
Nor let it only for vain fortune stand,
That I have seen thy visage—touch'd thy hand!"

I was sitting one morning beside our Editor, busily correcting proofs, when a visitor was announced, whose name, grumbled by a low ventriloquial voice, like Tom Pipes calling from the hold through the hatchway, did not resound distinctly on my tympanum. However, the door opened, and in came a stranger, a figure remarkable at a glance, with a fine head, on a small spare body, supported by two almost immaterial legs. He was clothed in sables, of a by-gone fashion, but there was something wanting, or something present about him, that certified he was neither a divine, nor a physician, nor a schoolmaster: from a certain neatness and sobriety in his dress, coupled with his sedate bearing, he might have been taken, but that such a costume would be anomalous, for a *Quaker* in black. He looked still more like (what he really was) a literary Modern Antique, a New-Old Author, a living Anachronism, contemporary at once with Burton the Elder, and Colman the Younger. Meanwhile he advanced with rather a peculiar gait, his walk was plantigrade, and with a cheerful "How d'ye," and one of the blandest, sweetest smiles that ever brightened a manly countenance, held out two fingers to the Editor. The two gentlemen in black soon fell into discourse; and whilst they conferred, the Lavater principle within me set to work upon the interesting specimen thus presented to its speculations. It was a striking intellectual face, full of wiry lines, physiognomical quips and cranks, that gave it great character. There was much earnestness about the brows, and a deal of speculation in the eyes, which were brown and bright, and "quick in turning;" the nose, a decided one, though of no established order; and there was a handsome smartness about the mouth. Altogether it was no common face —none of those *willow-pattern* ones, which nature turns out by thousands at her potteries;—but more like a chance specimen of the Chinese ware, one to the set—unique, antique, quaint. No one who had once seen it, could pretend not to know it again. It was no face to lend its countenance to any confusion of persons in a Comedy of Errors. You might have sworn to it piecemeal,—a separate affidavit for every feature. In short, his face was as original as his figure; his figure as his character; his character as his writings; his writings the most original of the age. After the literary business had been settled, the Editor invited his contributor to dinner, adding "we shall have a hare—"

"And—and—and—and many Friends!"

The hesitation in the speech, and the readiness of the allusion, were alike characteristic of the individual, whom his familiars will perchance have recognized already as the delightful Essayist, the capital Critic, the pleasant Wit and Humorist, the delicate-minded and large-hearted Charles Lamb! He was shy like myself with strangers, so, that despite my yearnings, our first meeting scarcely amounted to an introduction. We were both at dinner, amongst the hare's many friends, but our acquaintance got no farther, in spite of a desperate attempt on my part to attract his notice. His complaint of the Decay of Beggars presented another chance: I wrote on coarse paper, and in ragged English, a letter of thanks to him as if from one of his mendicant clients, but it produced no effect. I had given up all hope, when one night, sitting sick and sad, in my bed-room, racked with the rheumatism, the door was suddenly opened, the well-known quaint figure in black walked in without any formality, and with a cheerful "Well, boy, how are you?" and the bland, sweet smile, extended the two fingers. They were eagerly clutched of course, and from that hour we were firm friends.

Thus characteristically commenced my intimacy with C Lamb. He had recently become my neighbor, and in a few days called again, to ask me to tea, "to meet Wordsworth." In spite of any idle jests to the contrary, the name had a spell in it that drew me to Colebrooke Cottage * with more alacrity † than consisted with prudence, stiff joints, and a North wind. But I was willing to run, at least hobble, some risk, to be of a party in a parlor with the Author of Laodamia and Hartleap Well. As for his Betty Foy-bles, he is not the first man by many, who has met with a *simple* fracture through riding his theory-hack so far and so fast, that it broke down with him. If he has now and then put on a nightcap, so have his own next-door mountains. If he has babbled, sometimes, like an infant of *two* years old; he has also thought, and felt, and spoken, the beautiful fancies, and tender affections, and artless language, of the children who can say "We are *seven*." Along with food for babes, he has furnished strong meat for men. So I put on my great-coat, and in a few minutes found myself, for the first time, at a door, that opened to me as frankly as its master's heart;

* A cottage of Ungentility, for it had neither double coach-house nor wings. Like its tenant, it stood alone. He said, glancing at the Paternoster one, that he did not like "the Row." There was a bit of a garden, in which, being, as he professed, "more fond of Men Sects than of Insects," he made probably his first and last observation in Entomology. He had been watching a spider on a gooseberry bush, entrapping a fly. "I never saw such a thing," he said. "Directly he was caught in her fatal spinning, she darted down upon him, and in a minute turned him out, completely lapped in a shroud! It reminded me of the Fatal Sisters in Gray."

† A sort of rheumatic celerity, of which Sir W. Scott's favorite dramatiser seemed to have a very accurate notion. Those who remember "poor Terry's" deliberate delivery, will be able to account for the shout of laughter which once rang throughout the Adelphi green-room, at his emphatic manner of giving, from a manuscript play, the stage direction of "Enter ——, with — a—lack—ri—ty!"

for, without any preliminaries of hall, passage, or parlor, one single step across the threshold brought me into the sitting-room, and in sight of the domestic hearth. The room looked brown with "old bokes," and beside the fire sate Wordsworth, and his sister, the hospitable Elia, and the excellent Bridget. As for the bard of Rydal, his outward man did not, perhaps, disappoint one; but the *palaver*, as the Indians say, fell short of my anticipations. Perhaps my memory is in fault; 't was many years ago, and, unlike the biographer of Johnson, I have never made Bozziness my business. However, excepting a discussion on the value of the promissory notes issued by our younger poets, wherein Wordsworth named Shelley, and Lamb took John Keats for choice, there was nothing of literary interest brought upon the carpet. But a book man cannot always be bookish. A poet, even a Rydal one, must be glad at times to descend from Saddleback, and feel his legs. He cannot, like the Girl in the Fairy Tale, be always talking diamonds and pearls. It is a "Vulgar Error" to suppose that an author must be always authoring, even with his feet on the fender. Nevertheless, it is not an uncommon impression, that a writer sonnetizes his wife, sings odes to his children, talks essays and epigrams to his friends, and reviews his servants. It was in something of this spirit that an official gentleman to whom I mentioned the pleasant literary meetings at Lamb's, associated them instantly with his parochial mutual instruction evening schools, and remarked, "Yes, yes, all very proper and praiseworthy—of course, you go there *to improve your minds.*"

And very pleasant and improving, though not of set purpose, to both mind and heart, were those extempore assemblages at Colebrooke Cottage. It was wholesome for the soul but to breathe its atmosphere. It was a House of Call for All Denominations. *Sides* were lost in that *circle*, Men of all parties postponed their partizanship, and met as on a neutral ground. There were but two persons whom L. avowedly did not wish to encounter beneath his roof, and those two, merely on account of private and family differences. For the rest, they left all their hostilities at the door, with their sticks. This forbearance was due to the truly tolerant spirit of the Host, which influenced all within its sphere. Lamb, whilst he willingly lent a crutch to halting Humility, took delight in tripping up the stilts of Pretension. Anybody might trot out his Hobby; but he allowed nobody to ride the High Horse. If it was a High German one, like those ridden by the Devil and Doctor Faustus, he would chaunt

"Gëuty, Gëuty,
Is a great Beauty,"

till the rider moderated his gallop. He hated anything like Cock-of-the-Walk-ism; and set his face and his wit against all Ultraism, Transcendentalism, Sentimentalism, Conventional Mannerism, and above all, Separatism. In opposition to the Exclusives, he was emphatically an Inclusive.

As he once owned to me, he was fond of antagonising. Indeed in the sketch of himself, prefacing the Last Essays of Elia—a sketch for its truth to have delighted Mason the Self-Knowledge man—he says, "with the Religionist I pass for a Free-Thinker, while the other faction set me down for a Bigot." In fact, no politician ever labored more to preserve the Balance of Power in Europe, than he did to correct any temporary preponderances. He was always *trimming* in the nautical, not in the political, sense. Thus in his "magnanimous letter," as Hazlitt called it, to High Church Southey, he professed himself a Unitarian.* With a Catholic he would probably have called himself a Jew; as amongst Quakers, by way of a set-off against their own formality, he would indulge in a little extra levity. I well remember his chuckling at having spirited on his correspondent Bernard Barton, to commit some little enormities, such as addressing him as C. Lamb, *Esquire.*

My visits at Lamb's were shortly interrupted by a sojourn to unrheumatize myself at Hastings; but in default of other intercourse, I received a letter in a well-known hand, quaint as the sentences it conveyed.

* As regards his Unitarianism, it strikes me as more probable that he was what the unco guid people call "Nothing at all," which means that he was everything but a Bigot. As he was in spirit an Old Author, so he was in faith an Ancient Christian, too ancient to belong to any of the modern sub-hubbub-divisions of—Ists,—Arians, and—Inians.

"And what dost thou at the Priory? Cucullus non facit Monachum. English me that, and challenge old Lignum Janua to make a better.

"My old New River has presented no extraordinary novelties lately. But there Hope sits every day speculating upon traditionary gudgeons. I think she has taken the fisheries. I now know the reason why our forefathers were denominated East and West Angles. Yet is there no lack of spawn, for I wash my hands in fishets that come through the pump every morning, thick as motelings—little things that perish untimely, and never taste the brook. You do not tell me of those romantic Land Bays that be as thou goest to Lover's Seat, neither of that little Churchling in the midst of a wood (in the opposite direction nine furlongs from the town), that seems dropt by the Angel that was tired of carrying two packages: marry, with the other he made shift to pick his flight to Loretto. Inquire out and see my little Protestant Loretto. It stands apart from trace of human habitation, yet hath it pulpit, reading-desk, and trim front of massiest marble, as if Robinson Crusoe had reared it to soothe himself with old church-going images. I forget its Xtian name, and what She Saint was its gossip.

"You should also go to No. 13, Standgate Street, a Baker, who has the finest collection of marine monsters in ten sea counties; sea-dragons, polypi, mer-people, most fantastic. You have only to name the old Gentleman in black (not the Devil), that lodged with him a week (he'll remember) last July, and he will show courtesy. He is by far the foremost of the Savans. His wife is the funniest thwarting little animal! They are decidedly the Lions of green Hastings. Well, I have made an end of my say; —my epistolary time is gone by when I could have scribbled as long (I will not say as agreeable) as thine was to both of us. I am dwindled to notes and letterets. But in good earnest I shall be most happy to hail thy return to the waters of old Sir Hugh. There is nothing like inland murmurs, fresh ripples, and our native minnows.

> He sang in meads, how sweet the brooklets ran,
> To the rough ocean and red restless sands.

I design to give up smoking; but I have not yet fixed upon the equivalent vice. I must have quid pro quo, or quo pro *quid*, as Tom Woodgate would correct me. My service to him.

"C. L."

The letter came to hand too late for me to hunt the "Lions;" but on a subsequent visit to the same Cinque Port with my wife, though we verified the little Loretto, we could not find the Baker, or even his man, howbeit we tried at every shop that had the least sign of bakery or cakery in its window. The whole was a batch of *fancy* bread; one of those fictions which the writer was apt to pass off upon his friends.

The evening meetings at Colebrooke Cottage—where somebody, who *was* somebody, or a literary friend, was sure to drop in—were the more grateful to me, as the London Magazine was now in a rapid decline; some of its crack contributors had left it off, and the gatherings of the clan to eat, drink, and be merry, were few and far between. There was indeed one Venison Feast whereat, I have heard, the scent lay more than breast high, and the sport was of as rich a quality; but it was my chance to be absent from the pack. At former dinners, however, I had been a guest, and a sketch of one of them may serve to introduce some of the principal characters of our "London in the Olden Time."

On the right hand, then, of the Editor sits Elia, of the pleasant smile, and the quick eyes—Procter said of them that "they looked as if they could pick up pins and needles"—and a wit as quick as his eyes, and sure, as Hazlitt described, to stammer out the best pun and the best remark in the course of the evening. Next to him, shining verdantly out from the grave-colored suits of the literati, like a patch of turnips amidst stubble and fallow, behold our Jack i' the Green—John Clare! In his bright, grass-colored coat, and yellow waistcoat (there are greenish stalks, too, under the table), he looks a very Cowslip, and blooms amongst us as Goldsmith must have done in his peach-blossom. No wonder the door-keeper of the Soho Bazaar, seeing that *very countrified* suit, linked arm-in-arm with the Editorial sables, made a boggle at admitting them into his repository, having seen, perchance, such a made-up Peasant "playing at playing" at thimble-rig about the Square. No wonder the gentleman's gentleman, in the drab-coat and sealing-wax smalls, at W——'s, was for cutting off our Green Man, who was modestly the last in ascending the stairs, as an interloper, though he made amends afterwards by waiting almost exclusively on the Peasant, perfectly convinced that he was some eccentric Notable of the Corinthian order, disguised in Rustic. Little wonder, either, that in wending homewards on the same occasion through the Strand, the Peasant and Elia, *Sylvanus et Urban*, linked comfortably together; there arose the frequent cry of "Look at Tom and Jerry—there goes Tom and Jerry!" for truly, Clare in his square-cut green coat, and Lamb, in his black, were not a little suggestive of Hawthorn and Logic, in the plates to "Life in London."

But to return to the table. Elia—much more of House Lamb than of Grass Lamb—avowedly caring little or nothing for Pastoral; cottons, nevertheless, very kindly to the Northamptonshire Poet, and still more to his ale, pledging him again and again as "Clarissimus," and "Princely Clare," and sometimes so lustily, as to make the latter cast an anxious glance into his tankard. By his bright happy look, the Helpstone Visitor is inwardly contrasting the unlettered country company of Clod, and Hodge and Podge, with the delights of "London" society—Elia, and Barry, and Herbert, and Mr. Table-Talk, *cum multis aliis*—i. e. a multiplicity of all. But besides the tankard, the two "drouthie neebors" discuss Poetry in general,* and Montgomery's "Common Lot" in particular, Lamb insisting on the beauty of the tangental sharp turn at "O! she was fair!" thinking, mayhap, of his own Alice W——, and Clare swearing "Dal!" (a clarified oath) "Dal! if it isn't like a Dead Man preaching out of his coffin!" Anon, the Humorist begins to banter the Peasant on certain "Clare-obscurities" in his own

* Talking of Poetry, Lamb told me one day that he had just met with the most vigorous line he had ever read. "Where?" "Out of the Camden's Head, all in one line—

"*To One Hundred Pots of Porter* . . . . . £2 1 8."

verses, originating in a contempt for the rules of Priscian, where upon the accused, thinking with Burns,

> " What ser'es their grammars ?
> They'd better ta'en up spades and shools,
> Or knappin hammers,"

vehemently denounces all Philology as nothing but a sort of man-trap for authors, and heartily dals Lindley Murray for " inventing it."

It must have been at such a time, that Hilton *conceived* his clever portrait of C——, when he was " C. in alt." He was hardy, rough, and clumsy enough to look truly rustic—like an Ingram's rustic chair. There was a slightness about his frame, with a delicacy of features and complexion, that associated him more with the Garden than with the Field, and made him look the Peasant of a Ferme Ornée. In this respect he was as much beneath the genuine stalwart bronzed Plough-Poet, Burns, as above the Farmer's Boy, whom I remember to have seen in my childhood, when he lived in a miniature house, near the Shepherd and Shepherdess, now the Eagle tavern, in the City Road, and manufactured Æolian harps, and kept ducks. The Suffolk Giles had very little of the agricultural in his appearance ; he looked infinitely more like a handicraftsman, *town-made*.

Poor Clare !—It would greatly please me to hear that he was happy and well, and thriving ; but the transplanting of Peasants and Farmers' Boys from the natural into an artificial soil, does not always conduce to their happiness, or health, or ultimate well-doing. I trust the true Friends, who, with a natural hankering after poetry, because it is forbidden them, have ventured to pluck and eat of the pastoral sorts, as most dallying with the innocence of nature,—and who on that account patronised Capt. Lofft's protégé—I do trust and hope they took off whole editions of the Northamptonshire Bard. There was much about Clare for a Quaker to like ; he was tender-hearted, and averse to violence. How he recoiled once, bodily-taking his chair along with him,—from a young surgeon, or surgeon's friend, who let drop, somewhat abruptly, that he was just come "from seeing a child skinned !"—Clare, from his look of horror, evidently thought that the poor infant, like Marsyas, had been flayed *alive!* He was both gentle and simple. I have heard that on his first visit to London, his publishers considerately sent their porter to meet him at the inn; but when Thomas necessarily inquired of the gentleman in green, "Are you Mr. Clare?" the latter, willing to foil the traditionary tricks of London sharpers, replied to the suspicious query with "a positive negative." *

The Brobdignagdian next to Clare, overtopping him by the whole head and shoulders—a physical "Colossus of Literature," the grenadier of our corps—is Allan, not Allan Ramsay, " no, nor Barbara Allan neither," but Allan Cunningham,—"a credit," quoth Sir Walter Scott (he might have said a long credit) "to Caledonia." He is often called "honest Allan," to distinguish him, perhaps, from one Allan-a-Dale, who was apt to mistake his neighbors' goods for his own—sometimes, between ourselves, yclept the "C. of Solway," in allusion to that favorite "Allan Water," the Solway Sea. There is something of the true moody poetical weather observable in the barometer of his face, alternating from Variable to Showery, from Stormy to Set Fair. At times he looks gloomy and earnest and traditional—a little like a Covenanter—but he suddenly clears up and laughs a hearty laugh that lifts him an inch or two from his chair, for he rises at a joke when he sees one, like a trout at a fly, and finishes with a smart rubbing of his ample palms. He has store, too, of broad Scotch stories, and shrewd sayings; and he writes—no, he wrote rare old-new or new-old ballads. Why not now? Has his Pegasus, as he once related of his pony, run from under him? Has the Mermaid of Galloway left no little ones? Is Bonnie Lady Ann married, or May Morison dead? Thou wast formed for a poet, Allan, by nature, and by stature too, according to Pope—

> "To snatch a grace *beyond the reach* of Art."

And are there not Longman, or Tallboys, for thy Publishers?

* Somebody happened to say that the Peasant ought to figure in the Percy Anecdotes, as an example of uncultivated genius "And where will they stick me," asked Clare; "will they stick me in the instinct?"

But, alas! we are fallen on evil days for Bards and Barding, and nine tailors do more for a man than the Nine Muses. The only Lay likely to answer now-a-days would be an Ode (with the proper testimonials) to the Literary Fund!

The Reverend personage on the Editor's right, with the studious brow, deep-set eyes, and bald crown, is the mild and modest Cary—the same who turned Dante into Miltonic English blank verse. He is sending his plate towards the partridges, which he will relish and digest as though they were the Birds of Aristophanes. He has his eye, too, on the French made-dishes.* Pity, shame and pity, such a Translator found no better translation in the Church! Is it possible that, in some no-popery panic, it was thought by merely being Dragoman to Purgatory he had *Romed* from the true faith?

A very pleasant day we "Londoners" once spent at a Chiswick parsonage, formerly tenanted by Hogarth, along with the hospitable Cary, and, as Elia called them, his Caryatides! † The last time my eyes rested on the Interpreter (of the House Beautiful as well as of the Inferno) he was on the Library steps of the British Museum. Ere this, I trust he hath reached the tiptop—nay, hath perhaps attained being a Literary Worthy, even unto a Trusteeship, and had to buy, at Ellis's, a few yards of the Blue Ribbon of Literature!

Procter,—alias Barry Cornwall, formerly of the Marcian Colonnade, now of some prosaical Inn of Court—the kindly Procter, one of the foremost to welcome me into the Brotherhood, with a too-flattering Dedication (another instance against the jealousy of authors), is my own left-hand file. But what he says shall be kept as strictly confidential; for he is whispering it into my Martineau ear. On my other side, when I turn that way, I see a profile, a shadow of which ever confronts me on opening my writing-desk,—a sketch taken from memory, the

* I once cut out from a country newspaper what seemed to me a very good old English poem. It proved to be a *naturalization*, by Cary, of a French Song to April, by Remy Belleau.

† The father expressing an uncertainty to what profession he should devote a younger Cary, Lamb said, "Make him an Apothe-Cary."

day after seeing the original.* In opposition to the "extra man's size" of Cunningham, the party in question looks almost boyish, partly from being in bulk somewhat beneath Monsieur Quetelet's "Average Man," but still more so from a peculiar delicacy of complexion and smallness of features, which look all the smaller from his wearing, in compliment, probably, to the *Sampsons* of Teutonic Literature, his locks unshorn. Nevertheless whoever looks again,

> Sees more than marks the crowd of common men.

There is speculation in the eyes, a curl of the lip, and a general character in the outline, that reminds one of some portraits of Voltaire. And a Philosopher he is every inch. He looks, thinks, writes, talks and walks, eats and drinks, and no doubt sleeps philosophically—*i. e.* deliberately. There is nothing abrupt about his motions,—he goes and comes calmly and quickly—like the phantom of Hamlet, he is here—he is there—he is gone. So it is with his discourse. He speaks slowly, clearly, and with very marked emphasis,—the tide of talk flows like Denham's river, "strong without rage, without overflowing, full." When it was my frequent and agreeable duty to call on Mr. De Quincey (being an uncommon name to remember, the servant associated it, on the Memoria Technica principle, with a sore throat, and always pronounced it Quinsy), and I have found him at home, quite at home, in the midst of a German Ocean of *Literature*, in a storm,—flooding all the floor, the table and the chairs,—billows of books tossing, tumbling, surging open,—on such occasions I have willingly listened by the hour whilst the Philosopher, standing, with his eyes fixed on one side of the room, seemed to be less speaking than reading from a "handwriting on the wall." Now and then he would diverge, for a Scotch

* Unable to make anything "like a likeness," of a sitter for the purpose, I have a sort of Irish faculty for taking faces behind their backs. But my pencil has not been guilty of half the personalities attributed to it; amongst others "a formidable likeness of a Lombard Street Banker." Besides that one would rather draw on a Banker than at him, I have never seen the Gentleman alluded to, or even a portrait of him in my life.

mile or two, to the right or left, till I was tempted to inquire with Peregrine in John Bull (Colman's not Hook's), "Do you never deviate?"—but he always came safely back to the point where he had left, not lost the scent, and thence hunted his topic to the end. But look!—we are in the small hours, and a change comes o'er the spirit of that "old familiar face." A faint hectic tint leaves the cheek, the eyes are a degree dimmer, and each is surrounded by a growing shadow—signs of the waning influence of that Potent Drug whose stupendous Pleasures and enormous Pains have been so eloquently described by the English Opium Eater. Marry, I have one of his Confessions with his own name and mark to it:—an apology for a certain stain on his MS., the said stain being a large purplish ring. "Within that circle none durst drink but he,"—in fact the impression, colored, of "a tumbler of laudanum negus, warm, without sugar." *

That smart active person opposite with a game-cock-looking head, and the hair combed smooth, fighter fashion, over his forehead—with one finger hooked round a glass of champaigne, not that he requires it to inspirit him, for his wit bubbles up of itself—is our Edward Herbert, the Author of that true piece of Biography, the life of Peter Corcoran. He is "good with both hands," like that Nonpareil Randall, at a comic verse or a serious stanza—smart at a repartee—sharp at a retort,—and not averse to a bit of mischief. 'Twas he who gave the runaway ring at Wordsworth's Peter Bell. Generally, his jests, set off by a happy manner, are only ticklesome, but now and then they are sharp-flavored,—like the sharpness of the pine-apple. Would I could give a sample. Alas! What a pity it is that so many good things uttered by Poets, and Wits, and Humorists,

* On a visit to Norfolk, I was much surprised to find that Opium, or Opie, as it was vulgarly called, was quite in common use in the form of pills amongst the lower classes, *in the vicinity of the Fens*. It is not probable that persons in such a rank of life had read the Confessions,—or, might not one suspect that as Dennis Brulgruddery was driven to drink by the stale, flat and unprofitable prospects of Muckslush Heath, so the Fen-People in the dreary foggy cloggy boggy wastes of Cambridge and Lincolnshire, had flown to the Drug for the sake of the magnificent *scenery* that filled the splendid visions of its Historian?

at chance times—and they are always the best and brightest, like sparks struck out by Pegasus' own hoof, in a curvet amongs the flints—should be daily and hourly lost to the world for want of a recorder! But in this Century of Inventions, when a self-acting drawing-paper has been discovered for copying visible objects, who knows but that a future Niepce, or Daguerre, or Herschel, or Fox Talbot, may find out some sort of Boswellish writing-paper to repeat whatever it hears!

There are other Contributors—poor Hazlitt for instance—whose shades rise up before me: but I never met with them at the Entertainments just described. Shall we ever meet anywhere again? Alas! some are dead; and the rest dispersed; and days of *Social* Clubs are over and gone, when the Professors and Patrons of Literature assembled round the same steaming bowl, and Johnson, always best out of print, exclaimed, "Lads! who's for Poonch!"

* * * * * *

Amongst other notable men who came to Colebrooke Cottage, I had twice the good fortune of meeting with S. T. Coleridge. The first time he came from Highgate with Mrs. Gilman, to dine with "Charles and Mary." What a contrast to Lamb was the full-bodied Poet, with his waving white hair, and his face round, ruddy, and unfurrowed as a holy Friar's! Apropos to which face he gave us a humorous description of an unfinished portrait, that served him for a sort of barometer, to indicate the state of his popularity. So sure as his name made any temporary stir, out came the canvas on the easel, and a request from the artist for another sitting: down sank the Original in the public notice, and back went the copy into a corner, till some fresh publication or accident again brought forward the Poet; and then forth came the picture for a few more touches. I sincerely hope it has been finished! What a benign, smiling face it was! What a comfortable, respectable figure! What a model, methought, as I watched and admired the "Old Man eloquent," for a Christian bishop! But he was, perhaps, scarcely orthodox enough to be trusted with a mitre. At least, some of his voluntaries would have frightened a common everyday congregation from their propriety. Amongst other matters of discourse, he came to speak of the strange notions some literal-minded persons form of the joys of Heaven; joys they associated with mere temporal things, in which, for his own part, finding no delight in this world, he could find no bliss hereafter, without a change in his nature, tantamount to the loss of his personal identity. For instance, he said, there are persons who place the whole angelical beatitude in the possession of a pair of wings to flap about with, like '*a sort of celestial poultry*." After dinner he got up, and began pacing to and fro, with his hands behind his back, talking and walking, as Lamb laughingly hinted, as if qualifying for an itinerant preacher; now fetching a simile from Loddiges' garden, at Hackney; and then flying off for an illustration to the sugar-making in Jamaica. With his fine, flowing voice, it was glorious music, of the "never-ending, still-beginning" kind; and you did not wish it to end. It was rare flying, as in the Nassau Balloon; you knew not whither, nor did you care. Like his own bright-eyed Marinere, he had a spell in his voice that would not let you go. To attempt to describe my own feeling afterward, I had been carried, spiralling, up to heaven by a whirlwind intertwisted with sunbeams, giddy and dazzled, but not displeased, and had then been rained down again with a shower of mundane stocks and stones that battered out of me all recollection of what I had heard, and what I had seen!

On the second occasion, the author of Christabel was accompanied by one of his sons. The Poet, talking and walking as usual, chanced to pursue some argument, which drew from the son, who had not been introduced to me, the remark, "Ah, that's just like your crying up those foolish Odes and Addresses!" Coleridge was highly amused with this mal-àpropos, and, without explaining, looked slily round at me, with the sort of suppressed laugh one may suppose to belong to the Bey of *Tittery*. The truth was, he felt naturally partial to a book he had attributed in the first instance to the dearest of his friends.

"MY DEAR CHARLES,—This afternoon, a little, thin, mean-looking sort of a foolscap, sub-octavo of poems, printed on very dingy outsides, lay on the table, which the cover informed me was circulating in our book-club, so very Grub Streetish in all its appearance, internal as well as external, that I cannot explain by what accident of impulse (assuredly there was no *motive* in play) I came to look into it. Least of all, the title, Odes and Addresses to Great Men, which connected itself in my head with Rejected Addresses, and all the Smith and Theodore Hook squad. But, my dear Charles, it was certainly written by you, or under you, or *una cum* you. I know none of your frequent visitors capacious and assimilative enough of your converse to have reproduced you so honestly, supposing you had left yourself in pledge in his lock-up house. Gillman, to whom I read the spirited parody on the introduction to Peter Bell, the Ode to the Great Unknown, and to Mrs. Fry; he speaks doubtfully of Reynolds and Hood. But here come Irving and Basil Montagu.

"*Thursday Night,* 10 *o'clock.*—No! Charles, it is *you.* I have read them over again, and I understand why you have *anon'd* the book. The puns are nine in ten good—many excellent—the *Newgatory* transcendant. And then the *exemplum sine exemplo* of a volume of personalities and contemporaneities, without a single line that could inflict the infinitesimal of an unpleasance on any man in his senses; saving and except perhaps in the envy-addled brain of the despiser of your *Lays.* If not a triumph over him, it is at least an *ovation.* Then, moreover, and besides, to speak with becoming modesty, excepting my own self, who is there but you who could write the musical lines and stanzas that are intermixed?

"Here Gillman, come up to my garret, and driven back by the guardian spirits of four huge flower-holders of omnigenous roses and honeysuckles—(Lord have mercy on his hysterical olfactories! what will he do in Paradise? I must have a pair or two of nostril plugs, or nose-goggles laid in his coffin)—stands at the door, reading that to M'Adam, and the washerwoman's letter, and he admits *the facts.* You are found *in the manner,* as the lawyers say! so, Mr. Charles! hang yourself up, and send me a line, by way of token and acknowledgment. My dear love to Mary. God bless you and your Unshamabramizer,

"S. T. COLERIDGE."

It may be mentioned here, that instead of feeling "the infinitesimal of an unpleasance" at being Addressed in the Odes, the once celebrated Mr. Hunt presented to the Authors, a bottle of his best "Permanent Ink," and the eccentric Doctor Kitchiner sent an invitation to dinner.

From Colebrooke, Lamb removed to Enfield Chase,—a painful operation at all times, for, as he feelingly misapplied Wordsworth, "the *moving* accident was not his tradė." As soon as he was settled, I called upon him, and found him in a bald-looking yellowish house, with a bit of a garden, and a wasp's nest convanient, as the Irish say, for one stung my pony as he stood at the door. Lamb laughed at the fun; but, as the clown says, the whirligig of time brought round its revenges. He was one day bantering my wife on her dread of wasps, when all at once he uttered a horrible shout,—a wounded specimen of the species had slily crawled up the leg of the table, and stung him in the thumb. I told him it was a refutation well put in, like Smollet's timely snowball. "Yes," said he, "and a stinging commentary on Macbeth—

> "*By the pricking of my thumbs,*
> *Something wicked this way comes.*"

There were no pastoral yearnings concerned in this Enfield removal. There is no doubt which of Captain Morris's Town and Country Songs would have been most to Lamb's taste. "The sweet shady side of Pall-Mall" would have carried it all hollow. In courtesy to a friend, he would select a green lane for a ramble, but left to himself, he took the turnpike road as often as otherwise. "Scott," says Cunningham, "was a stout walker." Lamb was a *porter* one. He calculated Distances, not by Long Measure, but by Ale and Beer Measure. "Now I have walked a pint." Many a time I have accompanied him in these matches against Meux, not without sharing in the stake, and then, what cheerful and profitable talk! For instance, he once delivered to me orally the substance of the Essay on the Defect of Imagination in Modern Artists, subsequently printed in the Athenæum. But besides the criticism, there were snatches of old poems, golden lines and sentences culled from rare books, and anecdotes of men of note. Marry, it was like going a ramble with gentle Izaak Walton, minus the fishing.

To make these excursions more delightful to one of my temperament, Lamb never affected any spurious gravity. Neither did he ever act the Grand *Senior*. He did not exact that common copy-book respect, which some asinine persons would fain command on account of the mere length of their years. As if, forsooth, what is bad in itself, could be the better for keeping; as if intellects already *mothery*, got anything but *grandmothery* by lapse of time! In this particular, he was opposed to Southey, or rather (for Southey has been opposed to himself), to his Poem on the Holly Tree.

> So serious should my youth appear among
> The thoughtless throng;
> So would I seem among the young and gay
> *More grave than they.*

There was nothing of Sir Oracle about Lamb. On the contrary, at sight of a solemn visage that "creamed and mantled like a standing pool," he was the first to pitch a mischievous stone to disturb the duck-weed. "He was a boy-man," as he truly said of Elia; "and his manners lagged behind his years." He liked to herd with people younger than himself. Perhaps, in his fine generalizing way, he thought that, in relation to Eternity, we are all contemporaries. However, without reckoning birthdays, it was always "Hail fellow, well met;" and although he was my elder by a quarter of a century, he never made me feel, in our excursions, that I was "taking a walk with the schoolmaster." I remember, in one of our strolls, being called to account, very pompously, by the proprietor of an Enfield Villa, who asserted that my dog Dash, who never hunted anything in his dog-days, had chased the sheep; whereupon, Elia taking the dog's part, said very emphatically, "Hunt *Lambs*, sir? Why he has never hunted *me!*" But he was always ready for fun, intellectual or practical—now helping to pelt D*****, a modern Dennis, with puns; and then to persuade his sister, God bless her! by a vox et preterea nihil, that she was as deaf as an adder. In the same spirit, being requested by a young Schoolmaster to take charge of his flock for a day, "during the unavoidable absence of the Principal," he willingly undertook the charge, but made no other use of his "brief authority" than to give the boys a whole holiday.

As Elia supplied the place of the Pedagogue, so once I was substitute for Lamb himself. A prose article in the Gem was not from his hand, though it bore his name. He had promised a contribution, but being unwell, his sister suggested that I should write something for him, and the result was the "Widow" in imitation of his manner. It will be seen that the forgery was taken in good part.

"Dear Lamb,—You are an impudent varlet, but I will keep your secret. We dine at Ayrton's on Thursday, and shall try to find Sarah and her two spare beds for that night only. Miss M. and her Tragedy may be dished, so may *not* you and your rib. Health attend you. Yours,

Enfield. T. Hood, Esq.

Miss Bridget Hood sends love."

How many of such pleasant reminiscences revive in my memory, whilst thinking of him, like secret writing brought out by the kindly warmth of the fire! But they must be deferred to leave me time and space for other attributes—for example, his charity, in its widest sense, the moderation in judgment which, as Miller says, is "the Silken String running through the Pearl Chain of all Virtues." If he was intolerant of anything, it was of Intolerance. He would have been (if the foundation had existed, save in the fiction of Rabelais) of the Utopian order of Thelemites, where each man under scriptural warrant did what seemed good in his own eyes. He hated evil-speaking, carping, and petty scandal. On one occasion having slipped out an anecdote, to the discredit of a literary man, during a very confidential conversation, the next moment, with an expression of remorse, for having impaired even my opinion of the party, he bound me solemnly to bury the story in my own bosom. In another case he characteristically rebuked the backbiting spirit of a censorious neighbor. Some Mrs. Candor telling him, in expectation of an ill-natured comment, that Miss * * *, the teacher at the Ladies' School, had married a publican. "Has she so?" said Lamb, "then I'll have my beer there!"

"As to his liberality, in a pecuniary sense, he passed (says Lamb of Elia) with some people, through having a settled but moderate income, for a great miser. And in truth he knew the value of money, its power, its usefulness. One January night he told me with great glee that at the end of the late year he had been able to lay by—and then proceeded to read me a serio-comic lecture on the text, of "Keep your hand out of your Pocket." The truth is, Lamb, like Shakspeare, in the universality of his sympathies, could feel, pro tempore, what belonged to the character of a Gripe-all. The reader will remember his capital note in the "Dramatic Specimens," on "the decline of Misers, in consequence of the *Platonic* nature of an affection for Money," since Money was represented by "*flimsies*" instead of substantial coin, the good old solid sonorous dollars and doubloons, and pieces of eight, that might be handled, and hugged, and rattled, and perhaps kissed. But to this passion for hoarding he one day attributed a new origin. "A Miser," he said, "is sometimes a grand personification of Fear. He has a fine horror of Poverty. And he is not content to keep Want from the door, or at arm's length,—but he places it, by heaping wealth upon wealth, *at a sublime distance!*" Such was his theory: now for his practice. Amongst his other guests, you occasionally saw an elderly lady, formal, fair, and flaxen-wigged, looking remarkably like an animated wax doll,—and she *did* visit some friends, or relations, at a toyshop near St. Dunstan's. When she spoke, it was as if by an artificial apparatus, through some defect in her palate, and she had a slight limp and a twist in her figure, occasioned—what would Hannah More have said!—by running down Greenwich Hill! This antiquated personage had been Lamb's Schoolmistress—and on this retrospective consideration, though she could hardly have taught him more than to read his native tongue—he allowed her in her decline, a yearly sum, equal to—what shall I say?—to the stipend which some persons of fortune deem sufficient for the active services of an all-accomplished gentlewoman in the education of their children. Say, thirty pounds per annum!

Such was Charles Lamb. To sum up his character, on his own principle of antagonising, he was, in his views of human nature, the opposite of Crabbe; in Criticism, of Gifford; in Poetry, of Lord Byron; in Prose, of the last new Novelist; in Philosophy, of Kant; and in Religion, of Sir Andrew Agnew. Of his wit I have endeavored to give such samples as occurred to me; but the spirit of his sayings was too subtle and too much married to the circumstances of the time to survive the occasion. They had the brevity without the levity of wit—some of his puns contained the germs of whole essays. Moreover, like Falstaff, he seemed not only witty himself but the occasion of it by example in others. "There is M * * * * * *" said he, "who goes about dropping his good things as an ostrich lays her eggs without caring what becomes of them." It was once my good fortune to pick up one of Mr. M.'s foundlings, and it struck me as particularly in Lamb's own style, containing at once a pun and a criticism. "What do you think," asked somebody, "of the book called 'A Day in Stowe Gardens?'" Answer: "A Day ill be-stowed."

It is now some five years ago, since I stood with other mourners in Edmonton Church Yard, beside a grave in which all that was mortal of Elia was deposited. It may be a dangerous confession to make, but I shed no tear; and scarcely did a sigh escape from my bosom. There were many sources of comfort. He had not died young. He had happily gone before that noble sister, who not in selfishness, but the devotion of a unique affection, would have prayed to survive him but for a day, lest he should miss that tender care which had watched over him upwards from a little child. Finally he had left behind him his works, a rare legacy!—and above all, however much of him had departed, there was still more of him that could not die—for as long as Humanity endures, and man owns fellowship with man, the spirit of Charles Lamb will still be extant!

* * * * * *

On the publication of the Odes and Addresses, presentation copies were sent, at the suggestion of a friend, to Mr. Canning and Sir Walter Scott. The minister took no notice of the little volume; but the novelist did, in his usual kind manner. An eccentric friend in writing to me, once made a number of colons, semicolons, &c., at the bottom of the paper, adding

"And these are my points that I place at the foot
That you may put stops that I cant stop to put.'

It will surprise no one to observe that the author of Waverley had as little leisure for punctuation.

"Sir Walter Scott has to make thankful acknowledgments for the copy of the Odes to Great People with which he was favored and more particularly for the amusement he has received from the perusal. He wishes the unknown author good health good fortune and whatever other good things can best support and encourage his lively vein of inoffensive and humorous satire

"*Abbotsford Melrose 4th May*"

The first time I ever saw the Great Unknown, was at the private view of Martin's Picture of "Nineveh,"—when, by a striking coincidence, one of our most celebrated women, and one of our greatest men, Mrs. Siddons and Sir Walter Scott walked simultaneously up opposite sides of the room, and met and shook hands in front of the painting. As Editor of the Gem, I had afterwards occasion to write to Sir Walter, from whom I received the following letter, which contains an allusion to some of his characteristic partialities:—

"My dear Mr. Hood,—It was very ungracious in me to leave you in a day's doubt whether I was gratified or otherwise with the honor you did me to inscribe your whims and oddities to me I received with great pleasure this new mark of your kindness and it was only my leaving your volume and letter in the country which delayed my answer as I forgot the address

"I was favored with Mr. Cooper's beautiful sketch of the heart-piercing incident of the dead greyhound which is executed with a force and fancy which I flatter myself that I who was in my younger days and in part still am a great lover of dogs and horses and an accurate observer of their habits can appreciate. I intend the instant our term ends to send a few verses if I can make any at my years in acknowledgment. I will get a day's leisure for this purpose next week when I expect to be in the country . Pray inform Mr. Cooper of my intention though I fear I will be unable to do anything deserving of the subject. I am very truly your obliged humble servant

"*Edinburgh* 4 *March* WALTER SCOTT."

At last, during one of his visits to London, I had the honor of a personal interview with Sir Walter Scott at Mr. Lockhart's, in Sussex Place. The number of the house had escaped my memory; but seeing a fine dog down an area, I knocked without hesitation at the door. It happened, however, to be the wrong one. I afterwards mentioned the circumstance to Sir Walter. It was not a bad point, he said, for he was very fond of dogs; but he did not care to have his own animals with him, about London, "for fear he should be taken for Bill Gibbons." I then told him I had lately been reading the Fair Maid of Perth, which had reminded me of a very pleasant day spent many years before, beside the Linn of Campsie, the scene of Conachar's catastrophe. Perhaps he divined what had really occurred to me,—that the Linn, as a cataract, had greatly disappointed me; for he smiled, and shook his head archly, and said he had since seen it himself, and was rather ashamed of it. "But I fear, Mr. Hood, I have done worse than that before now, in finding a Monastery where there was none to be found; though there was plenty (here he smiled again) of Carduus Benedictus, or Holy Thistle."

In the mean time he was finishing his toilet, in order to dine at the Duchess of Kent's; and before he put on his cravat I had an opportunity of noticing the fine massive proportions of his bust. It served to confirm me in my theory that such mighty men are, and must be, physically, as well as intellectually, gifted beyond ordinary mortals; that their strong minds must be backed by strong bodies. Remembering all that Sir Walter Scott had done, and all that he had suffered, methought he had been in more than one sense "a Giant in the Land." After some more conversation, in the course of which he asked me if I ever came to Scotland, and kindly said he should be glad to see me at Abbotsford, I took my leave, with flattering dreams in my head that never were, and now, alas! never can be, realized!

* * * * *

And now, not to conclude in too melancholy a tone, allow me, gentle reader, to present to you the following genuine letter, the names, merely, for obvious reasons, being disguised.

To T. Hood, Esq.

"Thou'rt a comical chap—so am I; but thou possessest brains competent to write what I mean;—I don't—therefore Brother Comic wilt thou oblige me (if 'twas in my power I would you)—I'll tell you just what I want, and no more. Of late, Lord * * * has been endeavoring to raise a body of yeomanry in this county. Now there's a man at Bedfont—a compounder of nauseous drugs—and against whom I owe a grudge, who wishes to enter, but who's no more fit for a fighter than I for a punster. Now if you will just give him a palpable hit or two in verse, and transmit them to me by post, directed to A. B., Post Office, Bedfont, your kindness shall ever be remembered with feelings of the deepest sincerity and gratitude. His name is 'James Booker, Chemist,' Bedfont *of course*. If you disapprove of the above, I trust you will not abuse the confidence placed in you, by 'splitting.' You'll say, how can I?—by showing this letter to him. He knows the hand-writing full well—but you'll not do so, I hope. Perhaps, if you feel a disposition to oblige me, you will do so at your first convenience, ere the matter will be getting stale.

Yours truly,

A. B.

"Perhaps you will be kind enough to let me have an answer from you, even if you will not condescend to accede to my wish.

"Perhaps you've not sufficient particulars. He's a little fellow, flushed face, long nose, precious ugly, housekeeper as ugly, lives between the two Peacock Inns, is a single man, very anxious to get possession of Miss Boltbee, a ward in Chancery with something like 9000*l.* (WISH he may get it), is famous for his Gout Medicine, sells jalap (should like to make him swallow an ounce), always knows other people's business better than his own, used to go to church, now goes to chapel, and in the whole is a great rascal.

"Bedfont is thirteen miles from London."

THE LOST HEIR.

"Oh where, and oh where,
Is my bonny laddie gone?"—Old Song.

One day, as I was going by
That part of Holborn christened High,
I heard a loud and sudden cry
That chill'd my very blood;
And lo! from out a dirty alley,
Where pigs and Irish wont to rally,
I saw a crazy woman sally,
Bedaub'd with grease and mud.
She turn'd her East, she turn'd her West,
Staring like Pythoness possest,
With streaming hair and heaving breast,
As one stark mad with grief.
This way and that she wildly ran,
Jostling with woman and with man—
Her right hand held a frying-pan,
The left a lump of beef.
At last her frenzy seem'd to reach
A point just capable of speech,
And with a tone almost a screech,
As wild as ocean birds,
Or female Ranter mov'd to preach,
She gave her "sorrow words."

"O Lord! O dear, my heart will break, I shall go stick stark
staring wild!

Has ever a one seen anything about the streets like a crying lost-looking child ?
Lawk help me, I don't know where to look, or to run, if I only knew which way—
A Child as is lost about London streets, and especially Seven Dials, is a needle in a bottle of hay.
I am all in a quiver—get out of my sight, do, you wretch, you little Kitty M'Nab!
You promised to have half an eye to him, you know you did, you dirty deceitful young drab.
The last time as ever I see him, poor thing, was with my own blessed Motherly eyes,
Sitting as good as gold in the gutter, a playing at making little dirt pies.
I wonder he left the court where he was better off than all the other young boys,
With two bricks, an old shoe, nine oyster-shells, and a dead kitten by way of toys.
When his Father comes home, and he always comes home as sure as ever the clock strikes one,
He'll be rampant, he will, at his child being lost; and the beef and the inguns not done!
La bless you, good folks, mind your own consarns, and don't be making a mob in the street;
O serjeant M'Farlane! you have not come across my poor little boy, have you, in your beat?
Do, good people, move on! don't stand staring at me like a parcel of stupid stuck pigs;
Saints forbid! but he 's p'r'aps been inviggled away up a court for the sake of his clothes by the prigs;
He'd a very good jacket, for certain, for I bought it myself for a shilling one day in Rag Fair;
And his trowsers considering not very much patch'd, and red plush, they was once his Father's best pair.
His shirt, it 's very lucky I 'd got washing in the tub, or that might have gone with the rest;
But he 'd got on a very good pinafore with only two slits and a burn on the breast.

He 'd a goodish sort of hat, if the crown was sew'd in, and not
quite so much jagg'd at the brim.
With one shoe on, and the other shoe is a boot, and not a fit,
and you 'll know by that if it 's him.
Except being so well dress'd, my mind would misgive, some old
beggar woman in want of an orphan,
Had borrow'd the child to go a begging with, but I'd rather see
him laid out in his coffin!
Do, good people, move on, such a rabble of boys! I'll break
every bone of 'em I come near,
Go home—you 're spilling the porter—go home—Tommy Jones,
go along home with your beer.
This day is the sorrowfullest day of my life, ever since my
name was Betty Morgan,
Them vile Savoyards! they lost him once before all along of
following a Monkey and an Organ:
O my Billy—my head will turn right round—if he's got kid-
dynapp'd with them Italians,
They 'll make him a plaster parish image boy, they will, the
outlandish tatterdemalions.
Billy—where are you, Billy?—I'm as hoarse as a crow, with
screaming for ye, you young sorrow!
And shan't have half a voice, no more I shan't, for crying fresh
herrings to-morrow.
O Billy, you 're bursting my heart in two, and my life won't be
of no more vally,
If I'm to see other folks' darlins, and none of mine, playing
like angels in our alley,
And what shall I do but cry out my eyes, when I looks at the
old three-legged chair
As Billy used to make coach and horses of, and there a'n't no
Billy there!
I would run all the wide world over to find him, if I only know'd
where to run,
Little Murphy, now I remember, was once lost for a month
through stealing a penny bun,—
The Lord forbid of any child of mine! I think it would kill me
raily,

To find my Bill holdin' up his little innocent hand at the Old
Baily.
For though I say it as oughtn't, yet I will say, you may search
for miles and mileses
And not find one better brought up, and more pretty behaved,
from one end to t'other of St. Giles's.
And if I called him a beauty, it's no lie, but only as a Mother
ought to speak;
You never set eyes on a more handsomer face, only it hasn't
been washed for a week;
As for hair, tho' it's red, it's the most nicest hair when I've time
to just show it the comb;
I'll owe 'em five pounds, and a blessing besides, as will only
bring him safe and sound home.
He's blue eyes, and not to be call'd a squint, though a little cast
he's certainly got;
And his nose is still a good un, tho' the bridge is broke, by his
falling on a pewter pint pot;
He's got the most elegant wide mouth in the world, and very
large teeth for his age;
And quite as fit as Mrs. Murdockson's child to play Cupid on the
Drury Lane Stage.
And then he has got such dear winning ways—but O I never,
never shall see him no more!
O dear! to think of losing him just after nussing him back from
death's door!
Only the very last month when the windfalls, hang 'em, was at
twenty a penny!
And the threepence he'd got by grottoing was spent in plums,
and sixty for a child is too many.
And the Cholera man came and whitewash'd us all and, drat
him, made a seize of our hog.—
It's no use to send the Cryer to cry him about, he's such a
blunderin' drunken old dog;
The last time he was fetched to find a lost child, he was guzzling
with his bell at the Crown,
And went and cried a boy instead of a girl, for a distracted
Mother and Father about Town.

Billy—where are you, Billy, I say, come Billy, come home, to your best of Mothers!
I'm scared when I think of them Cabroleys, they drive so, they'd run over their own Sisters and Brothers.
Or may be he's stole by some chimbly sweeping wretch, to stick fast in narrow flues and what not,
And be poked up behind with a picked pointed pole, when the soot has ketch'd, and the chimbly's red hot.
Oh I'd give the whole wide world, if the world was mine, to clap my two longin' eyes on his face,
For he's my darlin of darlins, and if he don't soon come back, you'll see me drop stone dead on the place.
I only wish I'd got him safe in these two Motherly arms, and wouldn't I hug him and kiss him!
Lauk! I never knew what a precious he was—but a child don't not feel like a child till you miss him.
Why there he is! Punch and Judy hunting, the young wretch, it's that Billy as sartin as sin!
But let me get him home, with a good grip of his hair, and I'm blest if he shall have a whole bone in his skin!

AN UNDERTAKER.

Is an illwiller to the Human Race. He is by Profession an Enemy to his Species, and can no more look kindly at his Fellows than the Sheriff's Officer; for why, his Profit begins with an arrest for the Debt of Nature. As the Bailiff looks on a failing Man, so doth he, and with the same Hope, namely, to take the Body.

Hence hath he little Sympathy with his Kind, small Pity for the Poor, and least of all for the widow and the orphans, whom he regards Planter like, but as so many Blacks on his Estate. If he have any Community of Feeling, it is with the Sexton, who has likewise a Per Centage on the Bills of Mortality, and never sees a Picture of Health but he longs to ingrave it. Both have the same quick Ear for a Churchyard Cough, and both the same Relish for the same Music, to wit, the Toll of Saint Sepulchre. Moreover both go constantly in black—howbeit 'tis no Mourning Suit but a Livery—for he grieves no more for the Defunct than the Bird of the same Plumage, that is the Undertaker to a dead Horse.

As a Neighbor he is to be shunned. To live opposite to him is to fall under the Evil Eye. Like the Witch that forespeaks other Cattle, he would rot you as soon as look at you, if it could be done at a Glance; but that Magic being out of Date, he contents himself with choosing the very Spot on the House Front that shall serve for a Hatchment. Thenceforward he watches your going out and your coming in: your rising up and your lying down, and all your Domestic Imports of Drink and Victual, so that the veriest She Gossip in the Parish is not more familiar with your Modes and Means of Living, nor knows so certainly whether the Visitor, that calls daily in his Chariot, is a mere Friend or a Physician. Also he knows your Age to a Year, and your Height to an Inch, for he hath measured you with his Eye for a Coffin, and your Ponderosity to a Pound, for he hath an Interest in the Dead Weight, and hath so far inquired into your Fortune as to guess with what Equipage you shall travel on your last Journey. For, in professional Curiosity, he is truly a *Pall* Pry. Wherefore to dwell near him is as melancholy as to live in view of a Churchyard; to be within Sound of his Hammering is to hear the Knocking at Death's Door.

To be friends with an Undertaker is as impossible as to be the Crony of a Crocodile. He is by Trade a Hypocrite, and deals of Necessity in Mental Reservations and Equivoques. Thus he drinks to your good Health, but hopes, secretly, it will not endure. He is glad to find you so hearty—as to be Apoplectic; and rejoices to see you so stout—with a short Neck. He bids you beware of your old Gout—and recommends a Quack Doctor. He laments the malignant Fever so prevalent—and wishes you may get it. He compliments your Complexion—when it is Blue or Yellow: admires your upright Carriage,—and hopes it will break down. Wishes you good Day, but means everlasting Night; and commends his Respects to your Father and Mother—but hopes you do not honor them. In short, his good Wishes are treacherous; his Inquiries are suspicious; and his Civilities are dangerous; as when he proffereth the Use of his Coach—or to see you Home.

For the rest, he is still at odds with Humanity; at constant issue with its Naturalists, and its Philanthropists, its Sages, its Counsellors, and its Legislators. For example, he praises the Weather—with the Wind at East; and rejoices in a wet Spring and Fall, for Death and he reap with one Sickle, and have a good or a bad Harvest in common. He objects not to Bones in Bread (being as it were his own Diet), nor to ill Drugs in Beer, nor to Sugar of Lead or arsenical Finings in Wine, nor to ardent Spirits, nor to interment in Churches. Neither doth he discountenance the Sitting on Infants; nor the Swallowing of Plum Stones; nor of cold Ices at Hot balls,—nor the drinking of Embrocations, nay he hath been known to contend that the wrong Dose was the right one. He approves, *contra* the Physicians, of a damp Bed, and wet Feet,—of a hot Head and cold Extremities, and lends his own Countenance to the Natural Small Pox, rather than encourage Vaccination—which he calls flying in the Face of Providence. Add to these, a free Trade in Poisons, whereby the Oxalic Crystals may currently become Proxy for the Epsom ones; and the corrosive Sublimate as common as Salt in Porridge. To the same End he would give unto every Cockney a Privilege to shoot, within ten miles round London, without a Taxed License, and would never concur in a Fine or Deodand for Fast Driving, except the Vehicle were a Hearse. Thus, whatever the popular Cry, he runs counter: a Heretic in Opinion, and a Hypocrite in Practice, as when he pretends to be sorrowful at a Funeral; or, what is worse, affects to pity the ill-paid Poor, and yet helpeth to screw them down.

To conclude, he is a Personage of ill presage to the House of Life: a Raven on the Chimney Pot—a Dead-watch in the Wainscot,—a Winding Sheet in the Candle. To meet with him is ominous. His looks are sinister; his Dress is lugubrious; his Speech is prophetic; and his Touch is mortal. Nevertheless he hath one Merit, and in this our World, and in these our Times, it is a main one; namely, that whatever he *Undertakes* he *Performs*.

MISS KILMANSEGG AND HER PRECIOUS LEG.

A GOLDEN LEGEND.

"What is here?
Gold! yellow, glittering, precious gold?"
Timon of Athens.

HER PEDIGREE.

To trace the Kilmansegg pedigree,
To the very root of the family tree,
  Were a task as rash as ridiculous:
Through antediluvian mists as thick
As London fog such a line to pick
Were enough, in truth, to puzzle Old Nick,
  Not to name Sir Harris Nicholas.

It wouldn't require much verbal strain
To trace the Kill-man, perchance, to Cain;
  But waving all such digressions,
Suffice it, according to family lore,
A Patriarch Kilmansegg lived of yore,
  Who was famed for his great possessions.

Tradition said he feather'd his nest
Through an Agricultural Interest
  In the Golden Age of Farming;
When golden eggs were laid by the geese,
And Colchian sheep wore a golden fleece,
And golden pippins—the sterling kind
Of Hesperus—now so hard to find—
  Made Horticulture quite charming!

A Lord of Land, on his own estate,
He lived at a very lively rate,
  But his income would bear carousing;
Such acres he had of pasture and heath,
With herbage so rich from the ore beneath,
The very ewe's and lambkin's teeth
  Were turn'd into gold by browsing.

He gave, without any extra thrift,
A flock of sheep for a birthday gift
  To each son of his loins, or daughter:
And his debts—if debts he had—at will
He liquidated by giving each bill
  A dip in Pactolian water.

'Twas said that even his pigs of lead,
By crossing with some by Midas bred,
  Made a perfect mine of his piggery.
And as for cattle, one yearling bull
Was worth all Smithfield-market full
  Of the Golden Bulls of Pope Gregory.

The high-bred horses within his stud,
Like human creatures of birth and blood,
  Had their Golden Cups and flagons:
And as for the common husbandry nags,
Their noses were tied in money-bags,
  When they stopp'd with the carts and wagons.

Moreover, he had a Golden Ass,
Sometimes at stall, and sometimes at grass,
  That was worth his own weight in money—
And a golden hive, on a Golden Bank,
Where golden bees, by alchemical prank,
Gather'd gold instead of honey.

Gold! and gold! and gold without end!
He had gold to lay by, and gold to spend,
Gold to give, and gold to lend,

And reversions of gold *in futuro*.
In wealth the family revell'd and roll'd,
Himself and wife and sons so bold ;—
And his daughters sang to their harps of gold
"O bella eta del' oro!"

Such was the tale of the Kilmansegg Kin,
In golden text on a vellum skin,
Though certain people would wink and grin,
And declare the whole story a parable—
That the ancestor rich was one Jacob Ghrimes,
Who held a long lease, in prosperous times,
Of acres, pasture and arable.

That as money makes money, his golden bees
Were the five per cents, or which you please,
When his cash was more than plenty—
That the golden cups were racing affairs ;
And his daughters, who sang Italian airs,
Had their golden harps of Clementi.

That the Golden Ass, or Golden Bull,
Was English John, with his pockets full,
Then at war by land and water :
While beef, and mutton, and other meat,
Were almost as dear as money to eat,
And Farmers reaped Golden Harvests of wheat
At the Lord knows what per quarter!

HER BIRTH.

What different dooms our birthdays bring!
For instance, one little manikin thing
Survives to wear many a wrinkle ;
While Death forbids another to wake,
And a son that it took nine moons to make
Expires without even a twinkle!

Into this world we come like ships,
Launch'd from the docks, and stocks, and slips,

For fortune fair or fatal;
And one little craft is cast away
In its very first trip to Babbicome Bay,
While another rides safe at Port Natal.

What different lots our stars accord!
This babe to be hail'd and woo'd as a Lord!
And that to be shunned like a leper!
One to the world's wine, honey and corn,
Another, like Colchester native, born
To its vinegar, only, and pepper.

One is litter'd under a roof
Neither wind nor water proof,—
That's the prose of Love in a Cottage —
A puny, naked, shivering wretch,
The whole of whose birthright would not fetch,
Though Robins himself drew up the sketch,
The bid of "a mess of pottage."

Born of Fortunatus's kin,
Another comes tenderly usher'd in
To a prospect all bright and burnish'd:
No tenant he for life's back slums—
He comes to the world as a gentleman comes
To a lodging ready furnish'd.

And the other sex—the tender—the fair—
What wide reverses of fate are there
Whilst Margaret, charm' by the Bulbul rare,
In a garden of Gul reposes—
Poor Peggy hawks nosegays from street to street,
Till—think of that, who find life so sweet!—
She hates the smell of roses!

Not so with the infant Kilmansegg!
She was not born to steal or beg,
Or gather cresses in ditches;
To plait the straw, or bind the shoe,

Or sit all day to hem and sew,
As females must, and not a few—
  To fill their insides with stitches;

She was not doom'd, for bread to eat,
To be put to her hands as well as her feet—
  To carry home linen from mangles—
Or heavy-hearted, and weary-limb'd,
To dance on a rope in a jacket trimm'd
  With as many blows as spangles.

She was one of those who by Fortune's boon
Are born, as they say, with a silver spoon
  In her mouth, not a wooden ladle:
To speak according to poet's wont,
Plutus as sponsor stood at her font,
  And Midas rock'd the cradle.

At her first *début* she found her head
On a pillow of down, in a downy bed,
  With a damask canopy over.
For although by the vulgar popular saw
All mothers are said to be "in the straw,"
  Some children are born in clover.

Her very first draught of vital air
It was not the common chamelion fare
  Of plebeian lungs and noses,—
    No—her earliest sniff
    Of this world was a whiff
Of the genuine Otto of Roses!

When she saw the light it was no mere ray
Of that light so common—so everyday—
  That the sun each morning launches—
But six wax tapers dazzled her eyes,
From a thing—a gooseberry bush for size—
  With a golden stem and branches.

She was born exactly at half-past two,
As witness'd a timepiece in or-molu
That stood on a marble table—
Showing at once the time of day,
And a team of *Gildings* running away
As fast as they were able,
With a golden God, with a golden Star,
And a golden Spear, in a golden Car,
According to Grecian fable.

Like other babes, at her birth she cried;
Which made a sensation far and wide,
Ay, for twenty miles around her;
For though to the ear 'twas nothing more
Than an infant's squall, it was really the roar
Of a Fifty-thousand Pounder!
It shook the next heir
In his library chair,
And made him cry, "Confound her!'

Of signs and omens there was no dearth,
Any more than at Owen Glendower's birth,
Or the advent of other great people:
Two bullocks dropp'd dead,
As if knock'd on the head,
And barrels of stout
And ale ran about,
And the village-bells such a peal rang out,
That they crack'd the village-steeple.

In no time at all, like mushroom spawn,
Tables sprang up all over the lawn;
Not furnish'd scantly or shabbily,
But on scale as vast
As that huge repast,
With its loads and cargoes
Of drink and botargoes,
At the Birth of the Babe in Rabelais.

Hundreds of men were turn'd into beasts,
Like the guests at Circe's horrible feasts,
  By the magic of ale and cider;
And each country lass, and each country lad,
Began to caper and dance like mad,
And even some old ones appear'd to have had
  A bite from the Naples Spider.

  Then as night came on,
  It had scared King John,
Who considered such signs not risible,
  To have seen the maroons,
  And the whirling moons,
  And the serpents of flame,
  And wheels of the same,
That according to some were "whizzable."

Oh, happy Hope of the Kilmanseggs!
Thrice happy in head, and body, and legs,
  That her parents had such full pockets!
For had she been born of Want and Thrift,
For care and nursing all adrift,
It's ten to one she had had to make shift
  With rickets instead of rockets!

And how was the precious Baby drest?
In a robe of the East, with lace of the West,
Like one of Crœsus's issue—
  Her best bibs were made
  Of rich gold brocade,
And the others of silver tissue.

And when the Baby inclined to nap
She was lull'd on a Gros de Naples lap,
By a nurse in a modish Paris cap,
  Of notions so exalted,
She drank nothing lower than Curaçoa,
Maraschino, or pink Noyau,
  And on principle never malted.

From a golden boat, with a golden spoon,
The babe was fed night, morning, and noon;
And altho' the tale seems fabulous,
'Tis said her tops and bottoms were gilt,
Like the oats in that Stable-yard Palace built
For the horses of Heliogabalus.

And when she took to squall and kick—
For pains will wring and pins will prick
E'en the wealthiest nabob's daughter—
They gave her no vulgar Dalby or gin,
But liquor with leaf of gold therein,
Videlicet,—Dantzic Water.

In short, she was born, and bred, and nurst,
And drest in the best from the very first,
To please the genteelest censor—
And then, as soon as strength would allow,
Was vaccinated, as babes are now,
With virus ta'en from the best-bred cow
Of Lord Althorp's—now Earl Spencer.

HER CHRISTENING.

Though Shakspeare asks us, "What's in a name?"
(As if cognomens were much the same),
There's really a very great scope in it.
A name?—why, wasn't there Doctor Dodd,
That servant at once of Mammon and God,
Who found four thousand pounds and odd,
A prison—a cart—and a rope in it?

A name?—if the party had a voice,
What mortal would be a Bugg by choice?
As a Hogg, a Grubb, or a Chubb rejoice?
Or any such nauseous blazon?
Not to mention many a vulgar name,
That would make a door-plate blush for shame,
If door-plates were not so brazen!

A name ?—it has more than nominal worth,
And belongs to good or bad luck at birth—
  As dames of a certain degree know,
In spite of his Page's hat and hose,
His Page's jacket, and buttons in rows,
Bob only sounds like a page of prose
  Till turn'd into Rupertino.

Now to christen the infant Kilmansegg,
For days and days it was quite a plague,
  To hunt the list in the Lexicon:
And scores were tried, like coin, by the ring,
Ere names were found just the proper thin
  For a minor rich as a Mexican.

Then cards were sent, the presence to beg
Of all the kin of Kilmansegg,
  White, yellow, and brown relations:
Brothers, Wardens of City Halls,
And Uncles—rich as three Golden Balls
  From taking pledges of nations.

Nephews, whom Fortune seem'd to bewitch,
  Rising in life like rockets—
Nieces whose dowries knew no hitch—
Aunts as certain of dying rich
  As candles in golden sockets—
Cousins German, and cousins' sons,
All thriving and opulent—some had tons
  Of Kentish hops in their pockets!

For money had stuck to the race through life
(As it did to the bushel when cash so rife
Pozed Ali Baba's brother's wife)—
  And down to the Cousins and Coz-lings,
The fortunate brood of the Kilmanseggs,
As if they had come out of golden eggs,
  Were all as wealthy as "Goslings."

It would fill a Court Gazette to name
What East and West End people came
  To the rite of Christianity:
The lofty Lord, and the titled Dame,
  All di'monds, plumes, and urbanity:
His Lordship the May'r with his golden chain
And two Gold Sticks, and the Sheriffs twain,
Nine foreign Counts, and other great men
With their orders and stars, to help M or N
  To renounce all pomp and vanity.

To paint the maternal Kilmansegg
The pen of an Eastern Poet would beg,
  And need an elaborate sonnet;
How she sparkled with gems whenever she stirred,
And her head niddle-noddled at every word,
And seem'd so happy, a Paradise Bird
  Had nidificated upon it.

And Sir Jacob the Father strutted and bow'd,
And smiled to himself, and laugh'd aloud,
  To think of his heiress and daughter—
And then in his pockets he made a grope,
And then, in the fulness of joy and hope,
Seem'd washing his hands with invisible soap,
  In imperceptible water.

He had roll'd in money like pigs in mud,
Till it seemed to have enter'd into his blood
  By some occult projection:
And his cheeks, instead of a healthy hue,
As yellow as any guinea grew,
Making the common phrase seem true
  About a rich complexion.

And now came the nurse, and during a pause,
Her dead-leaf satin would fitly cause
  A very autumnal rustle—
So full of figure, so full of fuss,

As she carried about the babe to buss,
  She seemed to be nothing but bustle.

A wealthy Nabob was God-papa,
And an Indian Begum was God-mamma,
  Whose jewels a Queen might covet—
And the Priest was a Vicar, and Dean withal
Of that Temple we see with a Golden Ball,
  And a Golden Cross above it.

The Font was a bowl of American Gold,
Won by Raleigh in days of old,
  In spite of Spanish bravado;
And the Book of Prayer was so overrun
With gilt devices, it shone in the sun
Like a copy—a presentation one—
  Of Humboldt's "El Dorado."

Gold! and gold! and nothing but gold!
The same auriferous shrine behold
  Wherever the eye could settle!
On the walls—the sideboard—the ceiling-sky—
On the gorgeous footmen standing by,
In coats to delight a miner's eye
  With seams of the precious metal.

Gold! and gold! and besides the gold,
The very robe of the infant told
A tale of wealth in every fold,
  It lapp'd her like a vapor!
So fine! so thin! the mind at a loss
Could compare it to nothing except a cross
  Of cobweb with bank-note paper.

Then her pearls—'twas a perfect sight, forsooth,
To see them, like "the dew of her youth,"
  In such a plentiful sprinkle.
Meanwhile, the Vicar read through the form,
And gave her another, not over-warm,
  That made her little eyes twinkle.

Then the babe was cross'd and bless'd amain;
But instead of the Kate, or Ann, or Jane,
  Which the humbler female endorses—
Instead of one name, as some people prefix,
Kilmansegg went at the tails of six,
  Like a carriage of state with its horses.

Oh, then the kisses she got and hugs!
The golden mugs and the golden jugs
  That lent fresh rays to the midges!
The golden knives, and the golden spoons,
The gems that sparkled like fairy boons,
It was one of the Kilmansegg's own saloons,
  But looked like Rundell and Bridge's!

Gold! and gold! the new and the old!
The company ate and drank from gold,
  They revell'd, they sang, and were merry,
And one of the Gold Sticks rose from his chair,
And toasted "the Lass with the golden hair,"
  In a bumper of golden Sherry.

Gold! still gold! it rain'd on the nurse,
Who, unlike Danäe, was none the worse;
There was nothing but guineas glistening!
  Fifty were given to Doctor James,
  For calling the little Baby names,
    And for saying, Amen!
    The Clerk had ten,
And that was the end of the Christening.

HER CHILDHOOD.

Our youth! our childhood! that spring of springs!
'Tis surely one of the blessedest things
  That nature ever invented!
When the rich are wealthy beyond their wealth,
And the poor are rich in spirits and health,
  And all with their lots contented!

There's little Phelim, he sings like a thrush,
In the selfsame pair of patchwork plush,
With the selfsame empty pockets,
That tempted his daddy so often to cut
His throat, or jump in the water-butt—
But what cares Phelim? an empty nut
Would sooner bring tears to their sockets.

Give him a collar without a skirt,
That's the Irish linen for shirt,
And a slice of bread, with a taste of dirt,
That's Poverty's Irish butter,
And what does he lack to make him blest?
Some oyster-shells, or a sparrow's nest,
A candle-end and a gutter.

But to leave the happy Phelim alone,
Gnawing, perchance, a marrowless bone,
For which no dog would quarrel—
Turn we to little Miss Kilmansegg,
Cutting her first little toothy-peg
With a fifty guinea coral—
A peg upon which
About poor and rich
Reflection might hang a moral.

Born in wealth, and wealthily nursed,
Capp'd, papp'd, napp'd and lapp'd from the first
On the knees of Prodigality,
Her childhood was one eternal round
Of the game of going on Tickler's ground
Picking up gold—in reality.

With extempore carts she never play'd,
Or the odds and ends of a Tinker's trade,
Or little dirt pies and puddings made,
Like children happy and squalid;
The very puppet she had to pet,
Like a bait for the "Nix my Dolly" set,
Was a Dolly of gold—and solid!

Gold! and gold! 'twas the burden still!
To gain the Heiress's early goodwill
There was much corruption and bribery—
  The yearly cost of her golden toys
Would have given to half London's Charity Boys
And Charity Girls the annual joys
  Of a holiday dinner at Highbury.

Bon-bons she ate from the gilt cornet;
And gilded queens on St. Bartlemy's day;
  Till her fancy was tinged by her presents—
And first a goldfinch excited her wish,
Then a spherical bowl with a Golden fish,
  And then two Golden Pheasants.

Nay, once she squall'd and scream'd like wild—
And it shows how the bias we give to a child
Is a thing most weighty and solemn:—
But whence was wonder or blame to spring
If little Miss K.,—after such a swing—
Made a dust for the flaming gilded thing
  On the top of the Fish Street column?

HER EDUCATION.

According to metaphysical creed,
To the earliest books that children read
  For much good or much bad they are debtors—
But before with their A B C they start,
There are things in morals, as well as art,
That play a very important part—
  "Impressions before the letters."

Dame Education begins the pile,
Mayhap in the graceful Corinthian style,
  But alas for the elevation!
If the Lady's maid or gossip the Nurse
With a load of rubbish, or something worse,
  Have made a rotten foundation.

Even thus with Little Miss Kilmansegg,
Before she learnt her E for egg,
  Ere her Governess came, or her Masters—
Teachers of quite a different kind
Had "cramm'd" her beforehand, and put her mind
  In a go-cart on golden castors.

Long before her A B and C,
They had taught her by heart her L. S. D.,
  And as how she was born a great Heiress;
And as sure as London was built of bricks,
My Lord would ask her the day to fix,
To ride in her fine gilt coach and six,
  Like her Worship the Lady May'ress.

Instead of stories from Edgeworth's page,
The true golden lore for our golden age,
  Or lessons from Barbauld and Trimmer,
Teaching the worth of Virtue and Health,
All that she knew was the Virtue of Wealth,
Provided by vulgar nursery stealth,
  With a Book of Leaf Gold for a Primer.

The very metal of merit they told,
And praised her for being as "good as gold!"
  Till she grew as a peacock haughty:
Of money they talk'd the whole day round,
And weigh'd desert like grapes by the pound,
Till she had an idea from the very sound
  That people with naught were naughty.

They praised—poor children with nothing at all!
Lord! how you twaddle and waddle and squall
  Like common-bred geese and ganders!
What sad little bad little figures you make
To the rich Miss K., whose plainest seed-cake
  Was stuff'd with corianders!

They praised her falls, as well as her walk,
Flatterers make cream cheese of chalk,

They praised—how they praised—her very small talk,
  As if it fell from a Solon ;
Or the girl who at each pretty phrase let drop
A ruby comma, or pearl full-stop,
  Or an emerald semi-colon.

They praised her spirit, and now and then,
The Nurse brought her own little "nevy" Ben,
  To play with the future May'ress,
And when he got raps, and taps, and slaps,
Scratches, and pinches, snips, and snaps,
  As if from a Tigress or Bearess,
They told him how Lords would court that hand,
And always gave him to understand,
    While he rubb'd, poor soul,
    His carroty poll,
  That his hair had been pull'd by "a *Hairess.*"

Such were the lessons from maid and nurse,
A Governess help'd to make still worse,
Giving an appetite so perverse
  Fresh diet whereon to batten—
Beginning with A. B. C. to hold
Like a royal playbill printed in gold
  On a square of pearl-white satin.

The books to teach the verbs and nouns,
And those about countries, cities, and towns,
Instead of their sober drabs and browns,
  Were in crimson silk, with gilt edges :—
Her Butler, and Enfield, and Entick—in short
Her "Early Lessons" of every sort,
  Look'd like Souvenirs, Keepsakes, and Pledges.

Old Johnson shone out in as fine array
As he did one night when he went to the play ;
Chambaud like a beau of King Charles's day—
  Lindley Murray in like conditions—

Each weary, unwelcome, irksome task,
Appear'd in a fancy dress and a mask—
If you wish for similar copies ask
  For Howell and James's Editions.

Novels she read to amuse her mind,
But always the affluent match-making kind
  That ends with Promessi Sposi,
And a father-in-law so wealthy and grand,
He could give cheque-mate to Coutts in the Strand;
  So, along with a ring and posy,
He endows the Bride with Golconda off-hand,
  And gives the Groom Potosi.

Plays she perused—but she liked the best
Those comedy gentlefolks always possess'd
  Of fortunes so truly romantic—
Of money so ready that right or wrong
It always is ready to go for a song,
Throwing it, going it, pitching it strong—
They ought to have purses as green and long
  As the cucumber called the Gigantic.

Then Eastern Tales she loved for the sake
Of the Purse of Oriental make,
  And the thousand pieces they put in it—
But Pastoral scenes on her heart fell cold,
For Nature with her had lost its hold,
No field but the field of the Cloth of Gold
  Would ever have caught her foot in it.

What more? She learnt to sing, and dance,
To sit on a horse, although he should prance,
And to speak a French not spoken in France
  Any more than at Babel's building—
And she painted shells, and flowers, and Turks,
But her great delight was in Fancy Works
  That are done with gold or gilding.

Gold ! still gold !—the bright and the dead,
With golden beads, and gold lace, and gold thread,
She work'd in gold, as if for her bread ;
  The metal had so undermined her,
Gold ran in her thoughts and fill'd her brain,
She was golden-headed as Peter's cane
  With which he walk'd behind her.

HER ACCIDENT.

The horse that carried Miss Kilmansegg,
And a better never lifted leg,
  Was a very rich bay, called Banker—
A horse of a breed and a mettle so rare,—
By Bullion out of an Ingot mare,—
That for action, the best of figures, and air,
  It made many good judges hanker.

And when she took a ride in the Park,
Equestrian Lord, or pedestrian Clerk,
  Was thrown in an amorous fever,
To see the Heiress how well she sat,
With her groom behind her, Bob or Nat,
In green, half smother'd with gold, and a hat
  With more gold lace than beaver.

And then when Banker obtain'd a pat,
To see how he arched his neck at that !
  He snorted with pride and pleasure !
Like the Steed in the fable so lofty and grand,
Who gave the poor Ass to understand,
That *he* didn't carry a bag of sand,
  But a burden of golden treasure.

A load of treasure ?—alas ! alas !
Had her horse been fed upon English grass,
  And sheltered in Yorkshire spinneys,
Had he scour'd the sand with the Desert Ass,
  Or where the American whinnies—

But a hunter from Erin's turf and gorse,
A regular thorough-bred Irish horse,
Why, he ran away, as a matter of course,
  With a girl worth her weight in guineas!

Mayhap 'tis the trick of such pamper'd nags
To shy at the sight of a beggar in rags,
  But away, like the bolt of a rabbit,
Away went the horse in the madness of fright,
And away went the horsewoman mocking the sight—
Was yonder blue flash a flash of blue light,
  Or only the skirt of her habit?

Away she flies, with the groom behind,—
It looks like a race of the Calmuck kind,
  When Hymen himself is the starter:
And the Maid rides first in the fourfooted strife,
Riding, striding, as if for her life,
While the lover rides after to catch him a wife,
  Although it's catching a Tartar.

But the Groom has lost his glittering hat!
Though he does not sigh and pull up for that—
Alas! his horse is a tit for Tat
  To sell to a very low bidder—
His wind is ruin'd, his shoulder is sprung,
Things, though a horse be handsome and young,
  A purchaser *will* consider.

But still flies the Heiress through stones and dust,
Oh, for a fall, if fall she must,
  On the gentle lap of Flora!
But still, thank Heaven! she clings to her seat—
Away! away! she could ride a dead heat
With the dead who ride so fast and fleet,
  In the Ballad of Leonora!

Away she gallops!—it's awful work!
It's faster than Turpin's ride to York

On Bess that notable clipper!
She has circled the Ring!—she crosses the Park!
Mazeppa, although he was stripp'd so stark,
Mazeppa couldn't outstrip her!

The fields seem running away with the folks!
The Elms are having a race for the Oaks!
At a pace that all Jockeys disparages!
All, all is racing! the Serpentine
Seems rushing past like the "arrowy Rhine,"
The houses have got on a railway line,
And are off like the first-class carriages!

She'll lose her life! she is losing her breath!
A cruel chase, she is chasing Death,
As female shriekings forewarn her:
And now—as gratis as blood of Guelph—
She clears that gate, which has clear'd itself
Since then, at Hyde Park Corner!

Alas! for the hope of the Kilmanseggs!
For her head, her brains, her body, and legs,
Her life's not worth a copper!
Willy-nilly,
In Piccadilly,
A hundred hearts turn sick and chilly,
A hundred voices cry, "Stop her!"
And one old gentleman stares and stands,
Shakes his head and lifts his hands,
And says, "How very improper!"

On and on!—what a perilous run!
The iron rails seem all mingling in one,
To shut out the Green Park scenery!
And now the Cellar its dangers reveals,
She shudders—she shrieks—she's doom'd, she feels,
To be torn by powers of horses and wheels,
Like a spinner by steam machinery!

Sick with horror she shuts her eyes,
But the very stones seem uttering cries,
As they did to that Persian daughter,
When she climb'd up the steep vociferous hill,
Her little silver flagon to fill
With the magical Golden Water!

"Batter her! shatter her!
Throw and scatter her!"
Shouts each stony-hearted clatterer—
"Dash at the heavy Dover!
Spill her! kill her! tear and tatter her!
Smash her! crash her!" (the stones didn't flatter her!)
"Kick her brains out! let her blood spatter her!
Roll on her over and over!"

For so she gather'd the awful sense
Of the street in its past unmacadamized tense,
As the wild horse overran it,—
His four heels making the clatter of six,
Like a Devil's tattoo, played with iron sticks
On a kettle-drum of granite!

On! still on! she's dazzled with hints
Of oranges, ribbons, and color'd prints,
A Kaleidoscope jumble of shapes and tints,
And human faces all flashing,
Bright and brief as the sparks from the flints,
That the desperate hoofs keep dashing!

On and on! still frightfully fast!
Dover-street, Bond-street, all are past!
But—yes—no—yes!—they're down at last!
The Furies and Fates have found them!
Down they go with a sparkle and crash,
Like a Bark that's struck by the lightning flash—
There's a shriek—and a sob—
And the dense dark mob
Like a billow close around them!

* * * * *
* * * *

"She breathes!"
"She don't!"
"She'll recover!"
"She won't!"
"She's stirring! she's living, by Nemesis!"
Gold, still gold! on counter and shelf!
Golden dishes as plenty as delf!
Miss Kilmansegg's coming again to herself
On an opulent Goldsmith's premises!

Gold! fine gold!—both yellow and red,
Beaten, and molten—polish'd, and dead—
To see the gold with profusion spread
In all forms of its manufacture!
But what avails gold to Miss Kilmansegg,
When the femoral bone of her dexter leg
Has met with a compound fracture?

Gold may soothe Adversity's smart;
Nay, help to bind up a broken heart;
But to try it on any other part
Were as certain a disappointment,
As if one should rub the dish and plate,
Taken out of a Staffordshire crate—
In the hope of a Golden Service of State—
With Singleton's "Golden Ointment."

HER PRECIOUS LEG.

"As the twig is bent, the tree 's inclined,"
Is an adage often recall'd to mind,
Referring to juvenile bias:
And never so well is the verity seen,
As when to the weak, warp'd side we lean,
While Life's tempests and hurricanes try us.

Even thus with Miss K. and her broken limb,
By a very, very remarkable whim,

She show'd her early tuition:
While the buds of character came into blow
With a certain tinge that served to show
The nursery culture long ago,
As the graft is known by fruition!

For the King's Physician, who nursed the case,
His verdict gave with an awful face,
And three others concurr'd to egg it;
That the Patient to give old Death the slip,
Like the Pope, instead of a personal trip,
Must send her Leg as a Legate.

The limb was doom'd—it couldn't be saved!
And like other people the patient behaved,
Nay, bravely that cruel parting braved,
Which makes some persons so falter,
They rather would part, without a groan,
With the flesh of their flesh, and bone of their bone,
They obtain'd at St. George's altar.

But when it came to fitting the stump
With a proxy limb—then flatly and plump
She spoke, in the spirit olden;
She couldn't—she shouldn't—she wouldn't have wood!
Nor a leg of cork, if she never stood,
And she swore an oath, or something as good,
The proxy limb should be golden!

A wooden leg! what, a sort of a peg,
For your common Jockeys and Jennies!
No, no, her mother might worry and plague—
Weep, go down on her knees, and beg,
But nothing would move Miss Kilmansegg!
She could—she would have a Golden Leg,
If it cost ten thousand guineas!

Wood indeed, in Forest or Park,
With its sylvan honors and feudal bark,

Is an aristocratical article:
But split and sawn, and hack'd about town,
Serving all needs of pauper or clown,
Trod on! stagger'd on! Wood cut down
Is vulgar—fibre and particle!

And Cork!—when the noble Cork Tree shades
A lovely group of Castilian maids,
'Tis a thing for a song or sonnet!—
But, cork, as it stops the bottle of gin,
Or bungs the beer—the *small* beer—in,
It pierced her heart like a corking pin,
To think of standing upon it!

A Leg of Gold—solid gold throughout,
Nothing else, whether slim or stout,
Should ever support her, God willing!
She must—she could—she would have her whim,
Her father, she turn'd a deaf ear to him—
He might kill her—she didn't mind killing!
He was welcome to cut off her other limb—
He might cut her off with a shilling!

All other promised gifts were in vain,
Golden Girdle, or Golden Chain,
She writhed with impatience more than pain,
And utter'd "pshaws!" and "pishes!"
But a Leg of Gold! as she lay in bed,
It danced before her—it ran in her head!
It jump'd with her dearest wishes!

"Gold—gold—gold! Oh, let it be gold!"
Asleep or awake that tale she told,
And when she grew delirious:
Till her parents resolved to grant her wish,
If they melted down plate, and goblet, and dish,
The case was getting so serious.

So a Leg was made in a comely mould,
Of Gold, fine virgin glittering gold,

As solid as man could make it—
Solid in foot, and calf, and shank,
A prodigious sum of money it sank;
In fact 'twas a Branch of the family Bank,
And no easy matter to break it.

All sterling metal—not half-and-half,
The Goldsmith's mark was stamp'd on the calf—
'Twas pure as from Mexican barter!
And to make it more costly, just over the knee,
Where another ligature used to be,
Was a circle of jewels, worth shillings to see,
A new-fangled Badge of the Garter!

'Twas a splendid, brilliant, beautiful Leg,
Fit for the Court of Scander-Beg,
That Precious Leg of Miss Kilmansegg!
For, thanks to parental bounty,
Secure from Mortification's touch,
She stood on a member that cost as much
As a Member for all the County!

HER FAME.

To gratify stern ambition's whims,
What hundreds and thousands of precious limbs
On a field of battle we scatter!
Sever'd by sword, or bullet, or saw,
Off they go, all bleeding and raw,
But the public seems to get the lock-jaw,
So little is said on the matter!

Legs, the tightest that ever were seen,
The tightest, the lightest, that danced on the green,
Cutting capers to sweet Kitty Clover;
Shatter'd, scatter'd, cut, and bowl'd down,
Off they go, worse off for renown,
A line in the *Times*, or a talk about town,
Than the leg that a fly runs over!

But the Precious Leg of Miss Kilmansegg,
That gowden, goolden, golden leg,
  Was the theme of all conversation!
Had it been a Pillar of Church and State,
Or a prop to support the whole Dead Weight,
It could not have furnish'd more debate
  To the heads and tails of the nation!

East and west, and north and south,
Though useless for either hunger or drouth,—
The Leg was in everybody's mouth,
  To use a poetical figure,
Rumor, in taking her ravenous swim,
Saw, and seized on the tempting limb,
  Like a shark on the leg of a nigger.

Wilful murder fell very dead;
Debates in the House were hardly read;
In vain the Police Reports were fed
  With Irish riots and *rumpuses*—
The Leg! the Leg! was the great event,
Through every circle in life it went,
  Like the leg of a pair of compasses.

The last new Novel seem'd tame and flat,
The Leg, a novelty newer than that,
  Had tripp'd up the heels of Fiction!
It Burked the very essays of Burke,
And, alas! how Wealth over Wit plays the Turk!
As a regular piece of goldsmith's work,
  Got the better of Goldsmith's diction.

"A leg of gold! what of solid gold?"
Cried rich and poor, and young and old,—
  And Master and Miss and Madam—
'Twas the talk of 'Change—the Alley—the Bank—
And with men of scientific rank
It made as much stir as the fossil shank
  Of a Lizard coëval with Adam!

Of course with Greenwich and Chelsea elves,
Men who had lost a limb themselves,
  Its interest did not dwindle—
But Bill, and Ben, and Jack, and Tom,
Could hardly have spun more yarns therefrom,
  If the leg had been a spindle.

Meanwhile the story went to and fro,
Till, gathering like the ball of snow,
By the time it got to Stratford-le-Bow,
  Through Exaggeration's touches,
The Heiress and Hope of the Kilmanseggs
Was propp'd on *two* fine Golden Legs,
  And a pair of Golden Crutches!

Never had Leg so great a run!
'Twas the "go" and the "Kick" thrown into one!
The mode—the new thing under the sun,
  The rage—the fancy—the passion!
Bonnets were named, and hats were worn,
A la Golden Leg instead of Leghorn,
    And stockings and shoes
    Of golden hues,
  Took the lead in the walks of fashion!

The Golden Leg had a vast career,
It was sung and danced—and to show how near
  Low Folly to lofty approaches,
Down to society's very dregs,
The Belles of Wapping wore "Kilmanseggs,"
And St. Giles's Beaux sported Golden Legs
  In their pinchbeck pins and brooches!

HER FIRST STEP

Supposing the Trunk and Limbs of Man
Shared on the allegorical plan,
  By the Passions that mark humanity,
Whichever might claim the head, or heart,

The stomach, or any other part,
  The Legs would be seized by vanity.

There's Bardus, a six-foot column of fop,
A lighthouse without any light atop,
  Whose height would attract beholders,
If he had not lost some inches clear
By looking down at his kerseymere,
Ogling the limbs he holds so dear,
  Till he got a stoop in his shoulders.

Talk of Art, of Science, or Books,
And down go the everlasting looks,
  To his cruel beauties so wedded!
Try him, wherever you will, you find
His mind in his legs, and his legs in his mind,
All prongs and folly—in short a kind
  Of Fork—that is Fiddle-headed.

What wonder, then, if Miss Kilmansegg,
With a splendid, brilliant, beautiful leg,
Fit for the court of Scander Beg,
Disdain'd to hide it like Joan or Meg,
  In petticoats stuff'd or quilted?
Not she! 'twas her convalescent whim
To dazzle the world with her precious limb,—
  Nay, to go a little high-kilted.

So cards were sent for that sort of mob
Where Tartars and Africans hob-and-nob,
And the Cherokee talks of his cab and cob
  To Polish or Lapland lovers—
Cards like that hieroglyphical call
To a geographical Fancy Ball
  On the recent Post-Office covers.

For if Lion-hunters—and great ones too—
Would mob a savage from Latakoo,
Or squeeze for a glimpse of Prince Le Boo,

  That unfortunate Sandwich scion—
Hundreds of first-rate people, no doubt,
Would gladly, madly, rush to a rout,
  That promised a Golden Lion!

HER FANCY BALL.

Of all the spirits of evil fame,
That hurt the soul, or injure the frame,
  And poison what's honest and hearty,
There's none more needs a Mathew to preach
A cooling, antiphlogistic speech,
    To praise and enforce
    A temperate course,
Than the Evil Spirit of Party.

Go to the House of Commons, or Lords,
And they seem to be busy with simple words
  In their popular sense or pedantic—
But, alas! with their cheers, and sneers, and jeers,
They're really busy, whatever appears,
Putting peas in each other's ears,
  To drive their enemies frantic!

Thus Tories love to worry the Whigs,
Who treat them in turn like Schwalbach pigs,
Giving them lashes, thrashes, and digs,
  With their writhing and pain delighted—
But after all that's said, and more,
The malice and spite of Party are poor
To the malice and spite of a party next door,
  To a party not invited.

On with the cap and out with the light,
Weariness bids the world good-night,
  At least for the usual season;
But hark! a clatter of horses' heels;
And Sleep and Silence are broken on wheels,
  Like Wilful Murder and Treason!

Another crash—and the carriage goes—
Again poor Weariness seeks the repose
  That Nature demands imperious;
But Echo takes up the burden now,
With a rattling chorus of row-de-dow-dow,
Till Silence herself seems making a row,
  Like a Quaker gone delirious!

'Tis night—a winter night—and the stars
Are shining like winkin'—Venus and Mars
Are rolling along in their golden cars
  Through the sky's serene expansion—
But vainly the stars dispense their rays,
Venus and Mars are lost in the blaze
  Of the Kilmanseggs' luminous mansion!

Up jumps Fear in a terrible fright!
His bedchamber windows look so bright,
  With light all the Square is glutted!
Up he jumps, like a sole from the pan,
And a tremor sickens his inward man,
For he feels as only a gentleman can,
  Who thinks he's being "gutted."

Again Fear settles, all snug and warm;
But only to dream of a dreadful storm
From Autumn's sulphurous locker;
  But the only electric body that falls,
Wears a negative coat, and positive smalls,
And draws the peal that so appals
  From the Kilmanseggs' brazen knocker!

'Tis Curiosity's Benefit night—
And perchance 'tis the English Second-Sight,
  But whatever it be, so be it—
As the friends and guests of Miss Kilmansegg
Crowd in to look at her Golden Leg,
      As many more

Mob round the door
To see them going to see it!

In they go—in jackets, and cloaks,
Plumes, and bonnets, turbans, and toques,
As if to a Congress of Nations:
Greeks and Malays, with daggers and dirks
Spaniards, Jews, Chinese, and Turks—
Some like original foreign works,
But mostly like bad translations.

In they go, and to work like a pack,
Juan, Moses, and Shacabac,
Tom, and Jerry, and Spring-heel'd Jack,
For some of low Fancy are lovers—
Skirting, zigzagging, casting about,
Here and there, and in and out,
With a crush, and a rush, for a full-bodied rout
Is one of the stiffest of covers.

In they went, and hunted about,
Open-mouth'd, like chub and trout,
And some with the upper lip thrust out,
Like that fish for routing, a barbel—
While Sir Jacob stood to welcome the crowd,
And rubb'd his hands, and smiled aloud,
And bow'd, and bow'd, and bow'd, and bow'd,
Like a man who is sawing marble.

For Princes were there, and Noble Peers;
Dukes descending from Norman spears;
Earls that dated from early years;
And Lords in vast variety—
Besides the Gentry, both new and old—
For people who stand on legs of gold,
Are sure to stand well with society.

"But where—where—where?" with one accord
Cried Moses and Mufti, Jack and my Lord,

Wang-Fong and Il Bondocani—
When slow, and heavy, and dead as a dump,
They heard a foot begin to stump,
Thump! lump!
Lump! thump!
Like the Spectre in "Don Giovanni!"

And lo! the Heiress, Miss Kilmansegg,
With her splendid, brilliant, beautiful leg,
In the garb of a Goddess olden—
Like chaste Diana going to hunt,
With a golden spear—which of course was blun
And a tunic loop'd up to a gem in front,
To show the Leg that was Golden!

Gold! still gold! her Crescent behold,
That should be silver, but would be gold;
And her robe's auriferous spangles!
Her golden stomacher—how she would melt!
Her golden quiver, and golden belt,
Where a golden bugle dangles!

And her jewell'd Garter? Oh, Sin! Oh, Shame!
Let Pride and Vanity bear the blame,
That bring such blots on female fame!
But to be a true recorder,
Besides its thin transparent stuff,
The tunic was loop'd quite high enough
To give a glimpse of the Order!

But what have sin or shame to do
With a Golden Leg—and a stout one too?
Away with all Prudery's panics!
That the precious metal, by thick and thin,
Will cover square acres of land or sin,
Is a fact made plain
Again and again,
In morals as well as Mechanics.

A few, indeed, of her proper sex,
Who seem'd to feel her foot on their necks,
And fear'd their charms would meet with checks
From so rare and splendid a blazon—
A few cried "fie!"—and "forward"—and "bold!"
And said of the Leg it might be gold,
But to them it looked like brazen!

'Twas hard they hinted for flesh and blood,
Virtue, and Beauty, and all that's good,
To strike to mere dross their topgallants—
But what were Beauty, or Virtue, or Worth,
Gentle manners, or gentle birth,
Nay, what the most talented head on earth
To a Leg worth fifty Talents!

But the men sang quite another hymn
Of glory and praise to the precious Limb—
Age, sordid Age, admired the whim,
And its indecorum pardon'd—
While half of the young—ay, more than half—
Bow'd down and worshipp'd the Golden Calf,
Like the Jews when their hearts were harden'd.

A Golden Leg! what fancies it fired!
What golden wishes and hopes inspired!
To give but a mere abridgment—
What a leg to leg-bail Embarrassment's serf!
What a leg for a Leg to take on the turf!
What a leg for a marching regiment!

A Golden Leg!—whatever Love sings,
'Twas worth a bushel of "Plain Gold Rings"
With which the Romantic wheedles.
'Twas worth all the legs in stockings and socks—
'Twas a leg that might be put in the Stocks,
N.B.—Not the parish beadle's!

And Lady K. nid-nodded her head,
Lapp'd in a turban fancy-bred,

Just like a love-apple, huge and red,
 Some Mussul-womanish mystery;
  But whatever she meant
   To represent,
 She talk'd like the Muse of History.

She told how the filial leg was lost;
And then how much the gold one cost;
 With its weight to a Trojan fraction:
And how it took off, and how it put on;
And call'd on Devil, Duke, and Don,
Mahomet, Moses, and Prester John,
 To notice its beautiful action.

And then of the Leg she went in quest;
And led it where the light was best;
And made it lay itself up to rest
 In postures for painters' studies:
It cost more tricks and trouble by half,
Than it takes to exhibit a Six-Legg'd Calf
 To a boothful of country Cuddies.

Nor yet did the Heiress herself omit
The arts that help to make a hit,
 And preserve a prominent station.
She talk'd and laugh'd far more than her share;
And took a part in "Rich and Rare
Were the gems she wore"—and the gems were there,
 Like a Song with an Illustration.

She even stood up with a Count of France
To dance—alas! the measures we dance
 When Vanity plays the Piper!
Vanity, Vanity, apt to betray,
And lead all sorts of legs astray,
Wood, or metal, or human clay,—
 Since Satan first play'd the Viper!

But first she doff'd her hunting gear,
And favor'd Tom Tug with her golden spear,

To row with down the river—
A Bonze had her golden bow to hold,
A Hermit her belt and bugle of gold;
And an Abbot her golden quiver.

And then a space was clear'd on the floor,
And she walk'd the Minuet de la Cour,
With all the pomp of a Pompadour;
But although she began *andante*,
Conceive the faces of all the Rout,
When she finish'd off with a whirligig bout,
And the Precious Leg stuck stiffly out
Like the leg of a *Figurantê!*

So the courtly dance was goldenly done,
And golden opinions, of course, it won
From all different sorts of people—
Chiming, ding-dong, with flattering phrase,
In one vociferous peal of praise,
Like the peal that rings on Royal days
From Loyalty's parish-steeple.

And yet, had the leg been one of those
That dance for bread in flesh-color'd hose,
With Rosina's pastoral bevy,
The jeers it had met,—the shouts! the scoff!
The cutting advice to "take itself off,"
For sounding but half so heavy.

Had it been a leg like those, perchance,
That teach little girls and boys to dance,
To set, poussette, recede, and advance,
With the steps and figures most proper,—
Had it hopp'd for a weekly or quarterly sum,
How little of praise or grist would have come
To a mill with such a hopper!

But the Leg was none of those limbs forlorn—
Bartering capers and hops for corn—

That meet with public hisses and scorn,
Or the morning journal denounces—
Had it pleas'd to caper from morn till dusk,
There was all the music of "Money Musk"
In its ponderous bangs and bounces.

But hark!—as slow as the strokes of a pump,
Lump, thump!
Thump, lump!
As the Giant of Castle Otranto might stump
To a lower room from an upper—
Down she goes with a noisy dint,
For taking the crimson turban's hint,
A noble Lord at the Head of the Mint
Is leading the Leg to supper!

But the supper, alas! must rest untold,
With its blaze of light and its glitter of gold,
For to paint that scene of glamor,
It would need the Great Enchanter's charm,
Who waves over Palace, and Cot, and Farm,
An arm like the Goldbeater's Golden Arm
That wields a Golden Hammer.

He—only HE—could fitly state
THE MASSIVE SERVICE OF GOLDEN PLATE,
With the proper phrase and expansion—
The Rare Selection of FOREIGN WINES—
The ALPS OF ICE and MOUNTAINS OF PINES,
The punch in OCEANS and sugary shrines,
The TEMPLE OF TASTE from GUNTER'S DESIGNS—
In short, all that WEALTH with A FEAST combines,
In a SPLENDID FAMILY MANSION.

Suffice it each mask'd outlandish guest
Ate and drank of the very best,
According to critical conners—

And then they pledged the Hostess and Host,
But the Golden Leg was the standing toast,
And as somebody swore,
Walk'd off with more
Than its share of the "Hips!" and honors!

"Miss Kilmansegg!—
Full glasses I beg!—
Miss Kilmansegg and her Precious Leg!"
And away went the bottle careering!
Wine in bumpers! and shouts in peals!
Till the Clown didn't know his head from his heels,
The Mussulman's eyes danced two-some reels,
And the Quaker was hoarse with cheering!

HER DREAM.

Miss Kilmansegg took off her leg,
And laid it down like a cribbage-peg,
For the Rout was done and the riot:
The Square was hush'd; not a sound was heard;
The sky was grey, and no creature stirr'd,
Except one little precocious bird,
That chirp'd—and then was quiet.

So still without,—so still within;—
It had been a sin
To drop a pin—
So intense is silence after a din,
It seem'd like Death's rehearsal!
To stir the air no eddy came;
And the taper burnt with as still a flame,
As to flicker had been a burning shame,
In a calm so universal.

The time for sleep had come at last;
And there was the bed, so soft, so vast,
Quite a field of Bedfordshire clover;
Softer, cooler, and calmer, no doubt,

From the piece of work just ravell'd out,
For one of the pleasures of having a rout
  Is the pleasure of having it over.

No sordid pallet, or truckle mean,
Of straw, and rug, and tatters unclean;
But a splendid, gilded, carved machine,
  That was fit for a Royal Chamber.
On the top was a gorgeous golden wreath;
And the damask curtains hung beneath,
  Like clouds of crimson and amber.

Curtains, held up by two little plump things,
With golden bodies and golden wings,—
  Mere fins for such solidities—
    Two Cupids, in short,
    Of the regular sort,
  But the housemaid call'd them "Cupidities."

No patchwork quilt, all seams and scars,
But velvet, powder'd with golden stars,
  A fit mantle for *Night*-Commanders!
And the pillow, as white as snow undimm'd,
And as cool as the pool that the breeze has skimm'd,
Was cased in the finest cambric, and trimm'd
  With the costliest lace of Flanders.

And the bed—Of the Eider's softest down,
'Twas a place to revel, to smother, to drown
  In a bliss inferr'd by the Poet;
For if ignorance be indeed a bliss,
What blessed ignorance equals this,
  To sleep—and not to know it?

Oh, bed! oh, bed! delicious bed!
That heaven upon earth to the weary head;
But a place that to name would be ill-bred,
  To the head with a wakeful trouble—
'Tis held by such a different lease!

To one, a place of comfort and peace,
All stuff'd with the down of stubble geese,
To another with only the stubble!

To one, a perfect Halcyon nest,
All calm, and balm, and quiet, and rest,
And soft as the fur of the cony—
To another, so restless for body and head,
That the bed seems borrow'd from Nettlebed,
And the pillow from Stratford the Stony!

To the happy, a first-class carriage of ease,
To the Land of Nod, or where you please;
But, alas! for the watchers and weepers,
Who turn, and turn, and turn again,
But turn, and turn, and turn in vain,
With an anxious brain,
And thoughts in a train
That does not run upon *sleepers!*

Wide awake as the mousing owl,
Night-hawk, or other nocturnal fowl,—
But more profitless vigils keeping,—
Wide awake in the dark they stare,
Filling with phantoms the vacant air,
As if that Crook-Back'd Tyrant Care
Had plotted to kill them sleeping.

And oh! when the blessed diurnal light
Is quench'd by the providential night,
To render our slumber more certain,
Pity, pity the wretches that weep,
For they must be wretched who cannot sleep
When God himself draws the curtain!

The careful Betty the pillow beats,
And airs the blankets, and smoothes the sheets,
And gives the mattress a shaking—
But vainly Betty performs her part,

If a ruffled head and a rumpled heart
 As well as the couch want making.

There's Morbid, all bile, and verjuice, and nerves,
Where other people would make preserves,
 He turns his fruits into pickles :
Jealous, envious, and fretful by day,
At night, to his own sharp fancies a prey,
He lies like a hedgehog rolled up the wrong way,
 Tormenting himself with his prickles.

But a child—that bids the world good night
In downright earnest and cuts it quite—
 A Cherub no Art can copy,—
'Tis a perfect picture to see him lie
As if he had supp'd on dormouse pie
(An ancient classical dish by the by)
 With a sauce of syrup of poppy.

Oh, bed! bed! bed! delicious bed!
That heav'n upon earth to the weary head,
 Whether lofty or low its condition!
But instead of putting our plagues on shelves,
In our blankets how often we toss ourselves,
Or are toss'd by such allegorical elves
 As Pride, Hate, Greed, and Ambition!

The independent Miss Kilmansegg
Took off her independent Leg
 And laid it beneath her pillow,
And then on the bed her frame she cast,
The time for repose had come at last,
But long, long, after the storm is past
 Rolls the turbid, turbulent billow.

No part she had in vulgar cares
That belong to common household affairs—
Nocturnal annoyances such as theirs
 Who lie with a shrewd surmising

That while they are couchant (a bitter cup!)
Their bread and butter are getting up,
  And the coals—confound them!—are rising.

No fear she had her sleep to postpone,
Like the crippled Widow who weeps alone,
And cannot make a doze her own,
  For the dread that mayhap on the morrow,
The true and Christian reading to balk,
A broker will take up her bed and walk,
  By way of curing her sorrow.

No cause like these she had to bewail:
For the breath of applause had blown a gale,
And winds from that quarter seldom fail
  To cause some human commotion;
But whenever such breezes coincide
    With the very spring-tide
    Of human pride,
  There's no such swell on the ocean!

Peace, and ease, and slumber lost,
She turn'd, and roll'd, and tumbled, and toss'd,
  With a tumult that would not settle:
A common case, indeed, with such
As have too little, or think too much,
  Of the precious and glittering metal.

Gold!—she saw at her golden foot
The Peer whose tree had an olden root,
The Proud, the Great, the Learned to boot,
  The handsome, the gay, and the witty—
The Man of Science—of Arms—of Art,
The man who deals but at Pleasure's mart,
  And the man who deals in the City.

Gold, still gold—and true to the mould!
In the very scheme of her dream it told;
  For, by magical transmutation,

From her Leg through her body it seem'd to go,
Till, gold above, and gold below,
She was gold, all gold, from her little gold toe
  To her organ of Veneration!

And still she retain'd, through Fancy's art,
The Golden Bow, and the Golden Dart,
With which she had played a Goddess's part
  In her recent glorification.
And still, like one of the self-same brood,
On a Plinth of the self-same metal she stood
  For the whole world's adoration.

And hymns and incense around her roll'd,
From Golden Harps and Censers of Gold,—
For Fancy in dreams is as uncontroll'd
  As a horse without a bridle:
What wonder, then, from all checks exempt,
If, inspired by the Golden Leg, she dreamt
  She was turn'd to a Golden Idol?

HER COURTSHIP.

When leaving Eden's happy land
The grieving Angel led by the hand
  Our banish'd Father and Mother,
Forgotten amid their awful doom,
The tears, the fears, and the future's gloom,
On each brow was a wreath of Paradise bloom,
  That our Parents had twined for each other.

It was only while sitting like figures of stone,
For the grieving Angel had skyward flown,
As they sat, those Two, in the world alone,
  With disconsolate hearts nigh cloven,
That scenting the gust of happier hours,
They look'd around for the precious flow'rs,
And lo!—a last relic of Eden's dear bow'rs—
  The chaplet that Love had woven!

And still, when a pair of Lovers meet,
There's a sweetness in air, unearthly sweet,
That savors still of that happy retreat
  Where Eve by Adam was courted:
Whilst the joyous thrush, and the gentle Dove,
Woo'd their mates in the boughs above,
  And the Serpent, as yet, only sported.

Who hath not felt that breath in the air,
A perfume and freshness strange and rare,
A warmth in the light, and a bliss everywhere,
  When young hearts yearn together?
All sweets below, and all sunny above,
Oh! there's nothing in life like making love,
  Save making hay in fine weather!

Who hath not found amongst his flow'rs
A blossom too bright for this world of ours,
  Like a rose among snows of Sweden?
But to turn again to Miss Kilmansegg,
Where must love have gone to beg,
If such a thing as a Golden Leg
  Had put its foot in Eden!

And yet—to tell the rigid truth—
Her favor was sought by Age and Youth—
  For the prey will find a prowler!
She was follow'd, flatter'd, courted, address'd,
Woo'd, and coo'd, and wheedled, and press'd,
By suitors from North, South, East, and West,
  Like that Heiress, in Song, Tibbie Fowler!

But, alas! alas! for the Woman's fate,
Who has from a mob to choose a mate!
  'T is a strange and painful mystery!
But the more the eggs, the worse the hatch;
The more the fish, the worse the catch;
The more the sparks, the worse the match;
  Is a fact in Woman's history.

Give her between a brace to pick,
And, mayhap, with luck to help the trick,
She will take the Faustus, and leave the Old Nick—
  But her future bliss to baffle,
Amongst a score let her have a voice,
And she'll have as little cause to rejoice,
As if she had won the "Man of her choice"
  In a matrimonial raffle!

Thus, even thus, with the Heiress and Hope,
Fulfilling the adage of too much rope,
  With so ample a competition,
She chose the least worthy of all the group,
Just as the vulture makes a stoop,
And singles out from the herd or troop
  The beast of the worst condition.

A Foreign Count—who came incog.,
Not under a cloud, but under a fog,
  In a Calais packet's fore-cabin,
To charm some lady British-born,
With his eyes as black as the fruit of the thorn,
And his hooky nose, and his beard half-shorn,
  Like a half-converted Rabbin.

And because the Sex confess a charm
In the man who has slash'd a head or arm,
  Or has been a throat's undoing,
He was dress'd like one of the glorious trade,
At least when Glory is off parade,
With a stock, and a frock, well trimm'd with braid,
  And frogs—that went a-wooing.

Moreover, as Counts are apt to do,
On the left-hand side of his dark surtout,
At one of those holes that buttons go through
  (To be a precise recorder),
A ribbon he wore, or rather a scrap,
About an inch of ribbon mayhap,

That one of his rivals, a whimsical chap,
  Described as his "Retail Order."

And then—and much it help'd his chance—
He could sing, and play first fiddle, and dance,
Perform charades, and Proverbs of France—
  Act the tender, and do the cruel;
For amongst his other killing parts,
He had broken a brace of female hearts,
  And murder'd three men in a duel!

Savage at heart, and false of tongue,
Subtle with age, and smooth to the young,
  Like a snake in his coiling and curling—
Such was the Count—to give him a niche—
Who came to court that Heiress rich,
And knelt at her foot—one needn't say which—
  Besieging her castle of *Sterling*.

With pray'rs and vows he open'd his trench,
And plied her with English, Spanish, and French
  In phrases the most sentimental:
And quoted poems in High and Low Dutch,
With now and then an Italian touch,
Till she yielded, without resisting much,
  To homage so continental.

And then the sordid bargain to close,
With a miniature sketch of his hooky nose,
And his dear dark eyes, as black as sloes,
And his beard and whiskers as black as those,
  The lady's consent he requited—
And instead of the lock that lovers beg,
The count received from Miss Kilmansegg
A model, in small, of her Precious Leg—
  And so the couple were plighted!

But, oh! the love that gold must crown!
Better—better, the love of the clown,

Who admires his lass in her Sunday gown,
  As if all the fairies had dress'd her!
Whose brain to no crooked thought gives birth,
Except that he never will part on earth
  With his true love's crooked tester!

Alas! for the love that's link'd with gold!
Better—better, a thousand times told—
  More honest, happy and laudable,
The downright loving of pretty Cis,
Who wipes her lips, though there's nothing amiss,
And takes a kiss, and gives a kiss,
  In which her heart is audible!

Pretty Cis, so smiling and bright,
Who loves as she labors, with all her might,
  And without any sordid leaven!
Who blushes as red as haws and hips,
Down to her very finger-tips,
For Roger's blue ribbons—to her, like strips
  Cut out of the azure of Heaven!

HER MARRIAGE.

'T was morn—a most auspicious one!
From the Golden East, the Golden Sun
Came forth his glorious race to run,
  Through clouds of most splendid tinges;
Clouds that lately slept in shade,
    But now seem'd made
    Of gold brocade,
  With magnificent golden fringes.

Gold above, and gold below,
The earth reflected the golden glow,
  From river, and hill, and valley:
Gilt by the golden light of morn,
The Thames—it look'd like the Golden Horn,
And the Barge, that carried coal or corn,
  Like Cleopatra's Galley!

Bright as clusters of Golden-rod,
Suburban poplars began to nod,
With extempore splendor furnish'd;
While London was bright with glittering clocks,
Golden dragons, and Golden cocks,
And above them all,
The dome of St. Paul,
With its Golden Cross and its Golden Ball,
Shone out as if newly burnish'd!

And lo! for Golden Hours and Joys,
Troops of glittering Golden Boys
Danced along with a jocund noise,
And their gilded emblems carried!
In short, 't was the year's most Golden Day,
By mortals call'd the First of May,
When Miss Kilmansegg,
Of the Golden Leg,
With a Golden Ring was married!

And thousands of children, women, and men,
Counted the clock from eight till ten,
From St. James's sonorous steeple;
For next to that interesting job,
The hanging of Jack, or Bill, or Bob,
There's nothing so draws a London mob
As the noosing of very rich people.

And a treat it was for a mob to behold
The Bridal Carriage that blazed with gold!
And the Footmen tall, and the Coachman bold,
In liveries so resplendent—
Coats you wonder'd to see in place,
They seem'd so rich with golden lace,
That they might have been independent.

Coats that made those menials proud
Gaze with scorn on the dingy crowd,
From their gilded elevations;

Not to forget that saucy lad
(Ostentation's favorite cad),
The Page, who look'd, so splendidly clad,
  Like a Page of the "Wealth of Nations."

But the Coachman carried off the state,
With what was a Lancashire body of late
  Turn'd into a Dresden Figure;
With a bridal Nosegay of early bloom,
About the size of a birchen broom,
And so huge a White Favor, had Gog been Groom
  He would not have worn a bigger.

And then to see the Groom! the Count!
With Foreign Orders to such an amount,
  And whiskers so wild—nay, bestial;
He seem'd to have borrow'd the shaggy hair
As well as the Stars of the Polar Bear,
  To make him look celestial!

And then—Great Jove!—the struggle, the crush,
The screams, the heaving, the awful rush,
  The swearing, the tearing, and fighting,
The hats and bonnets smash'd like an egg—
To catch a glimpse of the Golden Leg,
Which, between the steps and Miss Kilmansegg,
  Was fully displayed in alighting!

From the Golden Ankle up to the Knee
There it was for the mob to see!
A shocking act had it chanced to be
  A crooked leg or a skinny:
But although a magnificent veil she wore,
Such as never was seen before,
In case of blushes she blush'd no more
  Than George the First on a guinea!

Another step, and lo! she was launch'd!
All in white, as Brides are *blanch'd*,

With a wreath of most wonderful splendor—
Diamonds, and pearls, so rich in device,
That, according to calculation nice,
Her head was worth as royal a price
As the head of the Young Pretender.

Bravely she shone—and shone the more
As she sail'd through the crowd of squalid and poor,
Thief, beggar, and tatterdemalion—
Led by the Count, with sloe-black eyes
Bright with triumph, and some surprise,
Like Anson on making sure of his prize
The famous Mexican Galleon!

Anon came Lady K., with her face
Quite made up to act with grace,
But she cut the performance shorter;
For instead of pacing stately and stiff,
At the stare of the vulgar she took a miff,
And ran, full speed, into Church, as if
To get married before her daughter.

But Sir Jacob walk'd more slowly, and bow'd
Right and left to the gaping crowd,
Wherever a glance was seizable;
For Sir Jacob thought he bowd like a Guelph,
And therefore bow'd to imp and elf,
And would gladly have made a bow to himself,
Had such a bow been feasible.

And last—and not the least of the sight,
Six "Handsome Fortunes," all in white
Came to help in the marriage rite,—
And rehearse their own hymeneals;
And then the bright procession to close,
They were followed by just as many Beaux,
Quite fine enough for Ideals.

Glittering men and splendid dames,
Thus they enter'd the porch of St. James',

Pursued by a thunder of laughter:
For the Beadle was forced to intervene,
For Jim the Crow, and his Mayday Queen,
With her gilded ladle, and Jack i' the Green,
Would fain have follow'd after!

Beadle-like he hush'd the shout;
But the temple was full "inside and out,"
And a buzz kept buzzing all round about,
Like bees when the day is sunny—
A buzz universal that interfered
With the rite that ought to have been revered,
As if the couple already were smear'd
With Wedlock's treacle and honey!

Yet wedlock's a very awful thing!
'Tis something like that feat in the ring
Which requires good nerve to do it—
When one of a "Grand Equestrian Troop"
Makes a jump at a gilded hoop,
Not certain at all
Of what may befall
After his getting through it!

But the Count he felt the nervous work
No more than any polygamous Turk,
Or bold piratical schipper,
Who, during his buccaneering search,
Would as soon engage "a hand" in church
As a hand on board his clipper!

And how did the bride perform her part?
Like any Bride who is cold at heart,
Mere snow with the ice's glitter;
What but a life of winter for her!
Bright but chilly, alive without stir,
So splendidly comfortless,—just like a Fir
When the frost is severe and bitter.

Such were the future man and wife!
Whose bale or bliss to the end of life
  A few short words were to settle—
    Wilt thou have this woman?
      I will—and then,
    Wilt thou have this man?
      I will, and Amen—
And those Two were one Flesh, in the Angels' ken.
  Except one Leg—that was metal.

Then the names were signed—and kiss'd the kiss·
And the Bride, who came from her coach a Miss,
  As a Countess walk'd to her carriage—
Whilst Hymen preen'd his plumes like a dove,
And Cupid flutter'd his wings above,
In the shape of a fly—as little a Love
  As ever look'd in at a marriage!

Another crash—and away they dash'd,
And the gilded carriage and footmen flash'd
  From the eyes of the gaping people—
Who turn'd to gaze at the toe-and-heel
Of the Golden Boys beginning a reel,
To the merry sound of a wedding peal
  From St. James's musical steeple.

Those wedding-bells! those wedding-bells!
How sweetly they sound in pastoral dells
  From a tow'r in an ivy-green jacket!
But town-made joys how dearly they cost;
And after all are tumbled and tost,
Like a peal from a London steeple, and lost
  In town-made riot and racket.

The wedding-peal, how sweetly it peals
With grass or heather beneath our heels,—
  For bells are Music's laughter!—
But a London peal, well mingled, be sure,
With vulgar noises and voices impure,

What a harsh and discordant overture,
 To the Harmony meant to come after!

But hence with Discord—perchance, too soon
To cloud the face of the honeymoon
 With a dismal occultation!
Whatever Fate's concerted trick,
The Countess and Count, at the present nick,
Have a chicken and not a crow to pick
 At a sumptuous Cold Collation.

A Breakfast—no unsubstantial mess,
But one in the style of Good Queen Bess,
 Who,—hearty as hippocampus,—
Broke her fast with ale and beef,
Instead of toast and the Chinese leaf,
 And in lieu of anchovy—grampus!

A breakfast of fowl, and fish, and flesh,
Whatever was sweet, or salt, or fresh;
 With wines the most rare and curious—
Wines, of the richest flavor and hue;
With fruits from the worlds both Old and New;
And fruits obtained before they were due
 At a discount most usurious.

For wealthy palates there be that scout
What is *in* season, for what is *out*,
 And prefer all precocious savor:
For instance, early green peas, of the sort
That costs some four or five guineas a quart:
 Where the *Mint* is the principal flavor.

And many a wealthy man was there,
Such as the wealthy City could spare,
 To put in a portly appearance—
Men whom their fathers had help'd to gild:
And men who had had their fortunes to build,
And—much to their credit—had richly fill'd
 Their purses by *pursy-verance*.

Men, by popular rumor at least,
Not the last to enjoy a feast!
  And truly they were not idle!
Luckier far than the chestnut tits,
Which, down at the door, stood champing their bitts,
  At a different sort of bridle.

For the time was come—and the whisker'd Count
Help'd his Bride in the carriage to mount,
  And fain would the Muse deny it,
But the crowd, including two butchers in blue
(The regular killing Whitechapel hue),
Of her Precious Calf had as ample a view,
  As if they had come to buy it!

Then away! away! with all the speed
That golden spurs can give to the steed,—
Both Yellow Boys and Guineas indeed,
  Concurr'd to urge the cattle—
Away they went, with favors white,
Yellow jackets, and pannels bright,
And left the mob, like a mob at night,
  Agape at the sound of a rattle.

Away! away! they rattled and roll'd,
The Count, and his Bride, and her Leg of Gold—
  That faded charm to the charmer!
Away,—through Old Brentford rang the din,
Of wheels and heels, on their way to win
That hill, named after one of her kin,
  The Hill of the Golden Farmer!

Gold, still Gold—it flew like dust!
It tipp'd the post-boy, and paid the trust;
In each open palm it was freely thrust;
  There was nothing but giving and taking!
And if gold could ensure the future hour,
What hopes attended that Bride to her bow'r,
But alas! even hearts with a four-horse pow'r
  Of opulence end in breaking!

HER HONEYMOON.

The moon—the moon, so silver and cold,
Her fickle temper has oft been told,
  Now shady—now bright and sunny—
But of all the lunar things that change,
The one that shows most fickle and strange,
And takes the most eccentric range
  Is the moon—so called—of honey!

To some a full-grown orb reveal'd,
As big and as round as Norval's shield,
  And as bright as a burner Bude-lighted;
To others as dull, and dingy, and damp,
As any oleaginous lamp,
Of the regular old parochial stamp,
  In a London fog benighted.

To the loving, a bright and constant sphere,
That makes earth's commonest scenes appear
  All poetic, romantic and tender:
Hanging with jewels a cabbage-stump,
And investing a common post, or a pump,
A currant-bush, or a gooseberry clump,
  With a halo of dreamlike splendor.

A sphere such as shone from Italian skies,
In Juliet's dear, dark, liquid eyes,
  Tipping trees with its argent braveries—
And to couples not favor'd with Fortune's boons,
One of the most delightful of moons,
For it brightens their pewter platters and spoons
  Like a silver service of Savory's!

For all is bright, and beauteous, and clear,
And the meanest thing most precious and dear
  When the magic of love is present:
Love, that lends a sweetness and grace
To the humblest spot and the plainest face—

Love that sweetens sugarless tea,
And makes contentment and joy agree
  With the coarsest boarding and bedding:
Love that no golden ties can attach,
But nestles under the humblest thatch,
And will fly away from an Emperor's match
  To dance at a Penny Wedding!

Oh, happy, happy, thrice happy state,
When such a bright Planet governs the fate
  Of a pair of united lovers!
'Tis theirs, in spite of the Serpent's hiss,
To enjoy the pure primeval kiss,
With as much of the old original bliss
  As mortality ever recovers!

There's strength in double joints, no doubt,
In double X Ale, and Dublin Stout,
That the single sorts know nothing about—
  And a fist is strongest when doubled—
And double aqua-fortis, of course,
And double soda-water, perforce,
  Are the strongest that ever bubbled!

There's double beauty whenever a Swan
Swims on a Lake, with her double thereon:
And ask the gardener, Luke or John,
  Of the beauty of double-blowing—
A double dahlia delights the eye;
And it's far the loveliest sight in the sky
  When a double rainbow is glowing!

There's warmth in a pair of double soles;
As well as a double allowance of coals—
  In a coat that is double-breasted—
In double windows and double doors;
And a double U wind is blest by scores
  For its warmth to the tender-chested.

There's a two-fold sweetness in double pipes,
And a double barrel and double snipes
  Give the sportsman a duplicate pleasure:
There's double safety in double locks;
And double letters bring cash for the box;
And all the world knows that double knocks
  Are gentility's double measure.

There's a double sweetness in double rhymes,
And a double at Whist and a double Times
  In profit are certainly double—
By doubling, the Hare contrives to escape:
And all seamen delight in a doubled Cape,
  And a double-reef'd topsail in trouble.

There's a double chuck at a double chin,
And of course there's a double pleasure therein,
  If the parties were brought to telling:
And however our Dennises take offence,
A double meaning shows double sense:
  And if proverbs tell truth,
    A double tooth
  Is Wisdom's adopted dwelling!

But double wisdom, and pleasure, and sense,
Beauty, respect, strength, comfort, and thence
  Through whatever the list discovers,
They are all in the double blessedness summ'd,
Of what was formerly double-drumm'd,
  The Marriage of two true Lovers!

Now the Kilmansegg Moon—it must be told—
Though instead of silver it tipp'd with gold—
Shone rather wan, and distant, and cold
  And before its days were at thirty,
Such gloomy clouds began to collect,
With an ominous ring of ill effect,
As gave but too much cause to expect
  Such weather as seamen call dirty!

And yet the moon was the "Young May Moon,"
And the scented hawthorn had blossom'd soon,
  And the thrush and the blackbird were singing—
The snow-white lambs were skipping in play,
And the bee was humming a tune all day
To flowers as welcome as flowers in May,
  And the trout in the stream was springing!

But what were the hues of the blooming earth,
Its scents—its sounds—or the music and mirth
  Of its furr'd or its feather'd creatures,
To a Pair in the world's last sordid stage,
Who had never look'd into Nature's page,
And had strange ideas of a Golden Age,
  Without any Arcadian features?

And what were joys of the pastoral kind
To a Bride—town-made—with a heart and mind
  With simplicity ever at battle?
A bride of an ostentatious race,
Who, thrown in the Golden Farmer's place,
Would have trimm'd her shepherds with golden lace,
  And gilt the horns of her cattle.

She could not please the pigs with her whim,
And the sheep wouldn't cast their eyes at a limb
  For which she had been such a martyr:
The deer in the park, and the colts at grass,
And the cows unheeded let it pass;
And the ass on the common was such an ass,
    That he wouldn't have swapp'd
    The thistle he cropp'd
  For her Leg, including the Garter!

She hated lanes, and she hated fields—
She hated all that the country yields—
  And barely knew turnips from clover;
She hated walking in any shape,
And a country stile was an awkward scrape,

Without the bribe of a mob to gape
  At the Leg in clambering over!

O blessed nature, "O rus! O rus!'
Who cannot sigh for the country thus,
  Absorbed in a worldly torpor—
Who does not yearn for its meadow-sweet breath
Untainted by care, and crime, and death,
And to stand sometimes upon grass or heath—
  That soul, spite of gold, is a pauper!

But to hail the pearly advent of morn,
And relish the odor fresh from the thorn,
  She was far too pamper'd a madam—
Or to joy in the daylight waxing strong,
While, after ages of sorrow and wrong,
The scorn of the proud, the misrule of the strong,
And all the woes that to man belong,
The lark still carols the self-same song
  That he did to the uncurst Adam!

The Lark! she had given all Leipsic's flocks
For a Vauxhall tune in a musical box;
  And as for the birds in the thicket,
Thrush or ousel in leafy niche,
The linnet or finch, she was far too rich
To care for a Morning Concert to which
  She was welcome without any ticket.

Gold, still gold, her standard of old,
All pastoral joys were tried by gold,
  Or by fancies golden and crural—
Till ere she had pass'd one week unblest,
As her agricultural Uncle's guest,
Her mind was made up and fully imprest
  That felicity could not be rural!

And the Count?—to the snow-white lambs at play,
And all the scents and the sights of May,

And the birds that warbled their passion,
His ears, and dark eyes, and decided nose,
Were as deaf and as blind and as dull as those
That overlook the Bouquet de Rose,
The Huile Antique,
And Parfum Unique,
In a Barber's Temple of Fashion.

To tell, indeed, the true extent
Of his rural bias so far it went
As to covet estates in ring fences—
And for rural lore he had learn'd in town
That the country was green, turn'd up with brown,
And garnish'd with trees that a man might cut down
Instead of his own expenses.

And yet had that fault been his only one,
The Pair might have had few quarrels or none,
For their tastes thus far were in common;
But faults he had that a haughty bride
With a Golden Leg could hardly abide—
Faults that would even have roused the pride
Of a far less metalsome woman!

It was early days indeed for a wife,
In the very spring of her married life,
To be chill'd by its wintry weather—
But instead of sitting as Love-Birds do,
Or Hymen's turtles that bill and coo—
Enjoying their "moon and honey for two"
They were scarcely seen together!

In vain she sat with her Precious Leg
A little exposed, *à la* Kilmansegg,
And roll'd her eyes in their sockets!
He left her in spite of her tender regards,
And those loving murmurs described by bards,
For the rattling of dice and the shuffling of cards,
And the poking of balls into pockets!

Moreover he loved the deepest stake
And the heaviest bets the players would make;
  And he drank—the reverse of sparely,—
And he used strange curses that made her fret:
And when he play'd with herself at piquet
    She found, to her cost,
    For she always lost,
That the Count did not count quite fairly.

And then came dark mistrust and doubt,
Gather'd by worming his secrets out,
  And slips in his conversations—
Fears, which all her peace destroy'd,
That his title was null—his coffers were void—
And his French Château was in Spain, or enjoy'd
  The most airy of situations.

But still his heart—if he had such a part—
She—only she—might possess his heart,
  And hold his affections in fetters—
Alas! that hope, like a crazy ship,
Was forced its anchor and cable to slip
When, seduced by her fears, she took a dip
  In his private papers and letters.

Letters that told of dangerous leagues;
And notes that hinted as many intrigues
  As the Count's in the "Barber of Seville"—
In short such mysteries came to light,
That the Countess-Bride, on the thirtieth night,
Woke and started up in affright,
And kick'd and scream'd with all her might,
And finally fainted away outright,
  For she dreamt she had married the Devil!

HER MISERY.

Who hath not met with home-made bread,
A heavy compound of putty and lead—

And home-made wines that rack the head,
  And home-made liqueurs and waters?
Home-made pop that will not foam,
And home-made dishes that drive one from home,
    Not to name each mess,
    For the face or dress,
  Home-made by the homely daughters?

Home-made physic, that sickens the sick;
Thick for thin and thin for thick;—
In short each homogeneous trick
  For poisoning domesticity?
And since our Parents, called the First,
A little family squabble nurst,
Of all our evils the worst of the worst
  Is home-made infelicity.

There's a Golden Bird that claps its wings,
And dances for joy on its perch, and sings
  With a Persian exultation:
For the Sun is shining into the room,
And brightens up the carpet-bloom,
As if it were new, bran new from the loom,
  Or the lone Nun's fabrication.

And thence the glorious radiance flames
On pictures in massy gilded frames—
Enshrining, however, no painted Dames,
  But portraits of colts and fillies—
Pictures hanging on walls which shine,
In spite of the bard's familiar line,
  With clusters of "gilded lilies."

And still the flooding sunlight shares
Its lustre with gilded sofas and chairs,
  That shine as if freshly burnish'd—
And gilded tables, with glittering stocks
Of gilded china, and golden clocks,

Toy, and trinket, and musical box,
  That Peace and Paris have furnish'd.

And lo! with the brightest gleam of all
The glowing sunbeam is seen to fall
  On an object as rare as splendid—
The golden foot of the Golden Leg
Of the Countess—once Miss Kilmansegg—
  But there all sunshine is ended.

Her cheek is pale, and her eye is dim,
And downward cast, yet not at the limb,
  Once the centre of all speculation;
But downward drooping in comfort's dearth,
As gloomy thoughts are drawn to the earth—
Whence human sorrows derive their birth—
  By a moral gravitation.

Her golden hair is out of its braids,
And her sighs betray the gloomy shades
  That her evil planet revolves in—
And tears are falling that catch a gleam
So bright as they drop in the sunny beam,
That tears of *aqua regia* they seem,
  The water that gold dissolves in!

Yet, not in filial grief were shed
  Those tears for a mother's insanity;
Nor yet because her father was dead,
For the bowing Sir Jacob had bow'd his head
  To Death—with his usual urbanity:
The waters that down her visage rill'd
Were drops of unrectified spirit distill'd
  From the limbeck of Pride and Vanity.

Tears that fell alone and uncheckt,
Without relief, and without respect,
Like the fabled pearls that the pigs neglect,
  When pigs have that opportunity—

And of all the griefs that mortals share,
The one that seems the hardest to bear
Is the grief without community.

How bless'd the heart that has a friend
A sympathizing ear to lend
To troubles too great to smother!
For as ale and porter, when flat, are restored,
Till a sparkling bubbling head they afford,
So sorrow is cheer'd by being pour'd
From one vessel into another.

But friend or gossip she had not one
To hear the vile deeds that the Count had done,
How night after night he rambled;
And how she had learn'd by sad degrees
That he drank, and smoked, and worse than these,
That he "swindled, intrigued, and gambled."

How he kiss'd the maids, and sparr'd with John;
And came to bed with his garments on;
With other offences as heinous—
And brought *strange* gentlemen home to dine,
That he said were in the Fancy Line,
And they fancied spirits instead of wine,
And call'd her lap-dog "Wenus."

Of "making a book" how he made a stir,
But never had written a line to her,
Once his idol and Cara Sposa:
And how he had storm'd, and treated her ill,
Because she refused to go down to a mill,
She didn't know where, but remember'd still
That the Miller's name was Mendoza.

How often he waked her up at night,
And oftener still by the morning light,
Reeling home from his haunts unlawful;
Singing songs that shouldn't be sung,

Except by beggars and thieves unhung—
Or volleying oaths, that a foreign tongue
  Made still more horrid and awful!

How oft, instead of otto of rose,
With vulgar smells he offended her nose,
  From gin, tobacco, and onion!
And then how wildly he used to stare!
And shake his fist at nothing, and swear,—
And pluck by the handful his shaggy hair,
Till he look'd like a study of Giant Despair
  For a new Edition of Bunyan!

For dice will run the contrary way,
As well is known to all who play,
  And cards will conspire as in treason:
And what with keeping a hunting-box,
        Following fox—
        Friends in flocks,
        Burgundies, Hocks,
        From London Docks;
        Stultz's frocks,
        Manton and Nock's
        Barrels and locks,
        Shooting blue rocks,
        Trainers and jocks,
        Buskins and socks,
        Pugilistical knocks,
        And fighting-cocks,
If he found himself short in funds and stocks,
  These rhymes will furnish the reason!

His friends, indeed, were falling away—
Friends who insist on play or pay—
And he fear'd at no very distant day
  To be cut by Lord and by cadger,
As one who was gone or going to smash,
For his checks no longer drew the cash,

Because, as his comrades explain'd in flash,
  "He had overdrawn his badger."

Gold, gold—alas! for the gold
Spent where souls are bought and sold
  In Vice's Walpurgis revel!
Alas! for muffles, and bulldogs, and guns,
The leg that walks, and the leg that runs,
All real evils, though Fancy ones,
When they lead to debt, dishonor, and duns,
  Nay, to death, and perchance the devil!

Alas! for the last of a Golden race!
Had she cried her wrongs in the market-place,
  She had warrant for all her clamor—
For the worst of rogues, and brutes, and rakes,
Was breaking her heart by constant aches,
With as little remorse as the Pauper who breaks
  A flint with a parish hammer!

HER LAST WILL.

Now the Precious Leg while cash was flush,
Or the Count's acceptance worth a rush,
  Had never excited dissension;
But no sooner the stocks began to fall,
Than, without any ossification at all,
The limb became what people call
  A perfect bone of contention.

For alter'd days brought alter'd ways,
And instead of the complimentary phrase,
  So current before her bridal—
The Countess heard, in language low,
That her Precious Leg was precious slow,
A good 'un to look at but bad to go,
  And kept quite a sum lying idle.

That instead of playing musical airs,
Like Colin's foot in going up-stairs—

As the wife in the Scottish ballad declares—
  It made an infernal stumping,
Whereas a member of cork, or wood,
Would be lighter and cheaper and quite as good,
  Without the unbearable thumping.

P'rhaps she thought it a decent thing
To show her calf to cobbler and king,
  But nothing could be absurder—
While none but the crazy would advertise
Their gold before their servants' eyes,
Who of course some night would make it a prize,
  By a Shocking and Barbarous Murder.

But spite of hint, and threat, and scoff,
  The Leg kept its situation :
For legs are not to be taken off
  By a verbal amputation.

And mortals when they take a whim,
The greater the folly the stiffer the limb
  That stands upon it or by it—
So the Countess, then Miss Kilmansegg,
At her marriage refused to stir a peg,
Till the Lawyers had fastened on her Leg,
  As fast as the Law could tie it.

Firmly then—and more firmly yet—
With scorn for scorn, and with threat for threat,
  The Proud One confronted the Cruel :
And loud and bitter the quarrel arose,
Fierce and merciless—one of those,
With spoken daggers, and looks like blows,
  In all but the bloodshed a duel!

Rash, and wild, and wretched, and wrong,
Were the words that came from Weak and Strong,
  Till madden'd for desperate matters,
Fierce as tigress escaped from her den,

She flew to her desk—'twas open'd—and then,
In the time it takes to try a pen,
Or the clerk to utter his slow Amen,
  Her Will was in fifty tatters!

But the Count, instead of curses wild,
Only nodded his head and smiled,
As if at the spleen of an angry child ;
  But the calm was deceitful and sinister!
A lull like the lull of the treacherous sea—
For Hate in that moment had sworn to be
The Golden Leg's sole Legatee,
  And that very night to administer!

HER DEATH.

'Tis a stern and startling thing to think
How often mortality stands on the brink
  Of its grave without any misgiving:
And yet in this slippery world of strife,
In the stir of human bustle so rife,
There are daily sounds to tell us that Life
  Is dying, and Death is living!

Ay, Beauty the Girl, and Love the Boy,
Bright as they are with hope and joy,
  How their souls would sadden instanter,
To remember that one of those wedding bells,
Which ring so merrily through the dells,
      Is the same that knells
      Our last farewells,
  Only broken into a canter!

But breath and blood set doom at naught—
How little the wretched Countess thought,
  When at night she unloosed her sandal,
That the Fates had woven her burial-cloth,
And that Death, in the shape of a Death's Head Moth,
  Was fluttering round her candle!

As she look'd at her clock of or-molu,
For the hours she had gone so wearily through
  At the end of a day of trial—
How little she saw in her pride of prime
The dart of Death in the Hand of Time—
  That hand which moved on the dial!

As she went with her taper up the stair,
How little her swollen eye was aware
  That the Shadow which follow'd was double!
Or when she closed her chamber door,
It was shutting out, and for evermore,
  The world—and its worldly trouble.

Little she dreamt, as she laid aside
Her jewels—after one glance of pride—
  They were solemn bequests to Vanity—
Or when her robes she began to doff,
That she stood so near to the putting off
  Of the flesh that clothes humanity.

And when she quench'd the taper's light,
How little she thought as the smoke took flight
That her day was done—and merged in a night
  Of dreams and duration uncertain—
      Or, along with her own,
      That a Hand of Bone
Was closing mortalitv's curtain!

But life is sweet, and mortality's blind,
And youth is hopeful, and Fate is kind
  In concealing the day of sorrow;
And enough is the present tense of toil—
For this world is, to all, a stiffish soil—
And the mind flies back with a glad recoil
  From the debts not due till to-morrow.

Wherefore else does the Spirit fly
And bid its daily cares good-bye,

Along with its daily clothing?
Just as the felon condemned to die—
With a very natural loathing—
Leaving the Sheriff to dream of ropes,
From his gloomy cell in a vision elopes,
To caper on sunny greens and slopes,
Instead of the dance upon nothing.

Thus, even thus, the Countess slept,
While Death still nearer and nearer crept,
Like the Thane who smote the sleeping—
But her mind was busy with early joys,
Her golden treasures and golden toys,
That flash'd a bright
And golden light
Under lids still red with weeping.

The golden doll that she used to hug!
Her coral of gold, and the golden mug!
Her godfather's golden presents!
The golden service she had at her meals,
The golden watch, and chain, and seals,
Her golden scissors, and thread, and reels,
And her golden fishes and pheasants!

The golden guineas in silken purse—
And the Golden Legends she heard from her nurse,
Of the Mayor in his gilded carriage—
And London streets that were paved with gold—
And the Golden Eggs that were laid of old—
With each golden thing
To the golden ring
At her own auriferous Marriage!

And still the golden light of the sun
Through her golden dream appear'd to run
Though the night that roar'd without was one
To terrify seamen or gipsies—
While the moon, as if in malicious mirth,

Kept peeping down at the ruffled earth,
As though she enjoyed the tempest's birth,
  In revenge of her old eclipses.

But vainly, vainly, the thunder fell,
For the soul of the Sleeper was under a spell
  That time had lately embitter'd—
The Count, as once at her foot he knelt—
That Foot which now he wanted to melt!
But—hush!—'twas a stir at her pillow she felt—
  And some object before her glitter'd.

'Twas the Golden Leg!—she knew its gleam!
And up she started, and tried to scream,—
  But ev'n in the moment she started—
Down came the limb with a frightful smash,
And, lost in the universal flash
That her eyeballs made at so mortal a crash,
  The Spark, called Vital, departed!

* * * *

Gold, still gold! hard, yellow, and cold,
For gold she had lived, and she died for gold—
By a golden weapon—not oaken;
In the morning they found her all alone—
Stiff, and bloody, and cold as a stone—
But her Leg, the Golden Leg was gone,
  And the "Golden Bowl was broken!"

Gold—still gold! it haunted her yet—
At the Golden Lion the Inquest met—
  Its foreman, a carver and gilder—
And the Jury debated from twelve till three
What the Verdict ought to be,
And they brought it in as Felo de Se,
  "Because her own Leg had killed her!"

HER MORAL.

Gold! Gold! Gold! Gold!
Bright and yellow, hard and cold,
Molten, graven, hammer'd, and roll'd;
Heavy to get, and light to hold;
Hoarded, barter'd, bought, and sold,
Stolen, borrow'd, squander'd, doled:
Spurn'd by the young, but hugg'd by the old
To the very verge of the churchyard mould;
Price of many a crime untold;
Gold! Gold! Gold! Gold:
Good or bad a thousand-fold!
  How widely its agencies vary—
To save—to ruin—to curse—to bless—
As even its minted coins express,
Now stamp'd with the image of Good Queen Bess,
  And now of a Bloody Mary!

FAIR INES.

I.

O saw ye not fair Ines?
She's gone into the West,
To dazzle when the sun is down,
And rob the world of rest:
She took our daylight with her,
The smiles that we love best,
With morning blushes on her cheek,
And pearls upon her breast.

II.

O turn again, fair Ines,
Before the fall of night,
For fear the moon should shine alone,
And stars unrivall'd bright;
And blessed will the lover be
That walks beneath their light,
And breathes the love against thy cheek
I dare not even write!

III.

Would I had been, fair Ines,
That gallant cavalier,
Who rode so gaily by thy side,
And whisper'd thee so near!
Were there no bonny dames at home,
Or no true lovers here,
That he should cross the seas to win
The dearest of the dear?

IV.

I saw thee, lovely Ines,
Descend along the shore,
With bands of noble gentlemen,
And banners wav'd before;
And gentle youth and maidens gay,
And snowy plumes they wore;
It would have been a beauteous dream,
—If it had been no more!

V.

Alas, alas, fair Ines,
She went away with song,
With Music waiting on her steps,
And shoutings of the throng;
But some were sad and felt no mirth,
But only Music's wrong,
In sounds that sang Farewell, Farewell,
To her you've loved so long.

VI.

Farewell, farewell, fair Ines,
That vessel never bore
So fair a lady on its deck,
Nor danced so light before,—
Alas for pleasure on the sea,
And sorrow on the shore!
The smile that blest one lover's heart
Has broken many more!

BALLAD.

Spring it is cheery,
Winter is dreary,
Green leaves hang, but the brown must fly;
When he's forsaken,
Wither'd and shaken,
What can an old man do but die?

Love will not clip him,
Maids will not lip him,
Maud and Marian pass him by;
Youth it is sunny,
Age has no honey,—
What can an old man do but die?

June it was jolly,
O for its folly!
A dancing leg and a laughing eye;
Youth may be silly,
Wisdom is chilly,—
What can an old man do but die?

Friends they are scanty,
Beggars are plenty,
If he has followers, I know why;
Gold's in his clutches
(Buying him crutches!)—
What can an old man do but die?

RUTH.

She stood breast high amid tne corn,
Clasp'd by the golden light of morn,
Like the sweetheart of the sun,
Who many a glowing kiss had won.

On her cheek an autumn flush
Deeply ripened ;—such a blush
In the midst of brown was born,
Like red poppies grown with corn.

Round her eyes her tresses fell,
Which were blackest none could tell,
But long lashes veil'd a light,
That had else been all too bright.

And her hat, with shady brim,
Made her tressy forehead dim ;—
Thus she stood amid the stooks,
Praising God with sweetest looks :—

Sure, I said, heav'n did not mean,
Where I reap thou shouldst but glean,
Lay thy sheaf adown and come,
Share my harvest and my home.

AUTUMN.

THE Autumn is old,
The sere leaves are flying;—
He hath gather'd up gold,
And now he is dying;
Old age, begin sighing!

The vintage is ripe,
The harvest is heaping;
But some that have sow'd
Have no riches for reaping;—
Poor wretch, fall a weeping!

The year's in the wane,
There is nothing adorning;—
The night has no eve,
And the day has no morning;—
Cold winter gives warning.

The rivers run chill,
The red sun is sinking,
And I am grown old,
And life is fast shrinking;
Here's enow for sad thinking!

SONG.

O lady, leave thy silken thread
  And flowery tapestrie:
There's living roses on the bush,
  And blossoms on the tree;
Stoop where thou wilt, thy careless hand
  Some random bud will meet;
Thou canst not tread, but thou wilt find
  The daisy at thy feet.

'Tis like the birthday of the world,
  When earth was born in bloom;
The light is made of many dyes,
  The air is all perfume;
There's crimson buds, and white and blue—
  The very rainbow show'rs
Have turned to blossoms where they fell,
  And sown the earth with flowers.

There's fairy tulips in the East,
  The garden of the sun;
The very streams reflect the hues,
  And blossom as they run:
While Morn opes like a crimson rose,
  Still wet with pearly showers;
Then, lady, leave the silken thread
  Thou twinest into flowers!

ODE TO MELANCHOLY.

Come, let us set our careful breasts,
Like Philomel, against the thorn,
To aggravate the inward grief,
That makes her accents so forlorn;
The world has many cruel points,
Whereby our bosoms have been torn,
And there are dainty themes of grief,
In sadness to outlast the morn,—
True honor's dearth, affection's death,
Neglectful pride, and cankering scorn,
With all the piteous tales that tears
Have water'd since the world was born.

The world!—it is a wilderness,
Where tears are hung on every tree;
For thus my gloomy phantasy
Makes all things weep with me!
Come let us sit and watch the sky,
And fancy clouds, where no clouds be;
Grief is enough to blot the eye,
And make heaven black with misery.
Why should birds sing such merry notes,
Unless they were more blest than we?
No sorrow ever chokes their throats,
Except sweet nightingale; for she
Was born to pain our hearts the more
With her sad melody.
Why shines the sun, except that he

Makes gloomy nooks for Grief to hide,
And pensive shades for Melancholy,
When all the earth is bright beside?
Let clay wear smiles, and green grass wave,
Mirth shall not win us back again,
Whilst man is made of his own grave,
And fairest clouds but gilded rain!

I saw my mother in her shroud,
Her cheek was cold and very pale;
And ever since I've look'd on all
As creatures doom'd to fail!
Why do buds ope, except to die?
Ay, let us watch the roses wither,
And think of our loves' cheeks;
And oh! how quickly time doth fly
To bring death's winter hither!
Minutes, hours, days, and weeks,
Months, years, and ages, shrink to naught;
An age past is but a thought!

Ay, let us think of Him a while,
That, with a coffin for a boat,
Rows daily o'er the Stygian moat,
And for our table choose a tomb:
There's dark enough in any skull
To charge with black a raven plume;
And for the saddest funeral thoughts
A winding sheet hath ample room,
Where Death, with his keen-pointed style,
Hath writ the common doom.
How wide the yew tree spreads its gloom,
And o'er the dead lets fall its dew,
As if in tears it wept for them,
The many human families
That sleep around its stem!

How could the dead have made these stones,
With natural drops kept ever wet!

Lo! here the best, the worst, the world
Doth now remember or forget,
Are in one common ruin hurl'd,
And love and hate are calmly met;
The loveliest eyes that ever shone,
The fairest hands, and locks of jet.
Is 't not enough to vex our souls,
And fill our eyes, that we have set
Our love upon a rose's leaf,
Our hearts upon a violet?
Blue eyes, red cheeks, are frailer yet;
And sometimes at their swift decay
Beforehand we must fret:
The roses bud and bloom again;
But love may haunt the grave of love,
And watch the mould in vain.

O clasp me, sweet, whilst thou art mine,
And do not take my tears amiss;
For tears must flow to wash away
A thought that shows so stern as this:
Forgive, if somewhile I forget,
In wo to come, the present bliss.
As frighted Proserpine let fall
Her flowers at the sight of Dis,
Ev'n so the dark and bright will kiss.
The sunniest things throw sternest shade,
And there is ev'n a happiness
That makes the heart afraid!

Now let us with a spell invoke
The full-orb'd moon to grieve our eyes;
Not bright, not bright, but, with a cloud
Lapp'd all about her, let her rise
All pale and dim, as if from rest
The ghost of the late buried sun
Had crept into the skies.
The Moon! she is the source of sighs,

The very face to make us sad;
If but to think in other times
The same calm quiet look she had,
As if the world held nothing base,
Of vile and mean, of fierce and bad;
The same fair light that shone in streams,
The fairy lamp that charm'd the lad;
For so it is, with spent delights
She taunts men's brains, and makes them mad.

All things are touch'd with Melancholy,
Born of the secret soul's mistrust,
To feel her fair ethereal wings
Weigh'd down with vile degraded dust;
Even the bright extremes of joy
Bring on conclusions of disgust,
Like the sweet blossoms of the May,
Whose fragrance ends in must.
O give her, then, her tribute just,
Her sighs and tears, and musings holy.
There is no music in the life
That sounds with idiot laughter solely;
There's not a string attuned to mirth,
But has its chords of Melancholy.

THE END OF PART I.

PART SECOND.

PROSE AND VERSE.

THE GREAT CONFLAGRATION.

DREADFUL FIRE—DESTRUCTION OF BOTH HOUSES OF PARLIAMENT—THE SPEAKER'S HOUSE GUTTED—REPORTS OF INCENDIARISM.

It is our unexpected lot to announce that the Houses of Lords and Commons, so often threatened with combustion, are in a state of actual ignition. At this moment, both fabrics are furiously burning. We are writing this paragraph without the aid of lamp or candles; by the mere reflection of the flames. Nothing is known of the origin of the fire, although it is throwing a light upon everything else.—*Evening Star.*

The devouring element which destroyed Covent Garden and Drury Lane, the Royalty and the Pantheon, has made its appearance on a new stage, equally devoted to declamatory elocution. St. Stephen's Chapel is in flames! The floor which was trodden by the eloquent legs of a Fox, a Burke, a Pitt, and a Sheridan, is reduced to a heap of ashes; and the benches which sustained the Demosthenic weight of a Wyndham, a Whitbread, and a Wilberforce, are a mere mass of charcoal. The very roof that re-echoed the classicalities of Canning is nodding to its fall. In Parliamentary language, Fire is in possession of the House: the Destructive spirit is on its legs, and the Conservative principle can offer but a feeble opposition.—*Daily Post.*

The blow is struck. What we have long foreseen has come to pass. Incendiarism triumphs! The whole British Empire, as represented by the three estates, is in a blaze! The Throne, the Lords, and the Commons, are now burning. The cycle is complete. The spirit of Guy Fawkes revives in 1834!

England seems to have changed places with Italy; London with Naples. We stand hourly on the brink of a crater; every step we take is on a solfaterra—not a land of Sol Fa, as some musical people would translate it; but a frail crust, with a treacherous subsoil of ardent brimstone! At length the eyes of our rulers are opened; but we must ask, could nothing short of such an eruption awaken them to a sense of the perilous state of the country? For weeks, nay, months past, at the risk of being considered alarmists, we have called the attention of the legislature and magistracy to a variety of suspicious symptoms and signs of the times, and in particular to the multiplied chemical inventions, for the purpose of obtaining instantaneous lights. Well are certain matches or fire-boxes called Lucifers, for they may be applied to the most diabolical purposes! The origin of the fire cannot raise the shadow of a doubt in any reasonable mind. Accident is out of the question. Tell us not of tallies. We have just tried our milk-woman's, and it contained so much water, that nothing could make it ignite.—*Britannic Guardian.*

The Houses of Parliament are in flames. We shall stop the press to give full particulars. Our reporters are at the spot, and Mons. C——, the celebrated Salamander, is engaged to give a description of the blazing *interiors*, exclusively for this journal.—*Daily Times.*

FROM A CORRESPONDENT.

On Thursday evening, towards seven o'clock, I was struck by the singular appearance of the moon silvering the opposite chimneys with a blood-red light, a lunar phenomenon, which I conceived belonged only to our theatres. It speedily occurred to me that there must be a conflagration in my vicinity, and after a little hunting by scent as well as sight, I found myself in front of the Houses of Lords and Commons, which were burning with a rapidity and brilliancy that I make bold to say did not always characterize their proceedings. By favor of my natural assurance, which seemed to identify me with the firemen, I was allowed to pass through the lines of guards and policemen, who surrounded the blazing pile, and was thus enabled to select a favorable position for overlooking the whole scene. It was an imposing sight. The flames rose from the Peers' in a volume, as red as the Extraordinary Red Book, and the House of Commons was not at all behind-hand in voting supplies of timber and other combustibles. Westminster Hall reminded me vividly of a London cry, "Hall hot, Hall hot," that was familiar in our childhood—and the Gothic architecture of the Abbey seemed unusually *florid*. Instead of dingy stone, the venerable pile appeared to be built of the well-baked brick of the Elizabethan age. Indeed, so red-hot was its aspect, that it led to a ludicrous misapprehension on the part of the populace. A procession, bearing several male and female figures in a state of insensibility, naturally gave rise to the most painful conjectures, inferring loss of human life by the devouring element, but I have reason to believe it was only the Dean and Chapter saving the Wax-Work. As far as my own observation went, the first object carried out certainly bore a strong resemblance to General Monk.

In the mean time a select party had effected an entrance into the Hall, but not without some serious delay, occasioned, I believe, by somebody within bringing the wrong key, that belonged to a tea-caddy. However, at last they entered, and I followed their example. The first person I beheld was the veteran Higginbottom, so unfairly, but facetiously, put to death by the authors of the Rejected Addresses; for no man is more alive to his duty. But he was sadly hampered. First came one Hon. Gent. said to be Mr. Morrison, and insisted on directing the *Hose* department; and next arrived a noble Lord from Crockford's, who wouldn't sit out, but persisted in taking a hand, and playing, though everybody agreed that he played too high. I mention this, because some of the journals have imputed mismanagement to the engines, and have insinuated that the pipes wanted organizing; indeed, I myself overheard a noble director of the Academy of Music lamenting that the firemen did not "play in concert."

The same remark applies with greater force to the House of Commons. Here all was confusion worse confounded, and Higginbottom's station was enviable, compared with that of some of the poor fellows in St. Stephen's Chapel. A considerable number of members had arrived, and without any attention to their usual parliamentary rules, were all making motions at once, which nobody seconded. The most prominent, I was informed, were Mr. Hume, Mr. O'Connell, Mr. Attwood, Mr. Buckingham, Mr. Pease, Sir Andrew and Mr. Buxton—the latter almost covered with blacks. The clamor was terrific, and I really expected that the poor foremen who held the pipes would be torn in pieces. Everybody wanted to command the Coldstream. Nothing but shouts of "Here! here! here!" answered like an Irish echo by cries of "There! there! there!" "Oh, save my savings!"—"My poor, poor Bill!" "More water— more water for my Drunkenness!" "Work awa, lads, work awa—it's no the Sabbath, and ye may just play at what ye like!"

In pleasing contrast to this tumult, was the unusual and cordial unanimity of the members of both Houses, in rescuing whatever was portable from the flames. It was a delightful novelty to see the Lords helping the Commons in whatever they moved or carried. No party spirit—no Whig, pulling at one leg of the table, whilst a Tory tugged at another in the opposite direction. They seemed to belong to the Hand-in-Hand. Peers and Commoners were alike seen burthened with loads of papers or furniture. Mr. Calvert, in particular, worked like any porter. Of course, in rescuing the papers and parchments, there was no time for inspecting their contents, and some curious results were the consequence. Everybody remembers the pathetic story in the Tatler, of the lover who saved a strange lady from a burning theatre, under the idea that he was preserving the mistress of his affections, and some similar mistakes are currently reported to have occurred at the late conflagration—and equally to the chagrin of the parties. I go by hearsay, and cannot vouch for the facts, but it is said that the unpopular Six Acts, including what I believe is called the Gagging Act, were actually preserved by Mr. Cobbett. Mr. O'Connell saved the Irish Coercion Bill, whilst the Reform Bill was snatched like "a brand out of the fire," by a certain noble Duke, who resolutely set his face against it in all its stages! Amongst others, Mr. Ricardo saved an old tattered flag, which he thought was "the standard of value."

However deficient in general combination, and concentration

of energies, individual efforts were beyond all praise. The instances of personal exertion and daring were numerous. Mr. Rice worked amidst the flames till he was nearly baked; and everybody expected that Mr. Pease would be parched. The greatest danger was from the melted metal pouring down from the windows and roof. The heads of some of the Hon. Gentlemen were literally nothing but lead. Great apprehensions were entertained of the falling in of one of the walls, which eventually gave way, but fortunately everybody had retreated on the timely warning of a gentleman, Mr. O'Connell I believe, who declared that he saw a Rent in it.

I did not enter the House of Lords, which was now one mass of glowing fire, but directed my attention towards the Speaker's mansion, which was partially burning. The garden behind was nearly filled with miscellaneous property—and numbers of well-dressed gentlemen were every moment rushing into the house, from which they issued again, laden with spits, saucepans, and other culinary implements. I, myself, saw one zealous individual thus encumbered—with a stew-pan on his head, the meat-screen under one arm, the dripping-pan under the other, the frying-pan in his right hand, the gridiron in his left, and the rolling-pin in his mouth. Indeed, it is said that every article in the kitchen was saved down to the salt-box; and the cook declares that such was the anxiety to save her she was "cotched up in twelve gentlemen's arms, and never felt her feet till the corner of Abingdon Street."

The whole of the Foot Guards were in attendance, as well as a great number of the police, but the thieves had mustered in great force, and there was a good deal of plundering, which was however checked temporarily by a gentleman said to be one of the members and magistrates for Essex, who jumped up on a railing and addressed the populace to the following effect, "How do you hall dare!"

The origin of the fire is involved in much mystery; nor is it correctly ascertained by whom it was first discovered. Some say that one of the serjeants, in taking up the insignia, was astonished to find the mace as hot as ginger. Others relate that a Mr. Spell, or Shell, or Snell, whilst viewing the House, although no dancer, began suddenly, and in his boots, to the utter amazement of his companions and Mrs. Wright, the housekeeper, to jump and caper like a bear upon a hotted floor. This story certainly seems to countenance a report that the mischief originated in the warming apparatus, an opinion that is very current, but, for my own part, I cannot conceive that the Collective Wisdom, which knows how to lay down laws for us all, should not know how to lay down flues. Rumors of Incendiarism are also very generally prevalent, and stories are in circulation of the finding of half-burnt matches and other combustibles. But these facts rest on very frail foundations. The links said to have been found in the Speaker's garden have turned out to be nothing but German sausages; and another cock-and-a-bull that has got abroad will probably come to no better end. A Mr. Dudley affirms that he smelt the fire before it broke out, at Cooper's Hill; but such olfactories are too much like manufactories to be believed.

I am, Sir, your most obedient servant,

X. Y. Z.

ANOTHER ACCOUNT.

The writer of these lines, who resides in Lambeth, was first awakened to a sense of conflagration by a cry of "Fire" from a number of persons who were running in the direction of Westminster Bridge. Owning myself a warm enthusiast on the subject of ignition, and indeed not having missed a fire for the last fifty years, except one, and that was only a chimney, it may be supposed the exclamation in question had an electric effect. We are all the slaves of some physical bias, strange as it may appear to others with opposite tendencies. It is recorded of some great marshal that he disliked music, but testified the liveliest pleasure at a salvo of artillery or a roll of thunder, and the rumble of an engine has the same effect on the author of these lines. To say I am a guebre, or fire-worshipper, is only to confess the truth. I have a sort of observatory erected on the roof of my house, from which, if there be a break-out within the circuit of the metropolis, it may be discovered, and before going to bed I invariably visit this look-out.

Every man has his hobby-horse, and, figuratively speaking, mine was always kept harnessed and ready to run to a fire with the first engine. Many a time I have arrived before the turn-cocks, though I perhaps had to traverse half London, and I scarcely remember an instance that I did not appear long before the water. Habit is second nature—I verily believe I could sniff a conflagration by instinct; and if I was not, I ought to have been, the trainer of the firemen's dog, which at present attracts so much of the public attention, by his eager running along with the Sun, the Globe, the British and the Hand-in-Hand.

Of course I have seen a great many fires in my time—Rotherhithe, the theatres, the Custom-house, &c., &c. I remember in the days of Thistlewood and Co., when the metropolis was expected to be set on fire, I slept for three weeks in my clothes in order to be ready for the first alarm; for I had the good fortune to witness the great riots of 1780, when no less than eight fires were blazing at once, and a lamentable sight it was. I say lamentable, because it was impossible to be present at them all at the same time; but my good genius directed me to Langdale's the Distiller, which made (excuse the vulgar popular phrase) a very satisfactory flare-up.

The Rotherhithe fire, not the recent little job, but some fifteen or twenty years ago, was also on a grand scale, and very lasting. The engine-pipes were wilfully cut; and I remember some of my friends rallying me on my well-known propensity, jocularly accusing me of lending my knife and my assistance. The Custom-house was a disappointment; it certainly cleared itself effectually, but it was done by day-light, and consequently the long-room fell short of my anticipations. Drury-lane and Covent-garden were better; but I have observed generally that theatres burn with more attention to stage effect. They avoid the noon: a dark night to a fire is like the black letters in a benefit-bill, setting off the red ones.

The destruction of the Kent Indiaman I should like to have

witnessed, but contrary to the opinion of many experienced amateurs I conceive the Dartford Mills must have been a failure. Powder magazines make very indifferent conflagrations ; they are no sooner on fire than they are off,—all is over before you know where you are, and there is no getting under, which quite puts you out. But fires, generally, are not what they used to be. What with gas, and new police, steam, and one cause or other, they have become what one might call slow explosions. A body of flame bursts from all the windows at once, and before B 25 can call fi-er in two syllables, the roof falls in, and all is over. It was not so in *my* time. First a little smoke would issue from a window-shutter, like the puff of a cigar, and after a long spring of his rattle, the rheumatic watchman had time to knock double and treble knocks, from No. 9 to No. 35, before a spark made its appearance out of the chimney-pot. The Volunteers had time to assemble under arms, and muffle their drums, and the bell-ringers to collect in the belfry, and pull an alarm peal backwards. The parish engines even, although pulled along by the pursy churchwardens, and the paralytic paupers, contrived to arrive before the fire fairly broke out in the shape of a little squib-like eruption from the garret-window. The affrighted family, fourteen in number, all elaborately drest in their best Sunday clothes, saved themselves by the street-door, according to seniority, the furniture was carefully removed, and after an hour's pumping, the fire was extinguished without extending beyond the room where it originated, namely a bedroom on the second floor. Such was the progress *in my time* of a fire, but it is the fashion now to sacrifice everything to *pace*. Look at our race-horses, and look at our fox-hounds,—and I will add look at our conflagrations. All that is cared for is a burst—no matter how short, if it be but rapid. The devouring element never sits down now to a regular meal—it pitches on a house and *bolts* it.

But I am wandering from the point. The announcement of both Houses of Parliament being in flames thrilled through every fibre. It seemed to promise what I may call a crowning event to the Conflagrationary Reminiscences of an Octogenarian. I snatched up my hat, and rushed into the street, at eighty years of age, with the alacrity of eighteen, when I ran from Highgate to Horsleydown, to be present at the gutting of a ship chandler's. As the bard says—

> "Ev'n in our ashes live their wonted *fires*,"

and I could almost have supposed myself a fireman belonging to the Phœnix. My first step into the street discouraged me, the moonlight was so brilliant, and in such cases the most splendid blaze is somewhat "shorn of its beams." But a few steps re-assured me. Even at the Surrey side of the river the sparks and burning particles were falling like flakes of snow—I mean of course the red snow formerly discovered by Captain Ross, and the light was so great that I could have read the small print of the Police Gazette with the greatest ease, only I don't take it in. I of course made the best of my way towards the scene, but the crowd was already so dense that I could only attain a situation on the strand opposite Cotton Gardens, up to my knees in mud. Both Houses of Parliament were at this time in a blaze, and no doubt presented as striking objects of conflagration as the metropolis could offer. I say, "no doubt,"—for getting jammed against a barge with my back towards the fire, I am unable to state anything on my own authority as an eye-witness, excepting that the buildings on the Surrey side exhibited a glowing reflection for some hours. At last the flowing of the tide caused the multitude to retreat, and releasing me from my retrospective position allowed me to gaze upon the ruins. By what I hear, it was a most imposing sight—but in spite of my Lord Althorp, I cannot help thinking that Westminster Hall, with its long range, would have made up an admirable fire. Neither can I agree with the many that it was an Incendiary Act, that passed through both houses so rapidly. To enjoy the thing, a later hour and a darker night would certainly have been chosen. Fire-light and moon-light do not *mix well*:—they are best *neat*. I am, Sir, Yours, &c.,

SENEX.

VARIOUS ACCOUNTS.

We are concerned to state that Sir Jacob Jubb the new member for Shrops was severely burnt, by taking his seat in the House, on a bench that was burning under him. The danger of his situation was several times pointed out to him, but he replied that his seat had cost him ten thousand pounds, and he wouldn't quit. He was at length removed by force.—*Morning Ledger.*

A great many foolish anecdotes of the fire are in circulation. One of our contemporaries gravely asserts that the Marquis of Culpepper was the last person who left the South Turret, a fact we beg leave to question, for the exquisite reason that the noble Lord alluded to is at present at Constantinople.—*The Real Sun.*

We are enabled to state that the individual who displayed so much coolness in the South Turret was Captain Back.—*The Public Journal.*

It is said that considerable interest was evinced by the members of the House of Commons who were present at the fire, as to the fate of their respective Bills. One honorable gentleman, in particular, was observed anxiously watching the last scintillations of some burnt paper. "Oh, my Sabbath Observance!" he exclaimed, "There 's an end of religion! There go the Parson and Clerk!"—*Public Diary.*

The Earl of M. had a very narrow escape. His Lordship was on the point of kicking a bucket when a laborer rushed forward and snatched it out of the way. The individual's name is M'Farrel. We understand he is a sober, honest, hard-working man, and has two wives, and a numerous family; the eldest not above a year old.—*Daily Chronicle.*

The exclamation of a noble Lord, high in office, who was very active at the fire, has been very incorrectly given. The words were as follows:—"Blow the Commons! let 'em flare up —but oh,—for a save-all! a save-all."—*Morning News.*

The public attention has been greatly excited by the extraordinary statement of a commercial gentleman, that he smelt the fire at the Cock and Bottle, in Coventry. He asserts that he mentioned the fact in the commercial room to a deaf gentleman, and likewise to a dumb waiter, but neither have any recollection of the circumstance. He has been examined before the Common Council, who have elicited that he actually arrived at Coventry on the night in question, by the Tally-ho! and the near leader of that coach has been sent for by express.—*New Monitor.*

We were in error in stating that the Atlas was the first engine at the scene of action. So early as five o'clock Mr. Alderman A. arrived with his own garden engine, and began immediately to play upon the Thames.—*British Guardian.*

It must have struck every one who witnessed the operations in the House of Commons, that there was a lamentable want of "order! order! order!" A great many gentlemen succeeded in making pumps of themselves, without producing any check on the flames. The conduct of the military also was far from unexceptionable. On the arrival of the Coldstream at the fire, they actually refused to fall in. Many declined to stand at ease on the burning rafters—but what is the public interest to a private?—*Public Advertiser.*

MONSIEUR C.'S ACCOUNT. (EXCLUSIVE.)

When I am come first to the fire, it was not long burnt up; and I was oblige to walk up and down the floor to keep myself warm. At last, I take my seat on the stove quite convenient to look about. In the House of Commons there was nobody, and I am all alone. The first thing I observe was a great many rats, ratting about—but they did not know which way to turn. So they were all burnt dead. The flames grew very fast: and I am interested very much with the seats, how they burned, quite different from one another. Some seats made what you call a great splutter, and popped and bounced, and some other seats made no noise at all. Mr. Bulwer's place burned of a blue color; Mr. Buckstone's turned quite black; and there was one made a flame the color of a drab. I observe one green flame and one orange, side by side, and they hiss and roar at one another very furious.

The gallery cleared itself quite quickly, and the seat of Messieurs the reporters exploded itself like a cannon of forty-eight pounds. The speaking chair burnt without any sound at all.

When everything is quite done in the Commons I leave them off, and go to the House of Lords, where the fire was all in one sheet, and almost the whole of its inside burnt out. I was able in this room to take off my greatcoat. I could find nothing to be saved except one great ink-stand that was red hot, and which I carry away in my two hands. Likewise here, as well as in the Commons, I bottled up several bottles of smoke, to distribute afterwards, at five guineas a piece, and may be more; for I know the English people admire such things, and are fond after reliques, like a madness almost. I did not make a long stop, for whenever I was visible, the pompiers was so foolish as play water upon me, and I was afraid of a catch-cold. In fact, when I arrive at home, I find myself stuffed in my head, and fast in my chest, and my throat was a little horse. I am going for it into a bath of boiling water, and cannot write any more at full length.

A LETTER TO A LABORING MAN.

Bushell,

When you made a holiday last Whitsuntide to see the Sights of London, in your way to the Waxwork and Westminster Abbey, you probably noticed a vast pile of buildings in Palace Yard, ard you stood and scratched that shock head of yours, and wondered whose fine houses they were. Seeing you to be a country clodpole, no doubt some well-dressed vagabond, by way of putting a hoax upon the hawbuck, told you that in those buildings congregated all the talent, all the integrity and public spirit of the country—that beneath those roofs the best and wisest, and the most honest men to be found in three kingdoms, met to deliberate and enact the most wholesome and just and judicious laws for the good of the nation. He called them the oracles of our constitution, the guardians of our rights, and the assertors of our liberties. Of course, Bushell, you were told all this; but nobody told you, I dare say, that within those walls your master had lifted up his voice, and delivered the only sound, rational, and wholesome, upright, and able speeches, that were ever uttered in St. Stephen's Chapel. No, nobody told you that. But when I come dome, Bushell, I will lend you all my printed speeches, and when you have spelt them, and read them, and studied them, and got them by heart, bumpkin as you are, Bushell, you will know as much of legislation as all our precious members together.

Well, Bushell, the fine houses you stood gaping at are burnt down, gutted, as the vulgar call it, and nothing is left but the bare walls. You saw Farmer Gubbins' house, or, at least, the shell of it, after the fire there; well, the Parliament Houses are exactly in the same state. There is news for you! and now Bushell, how do you feel? Why, if the well-dressed vagabond told you the truth, you feel as if you had had a stroke—for all the British Constitution is affected, and you are a fraction of it, that is to say, a British subject. Your bacon grows rusty in your mouth, and your table-beer turns to vinegar on your palate. You cannot sleep at night, or work by day. You have no heart for anything. You can hardly drag one clouted shoe after another. And how do you look? Why, as pale as a parsnip, and as thin as a hurdle, and your carrotty locks stand bolt upright, as if you had just met old Lawson's ghost with his head under his arm. I say thus you must feel and look, Bushell, if what the well-dressed vagabond told you is the truth. But is that the case? No. You drink your small beer with a sigh and smack of delight; and you bolt your bacon with a relish, as if, as the virtuous Americans say, you could "go the whole hog." Your clouted shoes clatter about as if you were counting hob-nails with the Lord Mayor, and you work like a young horse, or an old ass, and at night you snore like an oratorio of jews' harps. Your face is as bold and ruddy as the Red Lion's. Your carrotty locks lie sleek upon your poll, and as for poor old Lawson's ghost, you could lend him flesh and blood enough to set him up again in life. But what, say you, does all this tend to? I will tell you, Bushell. There are a great many well-dressed vagabonds, besides the one you met in Palace Yard, who would persuade a poor man that a House of Lords or Commons is as good to him as his bread, beer, beef, bacon, bed, and breeches; and therefore I address this to you, Bushell, to set such notions to rights by an appeal to your own back and belly. And now I will tell you what you shall do. You shall go three nights a week to the Red Lion (when your work is done), and you may score by a pint of beer, at my cost, each time. And when the parson, or the exciseman, or the tax-gatherer, or any such gentry, begin to talk of the deplorable great burning, and the national calamity, and such-like trash, you shall pull out my letter and read to them—I say, Bushell, you shall read this letter to them, twice over, loudly and distinctly, and tell them from me, that the burning of twenty Parliament Houses wouldn't be such a national calamity as a fire at No. 1, Bolt Court.

PRIVATE CORRESPONDENCE.

To Mary Price, *Fenny Hall, Lincolnshire.*

O Mary,—I am writing in such a quiver, with my art in my mouth, and my tung sticking to it. For too hole hours I've bean Doin nothink but taking on and going off, I mean into fits, or crying and blessing goodness for my miraclus escape. This day week I wear inwallopped in flams, and thinkin of roth to cum, and fire evverlasting. But thenks to Diving Providings, hear I am, althowgh with loss of wan high brew scotched off, a noo cap and my rite shew. But I hav bean terrifid to deth. Wen I was ate, or it might be nine, I fell on the stow, and hav had a grate dred of fire evver since. Gudge then how low I felt at the idear of burning along with the Lords and Communer's. It as bean a Warnin, and never, no never never never agin will I go to Clandestiny parties behind Missisis backs. I now see my errer, but temtashun prevaled, tho the clovin fut of the Wicked Wan had a hand in it all: Oh Mary, down on yure marrybones, and bless yure stars for sitiating you in a loanly stooped poky place, wear you can't be lead into liteness and gayty, if you was ever so inclind. Fore wipping willies and a windmill is a dullish luck out, shure enuff, but its better then moor ambishus prospex, and stairing at a grate fire, like a suckin pig, till yure eyes is reddy to drop out of yure hed!

You no wen Lady Manners is absent, a certin person always gives a good rowt:—and I had a card in Coarse. I went very ginteel, my Cloke cost I wont say Wot, and a hat and fethers to match. But it warnt to be. After takin off my things, I had barely set down, wen at the front dore there cums a dubble nock without any end to it, and a ring of the bell at the saim time, like a triangle keepin cumpany with a big drum. As soon as the door were opened, a man with a pail face asked for the buckits, and that was the fust news we had of the fire. Oh Mary, never trust to the mail sects! They are all Alick from the Botcher and Backer that flurts at the front dore, down to the deer dissevers you throw away yure arts upon. For all their fine purfessions, they are only filling yure ears with picrust, they make trifles of yure afections, and destroy your comfits for life. They think no more of perjuring themselves then I do of sweeping the earth. If yure wise you will sit yure face agin all menkind and luv nonsense, as I meen to in futer, or may be, wen you are dreeming of brid cake and wite fevers, you may find yureself left with nothink but breeches of prommis. John Futman is a proof in pint. Menny tims Ive give him a hiding at number fore, and he always had the best of the lardur at our stolin meatings, and God nose Ive offun alloud him to idelize me when I ort to have bean at my wurks, besides larning to rite for his sack. Twenty housis afire ort not to have a baited his warmth, insted of witch to jump up at the first allurm and run away, leaving me to make my hone shifts. A treu luver wood have staid to shear my fat. O Mary, if ever there was a terryfickle spectikle that was won! Flams before and flams behind, and flams over-head. Sich axing and hollowing out, and mobbing and pumpin, and cussing and swaring, and the peple's rushes into the Hous purvented all gitting out. For my hone parts, I climed up the dresser, and skreeked, but nobbody was man enuff to purtect. Men ant what they was. I am sick of the retches! It used to be femails fust, but now its furniter. I fully thort one gintleman was comin to cotch me up in arms, but he preferred the fish kettle. As for the sogers they marcht off to the wind seller, and the pantry, ware they maid beleave to preserve the gusberry gam. How I was reskewd at last Lord nose, for my hed was unsensible tell I found meself setten on the pickid pinted ralings of St. Margaret's Church, with my fethers all frizzild, and a shew off. But of all lossis, my ridiculo was most serius, for it had my puss in it.

How and ware it broke out is a mistery. Sum say both Howses was under minded. Sum say the Common members got over heatid in their fluency. A grate deal of property was burned, in spit of Lord Allthorp, who ingaged every cotch, cab, and gobbing porter as conveyancers. Westmunster may thenk his Lordship it did not lose its All. They say the Lords and Communs was connectid with a grate menny historicle associashuns, wich of coarse will hav to make good all dammage.

Fortnately, the Speker's mornin, noon, and evning services of plait was not at hom, or it mite hav sufferd, for they say goold and silver as stud the fire verry well, melted down when it got furthur off. • Tauking of plait a gentilman, who giv his card, Mr. William Soames, were verry kind and partickler in his inquerries efter Mr. Speker's vallybles. I hope he will hav a place givn him for his indevvers.

Ware the poor burnt-out creturs will go noboddy nose. Sum say Exter Hall, sum say the Refudge for the Destitut, and sum say the King will lend them his Bensh to set upon! All I no is, I've had a frite that will go with me to my grave. I am allways snifing fire by day and dreeming on it by nite. Ony last Fryday I allarmd the hole naberhood by screaching out of winder for the warter to be plugged up. Liting fires, or striking lite, or making tindur, throes me into fits.

I shall nevver be the womman I was; but that is no excus for John's unconstancy. I don't dare to take my close off to go to bed, and I practice clambering up and down by a rop in case, and I giv Police M 25 a shillin now and than to keep a specious eye to number fore, and be reddy to ketch anny won in his harms. But it cums to munny, and particly given the ingin keeper a pint of bear from time to time, and drams to the turn-cox; where there's nabers fires will happen, howevver cerefull and precocius you may be youreself. I dred our two nex dores; number three is a Gurmin fammily, and them orrid forriners think nothink of smocking siggars in bed, witch will ketch sum day to a certainty. Number fiv is wus; since his wif's death Mr. Sanders has betuck himself to comicle studis, and offin has a littel blo up amung his pistles and morters. O! Mary, how happy is them as livs lick you, as the song says, "Fur from the buzzy aunts of men." If you're inflamd its nobbody's folt but yure hone. Pray take the greatest car. Have yure eyes about you, and luck out for sparks; watever the men may say, don't allow backer pips or long snufs, and let evvery boddy be thurrowly put out. Don't neglect to rake out evvery nite, see that evvery sole in the hows is turned down xtinguished, and allways blo yureself out befour you go to yure piller. Thenk gudness you nevver larnd to reed, and therefor will not take anny bucks to bed with you. Allways ware stuff or woollin, insted of lite cottons and gingums, in case of the coles throwin out coffens or pusses, by witch menny persons gains their ends. In case of yure pettycots catchin don't forgit standin on yure head, as recommended by the Human Society, becoz fire burns uppards, but its a posishun as requiers practis. Have yure chimbly swept reglar wonce a munth, and wen visiters cum nevver put hot coles in the warmin pan, for fear you forgit and leave it in the spair bed. Remember fire is a good sarvent but a bad master, and sure enuff wen it is master it never gives a sarvent a munth's notis. To be shure we have won marsy in town that is unbenone in the country, and that there is Swingeing; is no cornstax or heyrix in St. Jims's Square. That is yure week pint, and I trembil for the barns; a rockite or a roaming candel mite set you in a blaze. But I hop and trust wat I say will nevver pruve the truth. Oppydildock is good for burns, and I am, dear Mary,

Yure old and afexionate feller sarvent,

Ann Gale.

THE JUBB LETTERS.

From Lady Jubb *to* Mrs. Phipps, *Housekeeper at the Shrubbery, Shrewsbury, Shrops.*

Mrs. Phipps:

You will prepare the house directly for the family's return, not that our coming back is absolutely certain, but events have happened to render our stay in Portland-Place very precarious. All depends upon Sir Jacob. In Parliament or out of Parliament his motions must guide ours. By this time what has happened will be known in Shropshire, but I forbid your talking. Politics belong to people of property, and those who have no voice in the country ought not to speak. In your inferior situations it's a duty to be ignorant of what you know. The nation is out of your sphere, and besides, people out of town cannot know the state of the country. I want to put you on your guard; thanks to the press, as Sir Jacob says, public affairs cannot be kept private, and the consequence is, the ignorant are as well informed as their betters. The burning of both Houses of Parliament I am afraid cannot be hushed up—but it is not a subject for servants, that have neither upper nor lower members amongst them, and represent nobody. I trust to you, Mrs. Phipps, to discourage all discussions in the kitchen, which isn't the place for parliamentary canvassing. The most ridiculous notions are abroad. I should not be surprised even to hear that Sir Jacob had lost his seat, because the benches were burnt, but we have been deprived of none of our dignities or privileges. You will observe this letter is *franked;* the fire made no difference to your master, he is not dissolved, whatever the Blues may wish—he is still Sir Jacob Jubb, Baronet, M. P.

The election of Sir Jacob at such a crisis was an act of Providence. His firmness at the fire affords an example to posterity; although the bench was burning under him he refused to retreat, replying emphatically, "I will sit by my order." As far as this goes you may mention, and no more. I enjoin upon all else a diplomatic silence. Sir Jacob himself will write to the bailiff, and whatever may be the nature of his directions, I desire that no curiosity may be indulged in, and above all, that you entertain no opinions of your own. You cannot square with the upper circles. I would write more, but I am going to a meeting, I need not say where, or upon what subject. I rely, Mrs Phipps, on your discretion, and am, &c.,

ARABELLA ANASTASIA JUBB

To T. CRAWFURD, *junior, Esquire, the Beeches, near Shrewsoury, Shrops.*

DEAR TOM:

Throw up your cap and huzza. There's glorious news, and so you'll say when I tell you. I could almost jump out of my skin for joy! Father's dismembered! The House of Commons caught fire, and he was dissolved along with the rest.

I've never been happy since we came up to London, and all through Parliament. The election was good sport enough. I liked the riding up and down, and carrying a flag; and the battle, with sticks, between the Blues and the Yellows, was famous fun; and I huzza'd myself hoarse at our getting the day at last. But after that came the jollup, as we used to say at Old Busby's. Theme writing was a fool to it. If father composed one maiden speech he composed a hundred, and he made me knuckle down and copy them all out, and precious stupid stuff it was. A regular physicker, says you, and I'd worse to take after it. He made us all sit down and hear him spout them, and a poor stick he made. —Dick Willis, that we used to call Handpost, was a dab at it compared to him. He's no better hand at figures, so much the worse for me. Did you ever have a fag, Tom, at the national debt? I don't know who owes it, but I wish he'd pay it, or be made bankrupt at once. I've worked more sums last month than ever I did at school in the half year,—geography the same. I had to hunt out Don Carlos and Don Pedro, all over the maps. I came in for a regular wigging one day, for wishing both the Dons were well peppered, as Tom Tough says. I've seen none of the sights I wanted to see. He wouldn't let me go to the play, because he says the theatres are bad schools, and would give me a vicious style of elocution. The only pleasure he promised me was to sit in the gallery at the Commons and see him present his petitions. Short-hand would have come next, that I might take down his speechifying—for he says the reporters all garble. An't I well out of it all—and a place he was to get for me besides, from the Prime Minister? I suppose the Navy Pay, to sit on a high stool and give Jack Junk one pound two and nine pence twice a year. I'd rather be Jack himself, wouldn't you, Tom? But father's lost his wicket, and huzza for Shropshire! In hopes of our soon meeting, I remain, my dear Tom,

Your old chum and schoolfellow,

FREDERICK JUBB.

P. S.—A court gentleman has just come in, with a knock-me-down-again. He says there's to be a new election. I wish you'd do something; it would be a real favor, and I will do as much for you another time. What I want of you is, to get your father to set up against mine. Do try, Tom—there's a good fellow. I will ask every body I know to give your side a plumper.

To MR. ROGER DAVIS, *Bailiff, the Shrubbery, near Shrewsbury.*

DAVIS,

I hope to God this will find you at home—I am writing in a state of mind bordering on madness. I can't collect myself to give particulars—you will have a newspaper along with this—read that, and your hair will stand on end. Incendiarism has reached its height like the flaming thing on the top of the Monument. Our crisis is come. To my mind—political suicide—is as bad as felo de se. Oh Whigs, Whigs, Whigs—what have you brought us to! As the Britannic Guardian well says—England is gone to Italy—London is at Naples—and we are all standing on the top of Vesuvius. I have heard and I believe it—that an attempt has been made to choke Aldgate Pump. A Waltham Abbey paper says positively that the mills were recently robbed of 513 barrels of powder, the exact number of the members for England and Wales. What a diabolical refinement—to blow up a government with its own powder! I can hardly persuade myself I am in England. God knows where it will spread to—I mean the incendiary spirit. The dry season is frightful—I suppose the springs are all dry. Keep the engine locked in the stable, for fear of a cut at the pipes. I'll send you down two more. Let all the laborers take a turn at them, by way of practice. I'm persuaded the Parliament houses were burnt on purpose. The flue story is ridiculous. Mr. Cooper's is a great deal more to the point. I believe everything I hear. A bunch of matches was found in the Speaker's kitchen. I saw something suspicious myself—some said treacle, but I say tar. Have your eyes about you—lock all the gates, day as well as night—and above all, watch the stacks. One Tiger is not enough—get three or four more, I should have said Cæsar, but you know I mean the house-dog. Good mastiffs,—the biggest and savagest you can get. The gentry will be attempted first—beginning with the M. P.'s. You and Barnes and Sam must sit up by turns—and let the maids sit up too—women have sharp ears and sharp tongues.—If a mouse stirs I would have them squall—danger or no danger. It's the only way to sleep in security—and comfort. I have read that the common goose is a vigilant creature—and saved Rome. Get a score of them—at the next market—don't stand about price—but choose them with good cackles. Alarm them now and then to keep them watchful. Fire the blunderbuss off every night, and both fowling-pieces and the pistols. If all the gentry did as much, it might keep the country quiet. If you were to ring the alarm-bell once or twice in the middle of the night, it would be as well—you would know then what help to depend upon. Search the house often from the garret to the cellar, for combustibles—if you could manage to go without candles, or any sort of light, it would be better. You'd find your way about in the dark after a little practice.

Pray don't allow any sweethearts; they may be Swings and Captain Rocks in disguise, and their pretended flames turn out real. I've misgivings about the maids. Tie them up, and taste their liver, before they eat it themselves—I mean the housedogs; but my agitation makes me unconnected. The scoundrels often poison them, before they attempt robbery and arson. Keep the cattle in the cowhouse for fear of their being houghed and hamstrung. Surely there were great defects somewhere. The Houses could not have been properly protected—if they had been watched as well as they were lighted—but it is too late to cast any blame on individuals. A paltry spirit of economy has been our bane. A few shillings would have purchased a watch-dog; and one or two geese in each house might have saved the capitol of the constitution! But the incendiary knew how to choose his time—an adjournment when there were none sitting. I say, incendiary, because no doubt can exist in any cool mind, that enters into the conflagration. I transcribe conclusive extracts from several papers, the editors of which I know to be upright men, and they all write on one side.

"We are confidently informed," says the Beacon, "that a quantity of tar-barrels was purchased at No. 2, High-street, Shadwell, about ten o'clock on the morning of the fire. There was abundant time before six A. M., for removing the combustibles to Westminster. The purchaser was a short, squat, down-looking man, and the name on his cart was I. Burns."

"Trifling circumstances," says the Sentinel, "sometimes point to great results. Our own opinion is formed. We have made it our business to examine the Guys in preparation for the impending anniversary of the Gunpowder Plot, and we affirm, that every one of the effigies bore a striking resemblance to some member or other of assemblies we need not name. These are signs of the times."

"We should be loth," says the Detector, "to impute the late calamity to any particular party: but we may reasonably inquire what relative stake in the country is possessed by the Whigs and the Tories. The English language may be taken as a fair standard. The first may lay claim to peri-*wig*, scratch-*wig*, tie-*wig*, bob-*wig*, in short, the whole family of peruques, with *whig*maleery. The latter, not to mention other good things, have a vested right in ora*tory*, his*tory*, terri*tory*, and vic*tory*.

Can a man of common patriotism have a doubt which side it is his interest to adhere to?"

That last paragraph, Davis, is what I call sound argument. Indeed I don't see how it is to be answered. You see they are all nem. con. as to our danger, and decidedly reckon fire an inflammatory agent. Take care what you read. Very pernicious doctrines are abroad, and especially across the Western Channel. The Irish are really frightful. I'm told they tie the cows' tails together, and then saw off their horns for insurrectionary bugles. The foundations of society are shaken all over the world—the Whiteboys in Ireland, and the Blacks in the West Indies, all seem to fight under the same colors. It's time for honest men to rally round themselves—but I'm sorry to say public spirit and love of one's country are at a low ebb. There's too much Americanism. One writer wants us to turn all our English wheat to Indian corn, and to grow no sort of apples but Franklin pippins. We want strong measures against associations and unions. There's demagogues abroad—and they wear white hats. By-the-bye, I more than half suspect that fellow Johnson is a delegate. Take him to the ale-house, and treat him freely—it may warm him to blab something. Besides, you will see what sort of papers the public-houses take in. You may drop a hint about their licenses. Give my compliments to Dr. Garratt, and tell him I hope he will preach to the times, and take strong texts. I wish I could be down amongst you, but I cannot desert my post. You may tell the tenantry, and electors—I'm burnt out and gutted—but my heart's in the right place—and devoted to constituents. Come what may, I will be an unshaken pillar on the basis of my circular letter. Don't forget any of my precautions. I am sorry I did not bring all the plate up to town—but at the first alarm bury it. Take in no letters or notices; for what you know they may be threatenings. If any Irishman applies for work, discharge him instantly. All the old spring-guns had better be set again, they are not now legal, but I am ministerial, and if they did go off, the higher powers would perhaps wink at them. But it's the fire that I'm afraid of, fire that destroyed my political roof, and may now assail my paternal one. Walk, as I may say, bucket in hand

and be ready every moment for a break out. You may set fire to the small faggot-stack, and try your hands at getting it under —there's nothing worse than being taken by surprise. Read this letter frequently, and impress these charges on your mind. It is a sad change for England to have become, I may say, this fiery furnace. I have not the least doubt, if properly traced, the burning cliff at Weymouth would be found to be connected with Incendiarism, and the Earthquakes at Chichester with our political convulsions. Thank Providence in your prayers, Davis, that your own station forbids your being an M.P., for a place in parliament is little better than sitting on a barrel of gunpowder. Honor forbids to resign, or I should wish I was nothing but a simple country gentleman. Remember, and be vigilant. Once more I cry Watch, Watch, Watch! By adopting the motions I propose, a conflagration may be adjourned sine die, which is a petition perpetually presented by

Your anxious
but uncompromising Master,
JACOB JUBB, M.P.

To LADY JUBB, *at* 45, *Portland Place.*

RESPECTED MADAM,

I received your Ladyship's obliging commands, and have used my best endeavors to conform to the wishes condescended therein. In respect to political controversy, I beg to say I have imposed a tacit silence on the domestic capacities as far as within the sphere of my control, but lament to say the Bailiff, Mr. Davis, is a party unamenable to my authority, and as such has taken liberties with decorum quite unconsistent with propriety and the decency due. However reluctant to censoriousness, duty compels to communicate subversive conduct quite unconformable to decency's rules and order in a well-regulated establishment. I allude to Mr. Davis's terrifically jumping out from behind doors and in obscure dark corners, on the female domestics, for no reasonable purpose I can discover, except to make them exert their voices in a very alarming manner. The house-maid, indeed, confirms me by saying in her own words, "he considered her skreek the best skreek in the family." If impropriety had proceeded no further, I should have hesitated to trouble your Ladyship with particulars; but Mr. Davis, not satisfied with thus working on the unsophisticated terrors of ignorant females, thought proper to horrify with inflammatory reports. One night, as a prominent instance, about twelve o'clock, he rang the alarm bell so violently, at the same time proclaiming conflagration, that the law of preservation became our paramount duty, and, as a consequence, we all escaped in a state of dishabille only to be ambiguously hinted at, by saying that time did not allow to put on my best lutestring to meet the neighboring gentry—and must add, with indignation, in the full blaze of a heap of straw, thought proper to be set on fire by Mr. Davis in the fore-court. I trust your Ladyship will excuse a little warmth of language, in saying it was highly reprehensible; but I have not depictured the worst. I, one evening, lighted up what I conceived to be a mould candle, and your Ladyship will imagine my undescribable fright when it exploded itself like a missile of the squib description, an unwarrantable mode, I must say, of convincing me, as Mr. Davis had the audaciousness to own to, that we may be made to be actors in our own combustion. To suppose at my years and experience, I can be unsensible of the danger of fire, must be a preposterous notion; but all his subsequent acts partake an agreeable character. For fear of being consumed in our beds, as he insidiously professed, he exerted all his influential arguments to persuade the females to sit up nocturnally all night, a precaution of course declined, as well as his following scheme being almost too much broached with absurdity to enumerate. I mean every retiring female reposing her confidence on a live goose in her chamber, as were purchased for the express purpose, but need not add were dispensed with by rational beings. I trust your Ladyship will acquit of uncharitableness if I suspect it was out of vindictive feelings at their opposition to the geese, that Mr. Davis insinuated a strict inquiry into every individual that came into the house, as far even as requiring to be personally present at all that passed between the dairymaid and her cousin. It escaped memory to say that when the feminine department refused to be deprived of rest, the male servants were equally adverse to go to bed, being spirited up by Mr. Davis to spend the night together, and likewise being furnished with the best strong ale in the cellar, by his imperious directions, which, by way of climax to assurance, was alleged to be by order of Sir Jacob himself. I say nothing reflectively on his repeatedly discharging his artillery at unseasonable hours, the shock principally concerning my own nervous constitution, which was so vibrated as to require calling in physical powers; and Doctor Tudor, considering advanced age and infirmity, is of opinion I may require to be under his professional hands for an ensuing twelvemonth. Of startling effects upon other parties I may make comments more unreserved, and without harsh extenuation must say, his letting off reports without due notice, frequently when the females had valuable cut glass and china in their hands, or on their trays, was blameable in the extreme, to express the least of it. Another feature which caused much unpleasantness, was Mr. Davis persisting to scrutinize and rummage the entire premises from top to bottom, but on this characteristic tediousness forbids to dwell, and more particularly as mainly affecting himself, such as the flow of blood from his nose, and two coagulated eyes, from the cellar door, through a peculiar whim of looking for everything in a state of absolute obscurity. I may add, by way of incident, that Mr. Davis walks lame from a canine injury in the calf of his leg, which I hope will not prove rabid in the end,—but the animals he has on his own responsibility introduced on the premises, really resemble, begging your Ladyship's pardon for the expression, what are denominated D.'s incarnate.

Such, your Ladyship, is the unpropitious posture of domestic affairs at the Shrubbery, originating, I must say, exclusively from the unprecedented deviations of Mr. Davis. A mild construction would infer, from such extraordinary extravagance of conduct, a flightiness, or aberration of mind in the individual, but I deeply lament to say a more obvious cause exists to put a negative on such a surmise. For the last week Mr. Davis has betrayed an unusual propensity to pass his evenings at the George Tavern, and in consequence has several times exhibited himself in a Bacchanalian character to our extreme discomforture, and on one occasion actually trespassed so far beyond the bounds of modesty, as to offer me the rudeness of a salute. I blush to impart such details to your Ladyship; but justice demands an explicit statement, however repulsive to violated reserve and the rules of virtue. Amongst less immoral actions, I must advert to the arrival of two new engines with a vast number of leathern buckets, I fear ordered by Mr. Davis at my honored master's expense, and which are periodically exercised in pumping every day, by the gardeners and the hinds, being induced thereto by extra beverages of strong beer. By such means the aquatic supply of the well is frequently exhausted by playing upon nothing,—and at this present moment I am justified in stating we have not sufficient water to fulfil culinary purposes, or the demands of cleanliness. I feel ashamed to say there is not a strictly clean cap in the whole household.

In short, Madam, we labor under an aggravated complication of insubordination, deprivation, discomfort, and alarm, daily and nightly, such as to shock my eyes whilst it grieves my heart, and I may almost say turns my head to be present at, without sufficient authority to dictate or power to enforce a course more consistent with the line of rectitude. As my sway does not extend to Mr. Davis, I humbly beseech your Ladyship's interference and influence in the proper quarter, in behalf, I may say, of a body of persecuted females, some of whom possess cultivated minds and sensitive feelings beyond their sphere.

I remain, respected Madam

Your Ladyship's most obliged and very humble Servant,

AMELIA PHIPPS.

P. S.—One of Mr. Davis's savage, bull-baiting dogs has just rushed with a frightful crash into the china-closet, in pursuit of the poor cat.

To SIR JACOB JUBB, *Baronet, M. P.*

HONNERD SUR,

Yure faver enclosin the Ruings of the Parlimint houses cam dully to hand, and did indeed put up all the hares on my hed. It cam like the bust of a thunder bolt. You mite hav nockt me down with the fether of a ginny ren. My bran swum. I seamed rooted to the hearth—and did not no weather I was a slip or a wack, on my hed or my heals. I was perfecly unconshunable, and could no more kollect meself than the Hirish tiths. I was a long Tim befor I cud perswade meself that the trooth was trew. But sich a dredful fire is enuff to unsettil wons resin. A thowsend ears mite role over our heds, and not prodeuce sich a blo to the constitushun. I was barley sensible. The Currier dropt from my hands wen I cam to the perrygraft witch says "Our hops are at an end. The Hous of Communs is a boddy of Flams, and so is the Hous of Pears! The Lords will be dun!"

Honnerd Sur, I beg to kondole as becums on yure missin yure seat. It must have bean the suddinest of shox, & jest wen goin to sit after standin for the hole county, on yure hone futting, at your sole expens. But I do hop and trust it will not be yure dissolushun, as sum report; I do hop it is onely an emty rummer pict up at sum publick Hous. At such an encindery crisus our wust frend wood be General Elixion, by stirrin up inflametory peple, particly if there was a long pole. You see, Sir Jacob, I konker in evvery sentashus sentemint in yure respected Letter. The Volkano you menshun I can enter into. Theres a great deal of combustibul sperits in the country that onely wants a spark to convart them into catarax:—and I greave to say evvery inflametory little demy Gog is nust, and has the caudle support of certin pappers. Im alludin to the Press. From this sort of countenins the nashunal aspec gits moor friteful evvery day. I see no prospex for the next generashun but rocking and swinging. I hav had a grate menny low thorts, for wat can be moor dispiritin then the loss of our two gratest Public Housis! There is nothin cumfortable. There is a Vesuvus under our feat, and evvery step brings us nearer to its brinks. Evvery reflective man must say we are a virgin on a precipus.

Honnerd Sur! In the mean tim I hav pade attenshuns to yure letter, and studid its epistlery direcshuns, witch I hav made meself very particlar in fulfiling to the utmost xtent. If the most zellus effuts have not sucksedid to wish I humbly beg no blame but wat is dew may fall on me, and hope other peples shears will visit their hone heds. The axident with the spring gun was no neglex of mine. After Barnes settin it himself, his tumblin over the wier must be lade to his hone dore along with his shot legs. I sent for two surgings to sea to him, and they cauld in too moor, so that he is certin of a good dressin, but he was very down-harted about gittin a livin, till I tolled him yure honner wood settle on him for the rest of his days. I may say the lik of the other axident to Sanders and Sam, who got badly woundid wile wotchin the stax, by apprehendin won another after a sanguine conflic by mistake for incinderies. I have promist in yure honners nam to reword them boath hansumly for their vigilings, but they stedfistly refus to padrol anny moor after dusk, tho they ar agreble by daylit, which leaves me at my whits ends for Firegards, as strange men would not be trussworthy.

Honnerd Sur—I am sorry I cood not git the mad servents to set up for theaves, even for wun nite runnin. I tried the Currier on them, but it didn't wurk on there minds; they tuck lites in their hands and waukd to there pillers as if they hadn't a car on there heds, and wen I insistid on their allarmin me they all give me warnin. As for the swetharts there's a duzzen domesticatted luvers in the kitchen, and I'm sorry to say I can't give them all a rowt. I ketchd the cook's bo gettin in at a winder, and sercht his pockets for feer of fosfrus, but he contaned nothin xcept a cruckid sixpens, a taler's thimbel, and a tin backy-box, with a lock of hare witch did not match with cook's. It is dangerus wurk. Becos I luck after the mades candels they tie strings to the banesters to ketch my fut, and I have twice pitcht from the hed to the fut of the stars. I am riting with my forrid brandid and brown pepperd, and my rite hand in a poltus from gropping in the dark for cumbustibils in the cole seller, and diskivering nothin but the torturous kat and her kittings.

Honnerd Sur—I got six capitol gees a bargin, but am verry dubbius weather they possess the property that ort to make them wakful and weary of nites. The old specious may be lost. The Roman gees you menshun wood certinly hav nevver sufferd themselvs to be stolen without a cakeling as our hone did too nites ago. As for the wotch dogs, to be candied, they were all errers in gudgment. There was to much Bul in the bread. The verry fust nite they were let lose they flew in a rag, and began to vent their caning propensites on each other's curcases. I regret to say too was wurried to deth before the next mourning, and the rest were so full of bad bits and ingeries in there vittles they were obligated to be kild. In shutting Seazer with the blunderbush, I lament to ad it hung fire, and in liftin it went off of its hone hed and shot the bucher's horse at the gait, and he has thretind to tak the law if he isn't made good, as he was verry vallyble.

Honnerd Sur—Accordin to orders I tuck Johnson the suspishus man evvery nite to the Gorge, and told him to caul for wat he likt, witch was allways an ot suppir and Punch. As yet he as diskivered nothin but sum lov nonsins about a deary-made, so that its uncertin weather he is a dillygate or not; but I shood say a desinin won, for by sum artful meens he allways manniged to make me drunk fust, and gennerally lent a hand to carry me home. I told the landlord to let him have aney thing he wantid and yure Honner wood pay the skore, but I think it was unprudent of Mr. Tapper to let him run up to ten pound. But it isn't all drink, but eating as well—Johnson has a very glutinous appetit, and always stix to the tabel as long as there is meet.

Honnerd Sur—Last fridy morning there was grate riotism and sines of the populus risin, and accordin I lost no time in berryin the plait as derected by yure ordirs. I am gratifid to say the disturbans turned out onely a puggleistical fit; but owen to our hurry and allarm, the spot ware the plait was berrid went out of our heads. We have since dug up the hole srubbery, but without turnin up anny thing in its shape. But it cant be lost, tho' it isnt to be found. The gardner swares the srubs will all di from being transplanted at unproper sesin—but I trust it is onely his old grumblin stile witch he cannot git over.

Honnerd Sur—The wust is to cum. In casis of Fire the trooth is shure to brake out sunner or latter, so I may as well cum to the catstrophy without any varnish on my tail. This morning, according to yure order, I hignitted the littel faggit stak, fust takin the precawshuny meshure of drawin up a line of men with buckits, from the dux-pond to the sene of combusting. Nothing can lay therefor on my sholders: it all riz from the men striking for bear, wen they ort to hav bean handin warter to won another. I felt my deuty to argy the pint, which I trust will be apruved, and wile we were cussin and discussin the fire got a hed that defide all our unitted pours to subdo. To confess the fax, the fire inguns ware all lokt up in a stabble with a shy key that had lost itself the day before, and was not to be had wen we wantid to lay hands on it. Not that we could have wurked the inguns if they had faverd with their presens, for want of hands. Evvery boddy had run so offen at the allarm bell that they got noboddy to go in there steed. It was an hawful site; the devowring ellemint swallerd won thing after another as sune as cotched, and rushed along roring with friteful violins. Were the finger of Providins is the hand as does we must not arrange it, but as the him says, "we must submit and humbel Bee." Heavin direx the winds, and not us. As it blue towards the sow the piggry sune cotchd, and that cotchd the foul housis, and then the barn cotchd with all the straw, and the granery cotched next, witch it wood not have dun if we had puld down the Cow Hous that stud between. That was all the cotching, excep the hay-stax, from Jenkins runnin about with a flamin tale to his smoak-frock. At last, by a blessin, when there was no moor to burn it was got under and squentched itself, prays be given without loss of lif or lim. Another comfit is all bein inshured in the Sun, enuff to kiver it; and I shud hop they will not refus to make gud on the ground that it was dun wilful by our hone ax and deeds. But fire officis are sumtimes verry unlibberal, and will ketch hold of a burning straw, and if fax were put on their oths I couldn't deni a bundil of rags, matchis, candel ends, and other combustibils pokt into the faggits, and then litin up with my hone hand. Tim will sho. In the meenwhile I am consienshusly easy, it was dun for the best, though turned out for the wust, and am gratifid to reflect that I hav omitted nothin, but have scruppleusly fulfild evvery particler of yure honner's instruxions, and in hap of approval of the saim, await the faver of furthir commands, and am,

Honnerd Sur Jacob,

Your humbel, faithful, and obedient Servint,

ROGER DAVIS.

A TALE OF A TRUMPET.

"Old woman, old woman, will you gc ɪ-shearing?
Speak a little louder, for I'm very hard of hearing."

OLD BALLAD

Of all old women hard of hearing,
The deafest, sure, was Dame Eleanor Spearing!
On her head it is true,
Two flaps there grew,
That served for a pair of gold rings to go through,
But for any purpose of ears in a parley,
They heard no more than ears of barley.

No hint was needed from D. E. F.
You saw in her face that the woman was deaf:
From her twisted mouth to her eyes so peery
Each queer feature ask'd a query;
A look that said in a silent way,
"Who? and What? and How? and Eh?
I'd give my ears to know what you say!"

And well she might! for each auricular
Was deaf as a post—and that post in particular
That stands at the corner of Dyott Street now,
And never hears a word of a row!
Ears that might serve her now and then
As extempore racks for an idle pen;
Or to hang with hoops from jewellers' shops
With coral, ruby, or garnet drops;
Or, provided the owner so inclined,

Ears to stick a blister behind;
But as for hearing wisdom, or wit,
Falsehood, or folly, or tell-tale-tit,
Or politics, whether of Fox or Pitt,
Sermon, lecture, or musical bit,
Harp, piano, fiddle, or kit,
They might as well, for any such wish,
Have been butter'd, done brown, and laid in a dish!

She was deaf as a post,—as said before—
And as deaf as twenty similes more,
Including the adder, that deafest of snakes,
Which never hears the coil it makes.

She was deaf as a house—which modern tricks
Of language would call as deaf as bricks—
  For her all human kind were dumb,
  Her drum, indeed, was so muffled a drum,
  That none could get a sound to come,
Unless the Devil who had Two Sticks!
She was deaf as a stone—say one of the stones
Demosthenes sucked to improve his tones;
And surely deafness no further could reach
Than to be in his mouth without hearing his speech!

She was deaf as a nut—for nuts, no doubt,
Are deaf to the grub that's hollowing out—
As deaf, alas! as the dead and forgotten—
(Gray has noticed the waste of breath,
In addressing the "dull, cold ear of death"),
Or the Felon's ear that was stuff'd with Cotton—
Or Charles the First, *in statue quo;*
Or the still-born figures of Madame Tussaud,
With their eyes of glass, and their hair of flax,
That only stare whatever you "ax,"
For their ears, you know, are nothing but wax.

She was deaf as the ducks that swam in the pond,
And wouldn't listen to Mrs. Bond,—

As deaf as any Frenchman appears,
When he puts his shoulders into his ears;
And—whatever the citizen tells his son—
As deaf as Gog and Magog at one!
Or, still to be a simile-seeker,
As deaf as dogs'-ears to Enfield's Speaker!

She was deaf as any tradesman's dummy,
Or as Pharaoh's mother's mother's mummy;
Whose organs, for fear of our modern sceptics,
Were plugg'd with gums and antiseptics.

She was deaf as a nail—that you cannot hammer
A meaning into, for all your clamor—
There never *was* such a deaf old Gammer!
So formed to worry
Both Lindley and Murray,
By having no ear for Music or Grammar!

Deaf to sounds, as a ship out of soundings,
Deaf to verbs, and all their compoundings,
Adjective, noun, and adverb, and particle,
Deaf to even the definite article—
No verbal message was worth a pin,
Though you hired an earwig to carry it in!

In short, she was twice as deaf as Deaf Burke,
Or all the Deafness in Yearsley's Work,
Who in spite of his skill in hardness of hearing,
Boring, blasting, and pioneering,
To give the dunny organ a clearing,
Could never have cured Dame Eleanor Spearing.

Of course the loss was a great privation,
For one of her sex—whatever her station—
And none the less that the Dame had a turn
For making all families one concern,
And learning whatever there was to learn
In the prattling tattling Village of Tringham—

A's who wore silk? and who wore gingham?
And what the Atkins's shop might bring 'em?
How the Smiths contrived to live? and whether
The fourteen Murphys all pigg'd together?
The wages per week of the Weavers and Skinners,
And what they boil'd for their Sunday dinners?
What plates the Bugsbys had on the shelf,
Crockery, china, wooden, or delf?
And if the parlor of Mrs. O'Grady
Had a wicked French print, or Death and the Lady?
Did Snip and his wife continue to jangle?
Had Mrs. Wilkinson sold her mangle?
What liquor was drunk by Jones and Brown?
And the weekly score they ran up at the Crown?
If the Cobbler could read, and believed in the Pope?
And how the Grubbs were off for soap?
If the Snobbs had furnished their room up-stairs,
And how they managed for tables and chairs,
Beds, and other household affairs,
Iron, wooden, and Staffordshire wares;
  And if they could muster a whole pair of bellows?
In fact, she had much of the spirit that lies
Perdu in a notable set of Paul Prys,
  By courtesy called Statistical Fellows—
A prying, spying, inquisitive clan,
Who have gone upon much of the self-same plan,
  Jotting the Laboring Class's riches;
And after poking in pot and pan,
  And routing garments in want of stitches,
Have ascertained that a working man
  Wears a pair and a quarter of average breeches!

But this, alas! from her loss of hearing,
Was all a sealed book to Dame Eleanor Spearing;
  And often her tears would rise to their founts—
Supposing a little scandal at play
'Twixt Mrs. O'Fie and Mrs. Au Fait—
  That she couldn't audit the Gossips' accounts.

'T is true, to her cottage still they came,
And ate her muffins just the same,
And drank the tea of the widow'd Dame,
And never swallowed a thimble the less
Of something the reader is left to guess,
For all the deafness of Mrs. S.,
Who *saw* them talk, and chuckle, and cough,
But to *see* and not share in the social flow,
She might as well have lived, you know,
In one of the houses in Owen's Row,
Near the New River Head, with its water cut off!

And yet the almond-oil she had tried,
And fifty infallible things beside,
Hot, and cold, and thick, and thin,
Dabb'd, and dribbled, and squirted in:
But all remedies fail'd; and though some it was clear
(Like the brandy and salt
We now exalt)
Had made a noise in the public ear,
She was just as deaf as ever, poor dear!

At last—one very fine day in June—
Suppose her sitting,
Busily knitting,
And humming she did n't quite know what tune;
For nothing she heard but a sort of a whizz,
Which, unless the sound of the circulation,
Or of Thoughts in the Process of fabrication,
By a Spinning-Jennyish operation,
It 's hard to say what buzzing it is,
However, except that ghost of a sound,
She sat in a silence most profound—
The cat was purring about the mat,
But her Mistress heard no more of that
Than if it had been a boatswain's cat,
And as for the clock the moments nicking,
The Dame only gave it credit for ticking.
The bark of her dog she did not catch;

Nor yet the click of the lifted latch;
Nor yet the creak of the opening door;
Nor yet the fall of a foot on the floor—
But she saw the shadow that crept on her gown
And turn'd its skirt of a darker brown.

And lo! a man! a Pedlar? ay, marry,
With the little back-shop that such tradesmen carry,
Stock'd with brooches, ribbons, and rings,
Spectacles, razors, and other odd things,
For lad and lass, as Autolycus sings;
A chapman for goodness and cheapness of ware,
Held a fair dealer enough at a fair,
But deem'd a piratical sort of invader
By him we dub the "regular trader,"
Who luring the passengers in as they pass
By lamps, gay pannels, and mouldings of brass,
And windows with only one huge pane of glass,
And his name in gilt characters, German or Roman,
If he isn't a Pedlar, at least is a Showman!

However, in the stranger came,
And, the moment he met the eyes of the Dame,
Threw her as knowing a nod as though
He had known her fifty long years ago;
And presto! before she could utter "Jack"—
Much less "Robinson"—open'd his pack—
   And then from amongst his portable gear,
With even more than a Pedlar's tact,—
(Slick himself might have envied the act)—
Before she had time to be deaf, in fact—
   Popped a Trumpet into her ear.

      "There, Ma'am! try it!
      You needn't buy it—
The last New Patent—and nothing comes nigh it
For affording the Deaf, at little expense,
The sense of hearing, and hearing of sense!
A Real Blessing—and no mistake,

Invented for poor Humanity's sake;
For what can be a greater privation
Than playing Dumby to all creation,
And only looking at conversation—
Great Philosophers talking like Platos,
And members of Parliament moral as Catos,
And your ears as dull as waxy potatoes!
Not to name the mischievous quizzers,
Sharp as knives, but double as scissors,
Who get you to answer quite by guess
Yes for No, and No for Yes."
("That's very true," says Dame Eleanor S.)

"Try it again! No harm in trying—
I'm sure you'll find it worth your buying,
A little practice—that is all—
And you'll hear a whisper, however small,
Through an Act of Parliament party-wall,—
Every syllable clear as day,
And even what people are going to say—
  I would n't tell a lie, I would n't,
  But my Trumpets have heard what Solomon's could n't;
And as for Scott he promises fine,
But can he warrant his horns like mine
  Never to hear what a Lady should n't—
Only a guinea—and can't take less."
("That's very dear," says Dame Eleanor S.)

"Dear!—Oh dear, to call it dear!
Why it is n't a horn you buy, but an ear;
Only think, and you'll find on reflection
You're bargaining, Ma'am, for the Voice of Affection;
For the language of Wisdom, and Virtue, and Truth,
And the sweet little innocent prattle of youth;
Not to mention the striking of clocks—
Cackle of hens—crowing of cocks—
Lowing of cow, and bull, and ox—
Bleating of pretty pastoral flocks—
Murmur of waterfall over the rocks—

Every sound that Echo mocks—
Vocals, fiddles, and musical-box—
And zounds! to call such a concert dear!
But I must n't swear with my horn in your ear.
Why in buying that trumpet you buy all those
That Harper, or any trumpeter, blows
At the Queen's Levees or the Lord Mayor's Shows,
At least as far as the music goes,
Including the wonderful lively sound
Of the Guards' key-bugles all the year round
Come—suppose we call it a pound!
Come," said the talkative Man of the Pack,
"Before I put my box on my back,
For this elegant, useful Conductor of Sound,
Come—suppose we call it a pound!

"Only a pound! it's only the price
Of hearing a Concert once or twice,
        It's only the fee
        You might give Mr. C.,
And after all not hear his advice,
But common prudence would bid you stump it;
        For, not to enlarge,
        It's the regular charge
At a Fancy Fair for a penny trumpet.
Lord! what's a pound to the blessing of hearing!"
("A pound's a pound," said Dame Eleanor Spearing.)

"Try it again! no harm in trying!
A pound's a pound there's no denying;
But think what thousands and thousands of pounds
We pay for nothing but hearing sounds:
Sounds of Equity, Justice and Law,
Parliamentary jabber and jaw,
Pious cant and moral saw,
Hocus-pocus, and Nong-tong-paw,
And empty sounds not worth a straw;
Why it costs a guinea, as I'm a sinner,

To hear the sounds at a Public Dinner!
One pound one thrown into the puddle,
To listen to Fiddle, Faddle, and Fuddle!
Not to forget the sounds we buy
From those who sell their sounds so high,
That, unless the Managers pitch it strong,
To get a Signora to warble a song
You must fork out the blunt with a haymaker's prong!

"It 's not the thing for me—I know it,
To crack my own Trumpet up and blow it;
But it is the best, and time will show it.
There was Mrs. F.
So very deaf,
That she might have worn a percussion cap,
And been knock'd on the head without hearing it snap,
Well, I sold her a horn, and the very next day
She heard from her husband at Botany Bay!
Come—eighteen shillings—that 's very low,
You 'll save the money as shillings go,
And I never knew so bad a lot,
By hearing whether they ring or not!
Eighteen shillings! it 's worth the price,
Supposing you 're delicate-minded and nice,
To have the medical man of your choice,
Instead of the one with the strongest voice—
Who comes and asks you how 's your liver,
And where you ache, and whether you shiver,
And as to your nerves so apt to quiver,
As if he was hailing a boat on the river!
And then, with a shout, like Pat in a riot,
Tells you to keep yourself perfectly quiet!

"Or a tradesman comes—as tradesmen will—
Short and crusty about his bill,
Of patience, indeed, a perfect scorner,
And because you 're deaf and unable to pay,
Shouts whatever he has to say,
In a vulgar voice that goes over the way,

Down the street and round the corner,
Come—speak your mind—it's 'No or Yes'"
("I've half a mind," said Dame Eleanor S.)

"Try it again—no harm in trying,
Of course you hear me, as easy as lying;
No pain at all, like a surgical trick,
To make you squall, and struggle, and kick,
Like Juno, or Rose,
Whose ear undergoes
Such horrid tugs at membrane and gristle,
For being as deaf as yourself to a whistle!

"You may go to surgical chaps if you choose,
Who will blow up your tubes like copper flues,
Or cut your tonsils right away,
As you 'd shell out your almonds for Christmas-day;
And after all a matter of doubt,
Whether you ever would hear the shout
Of the little blackguards that bawl about,
'There you go with your tonsils out!'
Why I knew a deaf Welshman who came from Glamorgan
On purpose to try a surgical spell,
And paid a guinea, and might as well
Have called a monkey into his organ!
For the Aurist only took a mug,
And pour'd in his ear some acoustical drug,
That instead of curing deafen'd him rather,
As Hamlet's uncle served Hamlet's father!
That 's the way with your surgical gentry!
And happy your luck
If you don't get stuck
Through your liver and lights at a royal entry,
Because you never answer'd the sentry!
Try it again, dear Madam, try it!
Many would sell their beds to buy it.
I warrant you often wake up in the night,
Ready to shake to a jelly with fright.

And up you must get to strike a light,
And down you go, in you know what,
Whether the weather is chilly or not,—
That 's the way a cold is got,—
To see if you heard a noise or not!

"Why, bless you, a woman with organs like yours
Is hardly safe to step out of doors!
Just fancy a horse that comes full pelt,
But as quiet as if he was 'shod with felt,'
Till he rushes against you with all his force,
And then I needn't describe of course,
While he kicks you about without remorse,
How awkward it is to be groomed by a horse,
Or a bullock comes, as mad as King Lear,
And you never dream that the brute is near,
Till he pokes his horn right into your ear,
Whether you like the thing or lump it,—
And all for want of buying a trumpet!

"I 'm not a female to fret and vex,
But if I belonged to the sensitive sex,
Exposed to all sorts of indelicate sounds,
I wouldn't be deaf for a thousand pounds.
  Lord! only think of chucking a copper
To Jack or Bob with a timber limb,
Who looks as if he was singing a hymn,
  Instead of a song that 's very improper!
Or just suppose in a public place
You see a great fellow a-pulling a face,
With his staring eyes and his mouth like an O,—
And how is a poor deaf lady to know,—
The lower orders are up to such games—
If he 's calling 'Green Peas,' or calling her names?'
(" They 're tenpence a peck!" said the deafest of Dames.

"'Tis strange what very strong advising,
By word of mouth, or advertising,

By chalking on walls, or placarding on vans,
With fifty other different plans,
The very high pressure, in fact, of pressing,
It needs to persuade one to purchase a blessing!
Whether the Soothing American Syrup,
A safety Hat, or a Safety Stirrup,—
Infallible Pills for the human frame,
Or Rowland's O-don't-o (an ominous name)!
A Doudney's suit which the shape so hits
That it beats all others into *fits ;*
A Mechi's razor for beards unshorn,
Or a Ghost-of-a-Whisper-Catching Horn!

"Try it again, Ma'am, only try!"
Was still the voluble Pedlar's cry;
"It's a great privation, there's no dispute,
To live like the dumb unsociable brute,
And to hear no more of the *pro* and *con*,
And how Society's going on,
Than Mumbo Jumbo or Prester John,
And all for want of this *sine quâ non ;*
Whereas, with a horn that never offends,
You may join the genteelest party that is,
And enjoy all the scandal, and gossip, and quiz,
And be certain to hear of your absent friends;—
Not that elegant ladies, in fact,
In genteel society ever detract,
Or lend a brush when a friend is black'd,—
At least as a mere malicious act,—
But only talk scandal for fear some fool
Should think they were bred at *charity* school.
Or, maybe, you like a little flirtation,
Which even the most Don Juanish rake
Would surely object to undertake
At the same high pitch as an altercation.
It 's not for me, of course, to judge
How much a Deaf Lady ought to begrudge;
But half-a-guinea seems no great matter—

Letting alone more rational patter—
Only to hear a parrot chatter:
Not to mention that feather'd wit,
The Starling, who speaks when his tongue is slit;
The Pies and Jays that utter words,
And other Dicky Gossips of birds,
That talk with as much good sense and decorum
As many *Beaks* who belong to the quorum.

" Try it—buy it—say ten and six,
The lowest price a miser could fix:
I don't pretend with horns of mine,
Like some in the advertising line,
To '*magnify sounds*' on such marvellous scales,
That the sounds of a cod seem as big as a whale's;
But popular rumors, right or wrong,—
Charity Sermons, short or long,—
Lecture, speech, concerto, or song,
All noises and voices, feeble and strong,
From the hum of a gnat to the clash of a gong,
This tube will deliver distinct and clear;
        Or, supposing by chance
        You wish to dance,
Why, it's putting a *Horn-pipe* into your ear!
          Try it—buy it!
          Buy it—try it!
The last New Patent, and nothing comes nigh it,
   For guiding sounds to proper tunnel:
Only try till the end of June,
And if you and the Trumpet are out of tune,
   I'll turn it gratis into a Funnel!"

In short, the pedlar so beset her,—
Lord Bacon couldn't have gammon'd her better,—
With flatteries plump and indirect,
And plied his tongue with such effect,—
A tongue that could almost have butter'd a crumpet,—
The deaf Old Woman bought the Trumpet.

* * * * *

* * * * *

The Pedlar was gone. With the Horn's assistance,
She heard his steps die away in the distance;
And then she heard the tick of the clock,
The purring of puss, and the snoring of Shock;
And she purposely dropped a pin that was little,
And heard it fall as plain as a skittle!

'Twas a wonderful Horn, to be but just!
Nor meant to gather dust, must, and rust;
So in half a jiffy, or less than that,
In her scarlet cloak and her steeple-hat,
Like old Dame Trot, but without her Cat,
The Gossip was hunting all Tringham thorough,
As if she meant to canvass the borough,
  Trumpet in hand, or up to the cavity;—
And, sure, had the horn been one of those
The wild Rhinoceros wears on his nose,
  It couldn't have ripp'd up more depravity!

Depravity! mercy shield her ears!
'Twas plain enough that her village peers
  In the ways of vice were no raw beginners;
For whenever she raised the tube to her drum,
Such sounds were transmitted as only come
  From the very Brass Band of human sinners!
Ribald jest and blasphemous curse
(Bunyan never vented worse),
With all those weeds, not flowers, of speech
Which the Seven Dialecticians teach;
Filthy Conjunctions, and Dissolute Nouns,
And Particles pick'd from the kennels of towns,
With Irregular Verbs for irregular jobs,
Chiefly active in rows and mobs,
Picking Possessive Pronouns' fobs,

And Interjections as bad as a blight,
Or an Eastern blast, to the blood and the sight;
Fanciful phrases for crime and sin,
And smacking of vulgar lips where Gin,
Garlic, Tobacco, and offals go in—
A jargon so truly adapted, in fact,
To each thievish, obscene, and ferocious act,
So fit for the brute with the human shape,
Savage Baboon, or libidinous Ape,
From their ugly mouths it will certainly come
Should they ever get weary of shamming dumb!

Alas! for the voice of Virtue and Truth,
And the sweet little innocent prattle of youth!
The smallest urchin whose tongue could tang,
Shock'd the Dame with a volley of slang,
Fit for Fagin's juvenile gang;
While the charity chap,
With his muffin-cap,
His crimson coat, and his badge so garish,
Playing at dumps, or pitch in the hole,
Cursed his eyes, limbs, body, and soul,
As if they didn't belong to the Parish!

'Twas awful to hear, as she went along,
The wicked words of the popular song;
Or supposing she listen'd—as gossips will—
At a door ajar, or a window agape,
To catch the sounds they allow'd to escape,
Those sounds belong'd to Depravity still!
The dark allusion, or bolder brag
Of the dexterous "dodge," and the lots of "swag,"
The plunder'd house—or the stolen nag—
The blazing rick, or the darker crime
That quench'd the spark before its time—
The wanton speech of the wife immoral—
The noise of drunken or deadly quarrel,—
With savage menaces, which threaten'd the life,

Till the heart seem'd merely a strop "for the knife;"
The human liver, no better than that
Which is sliced and thrown to an old woman's cat;
  And the head, so useful for shaking and nodding,
To be punch'd into holes, like "a shocking bad hat"
  That is only fit to be punch'd into wadding!

In short, wherever she turn'd the horn,
To the highly bred, or the lowly born,
The working man who look'd over the hedge,
Or the mother nursing her infant pledge,
  The sober Quaker, averse to quarrels,
Or the Governess pacing the village through,
With her twelve Young Ladies, two and two.
Looking, as such young ladies do,
  Truss'd by Decorum and stuff'd with morals—
Whether she listen'd to Hob or Bob,
      Nob or Snob,
      The Squire on his cob,
Or Trudge and his ass at a tinkering job,
To the Saint who expounded at "Little Zion"—
Or the "Sinner who kept the Golden Lion"—
The man teetotally wean'd from liquor—
The Beadle, the Clerk, or the Reverend Vicar—
Nay, the very Pie in its cage of wicker—
She gather'd such meanings, double or single,
      That like the bell
      With muffins to sell,
Her ear was kept in a constant tingle!

But this was naught to the tales of shame,
The constant runnings of evil fame,
Foul, and dirty, and black as ink,
That her ancient cronies, with nod and wink,
Pour'd in her horn like slops in a sink:
  While sitting in conclave, as gossips do,
With their Hyson or Howqua, black or green,
And not a little of feline spleen

Lapp'd up in "Catty packages," too,
To give a zest to the sipping and supping;
For still by some invisible tether,
Scandal and Tea are link'd together,
As surely as Scarification and Cupping;
Yet never since Scandal drank Bohea—
Or sloe, or whatever it happen'd to be,
For some grocerly thieves
Turn over new leaves
Without much amending their lives or their tea—
No, never since cup was fill'd or stirr'd
Were such vile and horrible anecdotes heard,
As blacken'd their neighbors, of either gender,
Especially that which is call'd the Tender,
But instead of the softness we fancy therewith,
As harden'd in vice as the vice of a smith.

Women! the wretches! had soil'd and marr'd
Whatever to womanly nature belongs;
For the marriage tie they had no regard,
Nay, sped their mates to the sexton's yard
(Like Madame Laffarge, who with poisonous pinches
Kept cutting off her L by inches),
And as for drinking, they drank so hard
That they drank their flat-irons, pokers, and tongs!

The men—they fought and gambled at fairs;
And poach'd—and didn't respect grey hairs—
Stole linen, money, plate, poultry, and corses;
And broke in houses as well as horses;
Unfolded folds to kill their own mutton,
And would their own mothers and wives for a button—
But not to repeat the deeds they did,
Backsliding in spite of all moral skid,
If all were true that fell from the tongue,
There was not a villager, old or young,
But deserved to be whipp'd, imprison'd, or hung,
Or sent on those travels which nobody hurries
To publish at Colburn's, or Longman's, or Murray's.

Meanwhile the Trumpet, *con amore,*
Transmitted each vile diabolical story;
And gave the least whisper of slips and falls,
As that Gallery does in the Dome of St. Paul's,
Which, as all the world knows, by practice or print,
Is famous for making the most of a hint.
Not a murmur of shame,
Or buzz of blame,
Not a flying report that flew at a name,
Not a plausible gloss, or significant note,
Not a word in the scandalous circles afloat
Of a beam in the eye or diminutive mote,
But vortex-like that tube of tin
Suck'd the censorious particle in;
And, truth to tell, for as willing an organ
As ever listen'd to serpent's hiss,
Nor took the viperous sound amiss,
On the snaky head of an ancient Gorgon!

The Dame, it is true, would mutter "shocking!"
And give her head a sorrowful rocking,
And make a clucking with palate and tongue,
Like the call of Partlett to gather her young,
A sound, when human, that always proclaims
At least a thousand pities and shames,
But still the darker the tale of sin,
Like certain folks when calamities burst,
Who find a comfort in "hearing the worst,"
The farther she poked the Trumpet in.
Nay, worse, whatever she heard, she spread
East and West, and North and South,
Like the ball which, according to Captain Z
Went in at his ear, and came out at his mouth.

What wonder between the horn and the Dame,
Such mischief was made wherever they came,
That the Parish of Tringham was all in a flame!
For although it requires such loud discharges,

Such peals of thunder as rumbled at Lear,
To turn the smallest of table-beer,
A little whisper breathed into the ear
Will sour a temper "as sour as varges."
In fact such very ill blood there grew,
From this private circulation of stories,
That the nearest neighbors the village through,
Look'd at each other as yellow and blue
As any electioneering crew
Wearing the colors of Whigs and Tories.

Ah! well the Poet said, in sooth,
That whispering tongues can poison Truth,—
Yea, like a dose of oxalic acid,
Wrench and convulse poor Peace, the placid,
And rack dear Love with internal fuel,
Like arsenic pastry, or what is as cruel,
Sugar of lead, that sweetens gruel,
At least such torments began to wring 'em
From the very morn
When that mischievous Horn
Caught the whisper of tongues in Tringham.

The Social Clubs dissolved in huffs,
And the Sons of Harmony came to cuffs,
While feuds arose, and family quarrels,
That discomposed the mechanics of morals,
For screws were loose between brother and brother,
While sisters fasten'd their nails on each other.
Such wrangles, and jangles, and miff, and tiff,
And spar, and jar—and breezes as stiff
As ever upset a friendship or skiff!
The plighted Lovers, who used to walk,
Refused to meet, and declined to talk;
And wish'd for *two* moons to reflect the sun,
That they mightn't look together on one;
While wedded affection ran so low,
That the oldest John Anderson snubbed his Jo—

And instead of the toddle adown the hill,
Hand in hand,
As the song has planned,
Scratch'd her, penniless, out of his will!

In short, to describe what came to pass
In a true, though somewhat theatrical way,
Instead of "Love in a Village"—alas!
The piece they perform'd was "The Devil to Pay!"

However, as secrets are brought to light,
And mischief comes home like chickens at night;
And rivers are track'd throughout their course,
And forgeries traced to their proper source;—
And the sow that ought
By the ear is caught,—
And the sin to the sinful door is brought;
And the cat at last escapes from the bag—
And the saddle is placed on the proper nag;
And the fog blows off, and the key is found—
And the faulty scent is pick'd out by the hound—
And the fact turns up like a worm from the ground—
And the matter gets wind to waft it about;
And a hint goes abroad, and the murder is out—
And the riddle is guess'd—and the puzzle is known—
So the truth was sniff'd, and the Trumpet was *blown!*

* * * * * * *

'Tis a day in November—a day of fog—
But the Tringham people are all agog;
Fathers, Mothers, and Mothers' Sons,—
With sticks, and staves, and swords, and guns,—
As if in pursuit of a rabid dog;
But their voices—raised to the highest pitch—
Declare that the game is "a Witch!—a Witch!"

Over the Green, and along by the George—
Past the Stocks, and the Church, and the Forge,

And round the Pound, and skirting the Pond,
Till they come to the whitewash'd cottage beyond,
And there at the door they muster and cluster,
And thump, and kick, and bellow, and bluster—
Enough to put Old Nick in a fluster!
A noise, indeed, so loud and long,
And mix'd with expressions so very strong,
That supposing, according to popular fame,
"Wise Woman" and Witch to be the same,
No Hag with a broom would unwisely stop,
But up and away through the chimney-top;
Whereas, the moment they burst the door,
Planted fast on her sanded floor,
With her Trumpet up to her organ of hearing,
Lo and behold!—Dame Eleanor Spearing!

Oh! then arises the fearful shout—
Bawl'd and scream'd, and bandied about—
"Seize her!—Drag the old Jezebel out!"
While the Beadle—the foremost of all the band,
Snatches the Horn from her trembling hand—
And after a pause of doubt and fear,
Puts it up to his sharpest ear.

"Now silence—silence—one and all!"
For the Clerk is quoting from Holy Paul!
        But before he rehearses
        A couple of verses
The Beadle lets the Trumpet fall;
For instead of the words so pious and humble,
He hears a supernatural grumble.

Enough, enough! and more than enough;
Twenty impatient hands and rough,
By arm, and leg, and neck, and scruff,
Apron, 'kerchief, gown of stuff—
Cap, and pinner, sleeve, and cuff—
Are clutching the Witch wherever they can,

With the spite of Woman and fury of Man ;
And then—but first they kill her cat,
And murder her dog on the very mat—
And crush the Infernal Trumpet flat ;—
And then they hurry her through the door
She never, never, will enter more !

Away ! away ! down the dusty lane
They pull her, and haul her, with might and main ;
And happy the hawbuck, Tom or Harry,
Dandy, or Sandy, Jerry, or Larry,
Who happens to get " a leg to carry !"
And happy the foot that can give her a kick,
And happy the hand that can find a brick—
And happy the fingers that hold a stick—
Knife to cut, or pin to prick—
And happy the Boy who can lend her a lick ,—
Nay, happy the Urchin—Charity-bred,
Who can shy very nigh to her wicked old head !

Alas ! to think how people's creeds
Are contradicted by people's deeds !
  But though the wishes that Witches utter
Can play the most diabolical rigs—
Send styes in the eye—and measle the pigs—
  Grease horses' heels—and spoil the butter ;
Smut and mildew the corn on the stalk—
And turn new milk to water and chalk,—
Blight apples—and give the chickens the pip—
And cramp the stomach—and cripple the hip—
And waste the body—and addle the eggs—
And give a baby bandy legs ;
Though in common belief a Witch's curse
Involves all these horrible things, and worse—
As ignorant bumpkins all profess,
No Bumpkin makes a poke the less
At the back or ribs of old Eleanor S. !
  As if she were only a sack of barley ;

Or gives her credit for greater might
Than the Powers of Darkness confer at night
  On that other old woman, the parish Charley!

Ay, now's the time for a Witch to call
On her Imps and Sucklings one and all—
Newes, Pyewacket, or Peck in the Crown
(As Matthew Hopkins has handed them down),
Dick, and Willet, and Sugar-and Sack,
Greedy Grizel, Jarmara the Black,
Vinegar Tom and the rest of the pack—
Ay, now's the nick for her friend Old Harry
To come "with his tail" like the bold Glengarry,
And drive her foes from their savage job
As a mad Black Bullock would scatter a mob:—
  But no such matter is down in the bond;
And spite of her cries that never cease,
But scare the ducks and astonish the geese,
  The Dame is dragg'd to the fatal pond!

And now they come to the water's brim—
And in they bundle her—sink or swim;
Though it's twenty to one that the wretch must drown,
With twenty sticks to hold her down;
Including the help to the self-same end,
Which a travelling Pedlar stops to lend.
A Pedlar!—Yes!—The same!—the same!
Who sold the Horn to the drowning Dame!
And now is foremost amid the stir,
With a token only reveal'd to her;
A token that makes her shudder and shriek,
And point with her finger, and strive to speak—
But before she can utter the name of the Devil,
Her head is under the water-level!

MORAL.

There are folks about town—to name no names—
Who much resemble that deafest of Dames;

And over their tea, and muffins, and crumpets,
Circulate many a scandalous word,
And whisper tales they could only have heard
Through some such Diabolical Trumpets!

Note.

The following curious passage is quoted for the benefit of such Readers as are afflicted, like Dame Spearing, with Deafness, and one of its concomitants, a singing or ringing in the head. The extract is taken from "Quid Pro Quo; or, A Theory of Compensations. By P. S." (perhaps Peter Shard), folio edition.

"Soe tenderly kind and gratious is Nature, our Mother, that She seldom or never puts upon us any Grievaunce without making Us some Amends, which, if not a full and perfect Equivalent, is yet a great Solace or Salve to the Sore. As is notably displaid in the Case of such of our Fellow Creatures as undergoe the Loss of Heering, and are thereby deprived of the Comfort and Entertainment of Natural Sounds. In lew whereof the Deaf Man, as testified by mine own Experience, is regaled with an inward Musick that is not vouchsafed unto a Person who hath the compleet Usage of his Ears. For note, that the selfsame Condition of Boddy which is most apt to bring on a Surdity,—namely, a general Relaxing of the delicate and subtile Fibres of the Human Nerves, and mainly such as belong and propinque to the Auricular Organ, this very Unbracing which silences the Tympanum, or drum, is the most instrumental Cause in producing a Consort in the Head. And, in particular, that affection which the Physitians have called Tinnitus, by reason of its Resemblance to a Ring of Bells. The Absence of which, as a National Musick, would be a sore Loss and Discomfort to any Native of the Low Countryes, where the Steeples and Church-Towers with their Carillons maintain an allmost endlesse Tingle; seeing that before one quarterly Chime of the Cloke hath well ended, another must by Time's Command strike up its Tune. On which Account, together with its manye waterish Swamps and Marshes, the Land of Flandres is said by the Wits to be Ringing Wet. Such campanulary Noises would alsoe be heavily mist and lamented by the Inhabitants of that Ringing Island described in Rabelais his Works, as a Place constantly filled with a Corybantick Jingle Jangle of great, middle-sized, and little Bells: wherewith the People seem to be as much charmed as a Swarm of Bees with the Clanking of brazen Kettles and Pans. And which Ringing Island cannot of a surety be Barbadoes, as certain Authors have supposed, but rather our own tintinnabulary Island of Brittain, where formerly a Saxon could not soe much as quench a Fire or a Candle but to the tune of a Bell. And even to this day, next to the Mother Tongue, the one mostly used is in a Mouth of Mettal, and withal so loosely hung, that it must needs wag at all Times and on all Topicks. For your English Man is a mighty Ringer, and besides furnishing Bells to a Bellfry, doth hang them at the Head of his Horse, and at the Neck of his Sheep—on the Cap of his Fool, and on the Heels of his Hawk. And truly I have known more than one amongst my Country Men, who would undertake more Travel, and Cost besides, to hear a Peal of Grandsires, than they would bestow to look upon a Generation of Grandchildren. But alack! all these Bells with the huge Muscovite, and Great Tom of Lincoln to boot, be but as Dumb Bells to the Deaf Man: wherefore, as I said, Nature kindly steps in with a Compensation, to wit a Tinnitus, and converts his own Head into a Bellfry, whence he hath Peals enow, and what is more without having to pay the Ringers."

BOZ IN AMERICA.

SINCE the voyages of Columbus in search of the New World, and of Raleigh in quest of El Dorado, no visit to America has excited so much interest and conjecture as that of the author of "Oliver Twist." The enterprise was understood to be a sort of Literary Expedition, for profit as well as pleasure: and many and strange were the speculations of the reading public as to the nature and value of the treasures which would be brought home by Dickens on his return. Some persons expected a philosophical comparison of Washington's Republic with that of Plato; others anticipated a Report on the Banking System and Commercial Statistics of the United States; and some few, perhaps, looked for a Pamphlet on International Copyright. The general notion, however, was that the Transatlantic acquisitions of Boz would transpire in the shape of a Tale of American Life and Manners—and moreover that it would appear by monthly instalments in green covers, and illustrated by some artist with the name of Phiz, or Whiz, or Quiz.

So strong indeed was this impression, that certain blue-stockinged prophetesses even predicted a new Avatar of the celebrated Mr. Pickwick in slippers and loose trousers, a nankeen jacket, and a straw-hat, as large as an umbrella. Sam Weller was to re-appear as his help, instead of a footman, still full of droll sayings, but in a slang more akin to that of his namesake, the Clock-maker: while Weller, senior, was to revive on the box of a Boston long stage,—only calling himself Jonathan, instead of Tony, and spelling it with a G. A Virginian widow Bardell was a matter of course—and some visionaries even foresaw a slave-owning Mr. Snodgrass, a coon-hunting Mr. Winkle, a wide-awake Joe, and a forest-clearing Bob Sawyer.*

The fallacy of these guesses and calculations was first proved by the announcement of "American Notes for General Circulation," a title that at once dissipated every dream of a Clock-case, or a Club, and cut off all chance of a tale. Encouraged by the technical terms which seemingly had some reference to their own speculations, the money-mongers still held on faintly by their former opinions:—but the Romanticists were in despair, and reluctantly abandoned all hopes of a Pennsylvanian Nicholas Nickleby affectionately *darning his mother*—a new Yorkshire Mr. Squeers *flogging creation*—a *black* Smike—a brown Kate, and a Bostonian Newman Noggs, alternately swallowing a *cock-tail* and a *cobbler*.†

Still there remained enough in the announcement of American Notes, by C. Dickens, to strop the public curiosity to a keen edge. Numerous had been the writers on the land of the stars and stripes—a host of travelled ladies and gentlemen, liberals and illiberals, utilitarians and inutilitarians—human bowls of every bias had trundled over the United States without hitting, or in the opinion of the natives, even coming near the jack. The Royalist, missing the accustomed honors of Kings and Queens, saw nothing but a republican pack of knaves; the High Churchman, finding no established church, declared that there was no religion—the aristocrat swore that all was low and vulgar, because there were no servants in drab turned up with blue, or in green turned down with crimson—the radical was shocked by the caucus, the enthralment of public opinion, and the timidity of the preachers—the metaphysical philosopher was disgusted with the preponderance of the real over the ideal—the adventurer took fright at Lynch law, and the saintly abolitionist saw nothing but black angels and white devils. An impartial account of America and the Americans was still to seek, and accordingly the reading public on both sides of the Atlantic looked forward with anxiety

* With the wishes of these admirers of Boz we can in some degree sympathize: for what could be a greater treat in the reading way than the perplexities of a *squatting* Mr. Pickwick, or a *settling* Mrs. Nickleby?

† Not a horse and shoe-maker, but two sorts of American drink

and eagerness for the opinions of a writer who had proved by a series of wholesome fictions that his heart was in the right place, that his head was not in the wrong one, and that his hand was a good hand at description. One thing at least was certain, that nothing would be set down in malice; for, compared with modern authors in general, Boz is remarkably free from sectarian or anti-social prejudices, and as to politics he seems to have taken the long pledge against party spirit. And doubtless one of the causes of his vast popularity has been the social and genial tone of his works,—showing that he feels and acts on the true principle of the "*homo sum*"—a sum too generally worked as one in long Division instead of Addition.

In the mean time the book, after long budding in advertisement, has burst into a full leaf, and however disconcerting to those persons who had looked for something quite different, will bring no disappointment to such as can be luxuriously content with good sense, good feeling, good fun, and good writing. In the very first half-dozen of pages the reader will find an example of that cheerful practical philosophy which makes the best of the worst—that happy healthy spirit which, instead of morbidly resenting the deception of a too flattering artist, who had lithographed the ship's accommodations, joined with him in converting a floating cup-board into a *state-room*, and a cabin "like a hearse with windows in it," into a handsome *saloon*. But we must skip the voyage, though pleasantly and graphically described, and at once land Boz in Boston, where, suffering from that true *ground* swell which annoys the newly landed, he goes rolling along the pitching passages of the Tremont hotel "with an involuntary imitation of the gait of Mr. T. P. Cooke in a new nautical melodrama."

Now, Boston is the modern Athens of America. Its inhabitants, many of them educated in the neighboring university of Cambridge, are decidedly of a literary turn, and of course were not indifferent to the arrival of so distinguished an author in their city. Modesty, however, prevents him from recording in print the popular effervescence—the only fact which transpires is, that the first day being Sunday he was offered pews and sittings in churches and chapels, "enough for a score or two of grown up families." These courtesies, one and all, the traveller is obliged to decline for want of a change of dress,—a fortunate circumstance so far, that whilst the curious but serious Bostonians were congregated elsewhere, he was enabled, accompanied by only a score or so of little boys and girls of no particular persuasion, to take a survey and a clever sketch (p. 59) of the city. On Monday, the case was evidently altered; for, after a visit to the State-House (p. 61), he was compelled to take refuge from the mob, in a place where he could not be made a sight or a show of—the Massachusetts Asylum for the Blind. Here he saw the interesting Laura Bridgman, a poor little girl, blind, deaf, dumb, destitute of the sense of smell, and almost of that of taste, yet, thanks to a judicious and humane education, not altogether dark within, nor hapless without. The following picture is deeply touching; a mist comes over the clear eye in reading it.

"Like other inmates of the house she had a green ribbon bound over her eyelids. A doll she had dressed lay near upon the ground. I took it up and saw that she had made a green fillet such as she wore herself, and fastened it about its mimic eyes."

But the mob has dispersed; at least the bulk of it, for not counting the children, there remain but fourteen autograph-hunters, six phrenologists, four portrait-painters, seven booksellers, five editors, and nineteen ladies, with handsomely-bound books in their hands or under their arms, on the steps and about the door of the Blind Asylum. And there they may be still, for somehow Boz has given them the slip, and in the turning of a leaf is at *South* Boston, in the state hospital for the insane—not however as a patient—for he was once deranged by proxy in some other person's intellects,—but witnessing and admiring the rational and humane mode of treatment which, as at our own Hanwell Asylum, has replaced the brutal, brainless practice of the good old times when insanity was treated as a criminal offence,—the tortures abolished for felons were retained for lunatics, and their poor over-heated brains had as much chance of cooling as under the Plombières of the Inquisition. Let the reader who has a mother turn to page 176 for a peep at a whimsical old lady, in the Hartford establishment, and then let him think that some fifty years ago the poor dear old soul would have been fettered, perhaps scourged, for only fancying herself an antediluvian! But to lighten a sad subject, let us smile at a characteristic interview between Boz and an Ophelia, in the same house.

"As we were passing through a gallery on our way out, a well-dressed lady, of quiet and composed manners, came up, and proffering a slip of paper and a pen, begged that I would oblige her with an autograph. I complied, and we parted. I hope *she* is not mad (quoth the visitor) for I think I remember having had a few interviews like that with ladies out of doors."

Huzza! whoo-oop! A mob has gathered again, and before he has gone a page, Boz is obliged to get into the Boston House of Industry, thence into the adjoining Orphan Institution, and from that, but not mortally crushed, into the Hospital, all highly creditable establishments, except in one iron feature, "the eternal, accursed, suffocating, redhot demon of a stove, whose breath would blight the purest air under heaven:" and so it does—parching the lungs with baked air. We have had some experience of the nuisance in Germany; and never saw it lighted without wishing for a washerwoman, exorbitant in her charges, to blow it up. But we must push on, or the observed of all observers will be divided from us by a square mile of the Lowell Factory Millicents, "all dressed out with parasols and silk-stockings," not white or flesh-color, but blue, for these young women are decidedly literary, and besides subscribing to the circulating libraries, actually get up a periodical of their own!

"The large class of readers, startled by these facts, will exclaim with one voice, 'How very preposterous!' On my deferentially inquiring why, they will answer, 'These things are above their station.' In reply to that observation I would beg leave to ask what that station is."

What?—why, according to some of our moral stationers, the proper station for such people is the station-house, to which actors, singers, and dancers have so often been consigned in this country for acting, singing, and dancing upon too moderate terms. But better times seem to dawn—the licensing Justices begin to outvote the Injustices, and perhaps some day we shall have Playing and Dancing as well as Singing for the Million. Why not? Why should not the cheerful, amusing treatment which has proved so beneficial to the poor mad people, be equally advantageous to the poor sane ones?

But to return to the Lowell lasses.—Pshaw! cries a literary fine gentleman, carelessly penning a sonnet, like Sir Roger de Coverly's ancestor, with his glove on, "they are only a set of *scribbling millers*." No such thing. In the opinion of a very competent judge they write as well as most of our gifted creatures and talented pens, and their "Offering" may compare advantageously with a great many of the English Annuals. An opinion not hastily formed, be it noted, but after the reading of "400 solid pages from the beginning to the end." No wonder the gratified Authoresses escorted the Critic—as of course they did, to the Worcester railway, which on the 5th of February, 1842, was beset of course by an unusual crowd, behaving, of course, as another mob did afterwards at Baltimore, but which Boz evidently mistook for only an every-day ebullition of national curiosity.

"Being rather early, those men and boys who happened to have nothing particular to do, and were curious in foreigners, came (according to custom) round the carriage in which I sat, let down all the windows; thrust in their heads and shoulders; hooked themselves on conveniently by their elbows; and fell to comparing notes on the subject of my personal appearance, with as much indifference as if I were a stuffed figure. I never gained so much uncompromising information with reference to my own nose and eyes, the various impressions wrought by my mouth and chin on different minds, and how my head looks when it's viewed from behind, as on these occasions. Some gentlemen were only satisfied by exercising their sense of touch; and the boys (who are surprisingly precocious in America) were seldom satisfied, even by that, but would return to the charge over and over again. Many a budding President has walked into my room with his cap on his head and his hands in his pockets, and stared at me for two whole hours: occasionally refreshing himself with a tweak at his nose, or a draught from the water-jug, or by walking to the windows and inviting other boys in the street below, to come up and do likewise: crying, 'Here he is!—Come on!—Bring all your brothers!' with other hospitable entreaties of that nature."

Here is another speculator on the Phenomenon, who evidently

could not make up his mind whether the hairy covering of Boz was that of a real, or of a metaphorical Lion, p. 56.

"Finding that nothing would satisfy him, I evaded his questions after the first score or two, and in particular pleaded ignorance respecting the fur whereof my coat was made. I am unable to say whether this was the reason, but that coat fascinated him ever afterwards; he usually kept close behind me when I walked, and moved as I moved, that he might look at it the better; and he frequently dived into narrow places after me, at the risk of his life, that he might have the satisfaction of passing his hand up the back and rubbing it the wrong way."

From Worcester, still travelling like a Highland chieftain with his tail on, or a fugitive with a tribe of Indians on his trail, the illustrious stranger railed on to Springfield; but there his voluntary followers were *fixed*. The Connecticut river being luckily unfrozen, Boz embarked, designedly, as it appears, in a steam-boat of about "half-a-pony power," and altogether so diminutive, that the few passengers the craft would carry "all kept in the middle of the deck, lest the boat should unexpectedly tip over." But some buzz about Boz had certainly got before him, for at a small town on the way, the tiny steamer, or rather one of its passengers, was saluted by a gun considerably bigger than the funnel! (p. 174.) At Hartford, however, thanks to the Deaf and Dumb School, the common Gaol, the State Prison, and the Lunatic Asylum, the Dickens enjoyed four quiet days, and then embarked for New York in the New York,—

"Infinitely less like a steam-boat than a huge floating bath. I could hardly persuade myself indeed, but that the bathing establishment off Westminster Bridge, which I had left a baby, had suddenly grown to an enormous size; run away from home; and set up in foreign parts for a steamer."

At New York, in the Broadway, an ordinary man may find elbow-room; but Boz is no ordinary man, and accordingly for a little seclusion is glad to pay a visit to the famous Prison called the Tombs. But the mob, the male part at least, again separates, and the gaol visitor ventures forth, as it appears, a little prematurely.

"Once more in Broadway! Here are the same ladies in bright colors, walking to and fro, in pairs and singly; yonder *the very same light blue parasol which passed and repassed the hotel window twenty times while we were sitting there.*"

Heavens! what a prospect for a modest and a married man! Popularity is no doubt pleasant, and Boz is extremely popular, but popularity in America is no joke. It is not down in the book, but we happen to know, that between 8 and 10 A. M., it was as much as Dickens could do, with Mrs. Dickens's assistance, to write the required autographs. It was more than he could do, between ten and twelve, to even look at the hospitable albums that were willing to take the stranger in. And now, not to forget the blue ladies in the Broadway, and the sulphur-colored parasol, if he should happen to be recognized by yonder group of admirers and well-wishers, he will have, before one could spell temperance, to swallow sangaree, ginsling, a mint julep, a cocktail, a sherry cobbler, and a timber doodle! In such a case the only resource is in flight, and like a hunted lion, rushing into a difficult and dangerous jungle, Boz plunges at once into the most inaccessible back-slums of New York.

"This is the place: these narrow ways, diverging to the right and left, and reeking everywhere with dirt and filth. Such lives as are led here, bear the same fruits here as elsewhere. The coarse and bloated faces at the doors, have counterparts at home, and all the wide world over. Debauchery has made the very houses prematurely old. See how the rotten beams are tumbling down, and how the patched and broken windows seem to scowl dimly, like eyes that have been hurt in drunken frays. Many of these pigs live here. Do they ever wonder why their masters walk upright in lieu of going on all fours? and why they talk instead of grunting?"

But what are "these pigs?" Why, the very swine whence, under the New Tariff, we are to derive American pork and bacon; and accordingly Boz considerately furnishes his countrymen with a sketch of the breed.

"They are the city scavengers, these pigs. Ugly brutes they are; having for the most part, scanty brown backs, like the lids of old horse-hair trunks, spotted with unwholesome black blotches. They have long gaunt legs, too, and such peaked snouts, that if one of them could be persuaded to sit for his portrait, nobody would recognize it for a pig's likeness."

No—for they have no choppers. We know the animals well,

or at least their German cousins and Belgian brothers-in-law; and moreover, have tasted the bacon, which only wants fat to be streaky. But here is a livelier sample of a pig, who seems to have had a notion of Lynch Law.

"As we were riding along this morning, I observed a little incident between two youthful pigs, which were so very human as to be inexpressibly comical and grotesque at the time, though I dare say in telling, it is tame enough.

"One young gentleman (a very delicate porker with several straws sticking about his nose, betokening recent investigations in a dunghill) was walking deliberately on, profoundly thinking, when suddenly his brother, who was lying in a miry hole unseen by him, rose up immediately before his startled eyes, ghostly with damp mud. Never was a pig's whole mass of blood so turned. He started back at least three feet, gazed for a moment, and then shot off as hard as ever he could go: his excessively little tail vibrating with speed and terror like a distracted pendulum. But before he had gone very far, he began to reason with himself as to the nature of this frightful appearance; and as he reasoned, he relaxed his speed by gradual degrees, until at last he stopped, and faced about. There was his brother with the mud upon him glazing in the sun, yet staring out of the very same hole, perfectly amazed at his proceedings. He was no sooner assured of this, and he assured himself so carefully, that one may almost say he shaded his eyes with his hand to see the better, than he came back at a round trot, pounced upon him, and summarily took off a piece of his tail, as a caution to him to be careful what he was about for the future, and never to play tricks with his family any more."

But as usual, Boz was not allowed exclusively to please the pigs; and being hunted all along shore, he was obliged, like a deer *fort couru*, to take to the water, and was carried to the Long Island Jail, by a boat belonging to the establishment, and rowed by a crew of prisoners "dressed in a striped uniform of black and buff, in which they looked like faded tigers." Not a bad retinue, by the way, for a black and white Lion. In the Gaol, the Madhouse, and the Refuge for the Destitute, he again found a temporary repose, but even these retreats becoming at last uncomfortably crowded, he set off by railway for Philadelphia, with a longing eye, of course, to its *Solitary* Prison. But that he did not enjoy much *un*popularity on this journey, we may guess, when the travelling in the same carriage with Boz was too much for even Foxite taciturnity, and a Friend made such a desperate effort, as follows, to become an Acquaintance:

> "A mild and modest young Quaker, who opened the discourse by informing me, in a grave whisper, that his grandfather was the inventor of cold-drawn castor-oil. I mention the circumstance here, thinking it probable that this is the first occasion on which the valuable medicine in question was ever used as a conversational aperient."

The genuine drab color of this anecdote is as true in tone as the tints of Claude, and gives a renewed faith in the artist. The following picture seems equally faithful, though reminding us of some of the Author's fancy pieces. Look at it, gentle reader, and then cry with us, "God forgive the inventor of the system of burying criminals alive in stone coffins!"

> "The first man I saw was seated at his loom at work. He had been there six years, and was to remain, I think, three more. He had been convicted as a receiver of stolen goods, but denied his guilt, and said he had been hardly dealt by. It was his second offence.
>
> "He stopped his work when we went in, took off his spectacles, and answered freely to everything that was said to him, but always with a strange kind of pause first, and in a low thoughtful voice. He wore a paper hat of his own making, and was pleased to have it noticed and commended. He had very ingeniously manufactured a sort of Dutch clock from some disregarded odds and ends; and his *vinegar-bottle* served for the pendulum. Seeing me interested in this contrivance, he looked up at it with a good deal of pride, and said that he had been thinking of improving it, and that he hoped the hammer and a little piece of broken glass beside it 'would play music ere long.'
>
> "He smiled as I looked at these contrivances to while away the time; but when I looked from them to him, I saw that his lip trembled, and could have counted the beating of his heart. I forgot how it came about, but some allusion was made to his having a wife. He shook his head at the word, turned aside, and covered his face with his hands.
>
> "'But you are resigned now!' said one of the gentlemen, after a short pause, during which he had resumed his former manner.
>
> "'Oh yes, oh yes! I am resigned to it.'
>
> "'And are a better man, you think?'
>
> "'Well, I hope so: I'm sure I may be.'
>
> "'And time goes pretty quickly?'
>
> "'Time is very long, gentlemen, between these four walls!'
>
> "He gazed about him—Heaven only knows how wearily! as he said these words; and in the act of doing so, fell into a strange stare, as if he

had forgotten something. A moment afterwards he sighed heavily, put on his spectacles, and resumed his work."

* * * * * * * *

"On the haggard face of every man among these prisoners the same expression sat. I know not what to liken it to. It had something of that strained attention which we see upon the faces of the blind and deaf, mingled with a kind of horror, as though they had all been secretly terrified. In every little chamber that I entered, and at every grate through which I looked, I seemed to see the same appalling countenance. It lives in my memory with the fascination of a remarkable picture. Parade before my eyes a hundred men, with one of them newly released from this solitary suffering, and I would point him out."

* * * * * * * *

"That it makes the senses dull, and by degrees impairs the bodily faculties, I am quite sure. I remarked to those who were with me in this very establishment at Philadelphia, that the criminals who had been there long were deaf."

Of course they were; and all more or less advanced towards a state (to adapt a new word) of idiosyncrasy. Again we say, Heaven forgive the inventors of such a course of slow mental torture! who could reduce a fellow-creature to become such a clock-maker! The truth is, no Solitary System is consonant with humanity or Christianity. Whenever there shall be persons too good for this world, they may have a right to thus excommunicate those who are too bad for it—but as Porson said, not till then!

Nevertheless to a gentleman mobbed, elbowed, jammed, stared at, and shouted after, a few hours in such a quiet hermitage would be a relief: nay, Boz tells us that it was once found endurable for a much longer term, by a voluntary prisoner, who, unable to resist the bottle, applied, as a favor, for a solitary cell. The Board refused, and recommended total abstinence and the long pledge, but the toper, to make sure of temperance, entreated to be put in the *stone jug*.

"He came again, and again, and again, and was so very earnest and importunate, that at last they took counsel together, and said, 'He will certainly qualify himself for admission, if we reject him any more. Let us shut him up. He will soon be glad to go away, and then we shall get rid of him.' So they made him sign a statement, which would prevent his ever sustaining an action for false imprisonment, to the effect that his incarceration was voluntary, and of his own seeking; they requested him to take notice that the officer in attendance had orders to release him at any hour of the day or night, when he might knock upon his door for that purpose; but desired him to understand that, once going out, he would not be admitted any more. These conditions agreed upon, and he still remaining in the same mind, he was conducted to the prison, and shut up in one of the cells.

"In this cell, the man who had not the firmness to leave a glass of liquor standing untasted on a table before him—in this cell, in solitary confinement, and working every day at his trade of shoe-making, this man remained nearly two years. His health beginning to fail at the expiration of that time, the surgeon recommended that he should work occasionally in the garden; and as he liked the notion very much, he went about this new occupation with great cheerfulness.

"He was digging here one summer-day very industriously, when the wicket in the outer gate chanced to be left open: showing, beyond, the well-remembered dusty road and sun-burnt fields. The way was as free to him as to any man living, but he no sooner raised his head and caught sight of it, all shining in the sun, than, with the involuntary instinct of a prisoner, he cast away his spade, scampered off as fast as his legs would carry him, and never once looked back."

At Washington Boz had an interview with the American President, and, as might be expected, the great drawing-room, and the other chambers on the ground-floor, were "crowded to excess." No wonder that as soon as released from the throng, our traveller turned his thoughts towards the wilds and forests of the Far West; with a vague hankering after the vast solitude and quiet of a Prairie! But such delights are to be reached by a course no smoother than that of true love,—as witness the coaching on a Virginian road, with an American Mr. Weller.

"He is a negro—very black indeed. He is dressed in a coarse pepper-and-salt suit excessively patched and darned (particularly at the knees), grey stockings, enormous unblacked high-low shoes, and very short trousers. He has two odd gloves: one of parti-colored worsted, and one of leather. He has a very short whip, broken in the middle, and bandaged up with string. And yet he wears a low-crowned, broad-brimmed, black hat: faintly shadowing forth a kind of insane imitation of an English coachman! But somebody in authority cries 'Go ahead!' as I am making these observations. The mail takes the lead, in a four-horse wagon, and all the coaches follow in procession headed by No. 1.

"By the way, whenever an Englishman would cry 'All right!' an American cries 'Go ahead!' which is somewhat expressive of the national character of the two countries.

"The first half mile of the road is over bridges made of loose planks laid across two parallel poles, which tilt up as the wheels roll over them, and IN the river. The river has a clayey bottom, and is full of holes, so that half a horse is constantly disappearing unexpectedly, and can't be found again for some time.

"But we get past even this, and come to the road itself, which is a series of alternate swamps and gravel-pits. A tremendous place is close before us, the black driver rolls his eyes, screws his mouth up very round, and looks straight between the two leaders, as if he were saying to himself, 'We have done this before, but *now* I think we shall have a crash.' He takes a rein in each hand; jerks and pulls at both; and dances on the splash-board with both feet (keeping his seat of course), like the late lamented Ducrow on two of his fiery coursers. We come to the spot, sink down in the mire nearly to the coach-window, tilt on one side at an angle of forty-five degrees, and stick there. The insides scream dismally; the coach stops; the horses flounder; all the other six coaches stop; and their four and twenty horses flounder likewise; but merely for company, and in sympathy with ours. Then the following circumstances occur.

"BLACK DRIVER (to the horses).—'Hi!'

"Nothing happens. Insides scream again.

"BLACK DRIVER (to the horses).—'Ho!'

"Horses plunge, and splash the black driver.

"GENTLEMAN INSIDE (looking out).—'Why, what on airth—'

"Gentleman receives a variety of splashes and draws his head in again, without finishing his question, or waiting for an answer.

"BLACK DRIVER (still to the horses).—'Jiddy! Jiddy!'

"Horses pull violently, drag the coach out of the hole, and draw it up a bank; so steep, that the black driver's legs fly up into the air, and he goes back among the luggage on the roof. But he immediately recovers himself, and cries (still to the horses),

"'Pill!'

"No effect. On the contrary, the coach begins to roll back upon No. 2, which rolls back upon No. 3, which rolls back upon No. 4, and so on until No. 7 is heard to curse and swear, nearly a quarter of a mile behind.

"BLACK DRIVER (louder than before).—'Pill!'

"Horses make another struggle to get up the bank, and again the coach rolls backward.

"BLACK DRIVER (louder than before).—'Pe-e-e-ill!'

"Horses make a desperate struggle.

"BLACK DRIVER (recovering spirits).—'Hi, Jiddy, Jiddy, pill."

"Horses make another effort.

"BLACK DRIVER (with great vigor).—'Ally Loo! Hi, Jiddy, Jiddy. Pill. Ally Loo!'

"Horses almost do it.

"BLACK DRIVER (with his eyes starting out of his head).—'Lee, den. Lee, dere. Hi. Jiddy, Jiddy. Pill. Ally Loo. Lee-e-e-e-e!'

"They run up the bank, and go down again on the other side at a fearful pace. It is impossible to stop them, and at the bottom there is a deep hollow, full of water. The coach rolls frightfully. The insides scream. The mud and water fly about us. The black driver dances like a madman. Suddenly, we are all right, by some extraordinary means, and stop to breathe.

"A black friend of the driver is sitting on a fence. The black driver recognizes him by twirling his head round and round like a harlequin, rolling his eyes, shrugging his shoulders, and grinning from ear to ear. He stops short, turns to me, and says:

"'We shall get you through, sa, like a fiddle, and hope a please you when we get you through, sa. Old 'ooman at home, sir,' chuckling very much. 'Outside gentleman, sa, he often remember old 'ooman at home, sa,' grinning again.

"'Ay, ay, we'll take care of the old woman. Don't be afraid.'

"The black driver grins again, but there is another hole, and beyond that another bank, close before us. So he stops short: cries (to the horses again), 'Easy—easy den—ease—steady—hi—Jiddy—pill—Ally—Loo," but never 'Lee!' until we are reduced to the very last extremity, and are in the midst of difficulties, extrication from which appears to be all but impossible.

"And so we do the ten miles or thereabouts in two hours and a half, breaking no bones, though bruising a great many; and in short, getting through the distance 'like a fiddle.'"

The next conveyance was by the Harrisburg Canal, on which there are two passage-boats, the Express and the Pioneer. For some reason, however, the Pioneers *would* come into the other boat, in which Boz was a passenger—an addition that drew out a certain thin-faced, spare-figured man, of middle age and stature, dressed in a dusty, drabbish-colored suit, and up to that moment as quiet as a lamb.

"'This may suit *you*, this may, but it don't suit *me*. This may be all very well with Down Easters, and men of Boston raising, but it won't suit my figure, no how; and no two ways about *that;* and so I tell you. Now, I'm from the brown forests of the Mississippi, I am; and when the sun shines on me, it does shine—a little. It don't glimmer where *I* live, the sun don't. No. I'm a brown forester, I am. I an't a Johnny Cake. There are no smooth skins where I live. We're rough men, there. Rather. If Down Easters and men of Boston raising are like this, I'm glad of it, but I'm none of that raising or of that breed. No. This company wants a little fixing—*it* does. I'm the wrong sort of a man for 'em. *I* am. They won't like me, *they* won't. This is piling of it up a little too mountainous, this is.'

"At the end of every one of these short sentences he turned upon his heel, and walked the other way; checking himself abruptly when he had finished another short sentence, and turning back again. It is impossible for me to say what terrific meaning was hidden in the words of this brown forester, but I know that the other passengers looked on in a sort of admiring horror, and that presently the boat was put back to the wharf, and as many of the Pioneers as could be coaxed or bullied into going away were got rid of."

It was perfectly natural, after this "touch of the earthquake," to desire to see the Shakers, whose peculiar *delirium tremens* had been reported as unspeakably absurd: but the elders had clearly received a hint of a chield coming, like Captain Grose, to make Notes and print them.

"Presently we came to the beginning of the village, and alighting at the door of a house where the Shaker manufactures are sold, and which is the head-quarters of the elders, requested permission to see the Shaker worship.

"Pending the conveyance of this request to some person in authority, we walked into a grim room, where several grim hats were hanging on grim pegs, and the time was grimly told by a grim clock, which uttered every tick with a kind of struggle, as if it broke the grim silence reluctantly and under protest. Ranged against the wall were six or eight stiff, high-backed chairs, and they partook so strongly of the general grimness that one would much rather have sat on the floor than incurred the smallest obligation to any of them.

"Presently there stalked into this apartment a grim old Shaker, with eyes as hard, and dull, and cold, as the great round metal buttons on his coat and waistcoat: a sort of calm goblin. Being informed of our desire, he produced a newspaper wherein the body of elders, whereof he was a member, had advertised but a few days before, that, in consequence of certain unseemly interruptions which their worship had received from strangers, the chapel was closed for the space of one year."

The chapel will now be opened: for the chield is in England, and his Notes are not only printed but published, and by this time have been abundantly circulated, read, quoted, and criticised. Many of them, that will be canvassed elsewhere, are here left untouched, for obvious reasons; and various desirable extracts are omitted through want of space; for example, a pretty episode of a little woman with a little baby at St. Louis, and sundry sketches of scenery, character, and manners, as superior as "chicken fixings" to "common doings." We have nevertheless worked out our original intention. The political will discuss the author's notions of the republican institutions; the analytical will scrutinize his philosophy; the critical his style, and the hypocritical his denunciations of cant. Our only aim has been, according to the heading of this article, to give the reader a glimpse of Boz in America.

COPYRIGHT AND COPYWRONG.

LETTER I.

To the Editor of the Athenæum:

My dear Sir,—I have read with much satisfaction the occasional exposures in your Journal of the glorious uncertainty of the Law of Copyright, and your repeated calls for its revision. It is high time, indeed, that some better system should be established; and I cannot but regret that the legislature of our own country, which patronizes the great cause of liberty all over the world, has not taken the lead in protecting the common rights of Literature. We have a national interest in each; and their lots ought not to be cast asunder. The French, Prussian, and American governments, however, have already got the start of us, and are concerting measures for suppressing those piracies, which have become, like the influenza, so alarmingly prevalent. It would appear, from the facts established, that an English book merely *transpires* in London, but is *published* in Paris, Brussels, or New York.

> 'Tis but to sail, and with to-morrow's sun
> The pirates will be *bound.*

Mr. Bulwer tells us of a literary gentleman, who felt himself under the necessity of occasionally going abroad to preserve his self-respect; and without some change, an author will equally be obliged to repair to another country to enjoy his circulation. As to the American reprints, I can personally corroborate your assertion, that heretofore a transatlantic bookseller "has taken five hundred copies of a single work," whereas he now orders none, or merely a solitary one, to set up from. This, I hope, is a matter as important as the little question of etiquette, which, according to Mr. Cooper, the fifty millions will have to adjust. Before, however, any international arrangements be entered into, it seems only consistent with common sense that we should begin at home, and first establish what copyright *is* in Britain, and provide for its protection from native pirates or Book-aneers. I have learned, therefore, with pleasure, that the state of the law is to be brought under the notice of Parliament by Mr. Serjeant Talfourd, who, from his legal experience and literary tastes, is so well qualified for the task. The grievances of authors have neither been loudly nor often urged on Lords or Commons; but their claims have long been lying on the library table, if not on the table of the House,—and methinks their wrongs have only to be properly stated to obtain redress. I augur for them at least a good hearing, for such seldom and low-toned appeals ought to find their way to organs as "deaf to clamor" as the old citizen of Cheapside, who said that "the more noise there was in the street, the more he didn't hear it." In the meantime, as an author myself, as well as proprietor of copyrights in "a small way," I make bold to offer my own feelings and opinions on the subject, with some illustrations from what, although not a decidedly serious writer, I will call my experiences. And here I may appropriately plead my apology for taking on myself the cause of a fraternity of which I am so humble a member; but, in truth, this very position, which forbids vanity on my own account, favors my pride on that of others, and thus enables me to speak more becomingly of the deserts of my brethren, and the dignity of the craft. Like P. P. the Clerk of the Parish, who with a proper reverence for his calling, confessed an elevation of mind in only considering himself as "a shred of the linen vestment of Aaron," I own to an inward exultation at being but a Precentor, as it were, in that worship, which numbers Shakspeare and Milton amongst its priests. Moreover, now that the rank of authors, and the nature and value of literary property, are about to be discussed, and I hope established for ever, it becomes the duty of every literary man--as much as of a Peer when his Order is in question—to assert his station, and stand up manfully for the rights, honors, and privileges of the Profession to which he belongs. The question is not a mere sordid one—it is not a simple inquiry in what way the emoluments of literature may be best secured to the author or proprietors of a work; on the contrary, it involves a principle of grave importance, not only to literary men, but to those who love letters,—and, I will presume to say, to society at large. It has a moral as well as commercial bearing; for the Legislature will not only have to decide *directly*, by a formal act, whether the literary interest is worthy of a place beside the shipping interest, the landed interest, the funded interest, the manufacturing, and other public interests, but also it will have *indirectly* to determine whether literary men belong to the privileged class,—the higher, lower, or middle class,—the working class,—productive or unproductive class,—or, in short, to any class at all.* "Literary men," says Mr. Bulwer, "have not with us any fixed and settled position as men of letters." We have, like Mr. Cooper's American lady, no precedence. We are, in fact, nobodies. Our place, in turf language, is nowhere. Like certain birds and beasts of difficult classification, we go without any at all. We have no more caste than the Pariahs. We are on a par—according as we are scientific, theologic, imaginative, dramatic, poetic, historic, instructive, or amusing—with quack doctors, street-preachers, strollers, ballad-singers, hawkers of last dying speeches, Punch-and-Judies, conjorers, tumblers, and other "divarting vagabonds." We are as the Jews in the East, the Africans in the West, or the gipsies anywhere. We belong to those to whom nothing can belong. I have even misgivings—heaven help us—if an author have a parish! I have serious doubts if a work be a qualification for the workhouse! The law apparently cannot forget, or forgive, that Homer was a vagrant, Shakspeare a deer-stealer, Milton a rebel. Our very cracks tell against us in the statute; Poor Stoneblind, Bill the Poacher, and Radical Jack have been the ruin of our gang. We have neither character to lose nor property to protect. We

* At a guess, I should say we were classed, in opposition to a certain literary sect, as Inutilitarians

are by law—outlaws, undeserving of civil rights. We may be robbed, libelled, outraged with impunity, being at the same time liable, for such offences, to all the rigor of the code. I will not adduce, as I could do, a long catalogue of the victims of this system which seems to have been drawn up by the "Lord of Misrule," and sanctioned by the "Abbot of Unreason." I will select, as Sterne took his captive, a single author. To add to the parallel, behold him in a prison! He is sentenced to remain there during the monarch's pleasure, to stand three times in the pillory, and to be amerced besides in the heavy sum of two hundred marks. The sufferer of this threefold punishment is one rather deserving of a triple crown, as a man, as an author, and as an example of that rare commercial integrity which does not feel discharged of its debts, though creditors have accepted a composition, till it has paid them in full. It is a literary offence—a libel, or presumed libel, which has incurred the severity of the law; but the same power that oppresses him, refuses or neglects to support him in the protection of his literary character and his literary rights. His just fame is depreciated by public slanderers, and his honest, honorable earnings are forestalled by pirates. Of one of his performances no less than twelve surreptitious editions are printed, and 80,000 copies are disposed of at a cheap rate in the streets of London. I am writing no fiction, though of one of fiction's greatest masters. That captive is—for he can never die—that captive author is Scott's, Johnson's, Blair's, Marmontel's, Lamb's, Chalmers's, Beattie's—good witnesses to character these!—every Englishman's, Britain's, America's, Germany's, France's, Spain's, Italy's, Arabia's; all the world's Daniel De Foe!

Since the age of the author of Robinson Crusoe, the law has doubtless altered in complexion, but not in character, towards his race. It no longer pillories an author who writes to the distaste, or like poor Daniel, above the comprehension of the Powers that be, because it no longer pillories any one; but the imprisonment and the fines remain in force. The title of a book is, in legal phrase, the worst title there is. Literary property is the lowest in the market. It is declared by law worth only so many years' purchase, after which the private right be comes common; and in the meantime, the estate being notoriously infested with poachers, is as remarkably unprotected by game laws. An author's winged thoughts, though laid, hatched, bred, and fed within his own domain, are less his property than is the bird of passage that of the lord of the manor, on whose soil it may happen to alight. An author cannot employ an armed keeper to protect his preserves; he cannot apply to a pindar to arrest the animals that trespass on his grounds;—nay, he cannot even call in a common constable to protect his purse on the King's highway! I have had thoughts myself of seeking the aid of a policeman, but counsel, learned in the law, have dissuaded me from such a course; there was no way of defending myself from the petty thief but by picking my own pocket! Thus I have been compelled to see ny own name attached to catchpenny works, none of mine, hawked about by placard-men in the street; I, who detest the puffing system, have apparently been guilty of the gross forwardness of walking the pavement by proxy for admirers, like the dog Bashaw! I have been made, nominally, to ply at stage-coach windows with my wares, like Isaac Jacobs with his cheap pencils, and Jacob Isaacs with his cheap pen-knives, to cut them with:—and without redress, for, whether I had placed myself in the hands of the law, or taken the law in my own hands, as any bumpkin in a barn knows, there is nothing to be thrashed out of a man of straw. Now, with all humility, if my poor name be any recommendation of a book, I conceive I am entitled to reserve it for my own benefit. What says the proverb?—"When your name is up you may lie abed;" but what says the law?—at least, if the owner of the name be an author. Why, that any one may steal his bed from under him and sell it; that is to say, his reputation, and the revenue which it may bring. In the meantime, for other street frauds there is a summary process: the vender of a flash watch, or a razor made to sell, though he appropriates no maker's name, is seized without ceremony by A 1, carried before B 2, and committed to C 3, as regularly as a child goes through its alphabet and numeration. They have defrauded the public, forsooth, and the public has its prompt remedy; but for the literary man, thus doubly robbed, of his money and his reputation, what is his redress but by injunction, or action against walking shadows,—a truly homœopathic remedy, which pretends to cure by aggravating the disease. I have thus shown how an author may be robbed; for if the works thus offered at an unusually low price be genuine, they must have been dishonestly obtained—the brooms were stolen ready made; if, on the contrary, they be counterfeit, I apprehend there will be little difficulty in showing how an author may be practically libelled with equal impunity. For anything I know, the Peripatetic Philosophy ascribed to me by the above itinerants, might be heretical, damnable, libellous, vicious, or obscene; whilst, for anything they knew to the contrary, the purchasers must have held me responsible for the contents of the volumes which went abroad so very publicly under my name. I know, indeed, that parties thus deceived have expressed their regret and astonishment that I could be guilty of such prose, verse, and worse, as they had met with under my signature. I believe I may cite the well-known Mr. George Robins as a purchaser of one of the counterfeits; and if he, perhaps, eventually knocked me down as a street-preacher of infidelity, sedition, or immorality, it was neither his fault nor mine. I may here refer, *en passant*—for illustrations are plenty as blackberries—to a former correspondence in the *Athenæum*, in which I had, in common with Mr. Poole and the late Mr. Colman, to disclaim any connexion with a periodical in which I was advertised as a contributor. There was more recently, and probably still is, one Marshall, of Holborn Bars, who publicly claims me as a writer in his pay, with as much right to the imprint of my name, as a print collector has to the engravings in another man's portfolio; but against this man I have taken no rash steps, otherwise called legal, knowing that I might as well appear to Martial Law versus Marshall, as to any other. As a somewhat whimsical case, I may add the following:—Mr. Chappell, the music-seller, agreed to give me a liberal sum for the use of any ballad I might publish; and another party, well known in the same line, applied to me for a formal permission to publish a little song of mine, which a lady had done me the honor of setting to an original melody. Here seemed to be a natural recognition of copyright, and the moral sense of justice standing instead of law; but in the meantime a foreign composer—I forget his name, but it was set in G——, took a fancy to some of my verses, and without the semiquaver of a right, or the demisemiquaver of an apology, converted them to his own use. I remonstrated, of course; and the reply, based on the assurance of impunity, not only admitted the fact, but informed me that Monsieur, not finding my lines agree with his score, had taken the liberty of altering them at my risk. Now, I would confidently appeal to the highest poets in the land, whether they do not feel it quite responsibility enough to be accountable for their own lays in the mother tongue; but to be answerable also for the attempts in English verse by a foreigner—and, above all, a Frenchman—is really too much of a bad thing!

Would it be too much to request of the learned Serjeant who has undertaken our cause, that he would lay these cases before Parliament? Noble Lords and Honorable Gentlemen come down to their respective Houses, in a fever of nervous excitement, and shout of "Privilege! Breach of Privilege!" because their speeches have been erroneously reported, or their meaning garbled in perhaps a single sentence; but how would they relish to see whole speeches,—nay, pamphlets,—they had never uttered or written, paraded, with their names, styles, and titles at full length, by those placarding walkers, who, like fathers of lies, or rather mothers of them, carry one staring falsehood pickaback, and another at the bosom? How would those gentlemen like to see extempore versions of their orations done into English by a native of Paris, and published, as the pig ran, down all sorts of streets? Yet to similar nuisances are authors exposed without adequate means of abating them. It is often better, I have been told, to abandon one's rights than to defend them at law,—a sentence that will bear a particular application to literary grievances. For instance, the law would have something to say to a man who claimed his neighbor's umbrella as his own parasol, because he had cut off a bit round the rim: yet, by something of a similar process, the better part of a book may be appropriated—and this is so *civil* an offence, that any satisfaction at law is only to be obtained by a very costly and doubtful course. There was even a piratical work, which,—to adopt Burke's paradoxical style,—disingenuously ingenuous and dishonestly honest, assumed the plain title of "The Thief," professing, with the connivance of the law, to steal all its materials. How this Thief died I know not; but as it was a literary thief, I would lay long odds that the law was not its finisher.

These piracies are naturally most injurious to those authors whose works are of a fugitive nature, or on topics of temporary interest; but there are writers of a more solid stamp—of a higher order of mind, or nobler ambition, who devote themselves to the production of works of permanent value and utility. Such works often creep but slowly into circulation and repute, but then become classics for ever. And what encouragement or reward does the law hold forth to such contributors to our Standard National Literature? Why, that after a certain lapse of years, coinciding probably with the term requisite to establish the sterling character of the work, or, at least, to procure its general recognition—then, aye, just then, when the literary property is realized, when it becomes exchangeable against the precious metals which are considered by some political and more practical economists as the standard of value—the law decrees that then all right or interest in the book shall expire in the author, and by some strange process, akin to the Hindoo transmigrations, revive in the great body of the booksellers. And here arises a curious question. After the copyright has so lapsed, suppose that some speculative publisher, himself an amateur writer, should think fit to abridge or expand the author's matter—extenuate or aggravate his arguments—French polish his style—Johnsonize his phraseology—or even, like Winifred Jenkins, wrap his own "bit of nonsense under his Honor's kiver,"—is there any legal provision extant to which the injured party could appeal for redress of such an outrage on all that is left to him, his reputation? I suspect there is none whatever. There is yet another singular result from this state of the law, which I beg leave to illustrate by my own case. If I may modestly appropriate a merit, it is that, whatever my faults, I have at least been a decent writer. In a species of composition, where, like the ignis fatuus that guides into a bog, a glimmer of the ludicrous is apt to lead the fancy into an indelicacy, I feel some honest pride in remembering that the reproach of impurity has never been cast upon me by my judges. It has not been my delight to exhibit the Muse, as it has tenderly been called, "high-kilted." I have had the gratification, therefore, of seeing my little volumes placed in the hands of boys and girls; and as I have children of my own, to, I hope, survive me, I have the inexpressible comfort of thinking that hereafter they will be able to cast their eyes over the pages inscribed with my name, without a burning blush on their young cheeks to reflect that the author was their father. So whispers Hope, with the dulcet voice and the golden hair; but what thunders Law, of the iron tone and the frizzled wig? "Decent as thy Muse may-be now—a *delicate* Ariel—she shall be indecent and indelicate hereafter! She shall class with the bats and the fowls obscene! The slow reward of thy virtue shall be the same as the prompt punishment of vice. Thy copyright shall depart from thee—it shall be everybody's and anybody's, and 'no man shall call it his own!'"

Verily, if such be the proper rule of copyright, for the sake of consistency two very old copywriters should be altered to match, and run thus:—"Virtue is its own *punishment*."—"Age commands *disrespect*!"

To return to the author, whose fame is slow and sure—to be its own reward,—should he be dependent, as is often the case, on the black and white bread of literature—should it be the profession by which he lives, it is evident that under such a system he must beg, run into debt, or starve. And many have been beggars—many have got into debt; it is hardly possible to call up the ghost of a literary hero, without the apparition of a catchpole at his elbow, for, like Jack the Giant-killer, our elder worthies, who had the Cap of Knowledge, found it equally convenient to be occasionally invisible, as well as to possess the Shoes of Swiftness,—and some have starved! Could the "Illustrious Dead" arise, after some Anniversary Dinner of the Literary Fund, and walk in procession round the table, like the resuscitated objects of the Royal Humane Society, what a melancholy exhibition they would make! I will not marshal them forth in order, but leave the show to the imagination of the reader. I doubt whether the Illustrious Living would make a much brighter muster. Supposing a general summons, how many day-rules—how many incognitos from abroad—how many visits to Monmouth Street would be necessary to enable the members to put in an appearance! I fear, heaven forgive me! some of our nobles even would show only Three Golden Balls in their coronets! If we do not actually starve or die by poison in this century, it is, perhaps, owing partly to the foundation of the Literary Fund, and partly to the invention of the Stomach Pump; but the truly abject state of Literature may be gathered from the fact, that, with a more accurate sense of the destitution of the Professors, than of the dignity of the Profession, a proposal has lately been brought forward for the erection of alms-houses for paupers of "learning and genius," who have fallen into the sere and yellow leaf, under the specious name of Literary *Retreats*, or, as a military man would technically and justly read such a record of our failures, Literary *Defeats*. Nor is this the climax: the proposal names half a dozen of these humble abodes to "make a beginning" with—a mere brick of the building—as if the projector, in his mind's eye, saw a whole Mile End Road of one-storied tenements in the shell, stretching from Number Six—and "to be continued!"

Visions of paupers, spare my aching sight,
Ye unbuilt houses, crowd not on my soul!

I do hope, before we are put into yellow-leather very small-clothes, muffin-caps, green-baize coats and badges,—and made St. Minerva's charity-boys at once,—for *that* must be the first step,—that the Legislature will interfere, and endeavor to provide better for our sere and yellow leaves, by protecting our black and white ones. Let the law secure to us a fair chance of getting our own, and perhaps, with proper industry, we may be able—who knows?—to build little snuggeries for ourselves. Under the present system, the chances are decidedly against a literary man's even laying a good foundation of French bricks. To further illustrate the nature of a copyright, we will suppose that an author retains it, or publishes, as it is called, on his own account. He will then have to divide amongst the trade, in the shape of commission, allowances, &c., from 40 to 45 per cent. of the gross proceeds, leaving the Stationer, Printer, Binder, Advertising, and all other expenses to be paid out of the remainder. And here arise two important contingencies. 1st. In order that the author may know the true number of the impression, and, consequently, the correct amount of the sale, it is necessary that his publisher should be honest. 2dly. For the author to duly receive his profits, his publisher must be solvent. I intend no disrespect to the trade in general by naming these conditions; but I am bound to mention them, as risks adding to the insecurity of the property: as two hurdles which the rider of Pegasus may have to clear in his course to be a winner. If I felt inclined to reflect on the trade, it would be to censure those dishonest members of it, who set aside a principle in which the interests of authors and booksellers are identical—the inviolability of copyright. I need not point out the notorious examples of direct piracy at home, which have made the foreign offences comparatively venial; nor yet those more oblique plagiarisms, and close parodies, which are alike hurtful in their degree. Of the evil of these latter practices I fear our bibliopoles are not sufficiently aware; but that man deserves to have his head published in foolscap, who does not see that whatever temporary advantages a system of piracy may hold out, the consequent swamping of Literature will be ruinous to the trade, till eventually it may dwindle down to Four-and-Twenty Booksellers all in a Row,—and all in "the *old* book line," pushing off back-stock and bartering remainders.

But my letter is exceeding all reasonable length, and I will reserve what else I have to say till next post.

LETTER II.

To the Editor of the Athenæum:

My Dear Sir,—I have, perhaps, sufficiently illustrated the state of copyright, bad as it is, without the help of Foreign intervention: not, however, without misgivings that I shall be suspected of quoting from some burlesque code, drawn up by a Rabelais in ridicule of the legislative efforts of a community of ourang-outangs—or a sample by Swift, of the Constitution of the Sages of Laputa. I have proved that literary property might almost be defined, reversing the common advertisement, as something of use to everybody but the owner. To guard this precarious possession I have shown how the law provides, 1st, That if a work be of temporary interest it shall virtually be free for any Bookaneer to avail himself of its pages and its popularity with impunity. 2dly. That when time has stamped a work as of permanent value, the copyright shall belong to anybody or nobody. I may now add,—as if to "huddle jest upon jest,"—that the mere registry of a work, to entitle it to this precious protection, incurs a fee of eleven copies—in value, it might happen, some hundreds of pounds! Then to protect the author,—"aye, such protection as vultures give to lambs,"—I have instanced how he is responsible for all he writes—and subject, for libel and so forth, to fines and imprisonments—how he may libel by proxy—and how he may practically be libelled himself without redress. I have evidenced how the law, that protects his brass-plate on the door, will wink at the stealing of his name by a brazen pirate; howbeit the author, for only accommodating himself by a forgery, might be transported beyond seas. I have set forth how, though he may not commit any breach of privilege, he may have his own words garbled, Frenchified, transmogrified, garnished, taken in or let out, like old clothes, turned, dyed and altered. I have proved, in short, according to my first position, that in the evil eye of the law, "we have neither character to lose nor property to protect,"—that there is "one law for the rich and another for the poor" (alias authors)—and that the weights and scales which Justice uses in literary matters ought to be broken before her face by the petty jury.

And now let me ask, is this forlorn state—its professors thus degradingly appreciated, its products thus shabbily appraised—the proper condition of literature? The liberty of the press is boasted of as a part of the British constitution: but might it not be supposed that, in default of a censorship, some cunning Machiavel had devised a sly underplot for the discouragement of letters—an occult conspiracy to present "men of learning and genius" to the world's eye in the pitiful plight of poor devils, starvelings, mumpers, paupers, vagrants, loose fish, jobbers, needy and seedy ones, nobodies, ne'er-do-weels, shy coves, strollers, creatures, wretches, objects, small debtors, borrowers, dependents, lackpennies, half-sirs, clapper-dudgeons, scamps, insolvents, maunderers, blue-gowns, bedesmen, scarecrows, fellows about town, sneaks, scrubs, shabbies, rascal deer of the herd, animals "wi' letter'd braw brass collars"—but poor dogs for all that? Our family tree is ancient enough, for it is coeval with knowledge; and Mythology, the original Herald's College, has assigned us a glorious blazonry. But would not one believe that some sneering Mephistopeles, willing to pull down "God Almighty's gentlemen," had sought to supply the images of their heraldry with a scurvier gloss; e. g. a Lady Patroness with an ægis, that gives more stones than bread: a Patron who dispenses sunshine in lieu of coal and candle: nine elderly spinsters, who have never married for want of fortune: a horse with wings, that failing oats he may fly after the chaff that is driven before the wind: a forked mount, and no knife to it: a lot of bay-leaves—and no custards: a spring of Adam's ale! In fact, all the standing jests and taunts at authors and authorship, have their point in poverty: such as Grub-street—first floors down the chimney—sixpenny ordinaries—second hand suits—shabby blacks, holes at the elbow—and true as epaulette to the shoulder the hand of the bumbailiff!

Unfortunately, as if to countenance such a plot as I have hypothetically assumed above, there is a marked disproportion, as compared with other professions, in the number of literary men who are selected for public honors and employments. So far indeed from their having, as a body, any voice in the senate, they have scarcely a vote at the hustings; for the system under which they suffer is hardly adapted to make them forty-shilling freeholders, much less to enable them to qualify for seats in the House. A jealous-minded person might take occasion to say, that this was but a covert mode of effecting the exclusion of men whom the gods have made poetical, and whose voices might sound more melodious and quite as pregnant with meaning as many a *vox et præterea nihil* that is lifted up to Mr. Speaker. A literary man, indeed,—Sheridan,—is affirmed by Lord Byron to have delivered the best speech that was ever listened to in Parliament,—and it would even add force to the insinuation that the rotten boroughs, averred to be the only gaps by which men merely rich in learning and genius could creep into the Commons, have been recently stopped up. Of course such a plot cannot be entertained; but in the meantime the effect is the same, and whilst an apparent slight is cast upon literature, the senate has probably been deprived of the musical wisdom of many wonderful Talking Birds, through the want of the Golden Waters. For instance, it might not only be profitable to hear such a man as Southey, who has both read history and written history, speak to the matter in hand, when the affairs of nations are discussed, and the beacon lights of the past may be made to reflect a guiding ray into the London-like fogs of the future. I am quite aware that literary genius *per se* is not reckoned a sufficient qualification for a legislator:—perhaps not—but why is not a poet as competent to discuss questions concerning the public welfare, the national honor, the maintenance of morals and religion, or the education of the people, as a gentleman, without a touch of poetry about him, who had been schooling his intellects for the evening's debate by a course of morning whist? Into some of these honorary memberships, so to speak, a few distinguished men of letters might be safely franked—and if they did not exactly turn up trumps—I mean as statesmen,—they would serve to do away with an awkward impression that literature, which as a sort of Natural religion is the best ally of the Revealed one, has been kindly denied any share in that affectionate relationship which obtains between Church and State. As for the Upper House, I will not presume to say whether the dignity of that illustrious assembly would have been impaired or otherwise by the presence of a Baron with the motto of *Poeta nascitur, non fit;* supposing Literature to have taken a seat in the person of Sir Walter Scott beside the Lords of law and war. It is not for me to decide whether the brain-bewitching art be worthy of such high distinction as the brain-bewildering art, or that other one described by a bard, himself a Peer; but in the absence of such creations it seems a peculiar hardship that men of letters should not have been selected for distinctions; the "Blue Ribbon of Literature" for instance, most legitimately their due. Finally, as if to aggravate these neglects, literary men have not been consoled, as is usual, for the loss of more airy gratifications by a share in what Justice Greedy would call "the substantials, Sir Giles, the substantials." They have been treated as if they were unworthy of public employments, at least with two exceptions—Burns, who held a post very much under Government, and Wordsworth, who shares the reproach of "the loaves and fishes" for penny rolls and sprats. The want of business-like habits, it is true, has been alleged against the fraternity; but even granting such deficiency, might not the most practical Idlers, Loungers and Ramblers of them all fill their posts quite as efficiently as those personages who are paid for having nothing to do, and never neglect their duty? Not that I am an admirer of sinecures, except in the Irishman's acceptation of the word;* but may not such bonuses to gentlemen who write as little as they well can, viz., their names to the receipts, appear a little like a wish to discountenance those other gentlemen who write as much as they well can, and are at the expense of printing it besides?

I had better here enter a little protest against these remarks being mistaken for the splenetic and wrathful ebullitions of a morbid or addled egotism. I have not "deviated into the gloomy vanity of drawing from self;" I charge the State, it is true, with backing literature as the champion backed Cato—that is to say, tail foremost—but I am far from therefore considering myself as an overlooked, underkept, wet-blanketed, hid-under-a-bushel, or lapped-in-a-napkin individual. I have never, to my knowledge, displayed any remarkable aptitude for business, any decided predilection for politics, or unusual mastery in political economy—any striking talent at "a multiplicity of talk,"—and

* One Patrick Maguire. He had been appointed to a situation the reverse of a place of all work; and his friends, who called to congratulate him, were very much astonished to see his face lengthen on receipt of the news. "A sinecure is it!" exclaimed Pat. "The divil thank them for that same. Sure I know what a sinecure is. It's a place where there's nothing to do, and they pay ye by the piece."

withal, I am a very indifferent hand at a rubber. I nave never, like Bubb Doddington, expressed a determined ambition "to make a public figure—I had not decided what, but a public figure I was resolved to make." Nay, more, in a general view, I am not anxious to see literary men "giving up to a party what was meant for mankind," or hanging like sloths on the "branches of the revenue," or even engrossing working situations, such as gauger-ships, to the exclusion of humbler individuals, who, like Dogberry, have the natural gifts of reading and writing, and nothing else. Neither am I eager to claim for them those other distinctions, titles and decorations, the dignity of which requires a certain affluence of income for its support. A few orders indeed, domestic or foreign, conferred through a bookseller, hang not ungracefully on an author, at the same time that they help to support his slender revenue; but there would be something too ludicrous even for my humor, in a star—and no coat; a Garter—and no stocking; a coronet—and no nightcap; a collar—and no shirt! Besides, the creatures have, like the glow-worm and the firefly (but at the head instead of the tail), a sort of splendor of their own, which makes them less in need of any adventitious lustre. If I have dwelt on the dearth of state patronage, public employments, honors and emoluments, it was principally to correct a Vulgar Error, not noticed by Sir Thomas Browne; namely, that poets and their kind are "marigolds in the sun's eye,"—the world's favorite and pet children; whereas they are in reality its snubbed ones. It was to show that Literature, neglected by the government, and unprotected by the law, was placed in a false position; whereby its professors present such anomalous phenomena as high priests of knowledge—without a surplus; enlarged minds in the King's Bench; schoolmasters obliged to be abroad; great scholars without a knife and fork and spoon; master minds at journeywork; moral magistrates greatly unpaid; immortals without a living; menders of the human heart breaking their own; mighty intellects begrudged their mite; great wits jumping into nothing good; ornaments to their country put on the shelf; constellations of genius under a cloud; eminent pens quite stumped up; great lights of the age with a thief in them; prophets to booksellers;—

my ink almost blushes from black to red whilst marking such associations of the divine ore with the earthly—but, methinks, 'tis the metal of one of the scales in which we are weighed and found wanting. Poverty is the badge of all our tribe, and its reproach. There is, for instance, a well-known taunt against a humble class of men, who live by their pens, which, girding not at the quality of their work, but the rate of its remuneration, twits them as penny-a-liners! Can the world be aware of the range of the shaft? What pray, was glorious John Milton, upon whom rested an after-glow of the holy inspiration of the sacred writers, like the twilight bequeathed by a mid-summer sun? Why he was, as you may reckon any time in his divine Paradise Lost, not even a ha'penny-a-liner! We have no proof that Shakspeare, the high priest of humanity, was even a farthing-a-liner, and we know that Homer not only sold his lines "gratis for nothing," but gave credit to all eternity! If I wrong the world I beg pardon—but I really believe it invented the phrase of the *republic* of letters, to insinuate that taking the whole lot of authors together, they have not got a *sovereign* amongst them!

I have now reduced Literature, as an arithmetician would say, to its lowest terms. I have shown her like Misery,—

For Misery is trodden on by many,
And, being low, never relieved by any,—

fairly ragged, beggar'd, and down in the dust, having been robbed of her last farthing by a pickpocket (that's a pirate). There she sits, like Diggon Davie—"Her was her while it was daylight, but now her is a most wretched wight," or rather like a crazy Kate; a laughing-stock for the mob (that's the world), unprotected by the constable (that's the law), threatened by the beadle (that's the law too), repulsed from the workhouse by the overseer (that's the government), and denied any claim on the parish funds. Agricultural distress is a fool to it! One of those counterfeit cranks, to quote from "The English Rogue," "such as pretend to have the falling sickness, and by putting a piece of white soap into the corner of their mouths will make the froth come boiling forth, to cause pity in the beholders."

If we inquire into the causes of this depression, some must undoubtedly be laid at the doors of literary men themselves; but perhaps the greater proportion may be traced to the want of any definite ideas amongst people in general, on the following particulars:—1. How an author writes. 2. Why an author writes. 3. What an author writes. And firstly, as to how he writes, upon which head there is a wonderful diversity of opinions; one thinks that writing is "as easy as lying," and pictures the author sitting carefully at his desk "with his glove on," like Sir Roger de Coverley's poetical ancestor. A second holds that "the easiest reading is d—d hard writing," and imagines Time himself beating his brains over an extempore. A third believes in inspiration, i. e., that metaphors, quotations, classical allusions, historical illustrations, and even dramatic plots—all come to the waking author by intuition; whilst ready-made poems, like Coleridge's Kubla Khan, are dictated to him in his sleep. Of course the estimate of his desert will rise or fall according to the degree of learned labor attributed to the composition: he who sees in his mind's eye a genius of the lamp, consuming gallons on gallons of midnight oil—will assign a rate of reward, regulated probably by the success of the Hull whalers; whilst the believer in inspiration will doubtless conceive that the author ought to be fed as well as prompted by miracle, and accordingly bid him look up, like the apostle on the old Dutch tiles, for a bullock coming down from heaven in a bundle. 2dly. *Why* an author writes; and there is as wide a patchwork of opinions on this head as on the former. Some think that he writes for the present—others, that he writes for posterity—and a few, that he writes for antiquity. One believes that he writes for the benefit of the world in general—his own excepted—which is the opinion of the law. A second conceives that he writes for the benefit of booksellers in particular—and this is the trade's opinion. A third takes it for granted that he writes for nobody's benefit but his own—which is the opinion of the green-room. He is supposed to write for fame—for money—for amusement—for political *ends*—and, by certain schoolmasters, "to improve his mind." Need it be wondered at, that in this uncertainty as to his motives, the world sometimes perversely gives him anything but the thing he wants. Thus the rich author, who yearns for fame, gets a pension; the poor one, who hungers for bread, receives a diploma from Aberdeen; the writer for amusement has the pleasure of a mohawking review in a periodical; and the gentleman in search of a place has an offer from a sentimental milliner! 3dly. *What* an author writes. The world is so much of a Champollion, that it can understand hieroglyphics, if nothing else; it can comprehend outward visible signs, and grapple with a tangible emblem. It knows that a man on a table stands for patriotism, a man in the pulpit for religion, and so on, but it is a little obtuse as to what it reads in King Cadmus's types. A book hangs out no sign. Thus persons will go through a chapter, enforcing some principal duty of man towards his Maker or his neighbor, without discovering that, in all but the name, they have been reading a sermon. A solid mahogany pulpit is wanting to such a perception. They will con over an essay, glowing with the most ardent love of liberty, instinct with the noblest patriotism, and replete with the soundest maxims of polity, without the remotest notion that, except its being delivered upon paper instead of *vivâ voce*, they have been attending to a speech. As for dreaming of the author as a being who could sit in Parliament, and uphold the same sentiments, they would as soon think of chairing an abstract idea. They must see a *bonâ fide* wagon, with its true blue orange or green flag, to arrive at such a conclusion. The material keeps the upperhand. Hence the sight of a substantial Vicar may suggest the necessity of a parsonage and a glebe; but the author is, according to the proverb, "out of sight, out of mind"—a spirituality not to be associated with such tangible temporalities as bread and cheese. He is condemned *par contumace*, to dine, *tête-à-tête*, with the Barmecide or Duke Humphrey, whilst, for want of a visible hustings, or velvet cushion, the small still voice of his pages is never conceived of as coming from a patriot, a statesman, a priest, or a prophet. As a case in point: there is a short poem by Southey, called the "Battle of Blenheim," which from the text of some poor fellow's skull who fell in the great victory—

> For many a thousand bodies there
> Lay rotting in the sun—

takes occasion to ask what they killed each other for? and what good came of it in the end? These few quaint verses contain the very essence of a primary Quaker doctrine; yet lacking the tangible sign—a drab coat or a broad-brimmed hat—no member of the sect ever yet discovered that, in all but the garb, the peace-loving author was a Friend, moved by the spirit, and holding forth in verse in a strain worthy of the great Fox himself! Is such poetry, then, a *vanity*, or something worthy of all quakerly patronage? Verily, if the copyright had been valued at a thousand pounds the Society ought to have purchased it—printed the poem as a tract—and distributed it by tens of thousands, yea, hundreds of thousands, till every fighting man in the army and navy had a copy, including the marines. The Society, however, has done nothing of the kind; and it has only acted like society in general towards literature, by regarding it as a vanity or a luxury rather than as a grand moral engine, capable of advancing the spiritual as well as the temporal interests of mankind. It has looked upon poets and their kind as common men, and not as spirits that, like the ascending and descending angels in Jacob's vision, hold commerce with the sky itself, and help to maintain the intercourse between earth and heaven.

I have yet a few comments to offer on the charges usually preferred against literary men, but shall reserve them for another and concluding letter.

LETTER III.

TO THE EDITOR OF THE ATHENÆUM:

My dear Sir,—Now to the sins which have been laid at the doors, or tied to the knockers, of literary men: those offences which are to palliate or excuse such public slights and neglects as I have set forth; or may be, such private ones as selling a presentation copy, perhaps a dedicatory one, as a bookseller would sell the Keepsake, with the author's autograph letters—without the *delicacy* of waiting for his death, or the *policy*; for, as Crabbe says, one's writings then fetch a better price, because there can be no more of them—at a sale of Evans's. Literary men, then, have been charged with being eccentric—and so are comets. They were not created to belong to that mob of undistinguishable—call them not stars, but sparks—constituting the Milky Way. It is a taunt, as old as Chesterfield's Letters, that they are not polished—no more was that Chesterfield's son. They do not dress fashionably, for, if they could afford it, they know better, in a race for immortal fame, than to be *outsiders* Some, it has been alleged, have run through their estates, which might have been easily traversed at a walk; and one and all have neglected to save half-a-crown out of sixpence a day. Their disinterestedness has been called imprudence, and their generosity extravagance, by parties who bestow their charity like miser Mould.* The only charge,—not a blank charge,—that has been discharged against them, their poverty, has been made a crime, and, what is worse, a crime of their own seeking. They have not, it is true, been notorious for hoarding or funding—the last would, in fact, require the creation of a stock on purpose for them—the Short Annuities. They have never any weight in the city, or anywhere else; in cash temperature their pockets are always at Zero. They are not the "warm with," but the "cold without;" but it is to their credit,—if they have any credit,—that they have not worshipped Plutus. The Muse and Mammon never were in partnership; and it would be a desperate speculation indeed to take to literature as the means of amassing money. He would be a simple Dick Whittington indeed who expected to find its ways paved with philosopher's stones; he must have Dantzic water, with its gold leaf in his head, who thinks to find Castaly a Pactolus; ass indeed must he be who dreams of browsing on Parnassus, like those asses which feed on an herb—(a sort of *mint!*)—that turns their very teeth to gold. A line-maker, gifted with brains the gods have made

* An illiterate personage, who always volunteered to go round with the hat, but was suspected of sparing his own pocket. Overhearing, one day, a hint to that effect, he made the following speech:—"Other gentlemen puts down what they thinks proper, and so do I. Charity's a private concern, and what I gives is *nothing to nobody.*"

poetical, has no chance of making an independence—like Cogia Hassan Alhabbal, the rope-maker, gifted only with a lump of lead. Look into any palm, and if it contain the lines of poetry, the owner's fortune may be foretold at once—viz., a hill very hard to climb, and no prospect in life from the top. It is not always even a Mutton Hill, Garlic Hill, or Cornhill (remember Otway), for meat, vegetable, or bread. Let the would-be Crœsus then take up a Bank pen, and address himself to the Old Lady in Threadneedle Street, but not to the Muse: she may give him some "pinch-back," and pinch-front too, but little of the precious metals. Authorship has been pronounced, by a judge on the bench, as but a hand-to-mouth business; and I believe few have ever set up in it as anything else: in fact, did not Crabbe, though a reverend, throw a series of summersets, at least mentally, on the receipt of a liberal sum from a liberal publisher, as if he had just won the capital prize in the grand lottery? Need it be wondered at, then, if men who embrace literature more for love than for lucre, should grasp the adventitious coins somewhat loosely; nay, purposely scatter abroad, like Boaz, a liberal portion of their harvest for those gleaners, with whom they have, perhaps, had a hand-and-glove acquaintance—Poverty and Want? If there be the lively sympathy of the brain with the stomach that physiologists have averred, it is more than likely that there is a similar responsive sensibility between the head and the heart; it would be inconsistent, therefore it would be unnatural, if the same fingers that help to trace the woes of human life were but as so many feelers of the polypus Avarice, grasping everything within reach, and retaining it when got. We, know, on the contrary, that the hand of the author of the "Village Poor House" was "open as day to melting charity;" so was the house of Johnson munificent in proportion to his means; and as for Goldsmith, he gave more like a rich citizen of the world than one who had not always his own freedom.

But graver charges than improvidence have been brought against the literary character—want of principle, and offences against morality and religion. It might be answered, pleading guilty, that in that case authors have only topped the parts allotted to them in the great drama of life—that they have simply acted like vagabonds by law, and scamps by repute, "who have no character to lose, or property to protect;" but I prefer asserting, which I do fearlessly, that literary men, as a body, will bear comparison in point of conduct with any other class. It must not be forgotten that they are subjected to an ordeal quite peculiar, and scarcely milder than the Inquisition. The lives of literary men are proverbially barren of incident, and consequently, the most trivial particulars, the most private affairs, are unceremoniously worked up, to furnish matter for their bald biographies. Accordingly, as soon as an author is defunct, his character is submitted to a sort of Egyptian post-mortem trial; or rather, a moral inquest, with Paul Pry for the coroner, and a Judge of Assize, a Commissioner of Bankrupts, a Jew broker, a Methodist parson, a dramatic licenser, a dancing-master, a master of the ceremonies, a rat-catcher, a bone collector, a parish clerk, a schoolmaster, and a reviewer, for a jury. It is the province of these personages to rummage, ransack, scrape together, rake up, ferret out, sniff, detect, analyze, and appraise, all particulars of the birth, parentage, and education, life, character and behavior, breeding, accomplishments, opinions, and literary performances, of the departed. Secret drawers are searched, private and confidential letters published, manuscripts, intended for the fire, are set up in type, tavern bills and washing bills are compared with their receipts, copies of writs re-copied, inventories taken of effects, wardrobe ticked off by the tailor's account, by-gone toys of youth—billets-doux, snuff-boxes, canes—exhibited, discarded hobby-horses are trotted out,—perhaps even a dissecting surgeon is called in to draw up a minute report of the state of the corpse and its viscera: in short, nothing is spared that can make an item for the clerk to insert in his memoir. Outrageous as it may seem, this is scarcely an exaggeration—for example: who will dare to say that we do not know, at this very hour, more of Goldsmith's affairs than he ever did himself? It is rather wonderful, than otherwise, that the literary character should shine out as it does after such a severe scrutiny. Moreover, it remains yet to be proved that the follies and failings attributed to men of learning and genius are any more their private property than their copyrights after they have expired. There are certain well-educated ignorant people who contend that a little learning is a dangerous thing—for the poor; and as authors are poor, as a class, these horn-book monopolists may feel bound, in consistency, to see that the common errors of humanity are set down in the bill to letters. It is, of course, the black and white schoolmaster's dogs in a manger that bark and growl at the slips and backslidings of literary men; but to decant such cant, and see through it clearly, it is only necessary to remember that a fellow will commit half the sins in the Decalogue, and all the crimes in the Calendar—forgery excepted—without ever having composed even a valentine in verse, or the description of a lost gelding in prose. Finally, if the misdeeds of authors are to be pleaded in excuse of the neglect of literature and literary men, it would be natural to expect to see these practical slights and snubbings falling heaviest on those who have made themselves most obnoxious to rebuke. But the contrary is the case. I will not invidiously point out examples, but let the reader search the record, and he will find, that the lines which have fallen in pleasant places have belonged to men distinguished for anything rather than morality or piety. The idea, then, of merit having anything to do with the medals, must be abandoned, or we must be prepared to admit a very extraordinary result. It is notorious, that a foreign bird, for a night's warbling, will obtain as much as a native bard—not a second-rate one either—can realize in a whole year: an actor will be paid a sum per night equal to the annual stipend of many a curate; and the twelvemonth's income of an opera-dancer will exceed the revenue of a dignitary of the church. But will any one be bold enough to say, except satirically, that these disproportionate emoluments are due to the superior morality and piety of the concert-room, the opera, and the theatre? They are, in a great measure, the acknowledgments of physical gifts—a well tuned larynx—a well-turned figure, or light fantastic toes, not at all discountenanced in their vocation for being associated with light fantastic behavior. Saving, then, an imputed infirmity of temper—and has it not peculiar trials?—the only well-grounded failing the world has to resent, as a characteristic of literary men, is their poverty, whether the necessary result of their position, or of a wilful neglect of their present interests, and improvidence for the future. But what is an author's future, as regards his worldly prosperity? The law, as if judging him incapable of having heirs, absolutely prevents his creating a property, in copyrights, that might be valuable to his descendants. It declares, that the interest of the literary man and literature are not identical, and commends him to the composition of catch-penny works—things of the day and hour; or, so to speak, encourages him to discount his fame. Should he, letting the present shift for itself, and contemning personal privations, devote himself, heart and soul, to some great work or series of works, he may live to see his right and temporal interest in his books pass away from himself to strangers, and his children deprived of what, as well as his fame, is their just inheritance. At the best he must forego the superintendance of the publication and any foretaste of his success, and like Cumberland, when he contemplated a legacy "for the eventual use and advantage of a beloved daughter," defer the printing of his MSS. till after his decease. As for the present tense of his prosperity, I have shown that his possession is as open to inroad as any estate on the Border Land in days of yore; such is the legal providence that watches over his imputed improvidence! The law, which takes upon itself to guard the interest of lunatics, idiots, minors, and other parties incapable of managing their own affairs, not merely neglects to commonly protect, but connives at the dilapidation of the property of a class popularly supposed to have a touch of that same incompetence. It is, perhaps, rather the indifference of a generous spirit, which remembers to forget its own profit; but even in that case, if the author, like the girl in the fairy tale, drops diamonds and pearls from his lips, without stooping to pick up any for himself, the world he enriches is bound to see that he does not suffer from such a noble disinterestedness. Suppose even that he be a man wide awake to the value of money, the power it confers, the luxuries it may purchase, the consideration it commands—that he is anxious to make the utmost of his literary industry—and literary labor is as worthy of its hire as any other—there is no just principle on which he can be denied the same protection as any other trader. It may happen, also, that his "poverty, and not his will," consents to such a course. In this imperfect world there is nothing without its earthly alloy ; and, whilst the mind of the poet is married to a body, he must perform the divine service of the muses without banishing his dinner-service to the roof of the house, as in that Brazilian cathedral, which, for want of lead, is tiled with plates and dishes from the Staffordshire potteries. He cannot dwell even in the temple of Parnassus, but must lodge sometimes in an humbler abode, like the old Scotch songsters,

With bread and cheese for its door-cheeks.
And pancakes the rigging o't

Moreover, as authors—Protestant ones, at least—are not vowed to celibacy, however devoted to poverty, fasting and mortification, there may chance to exist other little corporealities, sprouts, off-sets, or suckers, which the nature of the law, as well as the law of nature, refers for sustenance to the parent trunk. Should our bards, jealous of these evidences of their mortality, offer to make a present of them to the parish, under the plea of the *mens divinior*, would not the overseer, or may be the Poor Law Commissioners, shut the workhouse wicket in their faces, and tell them that "the mens divinior must provide for the men's wives and children?" Pure fame is a glorious draught enough, and the striving for it is a noble ambition ; but, alas! few can afford to drink it *neat*. Across the loftiest visions of the poet earthly faces will flit; and even whilst he is gazing on Castaly little familiar voices will murmur in his ear, inquiring if there are no fishes that can be eaten to be caught in its waters!

It has happened, according to some inscrutable dispensation, that the mantle of inspiration has commonly descended on shoulders clad in cloth of the humblest texture. Our poets have been Scotch ploughmen, farmers' boys, Northamptonshire peasants, shoe-makers, old servants, milk-women, basket-makers, steel-workers, charity-boys, and the like. Pope's protégé, Dodsley, was a footman, and wrote "The Muse in Livery"—you may trace a hint of the double vocation in his "Economy of Human

Life."* Our men of learning and genius have generally been born, not with silver spoons in their mouths, but wooden ladles. Poetry, Goldsmith says, not only found him poor, but kept him so; but has not the law been hitherto lending a hand in the same uncharitable task? Has it not favored the "Cormorants by the Tree of Knowledge"—the native Bookaneer?—and "a plague the Devil hath added," as Sir J. Overbury calls the foreign pirate.

To give a final illustration of the working of the Law of Copyright, Sir Walter Scott, besides being a mighty master of fiction, resembles Defoe in holding himself bound to pay in full all the liabilities he had incurred. But the amount was immense, and he died, no doubt prematurely, from the magnitude of the effort. A genius so illustrious, united with so noble a spirit of integrity, doubly deserved a national monument, and a subscription was opened for the purpose of preserving Abbotsford to his posterity, instead of a public grant to make it a literary Blenheim. I will not stop to inquire whether there was more joy in France when Malbrook was dead than sorrow in Britain, or rather throughout the world, when Scott was no more; but I must point out the striking contrast between two advertisements in a periodical paper which courted my notice on the same page. One was a statement of the amount of the Abbotsford subscription, the other an announcement of a rival edition of one of Sir Walter's works, the copyright of which had expired. Every one may not feel with me the force of this juxtaposition, but I could not help thinking that the interest of any of his immortal productions ought to have belonged either to the creditors or to the heritage. Can there be heir-looms, I asked myself, and not head-looms?—and looms, too, that have woven such rich tissues of romance? Why is a mental estate, any more than a landed one, made subject to such an Agrarian law?

In spite of all my knowledge of ethics, and all my ignorance of law, I have never yet been able to answer these questions to my own satisfaction. Perchance Mr. Serjeant Talfourd will be

* The man of emulation, who panteth after fame. "The example of eminent men are in his visions by night—*and his delight is to follow them* (query, with a gold-headed cane?) *all the day long.*"

prepared with a solution, but, if not, I trust he will give us "the benefit of the doubt," and make an author's copyright heritable property, only subject to alienation by his own act, or in satisfaction of the claims of creditors. Such a measure will tend to retrieve our worldly respectability: instead of being nobodys with nothing, we shall be, if not freeholders, a sort of copyholders, with something between the sky and the centre, that we can call our own. It may be but a nominal possession, but if it were of any value, why should it be made common for the benefit of the Company of Stationers? They drink enough out of our living heads, without quaffing out of our skulls, like the kings of Dahomey. As to the probability of their revivals of authors who were adored, but have fallen into neglect and oblivion,—remembering how the trade boggled at Robinson Crusoe, and the Vicar of Wakefield—there would be as much chance of a speculative lawyer reviving such dormant titles. For my own part, I am far from expecting, personally, any pecuniary advantages from such an arrangement; but I have some regard for the abstract right. There is always a certain sense of humiliation, attendant on finding that we are made exceptions, as if incapable or undeserving of the enjoyment of equal justice. And can there be a more glaring anomaly than that, whilst our private property is thrown open and made common, we daily see other commons enclosed, and made private property? One thing is certain, that, by taking this high ground at once, and making copyright analogous in tenure to the soil itself—and it pays its land tax in the shape of a tax upon paper—its defence may be undertaken with a better grace, against trespass at home, or invasion from abroad. For, after all, what does the pirate or Bookaneer commit at present, but a sort of practical anachronism, by anticipating a period when the right of printing will belong to everybody in the world, including the man in the moon!

Such, it appears to me, is the grand principle upon which the future law of copyright ought to be based. I am aware that I have treated the matter somewhat commercially: but I have done so, partly because in that light principally the legislature will have to deal with it; and still more, because it is desirable, for the sake of literature and literary men, that they should have every chance of independence, rather than be compelled to look to extraneous sources for their support. Learning and genius, worthily directed and united to common industry, surely deserve, at least, a competence; and that their possessors should be something better than a Jarkman; that is to say, "one who can write and read, yea, some of them have a smattering in the Latin tongue, which learning of theirs advances them in office *amongst the beggars*." The more moderate in proportion the rate of their usual reward, the more scrupulously ought every particle of their interests to be promoted and protected, so as to spare, if possible, the necessity of private benefactions or public collections for the present distress, and "Literary Retreats" for the future. Let the weight and worth of literature in the state be formally recognized by the legislature:—let the property of authors be protected, and the upholding of the literary character will rest on their *heads*. They will, perhaps, recollect that their highest office is to make the world wiser and better; their lowest, to entertain and amuse it without making it worse. For the rest, bestow on literary men their fair share of public honors and employments,—concede to them, as they deserve, a distinguished rank in the social system, and they will set about effacing such blots as now tarnish their scutcheons. The surest way to make a class indifferent to reputation is to give it a bad name. Hence Literature having been publicly underrated, and its professors having been treated as vagabonds, scamps, fellows "without character to lose or property to protect," we have seen conduct to match,—reviewers, forgetful of common courtesy, common honesty, and common charity, misquoting, misrepresenting, and indulging in the grossest personalities, even to the extent of ridiculing bodily defects and infirmities—political partizans bandying scurrilous names, and scolding like Billingsgate mermaids —and authors so far trampling on the laws of morals, and the rights of private life, as to write works capable of being puffed off as club books got up amongst the Snakes, Sneerwells, Candors, and Backbites, of the School for Scandal.

And now, before I close, I will here place on record my own obligations to Literature: a debt so immense, as not to be cancelled, like that of nature, by death itself. I owe to it something more than my earthly welfare. Adrift early in life upon the great waters—as pilotless as Wordsworth's blind boy afloat in the turtle-shell—if I did not come to shipwreck, it was, that, in default of paternal or fraternal guidance, I was rescued, like the ancient mariner, by guardian spirits, "each one a lovely light," who stood as beacons to my course. Infirm health, and a natural love of reading, happily threw me, instead of worse society, into the company of poets, philosophers, and sages—to me good angels and ministers of grace. From these silent instructors—who often do more than fathers, and always more than godfathers, for our temporal and spiritual interests,—from these mild monitors—no importunate tutors, teazing Mentors, moral task-masters, obtrusive advisers, harsh censors, or wearisome lecturers—But, delightful associates,—I learned something of the divine, and more of the human religion. They were my interpreters in the House Beautiful of God, and my guides among the Delectable Mountains of Nature. They reformed my prejudices, chastened my passions, tempered my heart, purified my tastes, elevated my mind, and directed my aspirations. I was lost in a chaos of undigested problems, false theories, crude fancies, obscure impulses, and bewildering doubts—when these bright intelligences called my mental world out of darkness like a new creation, and gave it "two great lights," Hope and Memory—the past for a moon, and the future for a sun.

Hence have I genial seasons—hence have I
Smooth passions, smooth discourse, and joyous thoughts;
And thus from day to day my little boat
Rocks in its harbor, lodging peaceably.
Blessings be with them, and eternal praise,
Who gave us nobler loves and nobler cares,
The poets, who on earth have made us heirs
Of truth and pure delight by heavenly lays!
Oh! might my name be number'd among theirs,
How gladly would I end my mortal days.

LETTER IV

To the Editor of the Athenæum:

Five years ago I ventured in your popular journal to publish my private thoughts on the nature and laws of Literary Property. In those letters, without underrating the International Question, it was recommended that we should begin at home, and first establish what Copyright is in Britain, and provide for its protection against Native Pirates or Bookaneers. It was contended, therefore, that the author's perpetual property in his works should be formally recognized, and that "by taking this high ground at once, and making Copyright analogous in tenure to the soil itself, its defence might be undertaken with a better grace against trespass at home or invasion from abroad."

The fate of the Bill subsequently framed by Serjeant Talfourd is well known. An opposition was set up by publishers, stationers, binders, printers, journeymen, devils, and hawkers; and Mr. Tegg even so far discomposed himself as to compose a pamphlet, in which the earnings and emoluments of Scott, Byron, Moore, Southey, Hook, &c., were summed up as if they had been so many great sinecurists fattening in idleness at the cost of our dear public. Messrs. Wakley and Warburton chimed in with the pamphleteer, and even one or two country gentlemen, who had set their ridge and furrow faces against cheap food for the body, were all in favor of cheap food for the mind, as if it were desirable to see the public like a huge ricketty child with its head a great deal bigger than its belly. Nevertheless, even this opposition might have failed if the tone of the House had remained at its original pitch. The eloquent speech of the learned Serjeant, on introducing his Bill, had a thrilling effect. And when he ceased, "those airy tongues that syllable men's names" filled up the pause, till the very walls seemed whispering "Chaucer!" "Spenser!" "Shakspeare!" "Milton!" whilst sadder echoes responded with Chatterton, Otway, and Burns! Every head with a heart to it, and every heart with a head to it, answered to the appeal. The accomplished nobleman, the gentleman of cultivated mind, the man of taste, the well-educated commoners. at once acknowledged, as debts of honor, their deep obligations to literature. They recalled with affectionate interest and honorable respect the poets of their youth and the philosophers of their manhood—their intimates of the closet—their familiars of the fields and forests—the intellectual ministers from whom they had derived amusement in leisure, wisdom in action, society in solitude, and consolation in travel. They remembered the friends of their souls. Even the opponents of the measure confessed the national importance and value of literature, and its beneficial influence on the community, by their very struggles to make it cheap for the public at the expense of all liberal feeling and common justice. Moreover, the question involved, more or less, nearly the hereditary principle—the law of property—the nature of freehold and copyhold—the protection of a native interest—and, in some opinions, the national honor. But, alas! the argument had fallen on evil days! The question did not suit the temper of the times or the ordinary tone of the place. It contained no political Ode to the Passions. There was no ardent overproof unrectified party spirit in it to excite a parliamentary *delirium tremens*. There was no side-bone of contention for Whig or Tory. It was a subject whereon political Montagues and Capulets might shake hands. Faction overcame Fiction. The accomplished nobleman, the gentleman of cultivated mind, the man of taste, the well educated commoners had other fish to fry—hotter broils and stews to arrange—and their gratitude and good will to literature chilled as rapidly as mutton gravy on a cold plate!

Since then, the reprinting of English works in America has progressed with steam celerity: whilst the King of the Belgians has openly recommended this literary piracy to his subjects, as a profitable branch of the national industry:—a speech, by the way, for which his Majesty deserves an especial address from our literati, whenever he thinks proper to revisit this country. The importation of the foreign reprints has also increased, and to an extent that has made our publishers quite as alarmed as the farmers and graziers, when they recently fancied themselves surrounded by outlandish bulls of Bashan, and bellowed out for protection against foreign oxen, all ready to invade Smithfield, and drive our own beasts, without drovers, clean out of the mar ket. But our author feeders have more cause for alarm than the cattle breeders, inasmuch as it appears that the foreign bullocks, though invited, will not come in, whereas the foreign books will enter in spite of being forbidden.

In this extremity, Lord Mahon has opportunely brought for ward a new bill, which has been supported by authors and booksellers with a harmony as strange as pleasant—a harmony not so attributable, I fear, to Wilhem's system, or Mr. Hullah's vocal exercises for singing in tune, as to the fact that the voices of the literati form a powerful and welcome addition to .he cry set up for protection against foreign piracy. On the extension of the term of Copyright, the trade is now liberally indifferent, but extremely anxious for some very stringent enactment to stop the smuggling of piratical reprints—and, of course, with a retrospective clause, which shall prohibit Flemish, French, or American impressions of Shakspeare and Milton, as well as of Harry Lorrequer or Zanoni. And why not a retrospective clause —for how is a man to protect his property if he may not shoot into the back garden as well as into the forecourt? Provided always, that the grounds in the rear be really the property, or at least in the legal occupation of the man with the blunderbuss. Of which more hereafter.

In the meantime, the new bill has not been discussed, in either House, without some opposition to its provisions, and, as usual, especially directed against the section intended for the benefit of the author. In the Commons, up jumped Mr. Wakley—perhaps a Coroner accustomed to violent and sudden deaths could not relish anything expiring so deliberately as with forty-two years' notice—however, up jumped Mr. Wakley, as vicious with poetry and poets as if he had just been kicked by Pegasus, or rejected in turn by all the Nine Sisters,—and after a flagrant assault on the Bard of Rydal, behind the back of Mr. Wordsworth, protested vehemently against any further protection of good-for-nothing books. As if, forsooth, our dear public could be injured by even a perpetual copyright in works which nobody but the author would ever think of reprinting! These good-for-nothing writers, it has been fashionable to estimate as ninety-nine out of one hundred, and, admitting the proportion, what is to become of the rara avis, the phœnix, the one of a hundred? Is he to receive no reward or encouragement which may stimulate others to go and do likewise? Let us suppose a school kept by Doctor Posterity, and which offers, as usual, a prize for the best scholar. The term is at an end, the reward is to be conferred, and the best boy of a hundred is desired to step forward. "Master Scott," says the Doctor, "it is my pleasing task to inform you that you have won the highest prize in this Classical Establishment. The talents bestowed on you have not been abused or neglected. Your genius has been equalled by your industry, and your performances have given universal satisfaction. Your themes and essays in original composition have particularly excited my admiration and approbation: I have read them with interest and delight. Master Scott, I have had few boys like you. You are an honor to the school, as you will be an ornament to your age and country. I have no difficulty in awarding the first prize intended for the encouragement of genius and learning. Behold this large gold medal! It is eminently your due. You have richly earned it—but, mind, I'm not going to give it you, and for this reason, that all your ninety-nine school-fellows, put together, are not worth a dump!"

Is this the way to encourage the production of standard works, and to improve the breed of authors? Is it on this system that we have sought to improve the breed of horses, horned cattle, and pigs? Is a prize ox ever denied the prize because there are so many lean beasts in the market? Would Boz, Ivanhoe, or Satirist be refused the gold cup at Ascot, because Dunce, Tony Lumkin, or King Log had been distanced in the race? Is it thus that merit is rewarded in other countries? My travelled readers have doubtless seen what is called, in France, a *Mât de Cocagne*—a tall well-greased pole—"Ah, who can tell how hard it is to climb!" with some public prize at the top. Many are the candidates, particularly sweeps and sailors, who attempt to swarm up the slippery mast; some heavy-sterned fellows only mounting half way; others scrambling almost within arm's length of the reward: but, alas! down, down, down they slide again like greased lightning, and cursing Sir Isaac Newton for inventing gravitation. At last some more fortunate or clever aspirant attempts the task—up he go—up he go—like the 'possum, till he actually reaches the tiptop, and clutches the tempting article. Lucky dog that he is, not to be an English author, and rewarded by English authorities! No one grudges him his success—no one objects that the nineteen other candidates have gone to the bottom of the pole. He has not only won the prize, but wears it, and perhaps literally in the shape of a new pair of breeches.

It has been said, indeed, that a writer would derive no advantage from an extended property in his works; but why should not long copyrights be as beneficial as long leases, long purses, long annuities, long legs, long heads, long lives, and other long things that are longed for? Much stress has been laid on the declarations of publishers, that they would give no more for forty-two years than for twenty-eight, or fourteen. And no doubt the parties were perfectly sincere in the declaration. There are persons who would not plant trees, however profitable ultimately, because the return would be distant and not immediate: and even so some publishers might not care to invest their capital in standard works for a sure, but slow, remuneration. But that money is to be made of books, even after twenty-eight years, is certain, or what becomes of Lord Brougham's statement, that publishers have been making large preparations, and incurring great expense for the purpose of bringing out works of which the copyrights were just expiring? Nay, is there not one bookseller in Cheapside, who is understood to have made hundreds and thousands, if not hundreds of thousands, by this sort of author-snatching? But to bring the question to issue, let us take a batch of writers who are all as dead as if they had been boiled, and yet at whose head and brains there is better sucking than in a quart of shrimps. For example, there is one Fielding, whose last novel was published a century ago, and, consequently, has been common spoil for some fourscore years. Will any one be bold enough to say, that a revived copyright of "Tom Jones" would be valueless in the market? Then we have one Smollett, and one Sterne, and one Goldsmith, all defunct fifty years since,—would an exclusive right in their works obtain no bidders? Not to name Shakspeare or Milton; would Johnson's Dictionary, as copyright, fetch nothing in the Row? or would the shade of Defoe again go a-begging from publisher to publisher, with his "Robinson Crusoe?" Why, in the Literary Stocks, there could hardly be a safer investment.

In the Upper House, the opposition to the Bill was led by Lord Brougham, not without expressions of great respect and "sincere affection" for literary men, whom he represented as claimants, not only on the justice, but on the benevolence of the house. To this last character, however, I for one must demur. There has been too much of this almsgiving tone used towards authors, so that an uninformed reader of the speeches would imagine that the poor dogs were on their hind legs begging for a bone, or a boon, as some pronounce it, instead of standing up like the kangaroo for their natural rights. For, be it remembered, by Tories, Conservatives, and Royal Oak Boys, that we have only been agitating to regain our usurped possessions—to effect not a Revolution, but a Restoration!

Apart from the above vile phrase, the compliments of Lord Brougham were highly flattering, and his sincere affection would no doubt be a valuable possession, but, alas! when it came to be tested, the tie, though showy, was no more binding than the flimsy gilt book-covers of the present day. His Lordship soon repented of his attachment to authors, and refused to "be led away, as many had been led away (and oh! that our state wheelers had never any other leaders!) by a generous, natural, and praise-worthy feeling." The Peers had listened too much to kind feelings, and he felt compelled to remind them of "the strict duties of the legislative office." A very superfluous injunction—for what has the legislature done for literature? How have our legislators "leaned towards the side towards which they must all wish to lean, and towards which all their prejudices and partialities must bear them?" Why, they found the authors in possession of a common law right, so called from being founded on common sense and common justice—and how did they show their amiable weakness, their partial warp and bias, their over-indulgent fondness for that spoiled child—a son of the Muses. To borrow a comparison, one of the most ill-used members of creation is that forlorn animal, a street dog. Every idle hand has a stone, every idle foot has a kick for him —every driver a whip, and every carpenter a cleft stick. He has only to look at a butcher's shop—merely to point at a sheep —to be snatched up instanter. Bang! goes the chopper! and off fly a few inches of his tail. He has only to be looked at by a bevy of young blackguards, and in a jiffy away he scours, encumbered with an old kettle. Even so it fared with the author. He was ragged in his coat, bare on his ribs, and tucked up in the flank—in short, he looked a very peltable, kickable, whipable, and curtailable dog, indeed. Accordingly, no sooner had Law caught sight of him, than it caught hold of him, docked his entail at a blow, and tied Stationers' Hall to the stump.

So much for the strict duties of the legislative office, to which we owe that we have only a lease of our own premises—a temporary usufruct in our own orchards—that we have been encouraged by a sequestration, and protected from retail privateering, on the condition of wholesale piracy hereafter!

To be sure it has been urged, that an extended copyright (an author's monopoly instead of a bookseller's) would damage the public interest—that it would enhance the price of books—at any rate, that it would prevent their re-issue at a reduced rate. But this speculation remains to be tested by experiment. The higher and wealthy classes do not compose, as formerly, the great mass of readers—the numbers have increased by millions, and our writers are quite as well aware as the trade of the superior advantage of a cheap and large circulation. They have the double temptation of popularity and profit. One can even fancy an author publishing without hope of pecuniary reward, nay, at a certain loss, provided it would insure his numbers a Bozzian diffusion; whereas it is difficult to imagine a writer setting so high a price on his own book as would necessarily confine its perusal to a very select circle. On these points I am competent to speak, having re-issued the majority of my own humble works, at a price quite in accordance with the demand for cheap literature—and most certainly not enhanced by the time my copyrights had been in existence. It is true that the cost of a volume has occasionally been purposely hoisted up, for instance, by wilfully destroying the wood-blocks and copper plates, as in the case of Dr. Dibdin's "Bibliographical Decameron," but such dog-in-the-mangery acts have been committed at or before publication: for even the maddest Bibliomaniac would hardly dream of making a work "scarce," after a sale of forty-two years. It follows, then, that the shorter the copyright the longer the price of the book! for supposing the term cut down to one year for the writer to sow, reap, and gather in his harvest, what so likely to set him Dibdinizing as the brevity of his lease? "Odds books and buyers!" says he, "only twelve months market before me, less fifty-two Sundays! As my time is so scant, I must make the most of it!" So he stirs up the coals to a bonfire, pitches into it all his costly wood-cuts, as if they were so many logs, and enhances the price of his volume to ten guineas a copy!

Apropos of cheapness, it seems never to have occurred to the sticklers for it, that an article may become unreasonably reasonable—that the consumer may be benefited overmuch. For example, there have been certain staring shop announcements to be seen about London, in which the low price of the commodities was vouched for by the ruin of the manufacturer—broad proclamations that the "Great Bargains in Cotton" had shut up the mills, and that the "Wonderfully Reduced Silks" had exhausted not only the bowels of the worm but those of the weaver. But is such a consummation a favorable one, and devoutly to be wished, whatever the fabric? Is it really desirable to see our authors publicly advertised as "Unprecedented Sacrifices?" Or would anybody, except Mr. Wakley, or some useless Utilitarian, be actually gratified by reading such a placard as the following:

UNEXAMPLED DISTRESS IN GRUB STREET!
GREAT REDUCTION IN LITERATURE!!
PROSE UNDER PRIME COST!!! POETRY FOR NOTHING!!!!

It is certain, nevertheless, that new works, and especially periodical ones, have been projected and started, during the Rage for Cheap Literature, at rates so ruinously low, that they might afford brown bread and single Gloster to the Publishers or to the Writers, but certainly not for both. Thus, a few months since, I was applied to, myself, to contribute to a new journal, not exactly gratuitously, but at a very small advance upon nothing—and avowedly because the work had been planned according to that estimate. However, I accepted the terms conditionally; that is to say, provided the principle could be properly carried out. Accordingly, I wrote to my butcher, baker, and other tradesmen, informing them that it was necessary, for the sake of cheap literature and the interest of the reading public, that they should furnish me with their several commodities at a very trifling per-centage above cost price. It will be sufficient to quote the answer of the butcher:—

"Sir,—Respectin your note. Cheap literater be blowed. Butchers must live as well as other pepel—and if so be you or the readin publick wants to have meat at prime cost, you must buy your own beastesses, and kill yourselves. I remane, &c., John Stokes."

And, truly, why not cheap anything, or everything, as well as cheap literature? Cheap beef, cheap beer, cheap butter, and cheap bread? As to books, the probability is, that distant re-issues would be at reduced rates; but, even supposing them to remain at their original prices, why should Mr. Thomson of 1843 have his "Waverley" any cheaper than Mr. Thomson of 1814?

At any rate, the interests of *both* parties ought to be fairly considered. Nay, Consistency goes still farther, and hints that the literary interest should be especially favored. For, hark to Consistency! "Let the public," she says, "be cared for—let the public be *well* cared for,—and let the Authors be *particularly well* cared for, as the most public part of the public!"

"But if we give an extended term to the authors," cries Lord Brougham, "we must also give a longer day to the patentees." And why not, if they deserve and need it? But it is as easy to show cause against a patent being perpetual, as it is difficult to prove why a copyright should be limited. In the abstract, the absolute rights of both parties may be equal—but as the monopoly of a mechanical invention might be an enormous evil, Expediency, with propriety, steps in to protect the public interest when the private one has been amply gratified. In fact, the patentees of great and useful inventions have generally realized large fortunes within a few years; whereas the best and greatest of our writers have commonly made such little ones during their whole lives, that the Next-of-Kin never heard of anything to his advantage. And the reason was ably explained by the Bishop of London.

The merits of a mechanical invention can at once be tested: and are immediately recognized. The merest loggerhead can understand at a glance the advantage of a machine which impels a ship without wind and a coach without horses—howbeit the same dunderpate in twenty long years had never found out the use of "book larning." There is a gentleman of my acquaintance who derives a yearly sum for a patent clothes brush, the superiority of which, in brushing his master's coat, John Footman would detect ere he had whistled through "Nancy Dawson." But suppose instead of a machine of bristles, wire, and wood, my friend had composed a work, intended to brush off the dirt and dust of the human intellect, he might have been months in catching a publisher, and years upon years in getting hold of the public. But why talk of steam-engines, clothes brushes, and such utilities? There was one trifling instrument, for which, had the inventor secured a patent, the sale of the article, merely as a toy, would have certainly enriched the proprietor—for the dullest unit of humanity had but to put the tube to his or her eye to enjoy all the beautiful and varied patterns of the kaleidoscope. But suppose, instead of a tin machine with reflectors and bits of colored glass, the novelty had been a "Novum Organon," how many of those peeping thousands and millions might have looked through it and through it, by sunlight and lamplight, without discovering that it was rare food for the mind—prime intellectual Bacon. The truth is, we so far resemble the brutes, that we understand our physical wants and comforts, much more quickly than our mental or moral ones,—just as a turnspit would find out the value of a bottlejack long before that of a Bridgewater Treatise. Hence, the prompt recognition and remuneration of mechanical inventions and inventors. Nor must it be forgotten that government, as wide awake to the Physical, and as fast asleep to the Intellectual, as the loggerheaded dunce, John Footman, the kaleidoscopers, and the turnspit,—it ought not to be forgotten that government has sometimes bought his invention of a patentee, but has never purchased a copyright since the invention of printing. It will be time enough, then, when Sir Robert Peel begins to bargain with us for our works, on behalf of the nation, to say that we are on the same footing as the patentees.

The International Question—and Pirates Foreign and Domestic—in my next.—Yours, &c.,

---

LETTER V.

To the Editor of the Athenæum:

Problematical as some persons may consider the benefit of an extended copyright to authors, there can be no doubt of the immediate injury they must sustain, in common with publishers, from the piratical reprinting of the works in foreign countries—to wit, France, Belgium, and the United States. I am not aware whether Germany partakes in this disgraceful traffic: but there is a word for it in the language, and nothing is more favorable to Nachdruckerie than the contiguity of several petty principalities.

Of the character of the system, the very name that is applied to it is significant—a term which associates this over-free-trade with the buccaneering practices of the old robbers on the high seas. The literary pirate does not, indeed, dabble in blood, but in ink; but the object is the same, and pursued by the same means—the indiscriminate pillage of friend or foe. And here be it said, that if anything can palliate the foreign marauder, and render his offence comparatively venial, it is the example of English publishers pirating English works. It has always been reckoned unnatural for dog to eat dog, or for hawks to pick out hawks' eyes; and the Highland veteran, who stole droves of cattle without scruple, would have held it a heinous offence to lift a sucking calf belonging to any one of his own clan.

Nevertheless, of this heinous and unnatural conduct there have been too many instances, including a couple within the last few months. In the first case, a piracy was committed by a Firm not the least active in the opposition to the Bill of Sergeant Talfourd, and who, of course, held the poacher-like principle that the proper time for a copyright to expire was whenever they chose to kill it. The other party alluded to, once went so far as to assert to me that an author would not receive more, but less, for a longer term in his works—a declaration attributed at the time to mere natural blockheadism; but his theory of literary rights has since been illustrated by an injunction obtained against him by a brother bookseller, for pirating some popular metrical legends. Now in what but the pseudo-respectability of a double-fronted shop in Cornhill does this publisher rank above a man whom he would no doubt have designated as a little, low, dirty, shabby library-keeper in the suburbs, to whom I one day happened to mention a placard in a neighboring shop-window announcing a spurious "Master Humphrey's Clock."

"Sir," said the little, low, dirty, shabby library-keeper, "if you had observed the name, it was by Bos, not Boz—S, Sir, not Z; and, besides, it would have been no piracy, Sir, even with the Z, because Master Humphrey's Clock, you see, Sir, was not published as by Boz, but by Charles Dickens."*

These lax principles of our domestic pirates are not at all *braced* by a passage across the Atlantic. In America the system has reached its climax, and the types, used on a new work here, are only the antetypes of a reprint in Boston, Philadelphia, or New York. Of this, a flagrant example has recently occurred in the republication of Sir E. Bulwer's last new novel, "Zanoni," in a newspaper form, at the rate of ten copies for a dollar! In fact, as to natural rights, in the States there appear to be two classes very much on a par—our *read* men and the Indians.

It may be as well for me, before commenting on such transactions, to disown any prejudice, personal or political, against America or the Americans. I am none of the "Mr. H's" who have drawn, sketched, or caricatured them. The stars and

* Fact.

stripes do not affect me like a blight in the eye; nor does "Yankee Doodle" give me the ear-ache. I have no wish to repeal the Union of the United States; or to alter the phrase in the Testament into "Republicans and Sinners." In reality, I have rather a Davidish feeling towards Jonathan, remembering whence he comes, and what language he speaks; and holding it better in such cases to have the wit that traces resemblances, than the judgment that detects differences,—and perhaps foments them.

It is, therefore, to gratify no private spleen, spite, or jealousy, that my voice is raised against a system which has been condemned by some of the wisest and most distinguished of her own sons as prejudicial to the dignity and best interests of America —men, who do not care, perhaps, to see their Gog of a country indebted for all its prose and poetry to little Great Britain, just as the jolterheaded Giant at the gate of Kenilworth Castle was dependent for *his* literature on the dwarfish imp Flibbertigibbet.

And truly gigantic is Jonathan in his material works, and extra-fast in his physical progress; but will he really be satisfied with going ahead in everything but that in which the head is so distinguished an agent? He is first chop with the hatchet, and a crack with the rifle,—grand at a 'coon, mighty at a 'possum, and awful at a squirrel,—he can drive a nail with a bullet, or a bargain with a Jew pedlar,—whip his weight in wild cats,* grin Jesuit's bark into quinine, and, as some say, wring off the tail of a comet,—but where will be his exploits with the pen? Will he resemble or not the big Ben of the school, a dab at marbles, a first-rater at cricket, a top-sawyer at fives, and a good-'un at fisticuffs, but obliged to be obliged for his English themes and exercises to the least boy on the form? The picture is a mortifying one; but in some such character must Jonathan necessarily figure, if he consents to be a mere interloper—a Squatter, instead of a settler, in the Field of Letters.

That America, in the absence of an International Copyright, can never possess a native literature, has been foretold by the second-sighted on either side of the Atlantic. Indeed, accord-

* "Phoo! phoo!" said an old Anglo-Indian, in reference to this boast; "I can whip my own weight in elephants"

ing to Mr. Cornelius Mathews, in his speech at the public dinner given to Dickens at New York, the barren time is already come, and the field of letters, in the States, scarcely produces a prose thistle or a poetical dandelion. It would hardly feed a Learned Pig. Such must be the inevitable result of the republication of English works on a scale that totally precludes any native competition; and whatever may be the feeling of the trading partners, I can imagine nothing more mortifying to the spirit of a liberal, accomplished, and patriotic American, than to sit in his study, under a framed and glazed "Declaration of Independence," and to look at a Family Library, well stored indeed with books, but of which nothing save the paper and the covers are of home manufacture.

Of the character of the traffic there can be no doubt. No honorable man would wish to obtain mental food, any more than his bodily victual, without fairly paying for it. It makes no difference that the supply comes from another country; for who would object to pay his tradesman's bills on the plea that his American apples, his Ostend butter, and his French eggs, were of foreign production? Nor does it matter that the acquisition is not exactly so tangible as upholstery; it is as irregular to have your head furnished as your house at the expense of your neighbor.

But these are the consumers. As to the purveyors, they are precisely on a par with the remarkable cheap traders, who stôle ready-made brooms. They are not liable, it is true, to any legal penalty; but a severe punishment is awarded to a very similar offence. According to the comity of civilized countries, the national flag virtually protects not only the aggregate people, but every native individual—the British subject at Baltimore or Boston as much as the cockney in Cheapside. Even so the copyright of an English work attaches to the solitary copy that finds its way to New York as much as to the 1499 which remain in the dominions of Queen Victoria. It is a single bank note, but of a large issue; and its multiplication by spurious copies, particularly for circulation in our empire or its colonies, is surely as nefarious as the forgery of our "flimsies." The analogy is undeniable: and as the wholesale counterfeiting of a paper currency has only been practised heretofore between nations at war, it is incumbent on the Congress of a country with which we are at amity to put a stop to such hostilities.

And here, pray note, how a Perpetual Copyright, as I formerly stated, might be defended with a better grace from invasion from abroad. Indeed, if foreign piracy have any plea in extenuation, it is the evil example of the statute of 1709, which first put a boundary line to our possession. Jonathan is a great calculator, and may calculate that space as well as time may nullify a copyright; and to be candid, there is no very clear reason why it should not. To me it appears that 28 degrees of latitude might as justly and rationally alienate a property as 28 years of longitude; that my right may as consistently depart from me in a steamboat as in a calendar; and of the two, the Great Western seems the most tangible conveyancer. As to any work above 23 years old, its reprinting by Americans or New Zealanders can be no transgression. On No Man's Land there can be no trespass; where there is no right there can be no infringement; there can be no piracy, for there is no copyright, that which was called so being dead and gone; not transferred like other property, but annihilated; not a dormant title, but extinct. As a consequence, in a couple of months, every printer in the United States will have, legally, as much right and interest in Waverley as the son and heir of the immortal Novelist.

There is another injury, however, with which our authors are threatened besides reprinting, namely, translation,—not from English into American, for there is no such tongue, but from the language of a Monarchy into that of a Republic. Yes; our writers are actually to be done into Locofocos, Nullifiers, Federalists, Democrats, Sympathisers,—nay, perhaps, into Horse Alligators and Yellow Flowers of the Forest, according to the taste of the province in which they may be reprinted, or the predilections of the republisher! In fact, American editions are to represent in spirit, as well as in form, American *impressions!*

This transmogrification is plainly alluded to in the following paragraph of a Memorial to Congress got up at a meeting of publishers, printers, &c., at Boston, in April last, Mr. Goodrich, alias Peter Parley, in the chair:

"We would also suggest another point of vital import. If English authors obtain copyrights upon their works here, and our markets are supplied with them, it is apparent that, having no power to adapt them to our wants, our institutions, and our state of society, we must permit their circulation as they are. We shall thus have a London literature forced upon us, at once driving our own out of the field, and subjecting the community to its influence. So long as we have power over it—so long as we can shape it as may suit our taste and condition, we have nothing to fear; but when this privilege is taken away, and the vast preponderance of British capital has driven our own out of the trade, shall we not have in our bosom a power at war with our institutions, and dangerous to our prosperity? Is it not safer and better to let in this literature freely, but subject to the moulding of our wants and wishes, rather than to give it an ascendency, and entrench it behind the inviolable privilege of copyright?"

And that there may be no doubt about the meaning of the memorialists, hear Mr. Cornelius Mathews:

"I have said nothing—and I might have said much—of the mutilation of books by our American republishers—that outrageous wrong by which a noble English writer, speaking truths in London, dear to him as life, is made to say in New York that which his soul abhors!"

I am not aware of the exact tinge of the Boston complexion; but, whether pallid or rubicund, golden or brazen, was there no cheek capable of a blush at the reading of such a precious document! Did Mr. Goodrich—himself a writer—and a moralist for children—did Peter Parley feel no misgivings as to the propriety or fairness of casting the brains of English authors into American moulds and shapes, with as little ceremony as so much jelly? Is there no turpitude in the falsification of writings because they happen to be not in manuscript, but in print? On the contrary, the most dishonorable of misrepresentations is to make a man misrepresent himself, by attributing to him expressions he had never uttered, or principles he had never entertained—a proceeding quite as dirty as that of the Brobdignaggian baboon, when it crammed into the mouth of Gulliver the filth it had hoarded in its own pouches!

For my own part, I think that a man has quite as good a right to attach a sum, as a sentiment, to my signature—to use my name for the supply of his wants, as for the support of his principles—to turn me into cash, as to turn me into a republican. But there may be more novel notions on these matters on the opposite side of the Atlantic; where "another and better world" is supposed to be the new one.

As to the picture of "London literature"—guarded by international copyright—"driving their own out of the field"—it comes with peculiar grace from the advocates of an unrestrained reissue of English books at little more than the cost of paper and print. The very men who are scuttling the ship called authorship, to express fears of its being swamped by a sea! For it is obvious that the American, who thinks of literature as a profession, under such circumstances, might as well swarm up a lamp-post for a bee-tree—that if he hopes to enlighten his countrymen and be paid for his pains, he had better turn beaver, at once, and thrash mud with his tail.

And now farewell to Jonathan! It can be no unfriendly aspiration to wish that he may have Shakspeares and Miltons of his own—that he may breed Scotts, Wordsworths, Moores, Byrons, and Bulwers, as well as Washingtons, Jeffersons, Madisons, Clays, and General Jacksons. But if he desires to own any eternally everlasting, immortal names in literature, we must put down a traffic, particularly adapted to make a great country look little.

Turning eastward, and looking across another ocean, there is a little kingdom, wherein the Journeymen Minds of the capital have also greatly profited by the Master Minds of England—at least in the way of mammon. I allude to the Belgians, the most sordid, illiberal, and huckstering tradespeople in Europe, to whom Napoleon might justly have applied the epithet of "boutiquière," seeing that a "Banker" sometimes keeps his office in a back parlor, whilst his wife and daughters retail haberdashery in the front shop. A people whose revolution originated not in love of liberty, but love of money—not a religious repeal of an union of Catholic and Protestant—but a mere breeches-pocket change, from a desire to get rid of Dutch debt, and a Dutch-copartnership in commercial profits. A people, in short, who in spite of their getting rid of the Spaniards have retained their affection for "the Spanish"—and instead of combining opulence with a liberal expenditure, store up their wealth in miserly hiding places—just as a jackdaw deposits silver spoons, &c., in his rubbish saving banks, from a mere objectless propensity to hoarding.

Now, as regards literary piracy, the Americans may plead in mitigation, their common origin with the English, and their use—saving some uncommon odd phrases—of a common language. Jonathan can read and relish Hamlet or Paradise Lost, as well as John; and at any rate a large proportion of his reprints are for his own consumption. But there is no such excuse for the Belgians. Shakspeare and Milton! why, if they were translated expressly into Flemish, I should be sorry to guarantee the sale of fifty copies. There would be as much demand for them by the Flanders horses and marės that trot upon four legs, as by those that walk upon two. If they ever transplant from our Literature into their own Belles Lettres, it will be "Tate's Universal Cambist," or Somebody on Assurance For, sharpwitted as the Flemish may be at a bargain, in intellectual matters they are as Bœotian as if they had taken mud baths in their own bogs, and, as the old Bubble Man recommends, had given their heads the full benefit of the immersion.

It follows that the Brussels Printers cannot set up the pretence of the Boston ones—that they patriotically rob our great literary lamps, for the enlightenment of their own citizens. In Belgium there is a smoking, beer-drinking, estaminet-haunting, but no Reading Public. The books they consult are filled with "Flemish accounts"—the leaves they love are rolled up into cigars. In short, in the great March of Mind, the Flemish are as far behind as the baggage, or along with the suttlers, selling sausages and schnapps. It is a fair conclusion, then, that a great part of the English reprints must be intended for the London market, into which they can only be surreptitiously introduced, and, consequently, the Brussels publisher is not only a Pirate, but a smuggler—a Dick Hatteraick engrafted on Paul Jones. But I do injustice to the brave Buccaneer and the bold Freetrader by the comparison; there may be the same greed for gain, but there is no risk of life or limb to ennoble a traffic as paltry and fraudulent as the "sweating" of our Sovereigns.

Against these new "Brussels Sprouts," the vigilance of our customs ought to be particularly directed; and their confiscation should be strictly enforced. Of an International Copyright, there is no hope—looking at the sordid and unlettered character of the Belgians, the speech of the King, a commercial jealousy of England, and a general ill-will towards us. France and America may accede to our claims, and agree to protect our literary rights; but Belgium will be the last, the very last, to do justice *even* to the English.*

In the meantime let us hope that our own Legislature will extend all the protection it can afford to our Literature; as much security as it can give to the Publisher; and as much encouragement as it can bestow on the Author: Heaven knows he is in need of it! Hitherto he has only been robbed by the Statute of Anne, nor has the legal unkindness been atoned for by proportionate favor in other quarters. Where are his Honorary Distinctions? The highest honor ever conferred on an author—a peerage—was granted to Bubb Doddington—and then not for writing his life. Where are the lucrative Tellerships, Wardenships, Comptrollerships, Secretaryships, and Governorships dedicated as rewards to this species of Civil Merit?

"And Echo answers, where?"

Even the very few appointments heretofore allotted for its portion are going or gone. The examinership of Plays has passed from an Author to an Actor; and a prophetic soul augurs that the Laureateship, at the next vacancy, may go to a Painter.

So much for the distinctions bestowed on a Literary man during his life. Now for the honors paid to him at his death. We

* "We must be just even towards the English"—from the *Messager de Gand*, June 9, 1842.

all know how he lives. He writes for bread, and gets it short weight;—for money, and gets the wrong change;—for the Present, and he is pirated;—for the Future, and his children are disinherited for his pains. At last, he sickens, as he well may, and can write no more. He makes his will, but, for any literary property, might as well die intestate. His eldest son is his heir, but the Row administers. And so he dies, a beggar, with the world in his debt. Being poor, he is buried with less ceremony than Cock Robin. Had he been rich enough, he might have bought a "snug lying in the Abbey" of the Dean and Chapter of Westminster, who even then, true to the same style of treatment, would put him, were he the greatest and best of our Poets—as the mother puts the least and worst of her brats—into a Corner!

PROSPECTUS OF HOOD'S MAGAZINE.

WHATEVER may be thought of Dr. Dickson's theory, that the type of disease in general is periodical, there can be no doubt of its applicability to modern literature, which is essentially periodical, whether the type be long primer, brevier, or bourgeois. It appears, moreover, by the rapid consumption of monthlies, compared with the decline of the annuals, that frequent fits of publication are more prevalent and popular than yearly paroxysms.

Under these circumstances, no apology is necessary for the present undertaking; but custom, which exacts an overture to a new opera, and a prologue to a new play, requires a few words of introduction to a new monthly magazine.

One prominent object, then, of the projected publication, as implied by the sub-title of "Comic Miscellany," will be the supply of harmless "Mirth for the Million," and light thoughts, to a public sorely oppressed—if its word be worth a rush, or its complaints of an ounce weight—by hard times, heavy taxes, and those "eating cares" which attend on the securing of food for the day, as well as a provision for the future. For the relief of such afflicted classes, the editor, assisted by able humorists, will dispense a series of papers and woodcuts, which, it is hoped, will cheer the gloom of Willow Walk, and the loneliness of Wilderness Row—sweeten the bitterness of Camomile street and Wormwood street—smoothe the ruffled temper of Cross street, and enable even Crooked Lane to unbend itself! It is hardly necessary to promise that this end will be pursued without raising a maiden blush, much less a damask, in the nursery grounds of modesty—or trespassing, by wanton personalities, on the parks and lawns of private life. In a word, it will aim at being merry and wise, instead of merry and otherwise.

For the sedate, there will be papers of a becoming gravity; and the lover of poetry will be supplied with numbers in each number.

As to politics, the reader of HOOD'S MAGAZINE will vainly search in its pages for a panacea for agricultural distress, or a grand Catholicon for Irish agitation; he will uselessly seek to know whether we ought to depend for our bread on foreign farmers, or merely on foreign sea-fowl; or, if the repeal of the Union would produce low rents and only three quarter days. Neither must he hope to learn the proper terminus of reform, nor even whether a finality man means Campbell's last man, or an undertaker.

A total abstinence from such stimulating topics and fermented questions is, indeed, ensured by the established character of the editor, and his notorious aversion to party spirit. To borrow his own words, from a letter to the proprietors,—"I am no politician, and far from instructed on those topics which, to parody a common phrase, no gentleman's newspaper should be without. Thus, for any knowledge of mine, the Irish prosecutions may be for pirating the Irish melodies; the Pennsylvanians may have repudiated their wives; Duff Green may be a place, like Goose Green; Prince Polignac a dahlia or a carnation, and the Duc de Bordeaux a tulip. The Spanish affairs I could never master, even with a *Pronouncing* Dictionary at my elbow; it would puzzle me to see whether Queen Isabella's majority is or is not equal to Sir Robert Peel's; or, if the shelling the Barcelonese was done with bombs and mortars, or the nutcrackers. Prim may be a quaker, and the whole civil war about the Seville Oranges. Nay, even on domestic matters, nearer home, my profound political ignorance leaves me in doubt on questions concerning which the newsmen's boys and printers' devils have formed very decided opinions; for example, whether the corn law league ought to extend beyond three miles from Mark Lane —or the sliding scale should regulate the charges at the glaciarium—what share the Welsh whigs have had in the Welsh riots, and how far the Ryots in India were excited by the slaughter of the Brahmin Bull. On all such public subjects I am less *au fait* than that Publicist the Potboy, at the public-house, with the insolvent sign, The Hog in the Pound."

Polemics will be excluded with the same rigor; and especially the Tractarian schism. The reader of HOOD'S MAGAZINE must not hope, therefore, to be told whether an old Protestant church ought to be plastered with Roman cement; or if a design for a new one should be washed in with Newman's colors. And most egregiously will he be disappointed, should he look for controversial theology in our Poets' Corner. He might as well expect to see queens of Sheba, and divided babies, from wearing Solomon's spectacles!

For the rest, a critical eye will be kept on our current literature, a regretful one on the drama, and a kind one for the fine arts, from whose artesian well there will be an occasional *drawing*.

With this brief explanatory announcement, HOOD'S MAGAZINE AND COMIC MISCELLANY is left to recommend itself, by its own merits, to those enlightened judges, the reviewers; and to that impartial jury—too vast to pack in any case—the British public.

THE HAUNTED HOUSE;

A ROMANCE.

"A jolly place, said he, in days of old,
But something ails it now: the spot is curst."
HARTLEAP WELL, BY WORDSWORTH.

PART I.

SOME dreams we have are nothing else but dreams,
Unnatural and full of contradictions;
Yet others of our most romantic schemes
Are something more than fictions.

It might be only on enchanted ground;
It might be merely by a thought's expansion,
But in the spirit, or the flesh, I found
An old deserted mansion.

A residence for woman, child, and man,
A dwelling-place—and yet no habitation;
A house—but under some prodigious ban
Of excommunication.

Unhinged the iron gates half open hung,
Jarr'd by the gusty gales of many winters,
That from its crumbled pedestal had flung
One marble globe in splinters.

No dog was at the threshold, great or small;
No pigeon on the roof—no household creature—
No cat demurely dozing on the wall—
Not one domestic feature.

No human figure stirred, to go or come,
No face looked forth from shut or open casement;
No chimney smoked—there was no sign of home
From parapet to basement.

With shatter'd panes the grassy court was starr'd;
The time-worn coping-stone had tumbled after;
And thro' the ragged roof the sky shone, barr'd
With naked beam and rafter.

O'er all there hung a shadow and a fear,
A sense of mystery the spirit daunted,
And said, as plain as whisper in the ear,
The place is haunted!

The flow'r grew wild and rankly as the weed,
Roses with thistles struggled for espial,
And vagrant plants of parasitic breed
Had overgrown the dial.

But gay or gloomy, steadfast or infirm,
No heart was there to heed the hour's duration;
All times and tides were lost in one long term
Of stagnant desolation.

The wren had built within the porch, she found
Its quiet loneliness so sure and thorough;
And on the lawn—within its turfy mound—
The rabbit made his burrow.

The rabbit wild and grey, that flitted thro'
The shrubby clumps, and frisk'd, and sat, and vanish'd,
But leisurely and bold, as if he knew
His enemy was banish'd.

The wary crow—the pheasant from the woods—
Lull'd by the still and everlasting sameness,
Close to the mansion, like domestic broods,
Fed with a "shocking tameness."

The coot was swimming in the reedy pond,
Beside the water-hen, so soon affrighted;
And in the weedy moat the heron, fond
Of solitude, alighted.

The moping heron, motionless and stiff,
That on a stone, as silently and stilly,
Stood, an apparent sentinel, as if
To guard the water-lily.

No sound was heard except, from far away,
The ringing of the Whitwall's shrilly laughter,
Or, now and then, the chatter of the jay,
That Echo murmur'd after.

But Echo never mock'd the human tongue;
Some weighty crime, that Heaven could not pardon,
A secret curse on that old building hung,
And its deserted garden.

The beds were all untouch'd by hand or tool;
No footstep marked the damp and mossy gravel,
Each walk as green as is the mantled pool,
For want of human travel.

The vine unprun'd, and the neglected peach,
Droop'd from the wall with which they used to grapple;
And on the canker'd tree, in easy reach,
Rotted the golden apple.

But awfully the truant shunn'd the ground,
The vagrant kept aloof, and daring poacher;
In spite of gaps that thro' the fences round
Invited the encroacher.

For over all there hung a cloud of fear,
A sense of mystery the spirit daunted,
And said, as plain as whisper in the ear,
The place is haunted!

The pear and quince lay squander'd on the grass;
The mould was purple with unheeded showers
Of bloomy plums—a wilderness it was
Of fruits, and weeds, and flowers!

The marigold amidst the nettles blew,
The gourd embraced the rose-bush in its ramble,
The thistle and the stock together grew,
The holly-hock and bramble.

The bear-bine with the lilac interlac'd,
The sturdy burdock choked its slender neighbor,
The spicy pink. All tokens were effac'd
Of human care and labor.

The very yew formality had train'd
To such a rigid pyramidal stature,
For want of trimming had almost regain'd
The raggedness of nature.

The fountain was a-dry—neglect and time
Had marr'd the work of artisan and mason,
And efts and croaking frogs begot of slime,
Sprawl'd in the ruin'd bason.

The statue, fallen from its marble base,
Amidst the refuse leaves, and herbage rotten,
Lay like the idol of some by-gone race,
Its name and rites forgotten.

On ev'ry side the aspect was the same,
All ruin'd, desolate, forlorn, and savage:
No hand or foot within the precinct came
To rectify or ravage.

For over all there hung a cloud of fear
A sense of mystery the spirit daunted,
And said, as plain as whisper in the ear
The place is haunted!

PART II.

O, very gloomy is the House of Wo,
Where tears are falling while the bell is knelling,
With all the dark solemnities which show
That Death is in the dwelling!

O very, very dreary is the room
Where Love, domestic Love, no longer nestles,
But smitten by the common stroke of doom,
The corpse lies on the trestles!

But House of Wo, and hearse, and sable pall,
The narrow home of the departed mortal,
Ne'er looked so gloomy as that ghostly hall,
With its deserted portal!

The centipede along the threshold crept,
The cobweb hung across in mazy tangle,
And in its winding-sheet the maggot slept,
At every nook and angle.

The keyhole lodged the earwig and her brood,
The emmets of the steps had old possession,
And marched in search of their diurnal food
In undisturbed procession.

As undisturbed as the prehensile cell
Of moth or maggot, or the spider's tissue,
For never foot upon that threshold fell,
To enter or to issue.

O'er all there hung the shadow of a fear,
A sense of mystery the spirit daunted,
And said, as plain as whisper in the ear,
The place is haunted.

Howbeit, the door I pushed—or so I dreamed—
Which slowly, slowly gaped—the hinges creaking

With such a rusty eloquence, it seem'd
That time himself was speaking.

But Time was dumb within that mansion old,
Or left his tale to the heraldic banners
That hung from the corroded walls, and told
Of former men and manners.

Those tattered flags, that with the opened door,
Seemed the old wave of battle to remember,
While fallen fragments danced upon the floor
Like dead leaves in December.

The startled bats flew out—bird after bird—
The screech-owl overhead began to flutter,
And seemed to mock the cry that she had heard
Some dying victim utter!

A shriek that echoed from the joisted roof,
And up the stair, and further still and further,
Till in some ringing chamber far aloof
It ceased its tale of murther!

Meanwhile the rusty armor rattled round,
The banner shuddered, and the ragged streamer
All things the horrid tenor of the sound
Acknowledged with a tremor.

The antlers, where the helmet hung and belt,
Stirred as the tempest stirs the forest branches,
Or as the stag had trembled when he felt
The blood-hound at his haunches.

The window jingled in its crumbled frame,
And through its many gaps of destitution
Dolorous moans and hollow sighings came,
Like those of dissolution.

The wood-louse dropped, and rolled into a ball,
Touched by some impulse occult or mechanic;

And nameless beetles ran along the wall
In universal panic.

The subtle spider, that from overhead
Hung like a spy on human guilt and error,
Suddenly turned, and up its slender thread
Ran with a nimble terror.

The very stains and fractures on the wall,
Assuming features solemn and terrific,
Hinted some tragedy of that old hall,
Locked up in hieroglyphic.

Some tale that might, perchance, have solved the doubt,
Wherefore amongst those flags so dull and livid,
The banner of the BLOODY HAND shone out
So ominously vivid.

Some key to that inscrutable appeal,
Which made the very frame of nature quiver;
And every thrilling nerve and fibre feel
So ague-like a shiver.

For over all there hung a cloud of fear,
A sense of mystery the spirit daunted,
And said, as plain as whisper in the ear,
The place is haunted!

If but a rat had lingered in the house,
To lure the thought into a social channel!
But not a rat remained, or tiny mouse,
To speak behind the pannel.

Huge drops rolled down the walls, as if they wept;
And where the cricket used to chirp so shrilly,
The toad was squatting, and the lizard crept
On that damp hearth and chilly.

For years no cheerful blaze had sparkled there,
Or glanced on coat of buff or knightly metal;

The slug was crawling on the vacant chair,—
The snail upon the settle.

The floor was redolent of mould and must,
The fungus in the rotten seams had quickened;
While on the oaken table coats of dust
Perennially had thickened.

No mark of leathern jack or metal can,
No cup—no horn—no hospitable token,—
All social ties between that board and man
Had long ago been broken.

There was so foul a rumor in the air,
The shadow of a presence so atrocious;
No human creature could have feasted there,
Even the most ferocious!

For over all there hung a cloud of fear,
A sense of mystery the spirit daunted,
And said, as plain as whisper in the ear,
The place is haunted!

PART III.

'Tis hard for human actions to account,
Whether from reason or from impulse only—
But some internal prompting bade me mount
The gloomy stairs and lonely.

Those gloomy stairs, so dark, and damp, and cold,
With odors as from bones and relics carnal,
Deprived of rite, and consecrated mould,
The chapel vault, or charnel,

Those dreary stairs, where with the sounding stress
Of ev'ry step so many echoes blended,
The mind, with dark misgivings, feared to guess
How many feet ascended.

The tempest with its spoils had drifted in,
Till each unwholesome stone was darkly spotted,
As thickly as the leopard's dappled skin,
With leaves that rankly rotted.

The air was thick—and in the upper gloom
The bat—or something in its shape—was winging;
And on the wall, as chilly as a tomb,
The Death's-head moth was clinging.

That mystic moth, which, with a sense profound
Of all unholy presence, augurs truly;
And with a grim significance flits round
The taper burning bluely.

Such omens in the place there seemed to be,
At every crooked turn, or on the landing,
The straining eyeball was prepared to see
Some apparition standing.

For over all there hung a cloud of fear,
A sense of mystery the spirit daunted,
And said, as plain as whisper in the ear,
The place is haunted!

Yet no portentous shape the sight amazed;
Each object plain, and tangible, and valid;
But from their tarnished frames dark figures gazed,
And faces spectre-pallid.

Not merely with the mimic life that lies
Within the compass of Art's simulation:
Their souls were looking through their painted eyes
With awful speculation.

On every lip a speechless horror dwelt;
On every brow the burthen of affliction;
The old ancestral spirits knew and felt
The house's malediction.

Such earnest wo their features overcast,
They might have stirred, or sighed, or wept, or spoken;
But, save the hollow moaning of the blast,
The stillness was unbroken.

No other sound or stir of life was there,
Except my steps in solitary clamber,
From flight to flight, from humid stair to stair,
From chamber into chamber.

Deserted rooms of luxury and state,
That old magnificence had richly furnished
With pictures, cabinets of ancient date,
And carvings gilt and burnished.

Rich hangings, storied by the needle's art,
With scripture history, or classic fable;
But all had faded, save one ragged part,
Where Cain was slaying Abel.

The silent waste of mildew and the moth
Had marred the tissue with a partial ravage;
But undecaying frowned upon the cloth
Each feature stern and savage.

The sky was pale; the cloud a thing of doubt;
Some hues were fresh, and some decayed and duller;
But still the Bloody Hand shone strangely out
With vehemence of color!

The Bloody Hand that with a lurid stain
Shone on the dusty floor, a dismal token,
Projected from the casement's painted pane,
Where all beside was broken.

The Bloody Hand significant of crime,
That glaring on the old heraldic banner,
Had kept its crimson unimpaired by time,
In such a wondrous manner!

O'er all there hung the shadow of a fear,
A sense of mystery the spirit daunted,
And said, as plain as whisper in the ear,
The place is haunted!

The death-watch ticked behind the panneled oak,
Inexplicable tremors shook the arras,
And echoes strange and mystical awoke,
The fancy to embarrass.

Prophetic hints that filled the soul with dread,
But through one gloomy entrance pointing mostly
The while some secret inspiration said,
That chamber is the ghostly!

Across the door no gossamer festoon
Swung pendulous—no web—no dusty fringes,
No silky chrysalis or white cocoon,
About its nooks and hinges.

The spider shunned the interdicted room,
The moth, the beetle, and the fly were banished,
And where the sunbeam fell athwart the gloom
The very midge had vanished.

One lonely ray that glanced upon a Bed,
As if with awful aim direct and certain,
To show the BLOODY HAND in burning red
Embroidered on the curtain.

And yet no gory stain was on the quilt—
The pillow in its place had slowly rotted:
The floor alone retained the trace of guilt,
Those boards obscurely spotted.

Obscurely spotted to the door, and thence
With mazy doubles to the grated casement—
Oh what a tale they told of fear intense,
Of horror and amazement!

What human creature in the dead of night
Had coursed like hunted hare that cruel distance?
Had sought the door, the window in his flight,
Striving for dear existence?

What shrieking spirit in that bloody room
Its mortal frame had violently quitted?—
Across the sunbeam, with a sudden gloom,
A ghostly shadow flitted.

Across the sunbeam, and along the wall,
But painted on the air so very dimly,
It hardly veiled the tapestry at all,
Or portrait frowning grimly.

O'er all there hung the shadow of a fear,
A sense of mystery the spirit daunted,
And said, as plain as whisper in the ear,
The place is haunted!

LIFE IN THE SICK ROOM.*

Of all the know-nothing persons in this world, commend us to the man who has "never known a day's illness." He is a moral dunce; one who has lost the greatest lesson in life; who has skipped the finest lecture in that great school of humanity, the Sick Chamber. Let him be versed in mathematics, profound in metaphysics, a ripe scholar in the classics, a bachelor of arts, or even a doctor in divinity, yet is he as one of those gentlemen whose education has been neglected. For all his college acquirements, how inferior is he in wholesome knowledge to the mortal who has had but a quarter's gout, or a half-year of ague—how infinitely below the fellow-creature who has been soundly taught his tic-douloureux, thoroughly grounded in the rheumatics, and deeply red in the scarlet fever! And yet, what is more common than to hear a great hulking, florid fellow, bragging of an ignorance, a brutal ignorance, that he shares in common with the pig and the bullock, the generality of which die, probably, without ever having experienced a day's indisposition?

To such a monster of health the volume before us will be a sealed book; for how can he appreciate its allusions to physical suffering, whose bodily annoyance has never reached beyond a slight tickling of the epidermis, or the tingling of a foot gone to sleep? How should he, who has sailed through life with a clean bill of health, be able to sympathize with the feelings, or the quiet sayings and doings, of an invalid condemned to a life-long quarantine in his chamber? What should he know of Life in the Sick Room? As little as our poor paralytic grandmother knows of Life in London.

* Life in the Sick Room. By an Invalid. Moxon.

With ourselves it is otherwise. Afflicted for twenty years with a complication of disorders, the least of which is elephantiasis—bedridden on the broad of our back till it became narrow—and then confined to our chamber as rigidly as if it had been a cell in the Pentonville Penitentiary—we are in a fit state, body and mind, to appreciate such a production as Mr. Moxon—not the Effervescing Magnesian, but the worthy publisher—has forwarded with so much sagacity, or instinct, to our own sick ward. The very book for us! if, indeed, we are not actually the Anonymous of its dedication—the very fellow-sufferer on whose sympathy—"confidently reckoned on though unasked," the Invalid author so implicitly relies. We certainly do sympathize most profoundly; and as certainly we are a great sufferer,—the greatest, perhaps, in England, except the poor incurable man who is always being cured by Holloway's Ointment.

Enough of ourselves:—and now for the book. The first thing that struck us, on the perusal, was a very judicious omission. Most writers on such a topic as the sick-room would have begun by recommending some pet doctor, or favorite remedy for all diseases; whereas the author has preferred to advise on the selection of an eligible retreat for laying up for life, and especially of a window towards that good aspect, the face of Nature. And truly, a long term of infirm health is such a very bad look out, as to require some better prospect elsewhere. For, not to mention a church-yard, or a dead wall, what can be worse for a sick prisoner, than to pass year after year in some dull street, contemplating some dull house, never new-fronted, or even insured in a new fire-office, to add a new plate to the two old ones under the middle window? What more dreadful than to be driven by the monotony outside to the sameness within, till the very figures of the chintz curtain are daguerreotyped on the brain, or the head seems lined with a paper of the same pattern as the one on the wall? How much better, for soul and body, for the invalid to gaze on such a picture as this:—

"Between my window and the sea is a green down, as green as any field in Ireland; and on the nearer half of this down, haymaking goes forward in its season. It slopes down to a hollow, where the prior of old preserved his fish, there being sluices formerly at either end, the one opening upon the river, and the other upon the little haven below the priory, whose ruins still crown the rock. From the prior's fish-pond, the green down slopes upwards again to a ridge; and on the slope are cows grazing all summer, and half way into the winter. Over the ridge, I survey the harbor and all its traffic, the view extending from the light-houses far to the right, to a horizon of sea to the left. Beyond the harbor lies another county, with, first, its sandy beach, where there are frequent wrecks—too interesting to an invalid—and a fine stretch of rocky shore to the left; and above the rocks, a spreading heath, where I watch troops of boys flying their kites; lovers and friends taking their breezy walk on Sundays; the sportsman with his gun and dog; and the washerwomen converging from the farm-houses on Saturday evenings, to carry their loads, in company, to the village on the yet further height. I see them, now talking in a cluster, as they walk each with her white burden on her head, and now in file, as they pass through the narrow lane; and finally they part off on the village green, each to some neighboring house of the gentry. Behind the village and the heath, stretches the railroad; and I watch the train triumphantly careering along the level road, and puffing forth its steam above hedges and groups of trees, and then laboring and panting up the ascent, till it is lost between two heights, which at last bound my view. But on these heights are more objects; a windmill now in motion and now at rest; a lime-kiln, in a picturesque rocky field; an ancient church tower, barely visible in the morning, but conspicuous when the setting sun shines upon it; a colliery, with its lofty wagon-way, and the self-moving wagons running hither and thither, as if in pure wilfulness; and three or four farms, at various degrees of ascent, whose yards, paddocks, and dairies, I am better acquainted with than their inhabitants would believe possible. I know every stack of the one on the heights. Against the sky I see the stacking of corn and hay in the season, and can detect the slicing away of the provender, with an accurate eye, at the distance of several miles. I can follow the sociable farmer in his summer-evening ride, pricking on in the lanes where he is alone, in order to have more time for the unconscionable gossip at the gate of the next farm-house, and for the second talk over the paddock-fence of the next, or for the third or fourth before the porch, or over the wall, when the resident farmer comes out, pipe in mouth, and puffs away amidst his chat till the wife appears, with a shawl over her cap, to see what can detain him so long; and the daughter follows, with her gown turned over head (for it is now chill evening), and at last the social horseman finds he must be going, looks at his watch, and, with a gesture of surprise, turns his steed down a steep broken way to the beach, and canters home over the sands, left hard and wet by the ebbing tide, the white horse making his progress visible to me through the dusk. Then if the question arises which has most of the gossip spirit, he or I, there is no shame in the answer. Any such small amusement is better than harmless—is salutary—which carries the spirit of the sick prisoner abroad into the open air, and among country people. When I shut down my window, I feel that my mind has had an airing."

Here is another :—

"The sun, resting on the edge of the sea, was hidden from me by the walls of the old Priory: but a flood of rays poured through the windows of the ruin, and gushed over the waters, strewing them with diamonds, and then across the green down before my windows, gilding its furrows, and then lighting up the yellow sands on the opposite shore of the harbor, while the market-garden below was glittering with dew and busy with early bees and butterflies. Besides these bees and butterflies, nothing seemed stirring, except the earliest riser of the neighborhood, to whom the garden belongs. At the moment, she was passing down to feed her pigs, and let out her cows; and her easy pace, arms a-kimbo, and complacent survey of her early greens, presented me with a picture of ease so opposite to my own state, as to impress me ineffaceably. I was suffering too much to enjoy this picture at the moment: but how was it at the end of the year? The pains of all those hours were annihilated—as completely vanished as if they had never been; while the momentary peep behind the window-curtain made me possessor of this radiant picture for evermore."

The mention of pictures reminds us of certain ones, and a commentary whence the reader may derive either a recipe, or a warning, as he desires to be, or not to be, an invalid for the remainder of his life. O! those beautiful pictures by our favorite Cuyp, with their rich atmosphere as of golden sherry and water! That gorgeous light flooding the wide level pasture,—clinging to tree and stone, and trickling over into their shadows—a liquid radiance, we used to fancy we could wring out of the glowing herbage, and catch dripping from the sleek side of the dappled cow! Sad experience has made us personally acquainted with the original soil and climate of those scenes, and has painfully taught us that the rich glowing atmosphere was no such wholesome aërial negus as we supposed, but a mixture of sunshine and humid exhalations, lovely but noxious—a gilded ague, an illuminated fever, a glorified pestilence, —which poisons the springs of life at their source. Breathe it, in bad health, and your fugitive complaints will become chronic, —regular standards, entwined in all their branches by the parasitic low slow fever of the swamp. In short, you will probably be set in for a long season of foul bodily weather, and may at once consult our invalid how to play the part in a becoming manner, and "enjoy bad health" with something of the cheerful philosophic spirit of the family man, who on being asked if he had not a "sick-house," replied, "Yes—but I've a *well* staircase."

The first grand step towards laying up in ordinary is to get rid of the superb egotism and splendid selfishness of the condition. Lamb, in one of his essays, has vividly described the gloomy absolutism of the sick man, obsequiously waited on by his household slaves, eager to anticipate his every want and wish, and to administer to his merest whims and caprices. And, for a short reign, such a tyranny may pass, but the confirmed invalid must prepare for a more moderate rule; a limited monarchy instead of a despotism. It requires some self-sacrifice to renounce such autocratical power, and will need much vigilance to prevent a relapse. But who, save a domestic Nero, would wish to indulge in such *ill* behavior as the following, for a permanence?

> "I have known the most devoted and benevolent of women call up her young nurse from a snatch of sleep at two in the morning, to read aloud, when she had been reading aloud for six or seven hours of the preceding day. I have known a kind-hearted and self-denying man require of two or three members of his family to sit and talk and be merry in his chamber, two or three hours after midnight: and both for want of a mere intimation that it was night, and time for the nurse's rest. How it makes one shudder to think of this being one's own case!"

It is rather difficult to believe in the habitual benevolence or considerateness of the parties who needed a broad hint on such matters; and yet real illness may make even a self-denying nature somewhat *exigéant,* when mere fanciful ailment renders selfishness so intensely selfish. Ask the physician, surgeon, and apothecary, and they will tell you, that for every hard-hearted medical man, who refuses or delays to attend on the urgent seizures and accidents of the poor, there are thousands of practitioners dragged from their warm beds at night, through wind, rain, snow, sleet, hail, and thunder and lightning—over heaths ana tnrough marshes, and along country cross-roads—at the risk of catarrh, rheumatism, ague, bronchitis, and inflammation—of falls, fractures, and footpads—on the most frivolous pretences that wealth and the vapors can invent. There is even a perversity in some natures that would find a dirty comfort in the muddy discomfort of an Esculapius soused in provincial muck, like Doctor Slop, by an encounter with a coach-horse—for what right has the physician to enjoy more bodily ease than his patient? For such a spirit we imperatiৎely prescribe a chapter of "Life in the Sick-room," night and morning, until he learns that the very worst excuse a man can offer for selfishness is, that he is "not quite himself."

There is, however, another peril of invalidism, akin to the "damning of sins we have no mind to," described in Hudibras;—

> "We are in ever-growing danger of becoming too abstract,—of losing our sympathy with passing emotions,—and particularly with those shared by numbers. There was a time we went to public worship with others,—to the theatre,—to public meetings; when we were present at picnic parties and other festivals, and heard general conversation every day of our lives. Now, we are too apt to forget those times. The danger is, lest we should get to despise them, and to fancy ourselves superior to our former selves, because now we feel no social transports."

True. We have ourselves felt a touch of that peril in our weaker moments—on some dull, cold, wet day, when our pores, acting inversely, instead of throwing off moisture, take in as much as they can collect from the damp atmosphere, well chilled by an easterly wind. At such times a sort of Zimmermannishness has crept over us, like a moral gooseskin, inducing a low estimate enough of all gregarious enjoyments, public meetings, and public dinners; and, above all, those public choruses on Wilhem's method, at Exeter Hall. What sympathy can We-by-ourselves-We have with Music for a Million? But the fit soon evaporates, when, looking into the garden, we see Theophilus Junior, that second edition of our boyhood, in default of brothers or playmates, making a whole mob of himself, or at the least a troop of cavalry, commanding for the captain, huzzaing for the soldiers, blowing flourishes for the trumpeter, and even prancing, neighing, and snorting for all the horses! One dose of that joyous Socialism is a cure for our worst attack of the mopes. The truth is, an invalid's misanthropy is no more in earnest than the piety of the sick demon who wanted to be a monk, or the sentence about being weary of existence, to which Hypochondriasis puts a period with a Parr's Life Pill!

A more serious peril, from illness, concerns the temper. When the nerves are irritable, and the skin is irritable, and the stomach is irritable—not to be irritable altogether is a moral miracle; and especially in England, where, by one of the anomalies of the constitution, whilst a man cannot be tried twice for the same offence, his temper may be tried over and over again for no offence at all. Indeed, as our author says, "there are cases, and not a few, where an invalid's freedom from irritability is a merit of the highest order." For example, after soot in your gruel, tallow grease in your barley-water, and snuff over your light pudding, to have "the draught as before" poured into your wakeful eyes, instead of your open mouth, by a drunken Mrs. Gamp, or one of her stamp. To check at such a moment the explosive speech, is at least equal to spiking a cannon in the heat of battle. There is beyond denial an ease to the chest, or somewhere, in a passionate objurgation—("Swear, my dear," said Fuseli to his wife, "it will relieve you")—so much so, that a certain invalid of our acquaintance, doubly afflicted with a painful complaint, and an unmanageable hard-mouthed temper, regularly retains, as helper to the sick-nurse, a stone-deaf old woman, whom he can abuse without violence to her feelings.

How much better to have emulated the heavenly patience in sickness, of which woman—in spite of Job—has given the brightest examples;—Woman, who endures the severest trials, with a meekness and submission, unheard of amongst men, the quaker excepted, who merely said, when his throat was being cut rather roughly—"Friend, thee dost haggle."

It must not be concealed, however, as regards irritability of temper in the sick-room—there are faults on both sides—captious nurses as well as querulous nurselings. Cross-patches themselves, they willingly mistake the tones and accents of intolerable anguish, naturally sharp and hurried, for those of anger and impatience—and even accuse pain, in its contortions, of making faces, and set up their backs at the random speeches of poor delirium! Then there are your lecturers, who preach patience in the very climax of a paroxysm, when the sermon can scarcely be heard, certainly not understood—as if a martyr, leaping mad with the toothache, could be calmed by reading to him the advertisement of the American Soothing Syrup! And then there is the she-dragon, who bullies the sufferer into comparative quiet! Not that the best of attendants is the smooth-tongued. Our invalid objects wisely to the sick being flattered, in season or out, with false hopes and views. As much panada, sago, or arrowroot as you please, but no flummery.

"Let the nurse avow that the medicine is nauseous. Let the physician declare that the treatment will be painful. Let sister, or brother, or friend, tell me that I must never look to be well. When the time approaches that I am to die, let me be told that I am to die, and when. If I encroach thoughtlessly on the time or strength of those about me, let me be reminded; if selfishly, let me be remonstrated with. Thus to speak the truth with love is in the power of us all."

And so say we. There is nothing worse for soul or body than the feverish agitation kept up by the struggle between external assurances and the internal conviction; for the mind will cling with forlorn pertinacity to the most desperate chance, like the sailor, who, when the ship was in danger of sinking, lashed himself to the sheet-anchor because it was the emblem of Hope. Till the truth is known there can be no calm of mind. It is only after he has abandoned all prospects of pardon or reprieve, that the capital convict sleeps soundly and dreams of green fields. So with ourselves, once satisfied that our case was beyond remedy, we gave up without reserve all dreams of future health and strength, and prepared, instead, to compete with that very able invalid who was able to be knocked down with a feather. Thenceforward, free of those jarring vibrations between hope and fear, relieved from all tantalizing speculations on the weather's clearing up, our state has been one of comparative peace and ease. We would not give one of our Pectoral Lozenges to be told, we are looking better than a month ago—not a splinter of our broken crutch to be promised a new lease of life—a renewal of our youth like the eagle's! Such flatteries go in at one ear, the deaf one, and out at the other. We never shall be well again, till broken bones are mended with "soft-sawder."

Are we, therefore, miserable, hypped, disconsolate? Answer, ye book-shelves, whence we draw the consolations of Philosophy, the dreams of Poetry and Romance—the retrospections of History; and glimpses of society from the better novels; mirth, comfort, and entertainment even for those small hours become so long from an unhealthy vigilance. Answer, ye pictures and prints, a Portrait Gallery of Nature!—and reply in your own tones, dear old fiddle, so often tuned to one favorite sadly-sweet air, and the words of Curran:

"But since in wailing
There's naught availing,
But Death unfailing
Must strike the blow,
Then for this reason,
And for a season,
Let us be merry before we go!"

It is melancholy, doubtless, to retire, in the prime of life, from the whole wide world, into the narrow prison of a sick-room. How much worse if that room be a wretched garret, with the naked tiles above and the bare boards below—no swinging bookshelf—not a penny colored print on the blank wall! And yet that forlorn attic is but the type of a more dreadful destitution, an unfurnished mind! The mother of Bloomfield used to say, that to encounter Old Age, Winter, and Poverty, was like meeting three giants; she might have added two more as huge and terrible, Sickness, and Ignorance—the last not the least of the Monster Evils; for it is he who affects pauperism with a deeper poverty—the beggary of the mind and soul.

"I have said how unavailing is luxury when the body is distressed and the spirit faint. At such times, and at all times, we cannot but be deeply grieved at the conception of the converse of our own state, at the thought of the multitude of the poor suffering under privation, without the support and solace of great ideas. It is sad enough to think of them on a winter's night, aching with cold in every limb, and sunk as low as we in nerve and spirits, from their want of sufficient food. But this thought is supportable in cases where we may fairly hope that the greatest ideas are cheering them as we are cheered; that there is a mere set-off of their cold and hunger against our disease; and that we are alike inspired by spiritual vigor in the belief that our Father is with us—that we are only encountering the probations of our pilgrimage—that we have a divine work given us to carry out, now in pain and now in joy. There is comfort in the midst of the sadness and shame when we are thinking of the poor who can reflect and pray—of the old woman who was once a punctual and eager attendant at church—of the wasting child who was formerly a Sunday-scholar—of the reduced gentleman or destitute student who retain the privilege of their humanity—of 'looking before and after.' But there is no mitigation of the horror when we think of the savage poor, who form so large a proportion of the hungerers—when we conceive of them suffering the privation of all good things at once—suffering under the aching cold, the sinking hunger, the shivering nakedness—without the respite or solace afforded by one inspiring or beguiling idea.

"I will not dwell on the reflection. A glimpse into this hell ought to suffice (though we to whom imagery comes unbidden, and cannot be banished at will, have to bear much more than occasional glimpses); a glimpse ought to suffice to set all to work to procure for every one of these sufferers, bread and warmth, if possible, and as soon as possible; but above everything, and without the loss of an hour, an entrance upon their spiritual birthright. Every man, and every woman, however wise and tender, appearing and designing to be, who for an hour helps to keep closed the entrance to the region of ideas—who stands between sufferers and great thoughts (which are the angels of consolation sent by God to all to whom he has given souls), are, in so far, ministers of hell, not themselves inflicting torment, but intercepting the influences which would assuage or overpower it. Let the plea be heard of us sufferers who know well the power of ideas—our plea for the poor—that, while we are contriving for all to be fed and cherished by food and fire, we may meanwhile kindle the immortal vitality within them, and give them that ethereal solace and sustenance which was meant to be shared by all, 'without money and without price.'"

Never, then, tell a man, permanently sick, that he will again be a perfect picture of health when he has not the frame for it—nor hint to a sick woman, incurably smitten, that the seeds of her disease will flourish and flower into lilies and roses. Why deter them from providing suitable pleasures and enjoyments to replace those delights of health and strength of which they must take leave for ever? Why not rather forewarn them of the Lapland Winter to which they are destined, and to trim their lamps spiritual, for the darkness of a long seclusion? Tell them their doom; and let them prepare themselves for it, according to the Essays before us, so healthy in tone, though from a confirmed invalid—so wholesome and salutary, though furnished from a Sick Room.

AN AUTOGRAPH.

To D. A. A., Esq., *Edinburgh.*

I AM much flattered by your request, and quite willing to accede to it; but, unluckily, you have omitted to inform me of the sort of thing you want.

Autographs are of many kinds. Some persons chalk them on walls: others inscribe what may be called auto-lithographs, in sundry colors, on the flag stones. Gentlemen in love delight in carving their autographs on the bark of trees; as other idle fellows are apt to hack and hew them on tavern-benches and rustic seats. Amongst various modes, I have seen a shop-boy dribble his autograph from a tin of water on a dry pavement.

The autographs of the Charity Boys are written on large sheets of paper, illuminated with engravings, and are technically called "pieces." The celebrated Miss Biffin used to distribute autographs amongst her visitors, which she wrote with a pen grasped between her teeth. Another, a German Phenomenon, held the implement with his toes.

The Man in the Iron Mask scratched an autograph with his fork on a silver plate, and threw it out of the window. Baron Trenck smudged one with a charred stick: and Silvio Pellico, with his fore-finger dipped in a mixture of soot-and-water.

Lord Chesterfield wrote autographs on windows with a diamond pencil. So did Sir Walter Raleigh and Queen Elizabeth.

Draco, when Themis requested a few *sentences* for her album, dipped his stylus in human blood. Faust used the same fluid in the autograph he bartered with Mephistophiles.

The Hebrews write their Shpargotua backwards; and some of the Orientals used to clothe them in hieroglyphics. An ancient Egyptian, if asked for his autograph, would probably have sent to the collector a picture of what Mrs. Malaprop calls "An Allegory on the Banks of the Nile."

Aster, the Archer, volunteered an autograph and sent it bang into Phillip's right eye.

Some individuals are so chary of their hand-writing as to bestow, when requested, only a mark or cross:—others more liberally adorn a specimen of their penmanship with such extraneous flourishes as a corkscrew, a serpent, or a circumbendibus, not to mention such caligraphic fancies as eagles, ships, and swans.

Then again, there are what may be called Mosaic Autographs —*i. e.* inlaid with cockle-shells, blue and white pebbles, and the like, in a little gravel walk. Our grandmothers worked their autographs in canvass samplers; and I have seen one wrought out with pins' heads on a huge white pincushion—as thus:

WELCOME SWEET BABBY.

MARY JONES.

When the sweetheart of Mr. John Junk requested his autograph, and explained what it was, namely, "a couple of lines or so, with his name to it," he replied, that he would leave it to her in his Will, seeing as how it was "done with gunpowder on his left arm."

There have even been autographs written by proxy. For example, Dr. Dodd penned one for Lord Chesterfield; but to oblige a stranger in this way is very dangerous, considering how easily a few lines may be twisted into a rope.

According to Lord Byron, the Greek girls compound autographs as apothecaries make up prescriptions,—with such materials as flowers, herbs, ashes, pebbles, and bits of coal. Lord Byron himself, if asked for a specimen of his hand, would probably have sent a plaster cast of it.

King George the Fourth and the Duke of York, when their autographs were requested for a Keepsake,—royally favored the applicant with some of their old Latin-English exercises.

With regard to my own particular practice, I have often traced an autograph with my walking-stick on the sea-sand. I also seem to remember writing one with my fore-finger on a dusty table, and am pretty sure I could do it with the smoke of a candle on the ceiling. I have seen something like a very badly scribbled autograph made by children with a thread of treacle on a slice of suet dumpling. Then it may be done with vegetables. My little girl grew her autograph the other day in mustard and cress.

Domestic servants, I have observed, are fond of scrawling autographs on a teaboard with the slopped milk. Also of scratching them on a soft deal dresser, the lead of the sink, and, above all, the quicksilver side of a looking-glass—a surface, by the bye, quite irresistible to any one who *can* write, and does not bite his nails.

A friend of mine possesses an autograph—"REMEMBER JIM HOSKINS"—done with a red-hot poker on the back-kitchen door. This, however, is awkward to bind up.

Another—but a young lady—possesses a book of autographs, filled just like a tailor's pattern-book—with samples of stuff and fustian.

The foregoing, sir, are but a few of the varieties; and the questions that have occurred to me in consequence of your only naming the genus, and not the species, have been innumerable. Would the gentleman like it short or long? for Doppeldickius, the learned Dutchman, wrote an autograph for a friend, which the latter published in a quarto volume. Would he prefer it in red ink, or black,—or suppose he had it in Sympathetic, so that he could draw me out when he pleased? Would he choose it on white paper, or tinted, or embossed, or on common brown paper, like Maroncelli's? Would he like it without my name to it—as somebody favored me lately with his autograph in an anonymous letter? Would he rather it were like Guy Faux's to Lord Mounteagle (not Spring Rice), in a feigned hand? Would he relish it in the aristocratical style, *i. e.*, partially or totally illegible? Would he like it—in case he shouldn't like it—on a slate?

With such a maze to wander in, if I should not take the exact course you wish, you must blame the short and insufficient clue you have afforded me. In the mean time, as you have not forwarded to me a tree or a table,—a paving-stone or a brick wall,—a looking-glass or a window,—a teaboard or a silver plate,—a bill-stamp or a back-kitchen door,—I presume, to conclude, that you want only a common pen-ink-and-paper autograph; and in the absence of any particular direction for its transmission,—for instance, by a carrier-pigeon—or in a fire-balloon—or set adrift in a bottle—or per wagon—or favored by Mr. Waghorn—or by telegraph, I think the best way will be to send it to you in *print*.

I am, Sir,
Your most obedient Servant,
THOMAS HOOD.

DOMESTIC MESMERISM.

"Gape, sinner, and swallow."—*Meg Merrilies.*

It is now just a year since we reviewed Miss Martineau's "Life in the Sick Room," and left the authoress set in for a house-ridden invalid, alternating between her bed and the sofa; unable to walk out of doors, but enjoying through her window and a telescope the prospect of green downs and heath, an old priory, a lime-kiln, a colliery railway, an ancient church, a windmill, a farm, with hay and corn stacks, a market-garden, gossipping farmers, sportsmen, boys flying kites, washerwomen, a dairy maid feeding pigs, the lighthouses, harbor, and shipping of Newcastle-on-Tyne, and a large assortment of objects, pastoral, marine, and picturesque. There we left the "sick prisoner," as we supposed, quite aware of a condition beyond remedy, and cheerfully made up for her fate by the help of philosophy, laudanum, and Christian resignation.

There never was a greater mistake. Instead of the presumed calm submission in a hopeless case, the invalid was intently watching the progress of a new curative legerdemain, sympathizing with its repudiated professors, and secretly intending to try whether her own chronic complaint could not be conjured away with a "Hey, presto! pass and repass!" like a pea from under the thimble. The experiment, it seems, has been made, and lo! like one of the patients of the old quacksalvers, forth comes Miss Martineau on the public stage, proclaiming to the gaping crowd how her long-standing, inveterate complaint, that baffled all the doctors, has been charmed away like a wart, and that, from being a helpless cripple, she has thrown away her crutches, literal or metaphorical, and can walk a mile as well as any Milesian. And this miraculous cure, not due to Holloway, Parr, Morison, or any of the rest of the faculty, not to any marvellous ointment, infallible pills, or new discovery in medicine, but solely to certain magical gesticulations, as safe, pleasant, and easy as playing at cat's cradle—in short by mesmerism!

Now we are, as we have said before, the greatest invalid in England; with a complication of complaints requiring quite a staff of physicians, each to watch and treat the particular disease which he has made his peculiar study: as, one for the heart, another for the lungs, a third for the stomach, a fourth for the liver, and so on. Above all, we are incapable of pedestrian locomotion; lamer than Crutched Friars, and, between gout in our ankles and rheumatism in our knees, could as easily walk on our head, like Quilp's boy, as on our legs. It would delight us, therefore, to believe that by no painful operation, but only a little posture-making behind our back or to our face, we could be restored to the use of our precious limbs, to walk like a leaguer, and run again like a renewed bill. But, alas! an anxious examination of Miss Martineau's statements has satisfied us that there is no chance of such a desirable consummation; that, to use a common phrase, "the news is too good to be true." We have carefully waded through the Newcastle letters, occupying some two dozen mortal columns of the "Athenæum," and with something of the mystified feeling of having been reading by turns and snatches in Moore's Almanac, Zadkiel's Astrology, a dream-book, and a treatise on metaphysics, have come to the sorrowful conclusion that we have as much chance of a cure by mesmerism, as of walking a thousand miles in a thousand hours through merely reading the constant advertisements of the Patent Pedometer. A conviction not at all removed by an actual encounter with a professor, who, after experimenting on the palms of our hands without exciting any peculiar sensation, except that quivering of the diaphragm which results from suppressed laughter, gravely informed us—slipping through a pleasant loophole of retreat from all difficulties—that "we were not in a fit state."

The precise nature of Miss Martineau's complaint is not stated; nor is it material to be known except to the professional man; the great fact, that after five years' confinement to the house she can walk as many miles without fatigue, thanks to the mysterious Ism, "that sadly wants a new name," is a sufficient subject for wonder, curiosity, and common sense, to discuss. A result obtained, it appears, after two months *passed* under the hands of three several persons—a performance that must be reckoned rather slow for a miracle, seeing that if we read certain passages aright, a mesmerizer, "with a white hat and an illuminated profile, like a saint or an angel," is gifted with powers little, if at all, inferior to those of the old apostles. The delay, moreover, throws a doubt on the source of relief, for there are many diseases to which such an interval would allow of a natural remission.

In the curative process, the two most remarkable phenomena were—1st, That the patient, with a weasel-like vigilance, did not go as usual into the magnetic sleep or trance; and, 2dly, That every glorified object before her was invested with a peculiar light, so that a bust of Isis burnt with a phosphoric splendor, and a black, dirty, Newcastle steam-tug shone with heavenly radiance. Appearances, for which we at once take the lady's word, but must decline her inference, that they had any influence in setting her on her legs again. The nerves, and the optic ones especially, were, no doubt, in a highly excited state; but that a five-year-old lameness derived any relaxation from the effulgence we will believe, when the broken heart of a soldier's widow is bound up by a general illumination. Indeed, we remember once to have been personally visited with such lights, that we saw two candles instead of one—but we decidedly walked the worse for it.

On the subject of other visionary appearances Miss Martineau is less explicit, or rather tantalizingly obscure; for, after hinting that she has seen wonders above wonders, instead of favoring us with her revelations or mysteries, like Ainsworth or Eugene Sue, she plumply says that she means to keep them to herself.

"Between this condition and the mesmeric sleep there is a state, transient and rare, of which I have had experience, but of which I intend to give no account. A somnambule calls it a glimmering of the lights of somnambulism and clairvoyance. To me there appears nothing like glimmering in it The ideas that I have snatched from it, and now retain, are, of all ideas which ever visited me, the most lucid and impressive. It may be well that they are incommunicable—partly from their nature and relations, and partly from their unfitness for translation into mere words. I will only say that the condition is one of no 'nervous excitement,' as far as experience and outward indications can be taken as a test. Such a state of repose, of calm translucent intellectuality, I had never conceived of; and no reaction followed, no excitement but that which is natural to every one who finds himself in possession of a great new idea."

So that whether she obtained a glimpse of the New Jerusalem, or a peep into the World of Spirits, or saw the old gentleman himself, is left to wide conjecture. Our own guess, in the absence of all direction, is, that she enjoyed a mesmeric translation into another planet, and derived her great idea from the Man in the Moon!

This, however, is not the only suppression. For instance, it is said that one of the strongest powers of the girl J., the somnambulist, was the discernment of disease, its condition and remedies; that she cleared up her own case first, prescribing for herself very fluently, and then medically advised Miss Martineau, and that the treatment in both cases succeeded. Surely, in common charity to the afflicted, these infallible remedies ought to have been published; their nature ought to have been indicated, if only to enable one to judge of supernatural prescribing compared with professional practice; but so profound a silence is preserved on these points as to lead to the inevitable conclusion, that the mesmeric remedies, like the quack medicines, are to be secured by patent, and to be sold at so much a family bottle, stamp included. One recipe only transpires, of so common-place and popular a character, and so little requiring inspiration for its invention—so ludicrously familiar to wide-awake advisers, that our sides shake to record how Miss Martineau, restless and sleepless for want of her abandoned opiates, was ordered ale at dinner, and brandy and water for a nightcap. Oh J. J.! well does thy initial stand also for Joker!

In addition to these suppressions, one unaccountable omission has certainly staggered us, as much as if we had considered it through a couple of bottles of wine. In common with ourselves, our clever friend T. L., and many other persons—who all hear the music of the spheres, dumb bells, and other mute melodies as distinctly as the rest of the world, but of gross mundane sounds and noises are unconscious as the adder—Miss Martineau is very deaf indeed. Here then was an obvious subject for experiment, and having been so easily cured of one infirmity it seems only natural that it should have occurred to the patient to apply instanter to the same agency for relief from another disability—that she should have requested her mesmerizer to quicken her hearing as well as her pace. But on the contrary, her ears seem quite to have slipped out of her head; and at an advanced stage of the proceedings we find her awaiting J.'s revelations, "with an American friend repeating to her on the instant, on account of her deafness, every word as it fell." And to make the omission more glaring, it is in the midst of speculations on the mesmeric sharpening of another sense, till it can see through deal-boards, millstones, and "barricadoes as lustrous as ebony," that she neglects to ascertain whether her hearing might not be so improved as to perceive sounds through no denser medium than the common air! Such an interesting experiment in her own person ought surely to have preceded the trials whether "J." could see, and draw ships and churches with her eyes shut; and the still more remote inquiry whether at the day of judgment we are to rise with or without our bodies, including the auricular organs. If dull people can be cured of stone deafness by a few magnetic passes, so pleasant a fact ought not to be concealed; whatever the consequence to the proprietors of registered Voice Conductors and Cornets.

Along with the experiment, we should have been glad of more circumstantial references to many successful ones merely assumed and asserted. There is, indeed, nothing throughout the Letters more singular than the complacency with which we are expected to take disputed matters for granted; as if all her readers were in magnetic *rapport* with the authoress, thinking as she thinks, seeing as she sees, and believing as she believes. Thus the theory, that the mind of the somnambulist mirrors that of the mesmerizer, is declared pretty clearly proved, "*when* an ignorant child, ignorant especially of the Bible, discourses of the Scriptures and divinity with a clergyman, and of the nebulæ with an astronomer;" a *when* perfectly satisfactory to the writer, but which sticks in our throat like its namesake for *goître*. We should be delighted to know the whereabouts of that Wonderful Child, and its caravan. And here are more whens;—

"What becomes of really divine inspiration *when* the commonest people find they can elicit marvels of prevision and insight? What becomes of the veneration for religious contemplation *when* ecstacies are found to be at the command of very unhallowed—wholly unauthorized hands? What becomes of the respect in which the medical profession onght to be held, *when* the friends of the sick and suffering, with their feelings all alive, see the doctor's skill and science overborne and set aside by means at the command of an ignorant neighbor—means which are all ease and pleasantness? How can the profession hold its dominion over minds, however backed by law and the opinion of the educated, *when* the vulgar see and know that limbs are removed without pain, in opposition to the will of doctors, and in spite of their denial of the facts? What avails the decision of a whole college of surgeons, that such a thing could not be, *when* a whole town full of people know that it was? What becomes of the transmission of fluid *when* the mesmerist acts, without concert, on a patient a hundred miles off?"

To all of which Echo answers "When?"—whilst another memorable one adds "Where?" In fact, had the letters been delivered as speeches, the orator would continually have been interrupted with such cries, and for "name! name!"

In the same style we are told that we need not quarrel about the name to be given to a power "that can make the deaf and dumb hear and speak; disperse dropsies, banish fevers, asthmas and paralysis, absorb tumors, and cause the severance of nerve, bone, and muscle to be unfelt." Certainly not—nor about the name to be bestowed on certain newly-invented magnetic rings, that have appeared simultaneously with the Newcastle letters, and are said to cure a great variety of diseases. We only object—as we should in passing a tradesman's accounts—to take mere items for facts that are unsupported by vouchers. But it is obvious throughout that Miss Martineau forgets she is not addressing magnetizers; instead of considering herself as telling a ghost story to people who did not believe in apparitions, and consequently fortifying her narrative with all possible evidence, corroborative and circumstantial. This is evident, from the trusting simplicity with which she relates all the freaks and fancies of the somnambulist J., in spite of their glaring absurdities and inconsistencies. For instance, her vocabulary is complained of with its odd and vulgar phrases, so inferior to the high tone of her ideas, and the subjects of her discourse: whereas, like the child that talked of nebulæ, and was up to astronomical technicals, she ought to have used as refined language as her mesmerizer, the well-educated widow of a clergyman. So when a glass of proper magnetic water was willed to be porter on her palate, she called it obliquely "a nasty sort of beer," when, reflecting the knowledge of her mesmerizer, she should have recognized it by name as well as by taste; and again, in the fellow experiment, when the water was willed to be sherry, she described it as wine, "white wine;" and moreover, on drinking half a tumbler, became so tipsy, that she was afraid to rise from the chair or walk, or go down stairs, "for fear of falling and spoiling her face." The thing, however, was not original. Miss Martineau insinuates that mesmerism is much older than Mesmer; and in reality the reader will remember a sham-Abram feast of the same kind in the Arabian Nights, where the Barmecide willed ideal mutton, barley-broth, and a fat goose with sweet sauce—and how Shacabac, to humor his entertainer, got drunk on imaginary wine.

The whole interlude, indeed, in which J. figures, if not very satisfactory to the skeptical, is rather amusing. She is evidently an acute, brisk girl of nineteen, with a turn for fun—"very fond of imitating the bagpipes" in her merry moods—and ready to go the whole Magnetic Animal, even to the "mesmerizing herself,"—an operation as difficult, one would imagine, as self-tickling. She exhibits, in fact, a will of her own, and an independence quite at variance with the usual subjection to a superior influence. She wakes at her own pleasure from her trances—is not so abstracted in them as to forget her household errands, that she has to go to the shop over the way—and without any mesmeric introduction gets into *rapport* with the music next door, which sets her mocking all the instruments of an orchestra, dancing, and describing the company in a ball-room. Another day, when one of the phrenological organs was affected, she was thrown into a paroxysm of order, and was "almost in a frenzy of trouble because she could not make two pocket-handkerchiefs lie flat and measure the same size"—all very good fun, and better than stitching or darning. But she preferred higher game. "I like to look up and see spiritual things. I can see diseases, and I like to see visions!" And accordingly she did see a vision—by what must be called clairvoyance's long range—of a shipwreck, with all its details, between Gottenburg and Elsinore.

This "inexplicable anecdote" Miss Martineau gives with the usual amiable reliance on the reader's implicit credence, declaring that she cannot discover any chink by which deception could creep in; whereas there is a gaping gap as practicable as any breach ever made by battery. To give any weight whatever to such a tale, two conditions are absolutely essential; that the intelligence should not have been received in the town; and that if it had, the girl should have had no opportunity of hearing the news. And was this the case? By no means. On the contrary, J. *had been out on an errand*, and immediately on her return she was mesmerized, and related her vision; the news arriving by natural means, so simultaueously with the revelation, that she presently observed, "my aunt is below, telling them all about it and I shall hear all about it when I go down." To be expected to look on a maid of Newcastle as a she-Ezekiel, on such terms, really confirms us in an opinion we have gradually been forming, that Miss Martineau never in her life looked at a human gullet by the help of a table-spoon.

In justice, however, it must be said, that the letter-writer gives credit as freely as she requires it; witness the vision just referred to, which it is confidently said was impossible to be known by ordinary means, coupled with an equally rash assertion, that the girl had not seen her aunt, "the only person (in all Newcastle!) from whom tidings of the shipwreck could be obtained." The truth is, with a too easy faith, Miss Martineau greatly underrates the mischievous propensities and wicked capabilities of human nature. She says,

"I am certain that it is not in human nature to keep up for seven weeks, without slip or trip, a series of deceptions so multifarious; and I should say so of a perfect stranger as confidently as I say it of this girl, whom I know to be incapable of deception, as much from the character of her intel lect as of her *morale.*'

It is certain, nevertheless, that Mary Tofts, the Rabbit-breeder, Ann Moore, the Fasting Woman of Tutbury, Scratching Fanny, and other impostors, young and old, exhibited extraordinary patience and painful perseverance in their deceptions combined with an art and cunning that deluded doctors medical, spiritual, and lexicographical, with many people of quality of both sexes. These, it is true, were all superstitious or credulous persons, who believed all they could get to believe; and what else are those individuals now-a-days, who hold that mesmerism is as ancient as the Delphian Oracle, and that witchcraft was one of its forms? In common consistency such a faith ought to go all lengths with the American sea-serpent, the whole breadth of the Kraken, and not believe by halves in the merman and mermaid.

In one thing we cordially agree with Miss Martineau, namely, in repudiating the cant about prying into the mysteries of Providence, perfectly convinced that what is intended to be hidden from us will remain as hermetically sealed as the secrets of the grave. The Creator himself has implanted in man an inquisitive spirit, with faculties for research, which he obviously intended to be exercised, by leaving for its discovery so many important powers—for instance, the properties of the loadstone—essential to human comfort and progress, instead of making them subjects of special revelation. Let man, then, divinely supplied with intellectual deep sea-lines, industriously fathom all mysteries within their reach. What we object to is, that so many charts are empirically laid down without his taking proper soundings, and to his pronouncing off-hand, without examination by the plummet, that the bottom off a strange coast is rock, mud, stone, sand, or shells. Thus it is that in mesmerism we have so much rash assertion on one hand, and point blank contradiction on the other. To pass over such subtleties as the existence of an invisible magnetic fluid, and the mode of magnetic action, there is the broad problem, whether a man's leg can be lopped off as unconsciously as the limb of a tree! That such a question should remain in dispute or doubt, in spite of our numerous hospitals and their frequent operations, is disgraceful to all parties. But speculation seems to be preferred to proof. Thus Miss Martineau talks confidently of such painless amputations; yet, with a somnambulist at her fingers' ends, never assures herself by the prick of a pin of the probability of the fact. Nay, she is very angry with an experimentalist, who tried to satisfy himself of the reality of J.'s insensibility by a sudden alarm, without giving notice that he was going to surprise her; a violation, it seems, of the first rule of mesmeric practice, but certainly according to the rules of common sense.

"Another incident is noteworthy in this connexion. A gentleman was here one evening, who was invited in all good faith on his declaration that he had read all that had been written on mesmerism, knew all about it, and was philosophically curious to witness the phenomena. He is the only witness we have had who abused the privilege. I was rather surprised to see how, being put in communication with J., he wrenched her arm, and employed usage which would have been cruelly rough in her ordinary state: but I suppose it was because he 'knew all about it,' and found that she was insensible to his rudeness; and her insensibility was so obvious, that I hardly regretted it. At length, however, it became clear, that his sole idea was (that which is the sole idea of so many who cannot conceive of what they cannot explain) of detecting shamming; and, in pursuance of this aim, this gentleman, who 'knew all about it,' violated the first rule of mesmeric practice, by suddenly and violently seizing the sleeper's arm, without the intervention of the mesmerist. J. was convulsed, and writhed in her chair. At that moment, and while supposing himself *en rapport* with her, he shouted out to me that the house was on fire. Happily, this brutal assault on her nerves failed entirely. There was certainly nothing congenial in the *rapport*. She made no attempt to rise from her seat, and said nothing—clearly heard nothing; and when asked what had frightened her, said something cold had got hold of her. Cold, indeed! and very hard too!"

In the mean time, how many sufferers there are, probably, male and female, afflicted with cancers and diseased limbs, who are looking towards mesmerism for relief, and anxiously asking, is it true that a breast can be removed as painlessly as its boddice; or a leg cut off, and perhaps put on again—why not, by such a miraculous agency?—without the knowledge of its great or little toe? Such inquirers ought at once to have their doubts resolved, for, as we all know, there is nothing more cruel, when such issues are at stake, than to be kept dangling in a state of uncertainty.

On the subject of itinerant mesmerists, Miss Martineau is very earnest, and roundly denounces the profane fellows, who make no scruple of "playing upon the nerves and brains of human beings, exhibiting for money on a stage, states of mind and soul held too sacred in olden times to be elicited elsewhere than in temples by the hands of the priests of the gods!"

While the wise, in whose hands this power should be, as the priesthood to whom scientific mysteries are consigned by Providence, scornfully decline their high function, who are they that snatch at it, in sport or mischief—and always in ignorance? School-children, apprentices, thoughtless women who mean no harm, aud base men who do mean harm. Wherever itinerant mesmerists have been, are there such as these, throwing each other into trances, trying funny experiments, getting fortunes told, or rashly treating diseases.

* * * * *

"Thus are human passions and human destinies committed to reckless hands for sport or abuse. No wonder if somnambules are made into fortune tellers—no wonder if they are made into prophets of fear, malice, and revenge, by reflecting in their somnambulism the fear, malice, and revenge of their questioners;—no wonder if they are made even ministers of death, by being led from sick-bed to sick-bed in the dim and dreary alleys of our towns, to declare which of the sick will recover, and which will die!

* * * * *

"If I were to speak as a moralist on the responsibility of the *savans* of society to the multitude—if I were to unveil the scenes which are going forward in every town in England, from the wanton, sportive, curious, or mischievous use of this awful agency by the ignorant, we should hear no more levity in high places about mesmerism."

A statement strangely at variance with the following dictum, which as strangely makes Morality still moral, whatever her thoughts or her postures—and whether controlled by the volition of "thoughtless women who mean no harm," or "base men who do mean harm."

"The volitions of the mesmerist may actuate the movements of the patient's limbs, and suggest the material of his ideas; but they seem unable to touch his *morale*. In this state the *morale* appears supreme, as it is rarely found in the ordinary condition."

We can well understand the "social calamity" apprehended from a promiscuous use of the ulterior powers of mesmerism. But what class, we must ask, is to arrogate to itself and monopolize the exercise of miraculous powers, allied to, if not identical with, those bestowed aforetime on certain itinerant apostles? An inspired fisherman will prescribe as safely, prophesy as correctly, and see visions as clearly, as an inspired doctor of medicine or divinity. There seems to be, in the dispensation of the marvellous gift, no distinction of persons. Miss Martineau's maid mesmerizes her as effectually as Mr. Hall; and J. owes her first magnetic sleep, and all its beneficial results on her health and inflamed eyes, to the passes of the maid of the clergyman's widow. A domestic concatenation that suggests to us a curious kitchen picture—and an illustrative letter,

To MARY SMASH, *at No.* 1 *Chaney Walk, Chelsea.*

DEAR MARY,

This cums hoping yure well, and to advize you to larn Mismerising. Its done with yure Hands, and is as easy as taking sites at Pepel, or talking on yure fingers. If I was nigh you, I'd larn you in no time to make Passes, witch is only pawing, like, without touchin, at sumboddys face or back, which gives them a tittevating feeling on the galvanic nerves, And then off they go into a Trance in a giffy, and talk in their sleep like Orators, I should say Oracles, and anser whatever you ax. Whereby you may get your Fortin told, and find out other folkes sweathearts & luve secrets, And diskiver Theaves better than by Bible and Key, And have yure inward Disorders told, & wats good for them. Sukey's was the indigestibles, and to take as much rubbub as would hide a shillin. All which is done by means of the sombulist, thats the sleeper, seeing through every think quite transparent, in their Trance, as is called Clare Voying, so that they can pint out munny hid under the Erth & burried bones, & springs of water, and vanes of mettle, & menny things besides.

Yesterday I was mismerized meself into a Trance, & clare voyed the chork Gout in John's stomack as plane as Margit Clifts. So I prescribed him to take Collyflower, witch by rites should have been Collycinth, but I forgot the proper word. Howsumever, he did eat two large ones, and promises to cum round.

It would make you split your sides with laffing to see me mismerize our Thomas, & make him go into all sorts of odd postures & anticks & capers Like a Dotterel, for whatever I do he must coppy to the snapping of a finger, and cant object to nuthing, for, as the song says, I've got his Will and his Power. Likewise you can make the Sombulist taste watever you think propper, so I give him mesmerized Warter, witch at my Command is transmoggrified on his pallet to Shampain, & makes him as drunk as Old Gooseberry, and then he will jump Jim Crow, or go down on his bended knees and confess all his peckaddillos, Witch is as diverten as reading the Misteries of Parris.

The wust to mesmerize is Reuben the Cotchman, not that he s too wakeful, for he's generally beery, And goes off like a shot, but he wont talk in his sleep, only snores.

The Page is more passable and very clarevoying. He have twice seed a pot of goold in the middle flower-bed. But the gardner wont have it dug up. And he says there is a skelliton bricked into the staircase wall, so that we never dares at nite to go up alone. Also he sees Visions, and can profesy and have foretold two Earthquacks and a great Pleg.

Cook wants to mismerize too, but wat with her being so much at the fire, and her full habbit, she always goes off to sleep afore the Sombulist. But Sukey can do it very well. Tho in great distress about Mrs. Hardin's babby witch Sukey offered to mismerize in lieu of syrrup of Poppies or Godfrey's Cordial, but the pore Innocent wont wake up agin, nor havent for two hole days. As would be a real blessin to Muthers and Nusses in a moderate way, but mite be carried too far, and require a Crowners Quest. As yet that's the only Trial we have made out of the House, But we mean to mismerize the Baker, and get out of him who he really does mean to offer to, for he is quite a General Lover.

Sum pepel is very dubious about Mismerizing, and some wont have it at any price; but Missis is for it, very strong, and says she means to belive every attom about it till sumboddy proves quite the reverse. She practises making passes every day, and is studyin Frenology besides, for she says, between the two you may play on pepel's pennycraniums like a Piany, and put them into any Key you like. And of course her fust performance will be a Master-piece on the Head of the Fammily.

To be shure it seems a wonderful power to be give to one over ones Fellow Creturs, and as mite be turned to Divilish purposes, But witch I cant stop to pint out, for makin the beds. To tell the truth, with so much Mismerizing going on, our Wurks has got terrible behind hand. And the carpits has not been swep for a week. So no more at present in haste from

Your luving Friend,

ELIZA PASSMORE.

P. S. A most remarkable Profesy! The Page have foretold that the Monkey some day would bite Missis, & lo! and behold he have flone at her, and made his teeth meet in her left ear. If that ant profesying I don't know what is.

THE ELM TREE:

A DREAM IN THE WOODS.

And this our life, exempt from public haunt,
Finds tongues in trees.

As you like it

'Twas in a shady Avenue,
Where lofty Elms abound—
And from a Tree
There came to me
A sad and solemn sound,
That sometimes murmur'd overhead,
And sometimes underground.

Amongst the leaves it seem'd to sigh,
Amid the boughs to moan;
It mutter'd in the stem and then
The roots took up the tone;
As if beneath the dewy grass
The Dead began to groan.

No breeze there was to stir the leaves;
No bolts that tempests launch,
To rend the trunk or rugged bark;
No gale to bend the branch;
No quake of earth to heave the roots,
That stood so stiff and staunch.

No bird was preening up aloft,
To rustle with its wing;
No squirrel, in its sport or fear,

From bough to bough to spring;
The solid bole
Had ne'er a hole
To hide a living thing!

No scooping hollow cell to lodge
A furtive beast or fowl,
The martin, bat,
Or forest cat
That nightly loves to prowl,
Nor ivy nook so apt to shroud
The moping, snoring owl.

But still the sound was in my ear,
A sad and solemn sound,
That sometimes murmur'd overhead,
And sometimes underground—
'Twas in a shady Avenue
Where lofty Elms abound.

O hath the Dryad still a tongue
In this ungenial clime?
Have Sylvan Spirits still a voice
As in the classic prime—
To make the forest voluble,
As in the olden time?

The olden time is dead and gone;
Its years have fill'd their sum—
And e'en in Greece—her native Greece—
The Sylvan Nymph is dumb—
From ash, and beech, and aged oak,
No classic whispers come.

From Poplar, Pine, and drooping Birch,
And fragrant Linden Trees;
No living sound
E'er hovers round,
Unless the vagrant breeze,

The music of the merry bird,
  Or hum of busy bees.

But busy bees forsake the Elm
  That bears no bloom aloft—
The Finch was in the hawthorn-bush,
  The Blackbird in the croft;
And among the firs the brooding Dove,
  That else might murmur soft.

Yet still I heard that solemn sound,
  And sad it was to boot,
From ev'ry overhanging bough,
  And each minuter shoot;
From the rugged trunk and mossy rind,
  And from the twisted root.

From these,—a melancholy moan;
  From those,—a dreary sigh;
As if the boughs were wintry bare,
  And wild winds sweeping by—
Whereas the smallest fleecy cloud
  Was steadfast in the sky.

No sign or touch of stirring air
  Could either sense observe—
The zephyr had not breath enough
  The thistle-down to swerve,
Or force the filmy gossamers
  To take another curve.

In still and silent slumber hush'd
  All Nature seem'd to be;
From heaven above, or earth beneath,
  No whisper came to me—
Except the solemn sound and sad
  From that Mysterious Tree!

A hollow, hollow, hollow sound,
  As is that dreamy roar

When distant billows boil and bound
  Along a shingly shore—
But the ocean brim was far aloof,
  A hundred miles or more.

No murmur of the gusty sea,
  No tumult of the beach,
However they might foam and fret,
  The bounded sense could reach—
Methought the trees in mystic tongue
  Were talking each to each!—

Mayhap, rehearsing ancient tales
  Of greenwood love or guilt,
    Of whisper'd vows
    Beneath their boughs;
  Or blood obscurely spilt;
Or of that near-hand Mansion House
  A Royal Tudor built.

Perchance, of booty won or shared
  Beneath the starry cope—
Or where the suicidal wretch
  Hung up the fatal rope;
Or Beauty kept an evil tryste,
  Insnared by Love and Hope.

Of graves, perchance, untimely scoop'd
  At midnight dark and dank—
And what is underneath the sod
  Whereon the grass is rank—
    Of old intrigues,
    And privy leagues,
  Tradition leaves in blank.

Of traitor lips that mutter'd plots
  Of Kin who fought and fell—
God knows the undiscovered schemes,
  The arts and acts of Hell,

Perform'd long generations since,
  If trees had tongues to tell!

With wary eyes, and ears alert,
  As one who walks afraid,
I wander'd down the dappled path
  Of mingled light and shade—
How sweetly gleamed that arch of blue
  Beyond the green arcade!

How clearly shone the glimpse of Heav'n
  Beyond that verdant aisle!
All overarch'd with lofty elms,
  That quench'd the light the while,
      As dim and chill
      As serves to fill
Some old Cathedral pile!

And many a gnarlèd trunk was there,
  That ages long had stood,
Till Time had wrought them into shapes
  Like Pan's fantastic brood;
Or still more foul and hideous forms
  That Pagans carve in wood!

A crouching Satyr lurking here—
  And there a Goblin grim—
As staring full of demon life
  As Gothic sculptor's whim—
A marvel it had scarcely been
  To hear a voice from him!

Some whisper from that horrid mouth
  Of strange, unearthly tone;
Or wild infernal laugh, to chill
  One's marrow in the bone.
But no——it grins like rigid Death,
  And silent as a stone!

As silent as its fellows be,
  For all is mute with them—
The branch that climbs the leafy roof—
  The rough and mossy stem—
    The crooked root,
    And tender shoot,
  Where hangs the dewy gem.

One mystic Tree alone there is,
  Of sad and solemn sound—
That sometimes murmurs overhead,
  And sometimes underground—
In all that shady Avenue,
  Where lofty Elms abound.

Part II.

The Scene is changed! No green Arcade—
  No Trees all ranged a-row—
But scattered like a beaten host,
  Dispersing to and fro;
With here and there a sylvan corse,
  That fell before the foe.

The Foe that down in yonder dell
  Pursues his daily toil;
As witness many a prostrate trunk,
  Bereft of leafy spoil,
Hard by its wooden stump, whereon
  The adder loves to coil.

Alone he works—his ringing blows
  Have banish'd bird and beast;
The Hind and Fawn have canter'd off
  A hundred yards at least;
And on the maple's lofty top,
  The linnet's song has ceased.

No eye his labor overlooks,
  Or when he takes his rest;
Except the timid thrush that peeps
  Above her secret nest,
Forbid by love to leave the young
  Beneath her speckled breast.

The Woodman's heart is in his work,
  His axe is sharp and good:
With sturdy arm and steady aim
  He smites the gaping wood;
      From distant rocks
      His lusty knocks
  Re-echo many a rood.

His axe is keen, his arm is strong;
  The muscles serve him well;
His years have reached an extra span,
  The number none can tell;
But still his lifelong task has been
  The Timber Tree to fell.

Through Summer's parching sultriness,
  And Winter's freezing cold,
      From sapling youth
      To virile growth,
  And Age's rigid mould,
His energetic axe hath rung
  Within that Forest old.

Aloft, upon his poising steel
  The vivid sunbeams glance—
About his head and round his feet
  The forest shadows dance;
And bounding from his russet coat
  The acorn drops askance.

His face is like a Druid's face,
  With wrinkles furrow'd deep,

And tann'd by scorching suns as brown
  As corn that's ripe to reap;
But the hair on brow, on cheek, and chin,
  Is white as wool of sheep.

His frame is like a giant's frame;
  His legs are long and stark;
His arms like limbs of knotted yew;
  His hands like rugged bark.
    So he felleth still
    With right good will,
  As if to build an Ark!

Oh! well within *His* fatal path
  The fearful Tree might quake
Through every fibre, twig, and leaf,
  With aspen tremor shake;
    Through trunk and root,
    And branch and shoot,
  A low complaining make!

Oh! well to *Him* the Tree might breathe
  A sad and solemn sound,
A sigh that murmur'd overhead,
  And groans from underground;
As in that shady Avenue
  Where lofty Elms abound!

But calm and mute the Maple stands,
  The Plane, the Ash, the Fir,
The Elm, the Beech, the drooping Birch
  Without the least demur;
And e'en the Aspen's hoary leaf
  Makes no unusual stir.

The Pines—those old gigantic Pines,
  That writhe—recalling soon
The famous Human Group that writhes

With Snakes in wild festoon—
In ramous wrestlings interlaced
A Forest Läocoon—

Like Titans of primeval girth
By tortures overcome,
Their brown enormous limbs they twine
Bedew'd with tears of gum—
Fierce agonies that ought to yell,
But, like the marble, dumb.

Nay, yonder blasted Elm that stands
So like a man of sin,
Who, frantic, flings his arms abroad
To feel the Worm within—
For all that gesture, so intense,
It makes no sort of din!

An universal silence reigns
In rugged bark or peel,
Except that very trunk which rings
Beneath the biting steel—
Meanwhile the Woodman plies his axe
With unrelenting zeal!

No rustic song is on his tongue,
No whistle on his lips;
But with a quiet thoughtfulness
His trusty tool he grips,
And, stroke on stroke, keeps hacking out
The bright and flying chips.

Stroke after stroke, with frequent dint
He spreads the fatal gash;
Till lo! the remnant fibres rend,
With harsh and sudden crash,
And on the dull resounding turf
The jarring branches lash!

Oh! now the Forest Trees may sigh,
The Ash, the Poplar tall,
The Elm, the Birch, the drooping Beech,
The Aspens—one and all,
With solemn groan
And hollow moan
Lament a comrade's fall!

A goodly Elm, of noble girth,
That, thrice the human span—
While on their variegated course
The constant Seasons ran—
Through gale, and hail, and fiery bolt,
Had stood erect as Man.

But now, like mortal Man himself,
Struck down by hand of God,
Or heathen Idol tumbled prone
Beneath th' Eternal's nod,
In all its giant bulk and length
It lies along the sod!—

Ay, now the Forest Trees may grieve
And make a common moan
Around that patriarchal trunk
So newly overthrown;
And with a murmur recognize
A doom to be their own!

The Echo sleeps: the idle axe,
A disregarded tool,
Lies crushing with its passive weight
The toad's reputed stool—
The Woodman wipes his dewy brow
Within the shadows cool.

No Zephyr stirs: the ear may catch
The smallest insect-hum;
But on the disappointed sense

No mystic whispers come ;
No tone of sylvan sympathy,
The Forest Trees are dumb.

No leafy noise, nor inward voice,
No sad and solemn sound,
That sometimes murmurs overhead,
And sometimes underground ;
As in that shady Avenue,
Where lofty Elms abound !

Part III.

The deed is done : the Tree is low
That stood so long and firm ;
The Woodman and his axe are gone,
His toil has found its term ;
And where he wrought the speckled Thrush
Securely hunts the worm.

The Cony from the sandy bank
Has run a rapid race,
Through thistle, bent, and tangled fern,
To seek the open space ;
And on its haunches sits erect
To clean its furry face.

The dappled Fawn is close at hand,
The Hind is browsing near,—
And on the Larch's lowest bough
The Ousel whistles clear ;
But checks the note
Within his throat,
As choked with sudden fear !

With sudden fear her wormy quest
The Thrush abruptly quits—
Through thistle, bent, and tangled fern

The startled Cony flits;
And on the Larch's lowest bough
No more the Ousel sits.

With sudden fear
The dappled Deer
Effect a swift escape;
But well might bolder creatures start,
And fly, or stand agape,
With rising hair, and curdled blood,
To see so grim a Shape!

The very sky turns pale above;
The earth grows dark beneath;
The human Terror thrills with cold,
And draws a shorter breath—
An universal panic owns
The dread approach of DEATH!

With silent pace, as shadows come,
And dark as shadows be,
The grisly Phantom takes his stand
Beside the fallen Tree,
And scans it with his gloomy eyes,
And laughs with horrid glee—

A dreary laugh and desolate,
Where mirth is void and null,
As hollow as its echo sounds
Within the hollow skull—
"Whoever laid this tree along
His hatchet was not dull!

"The human arm and human tool
Have done their duty well!
But after sound of ringing axe
Must sound the ringing-knell;
When Elm or Oak
Have felt the stroke
My turn it is to fell!

"No passive unregarded tree,
  A senseless thing of wood,
Wherein the sluggish sap ascends
  To swell the vernal bud—
But conscious, moving, breathing trunks
  That throb with living blood!

"No forest Monarch yearly clad
  In mantle green or brown;
That unrecorded lives, and falls
  By hand of rustic clown—
But Kings who don the purple robe,
  And wear the jewell'd crown.

"Ah! little recks the Royal mind,
  Within his Banquet Hall,
While tapers shine and Music breathes
  And Beauty leads the Ball,—
He little recks the oaken plank
  Shall be his palace wall!

"Ah! little dreams the haughty Peer
  The while his Falcon flies—
Or on the blood-bedabbled turf
  The antler'd quarry dies—
That in his own ancestral Park
  The narrow dwelling lies!

"But haughty Peer and mighty King
  One doom shall overwhelm!
      The oaken cell
      Shall lodge him well
  Whose sceptre ruled a realm—
While he who never knew a home,
  Shall find it in the Elm!

"The tatter'd, lean, dejected wretch,
  Who begs from door to door,

And dies within the cressy ditch,
  Or on the barren moor,
The friendly Elm shall lodge and clothe
  That houseless man, and poor!

"Yea, this recumbent rugged trunk,
  That lies so long and prone,
With many a fallen acorn-cup,
  And mast, and firry cone—
This rugged trunk shall hold its share
  Of mortal flesh and bone!

"A Miser hoarding heaps of gold,
  But pale with ague-fears—
A Wife lamenting love's decay,
  With secret cruel tears,
Distilling bitter, bitter drops
  From sweets of former years—

"A Man within whose gloomy mind,
  Offence had darkly sunk,
Who out of fierce Revenge's cup
  Hath madly, darkly drunk—
Grief, Avarice, and Hate shall sleep
  Within this very trunk!

"This massy trunk that lies along,
  And many more must fall—
      For the very knave
      Who digs the grave,
  The man who spreads the pall,
And he who tolls the funeral bell,
  The Elm shall have them all!

"The tall abounding Elm that grows
  In hedgerows up and down;
In field and forest, copse and park,
  And in the peopled town,

With colonies of noisy rooks
  That nestle on its crown.

'And well th' abounding Elm may grow
  In field and hedge so rife,
In forest, copse, and wooded park,
  And 'mid the city's strife,
For, every hour that passes by,
  Shall end a human life!"

The Phantom ends: the shade is gone;
  The sky is clear and bright;
On turf, and moss, and fallen Tree,
  There glows a ruddy light;
And bounding through the golden fern
  The Rabbit comes to bite.

The Thrush's mate beside her sits
  And pipes a merry lay;
The Dove is in the evergreens;
  And on the Larch's spray
The Fly-bird flutters up and down,
  To catch its tiny prey.

The gentle Hind and dappled Fawn
  Are coming up the glade;
Each harmless furr'd and feather'd thing
  Is glad, and not afraid—
But on my sadden'd spirit still
  The Shadow leaves a shade.

A secret, vague, prophetic gloom,
  As though by certain mark
I knew the fore-appointed Tree,
  Within whose rugged bark
This warm and living frame shall find
  Its narrow house and dark.

That mystic Tree which breathed to me
  A sad and solemn sound,
That sometimes murmur'd overhead
  And sometimes underground;
Within that shady Avenue
  Where lofty Elms abound.

THE LAY OF THE LABORER.

It was a gloomy evening. The sun had set, angry and threatening, lighting up the horizon with lurid flame and flakes of blood-red—slowly quenched by slants of distant rain, dense and dark as segments of the old deluge. At last the whole sky was black, except the low-driving grey scud, amidst which faint streaks of lightning wandered capriciously towards their appointed aim, like young fire-fiends playing on their errands.

"There will be a storm!" whispered nature herself, as the crisp fallen leaves of autumn started up with a hollow rustle, and began dancing a wild round, with a whirlwind of dust, like some frantic orgy ushering in a revolution.

"There will be a storm!" I echoed, instinctively looking round for the nearest shelter, and making towards it at my best pace. At such times the proudest heads will bow to very low lintels; and setting dignity against a ducking, I very willingly condescended to stoop into "The Plough."

It was a small hedge alehouse, too humble for the refinement of a separate parlor. One large tap-room served for all comers, gentle or simple, if gentlefolks, except from stress of weather, ever sought such a place of entertainment. Its scanty accommodations were even meaner than usual: the Plough had suffered from the hardness of the times, and exhibited the bareness of a house recently unfurnished by the broker. The aspect of the public room was cold and cheerless. There was a mere glimmer of fire in the grate, and a single unsnuffed candle stood guttering over the neck of the stone bottle in which it was stuck, in the middle of the plain deal table. The low ceiling, blackened by smoke, hung overhead like a canopy of gloomy clouds; the walls were stained with damp, and patches of the plaster had peeled off from the naked laths. Ornament there was none, except a soli tary print, gaudily daubed in body-colors, and formerly glazed, as hinted by a small triangle of glass in one corner of the black frame. The subject, "the Shipwrecked Mariner," whose corpse, jacketed in bright sky-blue, rolled on a still brighter strip of yellow shingle, between two grass-green wheat-sheaves with white ears—but intended for foaming billows. Above all, the customary odors were wanting; the faint smell of beer and ale, the strong scent of spirits, the fumes of tobacco; none of them agreeable to a nice sense, but decidedly missed with a feeling akin to disappointment. Rank or vapid, they belonged to the place, representing, though in an infinitely lower key, the bouquet of Burgundy, the aroma of choice liqueurs—the breath of social enjoyment.

Yet there was no lack of company. Ten or twelve men, some young, but the majority of the middle age, and one or two advanced in years, were seated at the sordid board. As many glasses and jugs of various patterns stood before them; but mostly empty, as was the tin tankard from which they had been replenished. Only a few of the party in the neighborhood of a brown earthenware pitcher had full cups; but of the very small ale called Adam's. Their coin and credit exhausted, they were keeping up the forms of drinking and good fellowship with plain water. From the same cause, a bundle of new clay pipes lay idle on the table, unsoiled by the Indian weed.

A glance sufficed to show that the company were of the laboring class—men with tanned, furrowed faces, and hairy, freckled hands—who smelt "of the earth, earthy," and were clad in fustian and leather, in velveteen and corduroy, glossy with wear or wet, soiled by brown clay and green moss, scratched and torn by brambles, wrinkled, warped, and threadbare with age, and variously patched—garments for need and decency, not show;—for if, amidst the prevailing russets, drabs, and olives, there was a gayer scrap of green, blue, or red, it was a tribute not to vanity but expediency—some fragment of military broadcloth or livery plush.

As I entered, the whole party turned their eyes upon me, and having satisfied themselves by a brief scrutiny that my face and person were unknown to them, thenceforward took no more notice of me than their own shadows on the wall. I could have fancied myself invisible, they resumed their conversation with so little reserve. The topics, such as poor men discuss amongst themselves:—the dearness of bread, the shortness of work, the long hours of labor, the lowness of wages, the badness of the weather, the sickliness of the season, the signs of a hard winter, the general evils of want, poverty, and disease; but accompanied by such particular revelations, such minute details, and frank disclosures, as should only have come from persons talking in their sleep! The vulgar indelicacy, methought, with which they gossipped before me of family matters—the brutal callousness with which they exposed their private affairs, the whole history and mystery of bed, board, and hearth, the secrets of home! But a little more listening and reflection converted my disgust into pity and concern. Alas! I had forgotten that the lives of certain classes of our species have been laid almost as bare and open as those of the beasts of the field! The poor men had no domestic secrets—no private affairs! All were public—matters of notoriety—friend and foe concurring in the advertisement. The law had ferreted their huts, and scheduled their three-legged tables and bottomless chairs. Statistical Groses had taken notes, and printed them, of every hole in their coats. Political reporters had calculated their incomings and outgoings down to fractions of pence and half ounces of tea; and had supplied the minutiæ of their domestic economy for paragraphs and leading articles. Charity, arm in arm with curiosity, and clerical philanthropy, linked perhaps with a religious inquisitor, had taken an inventory of their defects moral and spiritual; whilst medical visitors had inspected and recorded their physical sores, cancerous and scrofulous, their humors, and their tumors.

Society, like a policeman, had turned upon them the full blaze of its bull's eye—exploring the shadiest recesses of their privacy, till their means, food, habits, and modes of existence were as minutely familiar as those of the animalculæ exhibited in Regent street by the solar microscope. They had no longer any decent appearances to keep up—any shabby ones to mask with a better face—any petty shifts to slur over—any household struggles to conceal. Their circumstances were known intimately, not merely to next-door neighbors, and kith and kin, but to the whole parish, the whole county, the whole country. It was one of their last few privileges to discuss in common with the parliament, the press, and the public, the deplorable details of their own affairs. Their destitution was a naked great fact, and they talked of it like proclaimed bankrupts, as they were, in the wide world's Gazette.

"What matters?" said a grey-headed man, in fustian, in answer to a warning nudge and whisper from his neighbor. "If walls has ears, they are welcome to what they can ketch—ay, and the stranger to boot—if so be he don't know all about us already—for it's all in print. What we yarn, and what we spend—what we eat, and what we drink—what we wear, and the cost on it from top to toe—where we sleep, and how many on us lie in a bed—our consarns are as common as waste land."

"And as many geese and donkeys turned on to them, I do think!" cried a young fellow in velveteens—"to hear how folk cackle and bray about our states. And then the queer remedies as is prescribed, like, for a starving man! A Bible says one—a reading made easy says another—a temperance medal says another—or maybe a hagricultural prize. But what is he to eat, I ax? Why, says one, a Corkassian Jew—says another, a cricket ball—says another, a may-pole—and says another, the Wenus bound for Horsetrailye."

"As if idle hands and empty pockets," said the grey-headed man, "did not make signs, of themselves, for work and wages—and a hungry belly for bread and cheese."

"That's true any how," said one of the water-drinkers. "I only wish that a doctor would come at this minute, and listen with his *telescope* on my stomach, and he would hear it a-talking as plain as our magpie, and saying, I wants wittles."

There was a general peal of mirth at this speech, but brief, and ending abruptly, as laughter does, when extorted by the odd treatment of a serious subject—a flash followed by deeper gloom. The conversation then assumed a graver tone; each man in turn recounting the trials, privations, and visitations, of himself, his wife, and children, or his neighbor's—not mentioned with fierceness, intermingling oaths and threats, not with bitterness—some few allusions excepted to harsh overseers or miserly masters—but as soldiers or sailors describe the hardships and sufferings they have had to encounter in their rough vocation, and evidently endured in their own persons with a manly fortitude. If the speaker's voice faltered, or his eyes moistened, it was only when he painted the sharp bones showing through the skin, the skin through the rags, of the wife of his bosom; or how the traditional wolf, no longer to be kept from the door, had rushed in and fastened on his young ones. What a revelation it was! Fathers, with more children than shillings per week—mothers travailing literally in the straw—infants starving before the parents' eyes, with cold, and famishing for food! Human creatures, male and female, old and young, not gnawed and torn by single woes, but worried at once by winter, disease, and want, as by that triple-headed dog, whelped in the realm of torments!

My ears tingled, and my cheeks flushed with self-reproach, remembering my fretful impatience under my own inflictions, no light ones either, till compared with the heavy complications of anguish, moral and physical, experienced by those poor men. My heart swelled with indignation, my soul sickened with disgust, to recall the sobs, sighs, tears, and hystericks—the lamentations and imprecations bestowed by pampered selfishness on a sick bird or beast, a sore finger, a swelled toe, a lost rubber, a missing luxury, an ill-made garment, a culinary failure!—to think of the cold looks and harsh words cast by the same eyes and lips, eloquent in self-indulgence, on nakedness, starvation, and poverty. Wealth, with his own million of money, pointing to the new half-farthings as fitting money to the million—gluttony, gorged with dainties, washed down by iced champagne, complacently commending his humble brethren to the brook of Elisha and the salads of Nebuchadnezzar; and fashion, in furs and velvet, comfortably beholding her squalid sisters shivering in robes de zephyr, woven by winter itself, with the warp of a north, and the woof of an east wind!

"The job up at Bosely is finished," said one of the middle-aged men. "I have enjoyed but three days' work in the last fortnight, and God above knows when I shall get another, even at a shilling a day. And nine mouths to feed, big and little—and nine backs to clothe—with the winter a-setting in—and the rent behind-hand —and never a bed to lie on, and my good woman, poor soul, ready to ——"—a choking sound and a hasty gulp of water smothered the rest of the sentence. "There must be something done for us—there MUST," he added, with an emphatic slap of his broad, brown, barky hand, that made the glasses jingle and the idle pipes clatter on the board. And every voice in the room echoed "there must," my own involuntarily swelling the chorus.

"Ay, there must, and that full soon," said the grey-headed man in fustian, with an upward appealing look, as if through the smoky clouds of the ceiling to God himself for confirmation of the necessity. "But come, lads, time's up, so let's have our chant, and then squander.

The company immediately stood up; and one of the elders with a deep bass voice, and to a slow sad air, began a rude song, the composition, probably, of some provincial poet of his own class, the rest of the party joining occasionally in a verse that served for the burden.

A spade! a rake! a hoe!
  A pickaxe, or a bill!
A hook to reap, or a scythe to mow,
  A flail, or what you will—
And here's a ready hand
  To ply the needful tool,
And skilled enough by lessons rough
  In labor's rugged school.

To hedge, or dig the ditch,
  To lop or fell the tree,
To lay the swarth on the sultry field,
  Or plough the stubborn lea,
The harvest stack to bind,
  The wheaten rick to thatch;
And never fear in my pouch to find
  The tinder or the match.

To a flaming barn or farm
  My fancies never roam;
The fire I yearn to kindle and burn
  Is on the hearth of home;
Where children huddle and crouch
  Through dark long winter days,
Where starving children huddle and crouch
  To see the cheerful rays,
A-glowing on the haggard cheek,
  And not in the haggard's blaze!

To Him who sends a drought
  To parch the fields forlorn,
The rain to flood the meadows with mud,
  The blight to blast the corn—
To Him I leave to guide
  The bolt in its crooked path,
To strike the miser's rick, and show
  The skies blood-red with wrath.

A spade! a rake! a hoe!
  A pickaxe, or a bill!
A hook to reap, or a scythe to mow,
  A flail, or what ye will—
The corn to thrash, or the hedge to plash,
  The market team to drive,
Or mend the fence by the cover side,
  And leave the game alive.

Ay, only give me work,
  And then you need not fear
That I shall snare his worship's hare,
  Or kill his grace's deer—
Break into his lordship's house,
  To steal the plate so rich,
Or leave the yeoman that had a purse
  To welter in the ditch.

Wherever nature needs,
  Wherever labor calls,
No job I'll shirk of the hardest work,
  To shun the workhouse walls;
Where savage laws begrudge
  The pauper babe its breath,
And doom a wife to a widow's life
  Before her partner's death.

My only claim is this,
  With labor stiff and stark,
By lawful turn my living to earn,
  Between the light and dark—
My daily bread and nightly bed,
  My bacon and drop of beer—
But all from the hand that holds the land,
  And none from the overseer!

No parish money or loaf,
  No pauper badges for me,
A son of the soil, by right of toil,
  Entitled to my fee.
No alms I ask, give me my task:
  Here are the arm, the leg,
The strength, the sinews of a man,
  To work, and not to beg.

Still one of Adam's heirs,
  Though doomed by chance of birth
To dress so mean, and eat the lean
  Instead of the fat of the earth;
To make such humble meals
  As honest labor can,
A bone and a crust, with a grace to God,
  And little thanks to man!

A spade! a rake! a hoe!
  A pickaxe, or a bill!
A hook to reap, or a scythe to mow,

A flail, or what ye will—
Whatever the tool to ply,
Here is a willing drudge,
With muscle and limb—and wo to him
Who does their pay begrudge.

Who every weekly score
Docks labor's little mite,
Bestows on the poor at the temple-door,
But robbed them over-night.
The very shilling he hoped to save,
As health and morals fail,
Shall visit me in the New Bastile,
The spital or the gaol!

As the last ominous word ceased ringing, the candle-wick suddenly dropped into the neck of the stone bottle, and all was darkness and silence.

* * * * * * * * * *

The vision is dispelled—the fiction is gone—but a fact and a figure remain.

Some time since a strong inward impulse moved me to paint the destitution of an overtasked class of females, who work, work, work, for wages almost nominal. But deplorable as is their condition, in the low deep, there is, it seems, a lower still—below that gloomy gulf a darker region of human misery—beneath that purgatory a hell—resounding with more doleful wailings and a sharper outcry—the voice of famishing wretches, pleading vainly for work! work! work!—imploring as a blessing, what was laid upon man as a curse—the labor that wrings sweat from the brow, and bread from the soil!

As a matter of conscience, that wail touches me not. As my works testify, I am of the working class myself, and in my humble sphere furnish employment for many hands, including papermakers, draughtsmen, engravers, compositors, pressmen, binders, folders, and stitchers—and critics—all receiving a fair day's wages for a fair day's work. My gains consequently are limited—not nearly so enormous as have been realized upon shirts, slops, shawls, &c.—curiously illustrating how a man or woman might be "clothed with curses as with a garment." My fortune may be expressed without a long row of those ciphers—those 0's at once significant of hundreds of thousands of pounds, and as many ejaculations of pain and sorrow from dependent slaves. My wealth might all be hoarded, if I were miserly, in a gallipot or a tin snuff-box. My guineas, placed edge to edge, instead of extending from the Minories to Golden Square, would barely reach from home to Bread Street. My riches would hardly allow me a roll in them, even if turned into the new copper mites. But then, thank God! no reproach clings to my coin. No tears or blood clog the meshes, no hair, plucked in desperation, is knitted with the silk of my lean purse. No consumptive sempstress can point at me her bony forefinger, and say, "For thee, *sewing in formâ pauperis*, I am become this living skeleton!" or hold up to me her fatal needle, as one through the eye of which the scriptural camel must pass ere I may hope to enter heaven. No withered work-woman, shaking at me her dripping suicidal locks, can cry, in a piercing voice, "For thee, and for six poor pence, I embroidered eighty flowers on this veil"—literally a veil of tears. No famishing laborer, his joints racked with toil, holds out to me in the palm of his broad hard hand seven miserable shillings, and mutters, "For these, and a parish loaf, for six long days, from dawn till dusk, through hot and cold, through wet and dry, I tilled thy land!" My short sleeps are peaceful; my dreams untroubled. No ghastly phantoms with reproachful faces, and silence more terrible than speech, haunt my quiet pillow. No victims of slow murder, ushered by the avenging fiends, beset my couch, and make awful appointments with me to meet at the Divine bar on the day of judgment. No deformed human creatures—men, women, and children, smirched black as negroes, transfigured suddenly, as demons of the pit, clutch at my heels to drag me down, down, down, an unfathomable shaft, into a gaping Tartarus. And if sometimes in waking visions I see throngs of little faces, with features preternaturally sharp, and wrinkled brows, and dull, seared orbs—grouped with pitying clusters of the young-eyed cherubim—not for me, thank Heaven! did those crippled children become prematurely old;

and precociously evaporate, like so much steam power, the "dew of their youth."

For me, then, that doleful cry from the starving unemployed, has no extrinsic horror; no peculiar pang, beyond that sympathetic one which must affect the species in general. Nevertheless, amidst the dismal chorus, one complaining voice rings distinctly on my inward ear; one melancholy figure flits prominently before my mind's eye—vague of feature, indeed, and in form with only the common outlines of humanity—but the Eidolon of a real person, a living, breathing man, with a known name. One whom I have never seen in the flesh, never spoken with; yet whose very words a still small voice is, even now, whispering to me, I know not whence, like the wind from a cloud.

For months past, that indistinct figure, associated, as in a dream, with other dim images, but all mournful—stranger faces, male and female, convulsed with grief—huge hard hands, and smaller and tenderer ones, wrung in speechless anguish, and everlasting farewells—involved with obscure ocean waves, and momentary glimpses of outlandish scenery—for months past, amidst trials of my own, in the intervals of acute pain, perchance even in my delirium, and through the variegated tissue of my own interests and affairs, that sorrowful vision has recurred to me, more or less vividly, with the intense sense of suffering, cruelty, and injustice, and the strong emotions of pity and indignation, which originated with its birth.

It may be, that some peculiar condition of the body, inducing a morbid state of mind—some extreme excitability of the nerves, and through them, of the moral sensibility, concurred to induce so deep an impression, to make so warm a sympathy attach itself to a mere phantom, the representative of an obscure individual, an utter stranger. The reader must judge: and, when the case of my unknown, unconscious, invisible client shall be laid before him, will be able to say, whether it required any unnatural sensitiveness of the system, any extraordinary softening of the heart or brain, to feel a strong human interest in the fate of Gifford White.

In the spring of the present year, this very unfortunate and very young man was indicted, at the Huntingdon Assizes, for throwing the following letter, addressed, externally, and internally, to the farmers of Bluntisham, Hunts, into a strawyard:—

"We are determined to set fire to the whole of this place, if you don't set us to work, and burn you in your beds if there is not alteration. What do you think the young men are to do, if you don't set them to work? They must do something. The fact is, we cannot go on any longer. We must commit robbery, and everything that is contrary to your wish.

"I am,

"AN ENEMY."

For this offence, admitted by his plea, the prisoner, aged eighteen, was sentenced by a judge since deceased, to transportation for life!

Far be it from me to palliate incendiarism. Least of all, when so many conflagrations have recently illuminated the horizon; and so near the time when the memory of that arch incendiary, Guy Faux, will be revived by effigies and bonfires. I am fully aware of the risk of even this appeal, at such a season, but with that pleading shade before me, dare the reddest reflections that may be cast on this paper.

Only catch a real incendiary, bring his guilt clearly home to him, and let him suffer the extreme penalty of the law. Hang him. Or, if absolutely opposed to capital punishment, and inclined towards the philanthropy of a very French philosophy, adopt the Christianly substitute recommended in the "Mysteries of Paris," and blind the criminal. Let fire avenge fire, and, according to the prescription for Prince Arthur, with irons hot burn out both his eyes. Cruel and extreme as such tortures may seem, they would scarcely expiate one of the most dastardly and atrocious of human crimes, inasmuch as the perpetrator can neither control its extent, nor calculate the results.

The truth is, my faith stops far short of the popular belief in the prevalence of wilful and malignant fire-raising—that an epidemic of that inflammatory character is so rife and raging as represented in the provinces. I am too jealous of the national character, too chary of the good name of my humble countrymen, and think too well of "a bold peasantry, our country's pride," to look on them, willingly, as a mere pack of Samson's foxes, running from farm to farm, with fire-brands tied to their tails. If there be any notable increase in the number of fires, some portion of the excess may be fairly attributable to causes which have converted simple risks into doubly hazardous; for example, the prevalence of cigar smoking, and especially, the substitution for the old tinder-box, of dangerous chemical contrivances, facile of ignition, and distributed by myriads throughout the country. Talismans that, like the Arabian ones, on a slight rubbing, place a demon at the command of the possesscr—spells which have subjected the fire spirit to the instant invocation not merely of the wicked, but of the weak and the witless, the infant and the idiot. Generally, we work and play with the element more profusely than formerly: witness the glowing flames, flakes, sparks, and cinders, that sweep across streets, over seas and rivers, and along railroads, from the chimneys, funnels, and furnaces, of the factories, and floating and flying conveyances of Pluto, Vulcan, and Company. Another cause, spontaneous combustion, has lately been convicted of the destruction of the railway station at New Cross; and there is no reason to suppose that conflagrations from carelessness, and excessive house-warmings from inebriety, are less common than of old. Children will still play with fire; servants, town and country, persist in snuffing long wicks, as well as noses, with finger and thumb; and agricultural distress has not so annihilated the breed of jolly farmers, but that one, here and there, is still capable of blowing himself out, and putting his candle to bed.

In the meantime, vulgar exaggeration ascribes every "rapid consumption" of property, not clearly traceable to accident, to a malicious design. The English public, according to Goldsmith, are prone to panics, and he instances them as arming themselves with thick gloves and stout cudgels against certain popular bugbears in the shapes of mad dogs. And a fatal thing it is, proverbially, for the canine race to get an ill name. But a panic becomes a far more tragical affair, when it arms one class of society against another; and, instead of mere brutes and curs of low degree, animals of our own species are hunted down and hung, or, at best, all but banished to another world, by transportation for life. It is difficult to believe that some such local panic did not influence the very severe sentence passed on Gifford White. Indeed, the existence of something of the kind seems intimated by the Judge himself, along with the extraordinary dictum that a verbal burn is worse than the actual cautery. Lord Abinger said :—

"The offence was of a most atrocious character; and it might almost be said, that the sending of letters threatening to burn the property of the parties to whom they were addressed was worse than putting the threat in execution; for when a man lost his property by fire, he at least knew the worst of it; but he to whom such threats were made, was made to live in a state of continual terror and alarm."

Very true—and very harshly applied. The farmers of Bluntisham are not of my acquaintance; but presuming them to be not more nervous and timorsome than farmers in general, might not their terror and alarm have been pacified on rather easier terms? Would not the banishment of the culprit for seven, or at most fourteen years, have allowed time, ample time, for the yeomanly nerves to have recovered their tone; for their affrighted hair, erect as stubble, to have subsided prone as rolled grass; nay, for the very name of Gifford White to have evaporated from their agricultural heads? Were I a Bluntisham farmer, I could not eat with relish another rasher of bacon, or swallow with satisfaction another glass of strong ale, without protesting publicly against such a sacrifice to my supposed aspen-fits, and setting on foot a petition amongst my neighbors for a mitigation of that severe and satirical sentence which condemned a fellow parishioner to expiate my fears by fifty-two years of penance—according to the scriptural calculation of human life—in the land of the kangaroo. I could not sleep soundly, and know that for my sake a son of the same soil had been rooted out like a common weed—severed from kith and kin; from hearth and home, if he had one; from his mother-country, hard step-mother though she had proved; from a familiar land and native air, to a foreign one and a new climate, with strange faces around him, and strange stars above him,—a banished man, not for a little while, or for a long while, but for ever!

But, methinks I hear a voice say, it was necessary to make an example—a proceeding always accompanied by a certain degree of hardship, if not injustice, as regards the party selected to be punished *in terrorem;* unless the choice be made of a criminal especially deserving such a painful preference—as for robbery with personal violence: whereas there appear to be no aggravations of the offence for which Gifford White was sentenced to a murderer's atonement. On the contrary, he pleaded guilty: a course generally admitted as an extenuation of guilt: his youth ought to have been a circumstance in his favor; and above all, the consideration that a threat does not necessarily involve the intent, much less the deed. All who have been led, by word or writing, to hope or fear for good or evil, have had reason to know how far is promise from performance,—as far as England from New South Wales. Expectants never die the sooner for golden prospects held out to them; and threatened folks are long-lived, to a proverb. And why? Because the enemy who announces his designs is the least dangerous; as the Scotch say, "his bark is waur than his bite." The truth is, menaces are about the most abundant, idle, and empty of human vaporings; the mere puffings, blowings, gruntings, and growlings from the safety-valves and waste-pipes of high-pressure engines. The promissory notes of threateners to large amounts are ludicrously associated, instead of payment, with "no effects." Who of us has not heard a good mother, a fond mother, a doting mother, but sharp-tempered, promise her own dear but troublesome offspring, her very pets, such savage inflictions, such breaking of bones and knocking off plaguy little heads, as ought, sincerely uttered, to have consigned her to the custody of the police? There, as my Uncle Toby says, she found vent. Who has never known a friend, a worthy man, but a passionate one, to indulge in such murderous threats against the life, body, and limbs of a tight boot-maker, or a loose tailor; a blunt creditor, or a sharp critic; as ought, if in earnest, to have placed him in handcuffs and a strait waistcoat? But nobody mistakes these blazes of temper for the burnings of settled malignity—these harmless flashes of sheet lightning for the destructive gleam of the forked. It is quite possible, therefore, that the incendiary letter of Gifford

White, though breathing Congreves and Lucifers, was purely theoretical; albeit read by the judge as if in serious earnest, like the fulminating prospectuses of the Duc de Normandie or Captain Warner.

I confess to have searched, in vain, through the epistle for any animus of peculiar atrocity. Its address, generally to the farmers, shows it not to have been the inspiration of personal malice or private revenge. The threat is not a direct and positive one, as in resolved retaliation for some by-gone wrong; but put hypothetically, and rather in the nature of a warning of probable consequences, dependent on future contingencies. The wish of the writer is obviously not father to the menace: on the contrary, he expostulates, appeals, methinks most touchingly, to the reason, the justice, even the compassion, of the very parties —to be burnt in their beds. So clear a proof, to me, of the absence of any serious intent, or malice prepense, that the only agitation from the fall of such a missive in my farm-yard, if I had one, would be the flutter amongst the poultry. At least theirs would be the only personal terror and alarm,—for, with other feelings, who could fail to be moved by a momentous question and declaration reëchoed by hundreds and thousands of able and willing but starving laborers? "What are we to do if you don't set us to work? We must do something. The fact is, we cannot go on any longer!"

Can the wholesale emigration, so often proposed, be only transportation in disguise for using such language in common with Gifford White.

To me—speaking from my heart, and recording my deliberate opinions on a material that, frail as it is, will long outlast my own fabric,—there is something deeply affecting in the spectacle of a young man, in the prime of health and vigor, offering himself, a voluntary slave, in the labor-market without a purchaser—eagerly proffering to barter the use of his body, the day-long exertion of his strength, the wear and tear of flesh and blood, bone and muscle, for the common necessaries of life—earnestly craving for bread on the penal conditions prescribed by his Creator—and in vain—in vain! Well for those who enjoy each blessing of earth that there are volunteers to work out the curse! Well for the drones of the social hive that there are bees of so industrious a turn, willing for an infinitesimal share of the honey to undertake the labor of its fabrication!

Let these considerations avail an unfortunate man, or rather youth, perhaps an oppressed one, subject to the tyranny of some such ticket system as lately required the interference of the home secretary, in behalf of the laborers of another county.——

Methinks I see him, poor phantom! an impertinent unit of a surplus population, humbly pleading for bread, and offered an acre of stones—to be cleared at five farthings a rood. Work and wages for the asking!—with the double alternative of the Union-house, or a free passage—the North-West one—to the still undiscovered coast of Bohemia!——

Is a rash youth, so wrought on, to be eternally Ex-Isled from this sweet little one of our own, for only throwing a few intemperate "thoughts that breathe and words that burn" into an anonymous letter?

Let these things plead for a fellow-creature, goaded, perhaps, by the sense of wrong, as well as the physical pangs of hunger, and driven by the neglect of all milder applications to appeal to the selfish fears of men who will neither read the signs of the times, nor heed warnings, unless written, like Belshazzar's, in letters of fire!

One thing is certain. These are not times for visiting with severity the offences of the laboring poor; a class who, it is admitted by all parties, have borne the severest trials that can afflict the soul and body of man, with an exemplary fortitude, and a patience almost superhuman. A great fact at which every true Englishman should exult, as at a national victory, as in moral heroism it is. I, for one, am proud of my poor countrymen, and naturally loth to believe that a character which so reluctantly combines with disaffection, and indulges so sparely in outbreak, will freely absorb so vile a spirit as that of incendiarism. At any rate, before rashly adopting such a conclusion, common justice and common sense bid me look elsewhere for the causes of any unusual number of fires in the rural districts. As a mere matter of patriotism, one would rather ascribe such unfilial outrages to an alien than to a son of the soil. We have lately seen a foreign prince, an ally, in a time of peace speculating with much playful naïveté on the best modes for squibbing our shipping and rocketing our harbors—the facility with which he could ignite the Thames and mull the Medway—sink the Cinque Ports—blow off Beachy's head, shiver Deal into splinters, and knock the two Reculver steeples into one. His Highness, it is true, contemplated a bellicose state, ceremoniously proclaimed according to the usage of polite nations; but suppose some outlandish savage, as uncivilized as unshorn, say from Terra del Fuego, animated with an insane hostility to England, and burning to test his skill in Pyrotechnics—might not such a barbarian be tempted to dispense with a formal declaration of war, and make a few experimental essays how to introduce his treacherous combustibles into our perfidious towns and hamlets? Foreign incendiaries for me, rather than native; and accident or spontaneous combustion before either! But if we must believe in it home-made—surely, in preference to the industrious laborer, suspicion should fall on those sturdy trampers that infest the country, the foremost to crave for food and money, the last to ask for work, and one of whom might light up a dozen parishes. If it be otherwise, if a class eminently loyal, patient, peaceable, and rational, have really become such madmen throwing about fire, it is high time, methinks, with universal Artesian borings, to begin to scuttle our island for fear of its being burnt. But no—that Shadow of an incendiary, with uplifted hands, and streaming repentant eyes, disavows with earnest gesture the foul intent; and shadow as he is, my belief acquits him, and makes me echo the imaginary sigh with which he fades again into the foggy distance between me and Port Sydney.

It is in your power, Sir James Graham! to lay the ghost that is haunting me. But that is a trifle. By a due intercession with the earthly fountain of mercy, you may convert a melancholy shadow into a happier reality—a righted man—a much pleasanter image to mingle in our waking visions, as well as in those dreams which, as Hamlet conjectures, may soothe or disturb us in our coffins. Think, sir, of poor Gifford White—inquire into his hard case, and give it your humane consideration, as that of a fellow-man with an immortal soul—a "possible angel"—to be met hereafter face to face.

To me, should this appeal meet with any success, it will be one of the dearest deeds of my pen. I shall not repent a wide deviation from my usual course; or begrudge the pain and trouble caused me by the providential visitings of an importunate phantom. In any case, my own responsibility is at an end. I have relieved my heart, appeased my conscience, and absolved my soul.

THE BRIDGE OF SIGHS.

"Drowned! drowned!"—HAMLET

ONE more Unfortunate,
Weary of breath,
Rashly importunate,
Gone to her death!

Take her up tenderly,
Lift her with care;——
Fashion'd so slenderly,
Young, and so fair!

Look at her garments
Clinging like cerements;
Whilst the wave constantly
Drips from her clothing
Take her up instantly,
Loving, not loathing.—

Touch her not scornfully;
Think of her mournfully,
Gently and humanly;
Not of the stains of her,
All that remains of her
Now, is pure womanly.

Make no deep scrutiny
Into her mutiny
Rash and undutiful;

Past all dishonor,
Death has left on her
Only the beautiful.

Still, for all slips of hers,
One of Eve's family—
Wipe those poor lips of hers
Oozing so clammily.

Loop up her tresses
Escaped from the comb,
Her fair auburn tresses;
Whilst wonderment guesses
Where was her home?

Who was her father?
Who was her mother?
Had she a sister?
Had she a brother?
Or was there a dearer one
Still, and a nearer one
Yet, than all other?

Alas! for the rarity
Of Christian charity
Under the sun!
Oh! it was pitiful!
Near a whole city full,
Home she had none.

Sisterly, brotherly,
Fatherly, motherly,
Feelings had changed:
Love, by harsh evidence,
Thrown from its eminence;
Even God's providence
Seeming estranged.

Where the lamps quiver
So far in the river,

With many a light
From window and casement,
From garret to basement,
She stood, with amazement,
Houseless by night.

The bleak wind of March
Made her tremble and shiver;
But not the dark arch,
Or the black flowing river:
Mad from life's history,
Glad to death's mystery,
Swift to be hurl'd—
Anywhere, anywhere
Out of the world!

In she plunged boldly,
No matter how coldly
The rough river ran,—
Over the brink of it,
Picture it,—think of it,
Dissolute Man!
Lave in it, drink of it
Then, if you can!

Take her up tenderly,
Lift her with care;
Fashion'd so slenderly,
Young, and so fair!

Ere her limbs frigidly
Stiffen too rigidly,
Decently,—kindly,—
Smoothe, and compose them;
And her eyes, close them,
Staring so blindly!

Dreadfully staring
Through muddy impurity,

As when with the daring
Last look of despairing
Fixed on futurity.

Perishing gloomily,
Spurred by contumely,
Cold inhumanity,
Burning insanity,
Into her rest.—
Cross her hands humbly,
As if praying dumbly,
Over her breast!

Owning her weakness,
Her evil behavior,
And leaving, with meekness,
Her sins to her Saviour!

THE LADY'S DREAM.

THE lady lay in her bed,
 Her couch so warm and soft,
But her sleep was restless and broken still;
 For turning often and oft
From side to side, she muttered and moan'd
 And toss'd her arms aloft.

At last she started up,
 And gazed on the vacant air,
With a look of awe, as if she saw
 Some dreadful phantom there—
And then in the pillow she buried her face
 From visions ill to bear.

The very curtain shook,
 Her terror was so extreme,
And the light that fell on the broidered quilt
 Kept a tremulous gleam;
And her voice was hollow, and shook as she cried,
 "Oh me! that awful dream!

That weary, weary walk,
 In the churchyard's dismal ground!
And those horrible things, with shady wings,
 That came and flitted round,—
Death, death, and nothing but death,
 In every sight and sound!

"And oh! those maidens young,
Who wrought in that dreary room,
With figures drooping and spectres thin,
And cheeks without a bloom;—
And the voice that cried, 'For the pomp of pride
We haste to an early tomb!'

"For the pomp and pleasures of pride;
We toil like the African slaves,
And only to earn a home at last,
Where yonder cypress waves;—
And then it pointed—I never saw
A ground so full of graves!

"And still the coffins came,
With their sorrowful trains and slow;
Coffin after coffin still,
A sad and sickening show;
From grief exempt, I never had dreamt
Of such a world of Wo!

"Of the hearts that daily break,
Of the tears that hourly fall,
Of the many, many troubles of life,
That grieve this earthly ball—
Disease, and Hunger, Pain, and Want,
But now I dream of them all!

"For the blind and the cripple were there,
And the babe that pined for bread,
And the houseless man, and the widow poor
Who begged—to bury the dead!
The naked, alas, that I might have clad,
The famished I might have fed!

"The sorrow I might have soothed,
And the unregarded tears;
For many a thronging shape was there,
From long forgotten years,

Ay, even the poor rejected Moor,
  Who raised my childish fears!

"Each pleading look, that long ago
  I scanned with a heedless eye;
Each face was gazing as plainly there,
  As when I passed it by;
Wo, wo for me if the past should be
  Thus present when I die!

"No need of sulphurous lake,
  No need of fiery coal,
But only that crowd of human kind
  Who wanted pity and dole—
In everlasting retrospect—
  Will wring my sinful soul!

Alas! I have walked through life
  Too heedless where I trod;
Nay, helping to trample my fellow worm,
  And fill the burial sod—
Forgetting that even the sparrow falls
  Not unmarked of God!

"I drank the richest draughts;
  And ate whatever is good—
Fish, and flesh, and fowl, and fruit,
  Supplied my hungry mood;
But I never remembered the wretched ones
  That starve for want of food!

"I dressed as the noble dress,
  In cloth of silver and gold,
With silk, and satin, and costly furs,
  In many an ample fold;
But I never remembered the naked limbs
  That froze with winter's cold.

"The wounds I might have healed!
  The human sorrow and smart!

And yet it never was in my soul
  To play so ill a part:
But evil is wrought by want of Thought,
  As well as want of Heart!"

She clasped her fervent hands,
  And the tears began to stream;
Large, and bitter, and fast they fell,
  Remorse was so extreme;
And yet, oh yet, that many a Dame
  Would dream the Lady's Dream!

THE SONG OF THE SHIRT.

WITH fingers weary and worn,
  With eyelids heavy and red,
A woman sat, in unwomanly rags,
  Plying her needle and thread–
Stitch! stitch! stitch!
  In poverty, hunger, and dirt
And still with a voice of dolorous pitch,
  She sang the "song of the Shirt!"

"Work! work! work!
  While the cock is crowing aloof!
And work—work—work!
  Till the stars shine through the roof!
It's oh! to be a slave
  Along with the barbarous Turk,
Where woman has never a soul to save
  If THIS is Christian work!

"Work—work—work!
  Till the brain begins to swim;
Work—work—work!
  Till the eyes are heavy and dim!
Seam, and gusset, and band,
  Band, and gusset, and seam,
Till over the buttons I fall asleep,
  And sew them on in my dream!

"Oh! men with sisters dear!
  Oh! men with mothers and wives!

It is not linen you're wearing out,
  But human creatures' lives!
Stitch—stitch—stitch!
  In poverty, hunger, and dirt,
Sewing at once, with a double thread,
  A SHROUD as well as a shirt!

"But why do I talk of death,
  That phantom of grisly bone;
I hardly fear his terrible shape,
  It seems so like my own—
It seems so like my own,
  Because of the fast I keep:
Oh God! that bread should be so dear,
  And flesh and blood so cheap!

"Work—work—work!
  My labor never flags;
And what are its wages? A bed of straw
  A crust of bread—and rags:
A shattered roof—and this naked floor—
  A table—a broken chair—
And a wall so blank my shadow I thank
  For sometimes falling there!

"Work—work—work!
  From weary chime to chime;
Work—work—work!
  As prisoners work, for crime!
Band, and gusset, and seam,
  Seam, and gusset, and band,
Till the heart is sick and the brain benumbed,
  As well as the weary hand!

"Work—work—work,
  In the dull December light;
And work—work—work!
  When the weather is warm and bright:
While underneath the eaves

The brooding swallows cling,
As if to show me their sunny backs,
And twit me with the Spring.

"Oh! but to breathe the breath
Of the cowslip and primrose sweet;
With the sky above my head,
And the grass beneath my feet:
For only one short hour
To feel as I used to feel,
Before I knew the woes of want,
And the walk that costs a meal!

"Oh! but for one short hour!
A respite, however brief!
No blessed leisure for love or hope,
But only time for grief!
A little weeping would ease my heart—
But in their briny bed
My tears must stop, for every drop
Hinders needle and thread!"

With fingers weary and worn,
With eyelids heavy and red,
A woman sat, in unwomanly rags,
Plying her needle and thread;
Stitch—stitch—stitch!
In poverty, hunger and dirt;
And still with a voice of dolorous pitch—
Would that its tone could reach the rich!—
She sung this "Song of the shirt!"

www.ingramcontent.com/pod-product-compliance
Lightning Source LLC
LaVergne TN
LVHW011157110826
845150LV00006B/1244

* 9 7 8 1 4 2 5 5 4 5 7 3 4 *